TRAINING THE SPEAKING VOICE

Training the Speaking Voice

By VIRGIL A. ANDERSON

Professor of Speech Pathology and Audiology
Stanford University

SECOND EDITION

NEW YORK

OXFORD UNIVERSITY PRESS

1961

Illinois Central College
Learning Resouce Center

05576

PN
4162
.A 6
1961

© 1961 by Oxford University Press, Inc.
Library of Congress Catalogue Card Number: 61-6294

First edition of *Training the Speaking Voice*, copyright 1942 by
Oxford University Press, Inc.

Sixth Printing, 1965

PRINTED IN THE UNITED STATES OF AMERICA

Preface to the Second Edition

Training the Speaking Voice was originally written for use in the study of Voice Training, Voice and Diction, Fundamentals of Speech, or in any course in Speech that stresses the use of the voice as a basic approach to the problems of self-expression and communication. It is obviously difficult, if not impossible, to provide one book that will prove equally effective in all of these teaching situations. I believe, however, that the present revision comes closer to this ideal than the original version did.

Perhaps the greatest variation in the organization, content, and methodology of courses in voice and diction as taught by various instructors over the country is to be found in the relative amount of emphasis given to theoretical background material dealing with such topics as the structure and functioning of the voice and speech mechanism, the nature of speech sounds, and the theory of voice development and training. While these and similar topics form very important components of certain courses in voice and diction, in others they are passed over lightly and the primary emphasis is upon drill and performance.

Mindful of these divergent needs, I have attempted to 'streamline' and simplify the theoretical background material as much as possible, stressing its practical application to problems of voice and speech training. I have felt, however, that a certain minimum core of such material must be provided for the benefit of those instructors who need it. On the other hand, there is no reason why it must be assigned or otherwise included in the course merely because it happens to appear in the text. To facilitate this flexibility I have shifted the chapter dealing with sound in relation to voice and speech into an appendix, where it is out of the way if the instructor wishes to omit it, but is readily available if the instructor happens to need it. If it is used, incidentally, it should be assigned at some time prior to the study of Chapter IV.

Perhaps a few observations are in order at this point relative to the relationship between theory and practice in the study or teaching of voice and diction. There is little value in knowing the facts of voice and speech science merely as isolated facts. Effective use of the voice is a *skill*, involving *doing* as well as knowing, and it is attained in the same way that any skill is acquired—through observation and study and, most important of all, *practice*.

There is considerable evidence to indicate, however, that an individual will progress faster in a learning situation if he is aware of what he is trying to accomplish, as well as understanding something of the mechanisms involved and the factors governing the learning process. In other words, we learn better if, in addition to being told *what* we are to do, we also understand *why* we are doing it. To this end, I have attempted to relate the theoretical background to a practical program of voice improvement and I have excluded from the book material which, in my judgment, did not make some contribution to the realization of its central objective— improvement of the speaking voice.

Perhaps the most important change in the book has been made in Part II, which has been completely re-done and greatly expanded. This part is devoted to the subject of *diction,* a term used in accordance with a meaning it has acquired in the field of speech—namely, to signify the manner of speaking with particular reference to clearness and 'correctness.' Used in this sense, it embraces the traditional concepts of pronunciation, enunciation, and articulation.

Greater emphasis has been placed in the revised Part II upon certain aspects of phonetic theory, and practice material has been supplied in the use of phonetic symbols primarily for purposes of ear training in the identification of English speech sounds.

The facility and accuracy with which phonetic symbols can be used after even a short learning period more than offset the small amount of time and effort required to learn them. A table of the symbols used, complete with key words, is included at the beginning of Part II. Phonetic symbols throughout this book are enclosed in brackets, thus, [t]. When the symbol is italicized, thus, *t,* it is the alphabet letter that is referred to. Throughout Part I key words are also supplied along with the phonetic symbols in all instances where the symbol is different from the ordinary alphabet letter.

Part II has also been expanded to include a detailed discussion of each individual speech sound, and practice material for each sound has been supplied. Additional general practice material for diction has also been added to Part II.

In both Parts I and II the revision features considerably more emphasis upon ear training than was included originally. This emphasis is introduced in Chapter I where the student is directed to begin his program of work with a detailed analysis and evaluation of his own voice and speech. Such an evaluation should result in an individual plan of improvement for each student against which his progress can be checked from time to time during the term.

More attention has also been given throughout this revision to the problem of carry-over, or transfer, of skills learned in the voice and diction course to other special speech activities and to the everyday uses of voice and speech in oral communication. This has been accomplished through the inclusion of more prose selections for practice, as well as other materials more closely resembling conversational speech. A number of special assignments involving informal talks, group discussions, and so forth, have also been added. Several such assignments, as well as additional practice selections, will be found at the end of Chapter V.

In those courses for which the instructor needs more general assignments than this book supplies, he might consider for use as a supplementary text one of the several handy speech notebooks presently available. Such notebooks, many of which have tear-out sheets, supply a wide variety of practical speech assignments which could be used to supplement those in this book and thus augment the carry-over of vocal skills to specific activities such as public speaking, group discussion, microphone speaking, and oral interpretation.

Despite the extensive changes and additions that have been made in this revision, it should be stressed that the basic 'philosophy' of voice training and the program which implements it remain essentially unchanged from their presentation in the original edition. Thus, while it is hoped that the present revision will be found to be more complete, more stimulating, and more generally effective than the original, it is still not basically different.

In preparing this revision I have found the comments and recommendations of individuals who have used the original version to be of inestimable value. Such reactions have provided me with most helpful information regarding the various kinds of courses for which the book has been used as a text. I have also learned a great deal about what instructors and students want and need in a text, and I have been made aware of the many different approaches and methods preferred by various instructors.

To the many individuals who shared with me their suggestions and reactions, not only to the original edition but to the revision as well, I express my sincere appreciation.

V. A. A.

Stanford University
December 1960

Acknowledgments

GRATEFUL acknowledgment is made to the following pub-
lishers and individuals for permission to quote or reprint
from their publications:

D. Appleton-Century Company, Inc. for a selection from *Her-
mione* by Don Marquis.

College Verse for 'Haunted' by Frederick Goshe.

Holt, Rinehart and Winston, Inc. for 'Mending Wall,' 'The
Runaway,' 'Stopping by Woods on a Snowy Evening,' and
a selection from 'New Hampshire' from the *Complete Poems
of Robert Frost* by Robert Frost, published by Henry Holt
and Co., copyright 1930, 1949; and for 'The Listeners' from
Collected Poems by Walter de la Mare.

Houghton Mifflin Company for 'Relieving Guard' and a selection
from 'Dickens in Camp' by Bret Harte; 'Sea Shell' and a
selection from 'Lilacs' from the *Complete Poetical Works of
Amy Lowell;* 'Identity' by T. B. Aldrich; and 'Robinson
Crusoe's Story' by C. E. Carryl.

Alfred A. Knopf, Inc. for 'Madman's Song' from *Collected Poems*
by Elinor Wylie and for 'The Microbe' from *Cautionary
Verses* by Hilaire Belloc.

The Macmillan Company for selections from 'The Dauber,' 'The
West Wind,' 'Tewkesbury Road,' and 'Sea-Fever' from *Poems*
by John Masefield; a selection from 'The Congo' by Vachel
Lindsay; 'The Shell' by James Stephens; and a selection from
'Isaac and Archibald' by E. A. Robinson.

Rand McNally and Company for 'The Pirate Don Burke of
Dowdee' by Mildred Plew Meigs from *Child Life Magazine,*
copyright 1923. Also by permission of Mrs. Marion P.
Ruckel.

Mrs. Lew Sarett for 'The Loon' from *Covenant with Earth* by
Lew Sarett, edited and copyrighted 1956 by Alma Johnson

Sarett, Gainesville: University of Florida Press, 1956; and
for 'The Wolf Cry' from *Many Many Moons* by Lew Sarett,
copyrighted 1920 by Henry Holt and Company, Inc., renewed 1948 by Lew Sarett. Both poems reprinted by permission of Mrs. Lew Sarett.

Charles Scribner's Sons for 'Bed in Summer,' 'Requiem,' 'The
Wind,' and a selection from *Travels with a Donkey* by Rob-
ert Louis Stevenson; and for selections from 'The Marshes of
Glynn' and 'The Pine and the Palm' by Sidney Lanier.

The Society of Authors for 'Old Susan' by Walter de la Mare and
'Jock O' Dreams' by Rose Fyleman. The latter also by permission of Miss Rose Fyleman.

Frederick A. Stokes Company for selections from 'The Barrel-
Organ' and 'A Song of Sherwood' from *Collected Poems,*
Volume I, by Alfred Noyes.

Virgil Markham for selections from 'The Man with the Hoe' by
Edwin Markham.

If any acknowledgment has been omitted from this list, it has
not been from willful neglect, but rather because the author
has been unable to trace the original publisher or holder of
the copyright.

Table of Contents

List of Figures

Illustrations drawn by Walter B. Schwarz

PART I
THE VOICE

I

The Effective Voice

EVER since the Greek orators and teachers of rhetoric first recognized the fundamental importance of delivery in achieving true effectiveness in public speaking, training of the speaking voice has been considered to be a very important and rewarding activity. Voice is obviously the principal tool by means of which all of the activities involving speech in any form, whether it be public speaking, business speaking, or ordinary conversation, are performed. The individual's success or failure in those activities will be substantially influenced by the efficiency of his vocal mechanism and the skill with which he uses it. It is becoming more apparent every day that in our relationship with those about us a pleasing, effective voice is an asset contributing materially to social and professional success.

Much has been said and written on the role which the voice is believed to play in expressing and revealing personality. We have been told that people take us for what we appear to be and that the qualities and characteristics of our voices and our speech are important in determining the impression we make upon others. There is little doubt that this is true. Whether we like it or not and whether we are aware of it or not, close ties have been established in the mind of the average individual between certain characteristics of voice and corresponding types and characteristics of personality.

A very important use is made of this commonly accepted relationship in the casting of character roles in drama; there is always a close correspondence between voice and the kind

3

of character or personality that is being portrayed. If the part is not 'type-cast' and the actor does not naturally possess the required vocal qualities for the part he is to play, he must cultivate them or simulate them. If he is to play the part of a hard, unyielding character, for example, he must *sound* like such a person, as well as behave like him in other respects.

Because these stereotypes or 'vocal images,' as they might be called, do in reality exist, there are important implications for all of us; we must be sure at all times that our voice conveys the impression we want people to have of us. If our voice gives the impression we are timid, unfriendly, or arrogant and we are actually not that kind of person at all, it is indeed unfortunate, for others will tend to react to us as if we were that kind of person.

Speech has been referred to as man's chief medium of social adaptation and control. As egocentric as it may appear on the surface, it is still true that we speak in order that we may bring about responses favorable to ourselves. This fact is quite obvious in such speech situations as those confronting the salesman or the political speaker, where the desired result is a tangible, overt response of acceptance leading to favorable action on the part of the listener. For the average individual concerned with the more common uses of speech, the desired response may be social approval and acceptance— we want people to like us—or it may be simply to gain attention—we want people to listen to what we have to say. In any case, however, regardless of what the immediate purpose of the speaker happens to be, his chances of success will be materially enhanced if his voice and speech naturally create a favorable impression.

LEARNING TO SPEAK WELL

Why do we need voice training at all? Why are not our voices naturally as effective and efficient as they could be? There are doubtless a number of plausible explanations, but prominent among them is the generally accepted fact that speech, unlike such functions as walking, eating, crying, or laughing, is an acquired function, a learned activity. While the individual would naturally get about, eat, and cry in the normal course of his development, he would never employ speech unless as a child he were taught to use it. Speech is entirely a product of the child's social environment and as such has been called an 'overlaid function,' because it makes use of organs and mechanisms of the body intended by nature to serve basic, biological needs.

Strictly speaking, there are no speech organs as such in the human animal. The larynx, for example, of first importance in speech, was originally developed as a valve to prevent foreign matter from entering the trachea. The lungs, which furnish the motive power for voice production, have as their primary purpose the ventilation of the blood by supplying it with oxygen and carrying off waste products arising from the process of metabolism. The primary functions of the mouth are concerned with the intake and mastication of food. Speech, therefore, is an activity 'invented' and developed by man for the purpose of better adjusting himself to his social and physical environments. It is no more a natural activity for him than is dancing or singing, probably not as much. The principal difference is that speech has come to have a much deeper social significance and psychological involvement.

Chief among the implications arising from these considerations is this: since speech is a learned activity, it follows that it can be poorly learned. The process of learning to talk is largely one of imitation; the child comes to use the kind of speech that he hears. Fortunate indeed, therefore, is the individual who has heard superior speech models from the beginning; good speech will be but second nature to him. Unfortunately, however, such situations are comparatively rare. Most of us at some time or another, at home, at school, or among our companions, have been subjected to influences tending to induce habits of carelessness, slovenliness, and misuse of the vocal mechanism. Such habits, formed at an early, impressionable period in our development, become deeply imbedded and are very difficult to eradicate when later training is attempted. In fact, it is often more difficult to break down the old habit pattern than it is to establish the new response in its place. Nevertheless, this first step must be accomplished before any satisfactory progress can be made with the second.

Another characteristic of an acquired skill such as speech is that, lacking constant care and attention, it is likely to deteriorate. Not that there is danger of our forgetting how to speak, but if we are oblivious of our voices, habits of misuse and abuse can easily creep into our speech response patterns. We can become careless, 'lip-lazy,' and slovenly in our speech without realizing it, because we grow so accustomed to the sound of our own voices that no longer is any impression made on us; we are unable to listen objectively. Consequently we have no way of checking up on ourselves unless noticeable qualities and characteristics are called to our attention by others or we are fortunate enough to hear a recording of our voice played back to us, in which case the inevitable response will be, 'Do I sound like *that?*'

Such attitudes as indifference and carelessness, as well as misuse of the speech mechanism, therefore, account for a majority of the poor voices we hear all around us; they are merely the product of improper vocal habits. It is true, of course, that occasionally voice defects result from some structural deficiency or abnormality or a general physiological condition of ill health. These cases are in the minority, however, and generally do not come under the scope of voice training; they are subjects for the physician or the speech pathologist. Fortunately, most cases of improper voice production are not so serious, and with proper attention given to them do yield readily to training.

One factor that has seriously hindered progress in voice training for speech is the belief held by some that such training leads to an artificial, conscious nicety of expression. It may be unnecessary to stress here that there is no place for this sort of training in modern speech education. There should be no hint in voice training properly presented and founded upon soundly established principles of anything suggesting the 'arty,' the affected, or the superficially 'cultivated.' The trained voice that calls adverse attention to itself because it is unnatural has been improperly trained. There is nothing inherently incompatible with ease, simplicity, and naturalness in such characteristics of good speech as smoothness of phrasing, purity of tone, and clearness of diction.

Voice training today must be practical. It must not be thought of as merely a specialized form of fine art suitable for acting, reading, or public speaking, but having little to do with real life. Rather, if an individual's voice is going to be an asset to him, it must enhance his personality, aid him in the whole process of communication, and add to his effectiveness generally. Unfortunately there is not always the carry-over one might wish for from the training and discipline of the classroom to the actual speech situations of real life.

There are two possible explanations for this failure of voice training to 'take' properly. One is to be found in the conviction referred to a moment ago that such training leads to a vocal technique constituting a special sort of polish to be reserved for special occasions—a kind of accomplishment to be 'displayed' when unusual situations call for unusual vocal powers. An individual harboring such notions has failed to see the essentially practical, useful nature of voice training for speech.

The second explanation, really an outgrowth of the first,

is to be found in the fact that all voice and speech training naturally tends to be specific not only for the type of material used as a basis for training but also for the situations in which the training was given. A student, for example, who has been trained largely in oral reading may learn to read beautifully but he may speak wretchedly. Similarly, an individual trained in public speaking may read a simple illustrative quotation quite badly. In a like manner there is danger that the voice training student may learn to perform his drills and exercises flawlessly and he may speak well as long as his attention is on good speech, but he too often fails to demonstrate any of his vocal accomplishments when he steps outside of the classroom.

Yet it must be obvious to anyone who has thought about the matter at all that good use of voice and speech must become an integral part of the individual's personality if it is to have real value for him. It cannot be a rare accomplishment to be reserved for special occasions. It is in the everyday speaking situation—at home, on the street, in the office, and at the social gathering—that the average individual most needs good speech. For him the special occasions will be rare; he stands or falls on his adjustment to his everyday environment. Therefore, it cannot be said that voice or speech training has been successful until a final carry-over from the learning situation to the actual situation has been effected.

It is a commonplace to remind ourselves that voice and speech reflect the moods, attitudes, thinking, and general behavior potentials that make up an individual's personality. With certain qualifications, we know this to be true. In the process of developing an effective voice, therefore, should the emphasis be placed upon merely training the physical mechanism of voice, or upon stimulating a type of mental and emotional activity within the individual which will manifest itself in desirable characteristics of voice? In other words, shall we train the mechanism or train the mind? The truth of the

matter is that neither of these methods of approach can be
ignored by the student of voice because both are definitely
involved in the problem. Bluntly stated, one may have a dull,
uninteresting, or unpleasant voice because his voice is defective or improperly used; but he may also have such a voice
because he is a dull, uninteresting, or unpleasant person. In
the one case, voice training appears to be the proper solution,
but in the other case it is obvious that the problem involves
much more than merely giving attention to the mechanical
aspects of voice production.

Yet, as was stated, neither point of view can be ignored in
a comprehensive program of vocal training. The final objective is a pleasing, expressive voice. In the process of acquiring
it the first step is to put the instrument itself, the vocal
mechanism, in good condition, and through training and
practice render it fully responsive to any demands which may
be made upon it. In addition it is also necessary that the
individual himself be stimulated by vivid thinking, genuine
feeling, and a motivating purpose, for in the final analysis,
other things being equal, expressiveness of voice merely reflects the speaker's awareness of the importance and true
meaning of what he is attempting to communicate. In other
words, there must be something to express from within the
personality as well as a responsive mechanism for expressing it.

This last, it might be argued, involves the entire field of
education and personality development and hence is properly
outside the immediate concern of a course in voice or speech
training. While this contention is to a degree true, it is just
as true that vocal training cannot take place in a vacuum;
such training must always proceed in relation to the personality and other social factors which influence the *use* of voice
and speech. Thus, in a sense, voice training is personality
training, in the same way that personality training is also
voice training.

The chief point for the student of voice to remember as he progresses through the various steps of the program set forth in this book is that this twofold relationship does exist and that he should never lose sight of it. Much depends upon his constant awareness of this fact, since the psychological factors contributing to expressive and pleasing speech are much less tangible and hence less teachable than the more easily seen and understood mechanical aspects of the problem. It is much easier to effect changes in the voice than in the personality. That is to say, the voice student can be taught to breathe properly, to produce good tone, and to speak distinctly much more readily than he can be stimulated to emotional response, made to see fine intellectual distinctions and relationships, or be awakened to a compelling purpose. In this the student must be his own teacher to a certain extent.

While the major emphasis throughout this book will be upon the mechanism of voice production and its development and training, the dependence of an expressive voice upon an expressive personality will by no means be forgotten. Whenever the psychological element is involved in any vocal problem, full cognizance will be taken of it, and the psychological approach will be freely utilized.

CHARACTERISTICS OF A GOOD VOICE

We have been told that America is becoming 'voice conscious'; that as a result of the widespread influence of radio and television, the spoken word has a potentiality today which it has never before enjoyed. Men and women in important positions are taking voice and speech lessons so that they may more readily gain favor and acceptance when they address millions of listeners over the air and from the public platform. Superior speaking has been credited with winning national elections.

Just what is 'voice consciousness'? Of what are we conscious? Certainly not of our own voices, in the majority of instances. In reality, the so-called consciousness or awareness probably does not extend beyond our favorable, or unfavorable, reaction to voices we hear, a reaction that is often vague and intuitive, but none the less real and potent. We react to the general effect of the total personality as manifested through the voice. Usually we are not aware of the separate qualities that contribute to this effect; we think of a voice as being pleasant or unpleasant, interesting or dull, expressive or monotonous as a result of the over-all impression which it makes upon us. Very seldom do we analyze it to determine what outstanding characteristics contribute to this impression. Yet if we are to become truly voice conscious, as we must if we are to substitute new habit patterns for old ones in our own speech, we must break down vocal expression into its component parts so that separate attention may be given to each one.

As a beginning step in that direction, let us consider what qualifications can be formulated as characterizing an effective speaking voice. The following are suggested as a working basis:

1. *Adequate Loudness.* Nothing is more distressing than the attempt to hear what a speaker is saying when all that reaches one's ear is a low, weak murmur out of which an intelligible phrase arises now and then. Individuals whose normal conversational voices are thin and light are distinctly handicapped; it is difficult for them to create an impression of confidence, assurance, and self-possession. If people frequently have to ask you to repeat what you have said, take warning and determine whether your voice possesses adequate loudness.

2. *Clearness and Purity of Tone.* Is your voice clear and of good quality, or could it be called 'fuzzy,' hoarse, breathy, wheezy, metallic, or throaty? The good voice must be free from disturbing, unpleasant elements in the tone.

3. *A Pleasing and Effective Pitch Level.* A voice should not rumble far down in one's throat like the pedal notes of an organ nor should it be high and piping. One does not like to hear a man's voice too low in pitch nor a woman's voice too high. Individuals differ somewhat in their best and most natural pitch level, but for every voice there will be found a basic level at which it performs most effectively and pleasantly.

4. *Ease and Flexibility.* The normal voice is responsive and is characterized by a degree of variety and melody contributing to what can be called expressiveness. Absence of this quality makes for monotony and dullness. Moreover, a good voice should not convey the impression of being forced or labored.

5. *A Vibrant, Sympathetic Quality.* Lack of this quality produces a harshness and flatness of tone suggesting a cold, unimaginative, unsympathetic personality. On the other hand, a voice possessing this quality can be said to have warmth and vibrancy; it is 'alive.'

6. *Clearness and Ease of Diction.* The good voice is easily intelligible without being conspicuously so. The speaker is readily understood because his diction is clear and distinct; he doesn't mutilate his speech by omitting or swallowing sounds and syllables, nor does it appear that it is an effort for him to speak clearly.

MATERIALS FOR VOICE ANALYSIS AND DIAGNOSIS

It is a physiological as well as a psychological reality that individuals do not hear their own voices as others hear them. For this reason serious vocal defects may persist for years without the individual's being aware of them. He has not heard them in his own voice and even his best friends haven't told him! The invariable response of a person who has just heard a recording of his voice played back to him for the first time is 'Do I sound like that?'; whatever his other re-actions to the experience may be, he is always surprised.

THE USE OF A VOICE-RECORDING DEVICE

In this reaction of surprise is to be found the most im-portant clue to the necessity of having some objective basis upon which to conduct a voice analysis and diagnosis. With-out this basis, time spent in attempting to describe such in-herently obscure yet very real aspects of voice and speech as vocal quality, speech melody, and vowel intonation, or even such relatively objective aspects of voice as pitch and loudness, is to a certain extent wasted. Unless the speaker himself can hear and identify the particular vocal problem in his own voice, he will have the greatest difficulty in under-standing what is meant and what is wanted, and as a result he will be seriously handicapped in his efforts to do anything about it. A good tape recorder, or other recording device, is of the greatest value in accomplishing this necessary pre-liminary step to successful voice training.

On the other hand, there is no magical benefit to be de-rived from the mere recording and playing back of a student's voice. Even after he hears his voice objectively, he will need help and guidance in appraising it and in organizing a pro-gram of training to improve it. As a matter of fact, routine recording and reproduction of voices without careful analy-sis and guidance may prove more harmful than beneficial in some instances. The strange sound of one's voice coming back to him is not only an occasion for surprise, but it may also result in something of an emotional shock, especially if the effect of the voice is decidedly unpleasant. Merely calling attention to vocal defects serves only to make the individual self-conscious and distressed about them, unless he is also shown what he can do about them and is given some assur-ance that improvement is possible.

Therefore when a recording device is used in connection

with classroom instruction, each recording should be followed by a conference in which the student and the instructor listen to the play-back together. A complete analysis and diagnosis of the voice problems should then be made, and a program of training set up to correct the faults observed and to develop whatever potentialities may be evident. Such a program, adjusted to the needs of the individual voice, must be laid out in terms not only of ultimate objectives to be attained, but also in terms of separate steps and specific problems to which special attention is to be given. The training program must be definite and concrete. Recordings of the voice made at intervals throughout the term serve to motivate and direct the student, and a comparison of the final recording at the end of the term with the one made at the beginning will provide some objective measure of the student's total progress.

OUTLINE FOR VOICE ANALYSIS AND DIAGNOSIS

The following outline may be used as a basis for appraisal and analysis of voice and speech performance. In it are listed the various items that should receive attention—aspects of voice and speech which are, for the most part, those presented in detail in later chapters of this book both in the general discussion and in the drills and exercise material. The outline is not presented as a check sheet; rather it is designed merely to bring into focus the most important items that should be kept in mind as a basis for appraisal of vocal performance. It could easily be converted into a rating scale, however, if quantitative values, say from one to five, were assigned to the items in the sub-headings, indicating the degree to which each particular item applied to the voice as a whole. For example, a rating of five under Nasal would indicate that this quality was present to a very marked degree; a rating of one would indicate only very slight nasality.

Analysis of Voice and Diction

I. RATE. Very Good ☐ Average ☐ Unsatisfactory ☐ (Indicate below)
  A. Too fast ....
  B. Too slow ....
  C. Unvarying, monotonous ....
  D. Poor phrasing; irregular rhythm of speaking ....
  E. Hesitations ....
  F. Other ....

II. LOUDNESS. Very Good ☐ Average ☐ Unsatisfactory ☐ (Indicate below)
  A. Too loud ....
  B. Too weak ....
  C. Lack of variety, monotony ....
  D. Force overused as a form of emphasis ....
  E. Other ....

III. PITCH. Very Good ☐ Average ☐ Unsatisfactory ☐ (Indicate below)
  A. General level too high ....
  B. General level too low ....
  C. Lack of variety, monotony ....
  D. Fixed pattern, stereotyped ....
  E. Exaggerated pitch changes ....
  F. Other ....

IV. QUALITY. Very Good ☐ Average ☐ Unsatisfactory ☐ (Indicate below)
  A. Nasal ....
  B. Denasal ....
  C. Hoarse, husky ....
  D. Breathy, aspirate ....
  E. Throaty, harsh ....
  F. Strained, strident, shrill ....
  G. Flat, lack of vibrato ....
  H. Falsetto ....
  I. Tremorous ....
  J. Other ....

V. DICTION. Very Good ☐ Average ☐ Unsatisfactory ☐ (Indicate below)
  A. Speech sounds: Omitted .... Added ....
      Substituted .... Defective ....
  B. Indistinct articulation, oral inactivity ....
  C. Slow, labored ....
  D. Rapid, slurring ....
  E. Foreign dialect ....
  F. Regional dialect ....
  G. Mispronunciation ....
  H. Affectation ....
  I. Other ....

VI. GENERAL IMPRESSION GAINED FROM THE VOICE.
  A. Favorable: suggesting friendliness, alertness, self-assurance, vitality, poise, or responsiveness.
  B. Unfavorable: suggesting indifference, timidity, tenseness, indecision, unfriendliness, affectation, unresponsiveness, or immaturity.

It will often be found that vocal problems involve more than one aspect of the voice. In learning to analyze voices, therefore, one should train himself to listen in terms of such dimensions as loudness, pitch, and quality separately. If the general impression gained from the voice is that of tenseness, for example, one may discover upon closer examination that the pitch is excessively high, the quality strident, and the diction perhaps rapid and slurring. The harsh voice may be pitched too low, it may be close to a monotone, the rate may be too slow, and the articulation indistinct, as another example. This break-down of the voice into its several components is a necessary prelude to the planning of a program of voice improvement, since individual attention may need to be given to specific problems involving pitch, rate, quality, and so on.

MATERIALS FOR RECORDING AND ARTICULATION TESTING

In making an analysis of the voice, whether with the aid of a recording or not, it is well to use a sample of spontaneous speech, as well as more highly structured material which the individual can read. The following selections can be used for the reading portion; since they contain a rather complete sampling of English vowels and consonants in the various positions, they afford a good test of diction.

1. The following articulation test contains all of the sounds of the English language. All consonants appear in each of the three positions—initial, medial, and final—in which they are regularly found in English. The consonants most commonly found to be defective, such as [l], [r], and [s], are repeated a number of times. All of the vowels and diphthongs occur at least once, and many of them are used in at least two of the three positions.

It is usually rather easy to reach the Virginia Theater. Board car number fifty-six somewhere along Churchill Street and ride to the highway. Transfer there to the Mississippi bus. When you arrive at Judge Avenue, begin walking toward the business zone. You will pass a gift shop displaying little children's playthings that often look so clever you will wish yourself young again: such things as books and toys, and, behind the counter, a playroom with an elegant red rug and smooth, shining mirrors. Beyond this shop are the National Bank and the Globe Garage. Turn south at the next corner; the theater is to your left.

2. The following selection, an adaptation of the first few paragraphs of the well-known story of 'Arthur, the Young Rat,' also contains all of the sounds of English.

Once there was a young rat named Arthur, who could never make up his mind. Whenever the other rats asked him if he would like to go out with them, he would answer, 'I don't know.' And when they said, 'Would you like to stop at home?' he wouldn't say yes or no either. He would always shirk at making a choice.

One day his aunt said to him, 'Now, look here. No one will ever care for you if you carry on like this; you have no more mind than a blade of grass!' The young rat just coughed and looked wise as usual, but said nothing.

'Don't you think so?' asked his aunt, stamping with her feet, for she couldn't bear to see the young rat so cold-blooded. 'I don't know' was all the young rat ever answered. And then he would calmly walk off and think for an hour whether he should stay in his cool hole in the ground or go out and walk.*

3. This paragraph also contains most of the sounds of English:

The lodgekeeper found an old chart written in a peculiar cypher. After careful study he was able to make it out and learned from it that a choice and rare old treasure chest was buried four or five feet underground on the very spot where the new school house stood. He was sure he could find it if he obeyed directions, however, and following several trials at last he did unearth it. But as he was lifting it out, the box fell to pieces and the contents fell back into the hole.

EASE AND NATURALNESS—THE KEY TO PROPER VOICE PRODUCTION

Despite the fact that speech, as we have seen, is an overlaid function and, considered strictly from the point of view of biology, a somewhat unnatural one, it is still true that the best method of voice training is the easiest method, the method that interferes as little as possible with the basic, biological functions of the organs which are also involved in speech. Voice production should be as simple and effortless as possible. No great amount of energy should be required to produce a vocal tone even of considerable loudness, nor should the vocal organs become fatigued or irritated even after prolonged, steady use under normal conditions. Ordi-

* The entire story of 'Arthur, the Young Rat' will be found in Chapter X.

narily there should be no feeling of strain or tension in the throat during vocalization.

The theory of voice training developed in this book is based upon the assumption that most of the more common defects of vocalization arise as a result of interference with the easiest, most natural functioning of the organs responsible for speech. Far too much effort is expended, often misdirected, in voice production generally. The result is strain arising from muscular tensions in the throat and mouth, which interferes with the free action of the tone-producing mechanism. Such vocal faults as rapid and jerky speech, hoarseness, harshness, high pitch, weakness of tone, and even complete loss of voice are often directly traceable to strain and tension in the organs of phonation and articulation.

In accordance with this point of view, therefore, many of the problems of voice training will be approached through a type of controlled relaxation, not only of the muscles directly and indirectly involved in the speech process, but of the body as a whole. Only through relaxation of the larger muscles of the throat and neck can the mechanism of the larynx be freed to perform its function of tone production. Only through relaxation can breathing be adequately controlled and the resonators of the throat and mouth be adjusted properly to produce a full, rich, vibrant tone. Only in this way can all of the muscles involved in phonation and articulation be made flexible and instantly responsive to the demands of pleasant, expressive, and clear voice and speech.

An Exercise in Voice Analysis

From the radio or television, or in a face-to-face or public speaking situation, choose an individual and analyze his voice and speech, using the analysis outline included earlier in this chapter. Begin by describing your general reaction to the voice, referring to such items, if you wish, as are included under item VI in the outline. Proceed from there to a more detailed analysis, beginning with item I. Do not make the task unduly difficult for yourself by choosing an individual with a generally superior voice. Extend this assignment to include at least three different voices, striving for as much contrast as possible in your choices. Include both men and women.

II

Breathing for Speech

THE breathing mechanism in relation to the voice can be compared to the bellows of an organ or accordion. Just as air compressed within the bellows is forced out around the reed, setting it into vibration and thus producing tone, so the air within the lungs, when put under pressure, vibrates the vocal folds when they are drawn together during exhalation and tone again results. And just as loudness is increased in the organ or accordion by applying more pressure to the bellows, so loudness and carrying power in the voice result primarily from increased action of the breathing mechanism.

However, breathing serves a more vital function in the body than merely providing the motive power for voice. Of all the fundamental biological drives, breathing is the strongest and the most persistent because the body's supply of oxygen must be renewed more frequently than that of any other substance which the organism requires. Since oxygen cannot be stored in the body as food or water can be, there is virtually no reserve supply. A few minutes without this vital substance, and the tissues of the body begin to break down, the higher levels of the nervous system being the first to suffer. This essential dependence of the body upon a constantly renewed supply of oxygen has imposed certain restrictions and limitations upon speech, which is also dependent upon the breathing mechanism. These will be discussed in more detail in a later section. For the present, a brief description of the anatomical structures involved in respiration will serve to make the entire process more understandable. The air passages themselves, which we shall consider first, consist of the nasal chambers and the mouth, the pharynx, the larynx, the trachea, bronchi, bronchioles, and finally the tiny air sacs, or alveoli, of the lungs.

THE MOUTH, NASAL PASSAGES, AND PHARYNX

Although inhaling through the mouth is recommended for speech because of the greater ease and freedom from possible disturbing noises with which mouth inhalation can be accomplished, nasal breathing should be practiced under all other conditions for the reason that the nasal passages are biologically designed for that purpose. Their structure is such that the air is warmed, moistened, and filtered as it comes in contact with the mucous membrane which lines the devious passageways of the nasal chambers (Figure 1). The position of the pharyngeal tonsil should also be observed while referring to this figure because it will be mentioned in connection with the condition known as adenoids in a later discussion of nasal resonance.

Although the pharynx, or throat, serves as a passageway to conduct the air from the mouth and nasal cavities to the trachea through the glottis (the space between the vocal folds), the mouth and in certain respects the pharynx are more closely associated with the intake of food than with breathing. Each, however, has an important speech function in resonance, and the mouth especially plays a leading role in articulation, both of which activities will be discussed in succeeding chapters.

TRACHEA AND BRONCHI

The trachea, or windpipe (Figures 1 and 2), is a membranous tube held open by a series of cartilaginous crescents, each one approximately two-thirds of a circle. The purpose of these crescents of stiff cartilage is, of course, to prevent the trachea from collapsing when air is drawn into the lungs, just as a suction hose is held open by steel rings imbedded in its walls. The trachea, approximately four inches long and one inch in diameter, is elastic, allowing the larynx to move up and down, within limits, in swallowing and in speaking.

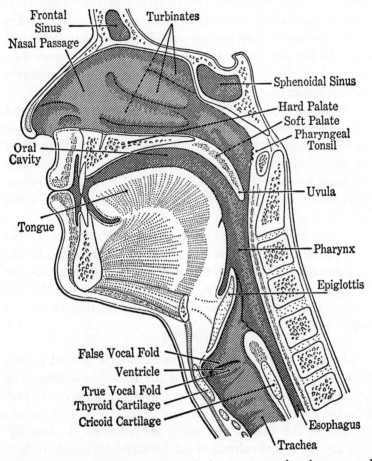

FIG. 1. Sagittal (mid-line) section of the nose, mouth, pharynx, and trachea. Only the right half of the nasal passage is illustrated, the thin, bony partition known as the septum, which divides the right from the left, not being shown because it lies directly in the line of section.

At its base the trachea divides into the two bronchi, right and left, which in turn divide into smaller and smaller tubes, or bronchioles.

THE LUNGS

The bronchioles terminate in clusters of tiny air sacs (alveoli) which make up the structure of the lungs. It is through the walls of these air sacs that actual respiration takes place, the oxygen of the air within the alveoli being exchanged for the excess carbon dioxide in the blood. The lungs as a whole are highly elastic, resembling minutely porous, conical sponges.

As can be seen from Figure 2, the lungs are concave and broad at the base, gradually becoming smaller as they taper up toward the apex. The right lung is somewhat larger than the left, consisting of three main divisions, or lobes. The left lung has only two lobes, and one of its chief characteristics is the deep notch on its under surface in which the heart lies.

In respiration the lungs are entirely passive, except for the force exerted by their elastic recoil upon the outgoing breath in exhalation. Otherwise they are solely responsive to the changes of pressure within the thorax occasioned by the action of the breathing muscles in altering the size of the chest cavity.

THE RIBS

The bony cage of the chest, or thorax, is formed principally by the vertebral column at the back; the sternum, or breast bone, in front; and twelve pairs of ribs, curved to provide the conformation of the chest. These ribs, with the exception of the two lowest pairs, are attached by movable joints to the spinal column at the back and by lengths of flexible cartilage to the sternum in front. The last two ribs on either side are attached only to the spinal column at the back and hence are called free, or floating, ribs.

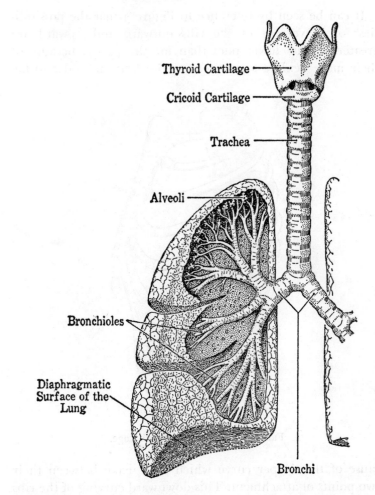

Thyroid Cartilage

Cricoid Cartilage

Trachea

Alveoli

Bronchioles

Diaphragmatic
Surface of the
Lung

Bronchi

FIG. 2. Portion of the respiratory tract with the right lung turned slightly outward so that its concave under-surface (diaphragmatic surface) might be more plainly seen. The interior of the lung is exposed to show the various divisions of the conducting system and their termination in the respiratory air sacs. The alveoli are disproportionately enlarged and the branchings of the bronchioles are likewise simplified.

It can be seen by reference to Figure 3 that the possibilities for movement of the ribs outward and upward are greater for the lower ones than for the upper, because of their more flexible attachment to the sternum and also be-

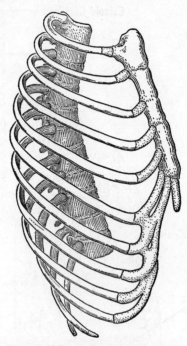

FIG. 3. Side view of the rib cage.

cause of the deeper curve which they make between their two points of attachment. This downward curving of the ribs is an important feature to bear in mind, since it explains how an upward pull upon the ribs can cause a cross-section, or lateral, expansion of the chest cavity by increasing the diameter from side to side. This action, often referred to as the 'bucket handle' action of the ribs, is illustrated in Figure 4.

THE MUSCLES OF RESPIRATION

With one or two exceptions, the muscles primarily responsible for getting air into the lungs are thoracic, or chest, muscles; those responsible for getting the air out under pres-

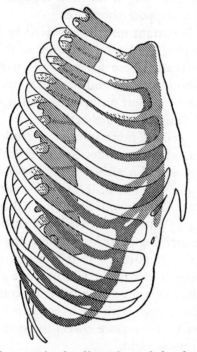

FIG. 4. Showing increase in the dimensions of the chest when the ribs are elevated in inhalation. The shaded portion represents the thorax after exhalation; the clear portion after the ribs have been raised at the end of inhalation.

sure are principally abdominal. However, in breathing for ordinary life purposes forced exhalation is rarely found; the natural force resulting from relaxation of the muscles of inhalation is sufficient to empty the lungs of air. This force is even adequate to support a quiet tone for a short length of time, or a phrase of speech. So far as breathing for speech is concerned, our interest centers particularly on the muscles responsible for getting an adequate supply of air into the lungs quickly and easily and on the control of the muscles responsible for parceling it out and regulating its pressure as it is needed to support phonation.

Among the important muscles involved in lifting the ribs and thus increasing the lateral diameter of the chest are the external intercostals, whose fibers, as the name implies, lie between the ribs themselves and slant upward and backward. Their function is to exert an upward pull upon the ribs, to accomplish the 'bucket handle' action.

The Diaphragm. Of more interest to students of voice is the diaphragm, which provides for a vertical expansion of the chest cavity and also assists in the upward and outward movement of the lower ribs. This important structure is a sheet of muscle and tendonous fiber, dome-shaped, or convex, in form, fitting up into the concave lower surface of the lungs and forming a dividing partition between the thorax and the abdominal cavity (Figure 5). It is attached to the sternum and to the lower border of the ribs in front and at the sides, and to the spinal column at the back. Its convex upper surface lies in close contact with the base of the lungs and heart, and its concave under surface covers the stomach on the left and the liver on the right.

The diaphragm is generally conceded to be the principal muscle involved in inhalation. When the muscular portion contracts, the central tendon or dome is pulled down, with the effect that the diaphragm is flattened and the vertical dimension of the chest cavity is considerably increased (Figure 6). This downward movement also causes some displacement of the visceral organs, the result of which is a slight expansion of the abdomen, particularly the upper portion located directly under the arch of the ribs in front.

The Mechanism of Breathing. Breathing is made possible by changes of air pressure within the thorax. Thus, when the diaphragm is depressed and the ribs are raised, the space

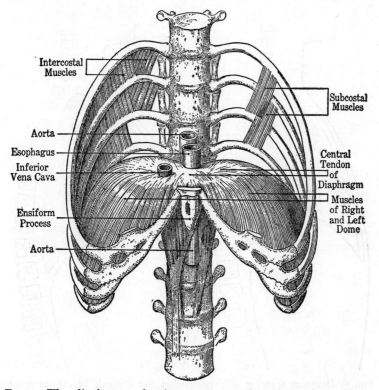

Fig. 5. The diaphragm, showing upper, or thoracic, surface; dome, or central tendon; and attachments to the lower ribs and the vertebrae.

within the chest cavity is substantially increased. The result is a rarefication, or a decrease in the pressure, of the air contained therein. To fill this partial vacuum, atmospheric pressure forces air into the only part of the thorax directly communicating with the air outside the body—the space within the lungs—until the pressures inside and outside the chest are again equalized. A reversal of this process forces air out of the lungs.

Again attention is called to the analogy of the bellows in the organ and accordion. When the bellows is pulled apart,

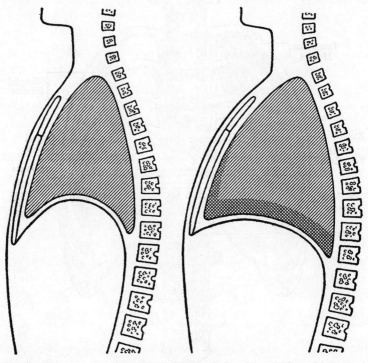

Fig. 6. Diagram showing enlargement of the thoracic breathing space during inhalation, with particular emphasis upon the role played by the diaphragm.

the volume inside is increased and air is thus drawn in to fill this space. When the bellows is squeezed together, the volume is decreased and air is forced out. So it is with breathing; the muscles of inhalation, principally the diaphragm and intercostals, expand the 'bellows,' while the abdominal muscles, with probably some help from the internal intercostals, are mainly responsible for decreasing its volume and forcing air out.

At the risk of giving undue attention to the obvious, it might be well to note that the part played by the air itself in this process is a purely passive one, as it is drawn into the lungs and then pushed out again by the mechanical action of the breathing mechanism.

As stated previously, passive exhalation as found in ordinary breathing results largely from a cessation of the activities responsible for inhalation with the accompanying relaxation and return to their normal positions of the muscles and other structures involved. Even though the process is ordinarily a passive one, the breath is expelled with appreciable force, which is derived from a number of factors, among them being the elastic recoil of the lungs and the return of the rib cage to its position of rest.

In forced, or active, exhalation, necessary to sustain all but very quiet phonation, the process referred to above is reinforced by contraction of the muscular walls of the abdomen, an action which forces the viscera up against the diaphragm. The viscera could be said to act like a piston, pushing the diaphragm back into its arched position and thus increasing the pressure on the air within the lungs. Note, however, that the diaphragm itself can exert no active force in adding to the pressure of the outgoing breath, since a muscle functions in only one way—by contracting and thus shortening itself. As we have already seen, contraction of the diaphragm flattens it, the effect of which is to increase the volume of the chest cavity and thus draw air in. So far as breathing is concerned, therefore, the diaphragm and the abdominal muscles are what are known as 'antagonists'; that is, they accomplish opposite results and work in opposite directions, so to speak.

The diaphragm can serve to influence the outflow of breath, therefore, only to the extent that its degree and rate of relaxation can be controlled to balance the upward pressure against it from the action of the abdominal muscles. This is a very important function, however; and in the control of exhalation, so necessary for effective vocalization, much depends upon the delicate balance achieved between the force exerted by the abdominal muscles and the restraining influence of the diaphragm.

By way of summary, it is misleading, therefore, to speak of 'supporting the tone from the diaphragm,' if by 'supporting' is meant attaining a degree of strength and projection. The function of the diaphragm in exhalation, as we have seen, is confined merely to that of exerting a measure of control over the rate at which the breath is allowed to escape; in other words, of parceling it out as needed to maintain phonation. Actual support—the building up of air pressure below the glottis—comes primarily from the abdominal muscles, especially those of the upper abdomen sometimes referred to as the 'belt muscles.'

THE BIOLOGICAL FUNCTION OF BREATHING

Students of voice and speech should not forget that the primary function of breathing is biological—the maintaining of life. In addition to the direct need for oxygen in the metabolism of the body, there are certain reflexive uses made of the breathing mechanism which are also concerned with fundamental life processes, such as sneezing, sobbing, and coughing. Because in the biological scale of development these activities are much older and much more important than speech, they will take precedence over speech and inhibit it whenever there is a conflict between the two. Thus, if one is speaking and has to cough, no matter how much he may desire to continue speaking, he stops speaking and coughs.

Although within certain limits breathing can be consciously controlled, under ordinary conditions it is an unconscious, automatic process. The respiratory center of the nervous system is located in the medulla at the base of the brain and it appears to be in close connection with the sensory fibers of virtually all of the cranial and spinal nerves, being responsive not only to visual and auditory stimuli, but also to pain, to various emotional states, and to almost any sudden and unexpected cutaneous sensation, such as a dash of cold water on the skin.

This sensitivity of the breathing mechanism to emotional stimulation presents a problem of considerable importance to voice training, as anyone can testify who has attempted to speak smoothly and breathe properly when suffering from stage fright. Frequently the rhythm and depth of breathing are so radically influenced by emotional and other disturbing factors as to make speech very difficult if not impossible. The expression 'breathless with fear' is far from being a mere figure of speech. Thus we find another argument in favor of giving careful attention to breathing in voice training, for to the extent that we are able to gain a measure of conscious control over the breathing mechanism we can insure a proper and dependable vocal response under the stress of adverse conditions.

Although for speech purposes somewhat more air may be taken in with each breath than would be used in normal breathing, there is still no close relationship between total breathing capacity and ability in speech or excellence in voice production. In other words, voices generally do not fail because sufficient air cannot be taken into the lungs, but rather because sufficient air is not taken in at the right time, or, if taken in, is not properly used. Therefore, exercises that have for their purpose merely the increase of chest expansion or of breathing capacity have but little value in voice training for the average individual. The important factor is not so much the total amount of air involved, as the use made of that air.

BREATHING FOR SPEECH

The points which we have just considered make it clear why in many instances proper breathing for speech must to a certain extent be learned and consciously controlled. The reasons for this will become even more apparent if the chief differences between breathing for speech and biological breathing are briefly reviewed.

1. Possibly the most important difference from the point of view of voice training is in the control of exhalation necessary when the outgoing breath is used to sustain tone. In normal respiration, exhalation is passive and relatively effortless. In fact, as has been pointed out, it results largely from relaxation after inhalation. But, since the vocal tone and in fact the whole speech process are entirely dependent upon the outgoing breath, it can clearly be seen that for voice production exhalation must be definitely regulated and prolonged. This regulation is of two kinds, involving first the control of relaxation of the muscles responsible for inhalation, principally the diaphragm, and second the control of the abdominal muscles involved in forced exhalation.

2. Another difference lies in the fact that for certain types of speaking breathing must be deeper and fuller than for ordinary life purposes, the type or depth of breathing required being determined by the speaker's attitude toward what he is saying, by the length of his phrases, and by the general circumstances under which he is speaking. That is, breathing becomes deeper as emotional tension is increased, and a 'big' idea requires more breath than a 'little' one. Some thoughts are best expressed in long, sustained phrases and sentences, while others naturally call for short, brisk sentences. Obviously the public speaker may need more breath than the individual engaged in quiet conversation.

3. Finally, the entire rhythm of breathing is quite different when speech is being produced from that which is ob-

served in ordinary biological breathing. The rhythm of breathing to sustain life is smooth, regular, and periodic, averaging about fifteen to twenty breaths per minute. For speech, however, the rhythm of breathing is largely determined, always within certain limits prescribed by biological necessity, by the rhythm of thinking. We think and speak not in terms of words, phrases, or sentences, but rather in terms of what have been called thought-groups. That is, each thought-group centers around a single idea, image, or concept which we wish to express. Appropriate words or phrases are chosen to express that single thought unit; it is uttered as a vocal unit; then there is a pause, and we pass to a new thought-group. This does not mean, however, that we inhale during every pause, but rather that whatever breath is taken should be taken during one of these pauses. Thus, whether we are always aware of it or not, we think, or 'get an idea,' take breath to express that idea, give voice to it, and then proceed to the next thought. This rhythm is ordinarily quite different from that of normal breathing, and the chief problem is to insure that both the speech and the biological needs are adequately served.

For speech purposes, therefore, a type of breathing is desired which will provide for (1) an adequate movement of air with a minimum of effort; (2) an inhalation that can be accomplished quickly and silently; (3) a sensitive and responsive control over the outgoing breath; and (4) a minimum of interference with the voice-producing mechanism in the throat. While speech can be produced as a result of any method of breathing that serves merely to draw air into the lungs and expel it under pressure, there is considerable evidence to indicate that the foregoing requirements can be met most adequately if the major activity is concentrated in the diaphragm and the lower ribs, with the diaphragm playing the dominant role. Contraction, or flattening, of the diaphragm provides for the vertical enlargement of the chest cavity and also facilitates the expansion of the lower ribs with an accompanying rise of the lower end of the sternum. Such a movement, exerting a downward pressure upon the abdominal organs, causes some distention of the abdomen, especially the upper portion, the most prominent of which movement will be noticed in the region of the so-called 'belt muscles,' and above, just under the arch of the ribs in front. The extreme upper portion of the chest should remain relaxed and passive.

Study of the description above discloses that there is nothing different or startling about the process recommended; it is the way a large number of individuals already breathe naturally and normally, both to sustain life and for speech purposes. The reasons why this way of breathing serves the purposes of voice production most effectively can be seen if the following features of the breathing mechanism are considered:

1. Since the lungs are conical in shape and hence have a larger cross-section area near the bottom than they have near the top, the greatest volume of air can naturally be moved with the least effort if the lower portion of the lungs is utilized. Such movement contributes to deeper, fuller breathing in contrast to the shallow breathing often found among those who employ chiefly the upper portion of the chest.

2. The control of the breath will be much more sensitive and flexible if the chief activity is centered in the middle of the body, since the inertia involved in the process is greatly lessened. When breathing is centered largely in the chest, especially the upper chest, the entire bony structure, including the twelve pairs of ribs, the sternum, and often the shoulders themselves, must be lifted for every inhalation. It is obvious that considerable weight and effort are involved in such a process. In contrast, when the diaphragm is brought into play, activity is primarily the result of flexible muscle tissue pulling against other muscles; no heavy structures are

involved. It is true that there is expansion of the widely arched and loosely attached lower ribs, but movement of the more rigid upper thorax is reduced to a minimum.

3. Finally, the diaphragm and the muscles attached to the lower ribs are functionally more independent of the laryngeal structures because of their more remote location than are the more adjacent muscles of the upper chest region. As a consequence, tensions resulting from the effort of breathing, especially forced exhalation to support speech, are much less likely to be transferred to the throat and to the muscles directly involved with the larynx. It is very difficult to contract one muscle or muscle group and at the same time keep other muscles relaxed if they are in close proximity. And it is highly essential, as we shall see in the following chapter, that interference with the free functioning of the vocal folds be kept to a minimum. The energy involved in supplying the motive power for voice through the breathing mechanism must not be allowed to 'spill over' into the laryngeal structure and hamper its functioning. Control becomes relatively easy when the major breathing effort can be concentrated in the middle of the body.

Proper Breathing, Merely One Means to an End. Without question, there has been much nonsense advocated from time to time on the subject of breathing for speech, a problem which has long been a center of keen interest and controversy among speech and voice teachers as well as research workers in the field. From time to time enthusiastic supporters have contended that this or that trick, notion, or 'system' of breathing was *the* one essential to effective voice production. In general, research has thus far produced somewhat inconclusive results. For example, a number of investigations have been conducted in which no significant relationship could be found between a type or method of breathing and certain aspects of voice production among the subjects studied. On the other hand, somewhat fewer studies have disclosed a significantly greater tendency toward diaphragmatic activity among superior speakers than among those with inferior voices. One such investigation, for example, discovered that individuals with voices judged to be superior exhibited a considerably greater movement of the diaphragm than did individuals with inferior voices. It also showed that the movement of the diaphragm tended to be steady and regular with the superior speakers, but jerky and irregular in the case of the inferior voices.*

In conclusion, no responsible voice teacher will contend that any one method or trick of breathing is the *sine qua non* of satisfactory voice production for speech. The whole process is much too complex for that, and breathing is only one of the elements involved in the total process of voice production. It is quite true that there are individuals with acceptable or even superior voices whose breathing does not conform with that recommended in this chapter. Whether or not these same individuals would have had still better voices if attention had been given to the most effective breathing for speech is a question that research has not as yet answered. The general results of research thus far cannot be interpreted to mean, therefore, that breathing can be safely disregarded in a program of voice improvement. A rather impressive rationale supports the contention that the student wishing to improve his speaking voice will be more likely to achieve success and achieve it with less time and effort if his training includes attention given to the control of exhalation and to the centering of breathing activity in the region of the upper abdomen and the lower chest area.

The program of exercises which follows has been organized toward the goal of making a controlled, centralized type of breathing an integrated part of the student's total normal speech activity. This development is accomplished first

* E. Mary Huyck and Kenneth D. A. Allen, 'Diaphragmatic Action of Good and Poor Speaking Voices,' *Speech Monographs*, 1937, Vol. iv, pp. 101-10.

through simple movements and activities designed primarily to make the individual aware of the muscular activities involved and thereby to give him control over those muscles.

Habituation of this process is accomplished through simple vocalization drills and exercises involving counting and the speaking of words and short phrases, and finally sentences, stanzas of poetry, and paragraphs of prose. Co-ordination of breathing with speaking should be the immediate aim at this point. Oral reading is helpful in establishing the rhythm of thinking, breathing, and speaking. Constant checking of the breathing for proper centering of activity in the middle of the body and for adequate control of exhalation is essential throughout the process of training. At all times, activity of the upper thorax should be at a minimum.

The student is reminded that while the present chapter is concerned exclusively with the problem of breathing in the general program of voice training, the subject should by no means be forgotten as the student progresses through the further stages of his training. The establishment of new habit patterns or the modification of old ones is a process involving continued observation and practice over an extended period of time if the final goal—the natural, unconscious use of the new patterns in everyday situations—is to be achieved.

BREATHING EXERCISES

ESTABLISHING CONSCIOUS CONTROL OF THE BREATHING PROCESS

Care should be taken at all times to insure that the greatest activity is in the central portion of the body directly under the arch of the ribs in front, with some expansion above and below this point as well as at the sides. At no time should the shoulders rise and fall in breathing nor should there be more than a slight secondary movement of the upper chest. The neck muscles should be kept relaxed.

Practice the following exercises either before a large mirror or with one hand held against the stomach and the other placed upon the chest to insure that the above conditions are observed. The purpose of these exercises is to make you conscious of the movement of the muscles responsible for the type of medial breathing which you are attempting to acquire. You will be able to use and control the muscles involved in medial breathing only when you learn what it feels like to use these muscles. Reinforce the kinesthetic sense with the visual by practicing before a mirror as suggested or by holding a book pressed against the midriff and watching its movements.

In connection with several of the exercises which follow keep in mind that there is a definite relationship between posture and ease and control of breathing. If you are standing, 'stand tall' with the back flat and the chest well supported; if you are sitting, 'sit up,' with your shoulders back and head held erect, but not in a stiff 'military' position. In either a sitting or standing position, slumping can only compress the ribs, making it difficult to expand the thoracic cavity and greatly hampering the freedom of movement which is one of the important goals of many of the exercises below.

1. Lie flat on your back in a relaxed condition and note the activity in the middle portion of your body as you breathe quietly. Place a book on your stomach and watch it rise and fall as you inhale and exhale. Get the 'feel' of this method of breathing.

2. Stand in an easy position with your back flat against the wall and with the edge of a book pressed against your stomach three or four inches below the end of the sternum. Exhale fully, forcing as much air as possible out of the body. If necessary, help this process along by pressing in on the book. When as much air as possible has been expelled, begin to inhale slowly, pushing the book away from you in the process by expanding that portion of the body against which it rests. Feel the action of the diaphragm pressing the upper viscera

out against the book. This exercise should be continued at intervals and in conjunction with those which follow until breathing has become easy and under perfect control.

3. Assume an easy standing position, but not against the wall this time, weight on the balls of the feet, chin in, chest up though not held rigid. Place the hands across the stomach with the finger tips touching at the position where the book was placed before. Breathe easily and quietly, feeling the expansion in front and at the sides. Take care to see that the upper portion of the chest remains passive and relaxed.

4. Repeat Exercise 3, taking an easy breath through the mouth and holding it for a second or two, then relaxing and exhaling. Try holding it for two seconds, then three, and up to five or six. Note that exhalation is accomplished merely by relaxing.

5. Following the procedure in Exercise 3, inhale through the nostrils; exhale quietly through the mouth.

6. Repeat Exercise 5, blowing the breath out with some pressure.

7. Inhale, a rather full breath, count 'one' in a firm, clear tone; then relax and allow the unused breath to escape. Pause momentarily, then repeat the process on 'two,' 'three,' and up to the count of ten. Take care that the tone is clear and pure and that only enough breath is used to speak the numbers, the rest being exhaled at the end of the count.

8. Repeat Exercise 7, counting from one to five on one breath, then relaxing, breathing, counting from six to ten, etc., up to twenty-five.

CONTROL OF EXHALATION

One of the most serious faults in the management of the breath for voice production is that of allowing a portion of it to escape before vocalization has begun. A person may take a good, full breath, but if he loses half of it before beginning to speak, he may find that he must replenish the supply in the middle of a thought-group or finish the phrase under strain by squeezing out the last bit of air within the lungs. The breath should not be wasted; it should be retained and used only as it is needed to sustain phonation. Since even a passive exhalation resulting merely from relaxation causes the breath to be expelled with considerable force, as was explained earlier in this chapter, the process of controlling exhalation for speech becomes to a certain extent a control of relaxation of the diaphragm and other muscles involved. Control thus involves a process of gradually parceling out the breath as it is needed to maintain speech. With this in mind, practice the following exercises.

1. To demonstrate the sustaining power of an exhalation that is purely passive, take a full breath, always from the middle of the body of course, start to sing the vowel [o] * and relax. That is, allow the production of the tone to be as passive as possible, exerting no active pressure from the breathing muscles. Time yourself to see how long the tone is maintained. Regulate the outflow of breath carefully, allowing only as much air to escape as is needed to produce a pure tone. Avoid excessive breathiness.

2. Repeat Exercise 1, but substitute counting for the sung vowel. Count at about the rate of two per second. Maintain complete relaxation except for the effort required to articulate the words. Allow no more break in the tone than is necessary between the counts, sustaining them on a relatively even pitch and volume. Do not allow waste breath to escape either between sounds or during the production of a sound. Continue counting as long as the breath supply naturally lasts; do not force it. Can you go as far as ten? Fifteen?

* A table of phonetic symbols will be found at the beginning of Part II.

3. Take a full breath without strain and, with controlled exhalation, gradually release it maintaining the sound [s]. Sustain the sound steadily and quietly, being careful to guard against fluctuations in the volume; don't allow the sound to become jumpy or irregular. In this drill the control of relaxation is evident. Practice until effective control has been attained.

4. Vary Exercise 3 by exerting pressure on the outgoing breath, thereby increasing the volume of the sound and shortening its duration. It is now much easier to maintain an even intensity. Why? What changes do you note in the action of the breathing mechanism?

5. Repeat Exercise 3, substituting a whispered [ɑ] for the [s]. Again give your full attention to maintaining an even sound. Place your hand over your 'diaphragm'; do you feel it gradually and steadily receding as a toy balloon deflates when the air is allowed to escape slowly?

6. Fix in your mind the average tempo of march time. Using this tempo, count aloud three bars of music, resting in each case on the fourth beat, thus: 1, 2, 3, —; 1, 2, 3, —; 1, 2, 3, —. This should all be done on one breath and an even tempo should be maintained, care being taken to observe a full quarter-note rest of silence where count 'four' would otherwise come. Neither replenish the supply of breath nor waste any of it during the rests. Can you do this exercise without closing the glottis during the rests, retaining the breath merely through control of the breathing muscles?

7. Speak the following sentences, breathing carefully before beginning each one and taking care to insure that no breath is lost before actual phonation begins.

   a. In truth, I know not why I am so sad.
   b. The weakest kind of fruit drops earliest to the ground.

   c. He is well paid that is well satisfied.

   d. Handsome is as handsome does.

   e. The only successful substitute for brains is silence.

   f. The person who is all wrapped up in himself is over-dressed.

   g. Smooth runs the water where the brook is deep.

   h. Silence is the unbearable repartee.

DEVELOPING ECONOMY OF BREATH

Wasted breath not only means lost energy for the speaker; it also contributes to an unpleasant quality of tone known as breathiness. The tendency for part of the exhaled breath to be lost even before phonation begins has already been mentioned. Breath is also often wasted between words or during pauses between thought-groups. One of the most important sources of wastage, however, occurs within words themselves when too much breath is used during the sounding of certain speech elements, such as the voiceless consonants, for example, which depend for their characteristic quality upon a considerable, but not excessive, outrush of air. It is known that the speech sounds requiring the greatest total expenditure of breath are the voiceless fricatives, such as [f], [s], and [ʃ]. Such a word as *success* therefore, unless carefully pronounced, will be wasteful of breath. For these sounds we must learn to produce the required acoustic result with a minimum volume of air. Moreover, the quality of the sounds themselves may be improved in this way, since excess breath used in the production of [s], for example, may result in a most unpleasant effect. The voiced fricatives, the voiceless and voiced plosives, and the nasals and so-called sonorants, such as [m], [l], and [r], require somewhat less breath in approximately the order mentioned. The vowels are the most efficient speech sounds of all, requiring the least expenditure of breath in relation to the phonetic power of the resulting tone.

Another source of difficulty might be called assimilation breathiness, in which the voicing of a vowel following a voiceless consonant is too long delayed and the breathy element of the consonant is carried over into what should be a clear vowel tone. In the word *far*, as an example, great care should be exercised to insure that [f] is held for only a very short time and that the beginning of the vowel [ɑ] is good tone, in which all of the breath is vocalized. Words beginning with a vowel preceded by a voiceless, or [h], approach also offer special difficulty if the voicing is excessively delayed or if the beginning of the vowel tone is allowed to become noticeably 'fuzzy' or breathy. This problem occurs in such words as *high, hot,* and *who.* However, breathiness properly belongs to the subject of tone production, and a more complete discussion of it, together with corrective exercises, will be presented in the following chapter. It is introduced here simply because it also involves wastage of the breath in speaking.

It can be seen, therefore, that control of the breath involves control of two different aspects of the speech mechanism: (1) The muscles of respiration, which are responsible for releasing the breath stream, and (2) the organs of phonation and articulation, which determine the efficiency with which the breath is used in the production of speech sounds.

It should be emphasized that several of the exercises which follow in this section are just that—exercises for purposes of diagnosis and training that do not have an immediate relationship to ordinary speech. For example, in communicative situations there is little practical value in seeing how far one can continue talking on one breath, since it is a simple matter to renew the breath supply at appropriate intervals. However, such exercises as the first four below can do much to disclose instances of needless breath wastage and can aid the individual to gain better control over his use of breath and improve the quality of many of the speech sounds.

EXERCISES TO DEVELOP ECONOMY OF BREATH

1. Take a full breath, avoiding undue strain or tension, especially in the throat, and count from one to twenty at a rate of slightly more than two counts per second. Bearing in mind the points discussed above, give special attention to such words as *two, three, four,* and *six.* Maintain a quiet, conversational volume.

2. Vary the exercise above by counting to twenty-five, thirty, thirty-five, and finally as far as your breath supply will carry you. Can you get to fifty on one breath? Avoid strain either at the beginning or at the end. Don't force the last few counts; always stop before your breath supply is entirely exhausted. Study your performance on this exercise to determine where you may be losing breath, or where you may be using more than is necessary.

3. Repeat Exercise 2, using the letters of the alphabet instead of digits. When you have finished with z, begin again without a break. Can you get through twice on one breath? Both in this and in the previous exercise you will find that your performance will improve markedly with practice. Why?

4. Read the following selection on one breath, observing a normal conversational tempo and paying attention to tone, articulation, and interpretation.

> Ring out, wild bells, to the wild sky,
> The flying cloud, the frosty light:
> The year is dying in the night;
> Ring out, wild bells, and let him die.

5. In reading the following selections, watch carefully for evidences of breath wastage on 'noisy' consonants, between words, and at the beginning of vowel sounds.

a. From the listless repose of the place, and the peculiar character of its inhabitants, who are descendants from the original

Dutch settlers, this sequestered glen has long been known by the name of Sleepy Hollow.

      b. Fair is foul, and foul is fair:
         Hover through the fog and filthy air.

    c. Success is full of promise till men get it; and then it is a last year's nest, from which the bird has flown.

    d. Apologizing—a very desperate habit; one that is rarely cured. Apology is only egotism wrong side out. Nine times out of ten, the first thing a man's companion knows of his short comings is from his apology.

      e. His beating heart is not at rest;
        And far and wide,
        With ceaseless flow,
        His beard of snow
      Heaves with the heaving of his breast.
             H. W. LONGFELLOW, 'The Building of the Ship'

f. Oh, somewhere in this favored land the sun is shining bright;
  The Band is playing somewhere, and somewhere hearts are
      light.
And somewhere men are laughing, and somewhere children
      shout;
But there is no joy in Mudville—mighty Casey has struck out.
           ERNEST LAWRENCE THAYER, 'Casey at the Bat'

    g. During the whole of a dull, dark, and soundless day in the autumn of the year, when the clouds hung oppressively low in the heavens, I had been passing alone, on horseback, through a singularly dreary tract of country, and at length found myself, as the shades of the evening drew on, within view of the melancholy House of Usher.
        EDGAR ALLAN POE, *The Fall of the House of Usher*

    h. The lunatic, the lover, and the poet
      Are of imagination all compact.
      One sees more devils than vast hell can hold,
      That is the madman. The lover, all as frantic,
      Sees Helen's beauty in a brow of Egypt:
      The poet's eye, in a fine frenzy rolling,
      Doth glance from heaven to earth, from earth to heaven;

And as imagination bodies forth
The forms of things unknown, the poet's pen
Turns them to shapes, and gives to airy nothing
A local habitation and a name.

SHAKESPEARE, *A Midsummer Night's Dream,* v. i

i. We, the people of the United States, in order to form a more perfect union, establish justice, insure domestic tranquillity, provide for the common defense, promote the general welfare, and secure the blessings of liberty to ourselves and our posterity, do ordain and establish this constitution for the United States of America.

Preamble to the Constitution of the United States

FLEXIBILITY OF BREATH CONTROL AND CO-ORDINATION WITH
SPEAKING

Acting, public reading, and frequently public speaking make far greater demands upon the voice than does ordinary conversation. Abrupt transitions, wide and sudden variations in loudness and tempo, and extremes of pitch range require a breathing mechanism that not only furnishes a firm support for the tone but also one that is flexible and instantly responsive to changes of thought and feeling as they are manifested in speech.

The co-ordination of breathing with speaking, determined largely by the thinking, as was explained earlier in this chapter, has become, through a process of conditioning, or habit, more or less automatic. However, when attention is called to the speech activity in the process of forming new habit patterns, or when we are self-conscious, as we often are before an audience or in a disturbing situation, this automatic process is inhibited and the co-ordination is in danger of being broken down. Under such conditions we may find ourselves at the beginning of a new sentence having forgotten to breathe or having taken in an insufficient supply of breath. Or, as sometimes happens, we may find ourselves with an excessive supply of air because we have breathed more deeply or more often than was necessary and have forgotten to empty the lungs of their surplus before refilling them with a fresh inhalation.

Special mention must also be made of the necessity for keeping some reserve supply of breath in the lungs at all times during phonation. Failure to observe this rule may result in a weak, thin tone which will give the impression that the speaker is out of breath. Such failure also often accounts for the disturbing practice, common among certain individuals, of allowing the voice to trail away at the ends of phrases and sentences into muffled unintelligibility. Or if the speaker attempts to maintain his loudness level despite his inadequate breath supply, a harsh throatiness, observable as the voice falls at the end of a phrase, may result from the effort to 'squeeze out' the tone from relatively empty lungs. In all speech activities the breathing and phrasing should be so managed that the speaker is assured of always having some reserve of breath even at the end of long phrases or sentences.

The ideal control of breathing, then, is one that provides instant and adequate response to all vocal demands made upon it and which supplies the speaker with just the right amount of breath, not too little and not too much, to carry him through the phrase or thought-group to the place where the supply can be replenished most conveniently. Nor should it ever be necessary for the speaker to exhaust his supply completely. It is with these aims in mind that the following exercises should be studied and practiced.

Exercises for Flexibility and Control of Breathing

1. Think of the count 'one'; inhale just enough breath to speak it and then pronounce it. Do the same for two, three, etc., up to ten. Practice this until you know just how much breath will be required each time.

2. Without taking time to think before each count, repeat Exercise 1, counting from one to ten at the rate of one count per second. Replenish the breath supply before each count with a slight catch of the breath, but gauge the amount so carefully that you will finish ten with the same amount of breath in the lungs with which you began. Be sure that the chief action of breathing is centered in the mid-region of the body.

3. Continue Exercise 2, but increase the rate of the counting. When the tempo has become so rapid that you can no longer alternately breathe and count, stop counting and increase the rate of your breathing until you are panting like a dog. Breathe through the mouth for this. Avoid a spasmodic, jerking, or 'pumping' movement and involve as little of the main bony cage of the thorax as possible. The action of the diaphragm should be smooth, rhythmical, and so relaxed that you could continue this drill for some time without fatigue or other discomfort.

4. Take a quick, spasmodic inhalation as you do when you are startled. Note the action in the mid-portion of the body. Repeat, saying 'oh!'—exclamation of startled surprise—immediately after you have caught your breath.

5. Think of counting from one to five on one breath, using a conversational style and tempo. Decide how much breath will be required and count as if it were a phrase you were speaking. You should finish with neither a surplus nor a deficiency of breath.

6. Vary Exercise 5 by counting from one to ten. Pause slightly after 'five,' but do not breathe; merely phrase the counts. Try one to fifteen and one to twenty, again pausing slightly at the end of each five counts.

7. Repeat Exercise 6, substituting the letters of the alphabet for the digits. Pause, think, and breathe before *a, h, l,* and *t.*

8. Apply the same routine to the following sentences:

    a. How do you do?

    b. Where are you going and what do you wish?

    c. Shut the door when you leave.

    d. I know of no one who could have done it better than he.

    e. If at first you don't succeed, try, try again.

    f. This is a very long road that leads into the sunset.

9. Chant the following selection, breathing as indicated by the dashes. Take just the right amount of breath to carry you through the phrase. Prolong the vowel tones, reading each phrase as a continuous unit with no break between words. (It is the Ghost speaking, from *Hamlet*.)

> —I am thy father's spirit—
> Doomed for a certain term to walk the night—
> And for the day confined to fast in fires—
> Till the foul crimes done in my days of nature—
> Are burnt and purged away.

10. Chant the following selection, allowing the pitch to rise and fall in accordance with the thought and feeling expressed. Prolong the vowel tones and read each phrase as a continuous unit with no break between words. Breathe as indicated.

> The day is done—and darkness
> Falls from the wings of night—
> As a feather is wafted downward—
> From an eagle in its flight.—
>
> And the night shall be filled with music—
> And the cares that infest the day—
> Shall fold their tents like the Arabs—
> And as silently steal away.
>
> H. W. LONGFELLOW, 'The Day Is Done'

11. Phrase the following selections carefully according to the thought-groups. Decide in advance where you should pause to breathe and how much breath will be needed to speak each unit. Speak the lines naturally.

a. Listen, my children, and you shall hear
   Of the midnight ride of Paul Revere,
   On the eighteenth of April, in Seventy-five;
   Hardly a man is now alive
   Who remembers that famous day and year.

   He said to his friend, 'If the British march
   By land or sea from the town to-night,
   Hang a lantern aloft in the belfry-arch
   Of the North Church tower as a signal light,—
   One, if by land, and two, if by sea;
   And I on the opposite shore will be,
   Ready to ride and spread the alarm
   Through every Middlesex village and farm,
   For the country folk to be up and to arm.'

   H. W. LONGFELLOW, 'Paul Revere's Ride'

b. Others may praise what they like;
   But I, from the banks of the running Missouri, praise nothing
      in art or ought else,
   Till it has well inhaled the atmosphere of this river, also the
      western prairie-scent,
   And exudes it all again.

   WALT WHITMAN, 'Others May Praise What They Like'

c. Friends, Romans, countrymen, lend me your ears;
   I come to bury Caesar, not to praise him.
   The evil that men do lives after them,
   The good is oft interred with their bones;
   So let it be with Caesar.

   SHAKESPEARE, *Julius Caesar*, III. ii

d. On my Northwest coast in the midst of the night a fishermen's
      group stands watching,
   Out on the lake that expands before them, others are spearing
      salmon,
   The canoe, a dim shadowy thing, moves across the black water,
   Bearing a torch ablaze at the prow.

   WALT WHITMAN, 'The Torch'

e. Thinking cannot be clear till it has had expression. We
must write, or speak, or act our thoughts, or they will remain in
half torpid form. Our feelings must have expression, or they will

be as clouds, which, till they descend in rain, will never bring up fruit or flower. So it is with all the inward feelings; expression gives them development. Thought is the blossom; language the opening bud; action the fruit behind it.

HENRY WARD BEECHER

SUPPORTING THE TONE *

Increase of loudness results primarily from an increase in the breath pressure below the larynx, and not from tensions in the muscles of the throat. Many of the most common faults of tone quality, including stridency, harshness, shrillness, and certain forms of hoarseness, are directly traceable to strain in the muscles surrounding the larynx. It is often true that this habit of speaking arises as a result of faulty breathing, since it is very difficult, if breathing is centered high in the chest, to produce strong, full tones without tightening the throat. Practice the following exercises, centering the activity in the middle of the body and maintaining a condition of openness and relaxation of the pharynx. Feel that the force producing the tone is coming from the muscles of breathing rather than from the muscles of phonation. Can you achieve the desired loudness and projection in the following exercises and still keep the basic pitch of your voice down to a comfortable level?

1. 'Count off' in military fashion, first inhaling slightly before each count, and later taking several counts on each breath. Place one hand over the midriff and observe the action of the breathing muscles. Do you feel a definite impulse coinciding with each count? Take care that the throat remains passive and relaxed.

2. Pronounce the following words and phrases as commands, warnings, or strong statements. Feel as if the tone were being supported from the middle of the body.

---

* The principal block of exercises dealing with projection and strength of tone will be found near the end of Chapter IV. The instructor may wish to combine some of this material with the present unit.

a. No! Hey! Look out! Get out! Halt! March!
   Who goes there!
   Left! Right! Left! Right! (Marching)

b. You are commanding a group of soldiers—
   Ready! Aim! Fire! (You are right by your men)
   Ready!! Aim!! Fire!! (They are across the street)
   Ready!!! Aim!!! Fire!!! (They are a block away)

    c. 'Halt!'—the dust-brown ranks stood fast.
       'Fire!'—out blazed the rifle-blast.

    d. 'Forward the light brigade!
       Charge for the guns!' he said.

e. Open; 'tis I, the king! Art thou afraid?

f. Hence! home, you idle creatures, get you home!

    g. 'Strike—till the last armed foe expires,
       Strike—for your altars and your fires,
       Strike—for the green graves of your sires,
       God—and your native land!'

h. If I were an American as I am an Englishman, and a foreign troop were landed in my country, I would never lay down
my arms. Never! Never!! Never!!!

i. Who fought your naval battles in the last war? Who led you
on to victory after victory on the ocean and the lakes? Whose
was the triumphant prowess before which the red cross of England paled with unwonted shame? Were they not men of New
England? Were these not foremost in those maritime encounters
which humbled the pride and power of Great Britain?

    j. 'Who dares'—this was the patriot's cry,
       As striding from the desk he came—
       'Come out with me, in Freedom's name,
       For her to live, for her to die?'
       A hundred hands flung up reply,
       A hundred voices answered 'I!'

               T. BUCHANAN READ, 'The Rising'

III

The Production of Vocal Tone

AN ESSENTIAL similarity between the voice and certain musical instruments was pointed out in the previous chapter when the breathing mechanism was compared with the bellows of an organ or accordion. The vocal folds which are set into vibration to produce the tone in the voice were compared to the reeds in these instruments. They also correspond in a rough way to the strings of the violin, and the reed of the clarinet, but they resemble the lips of the trumpet player more closely.

In addition to a source of energy and a vibrator, most musical instruments also provide for some method of resonance to amplify the tone. Resonance in the voice will be discussed in the following chapter. Meanwhile, let us take a closer look at this sound-producing mechanism, the larynx, for it is one of the more interesting organs in your body.

THE BIOLOGICAL FUNCTIONS OF THE LARYNX

Biologically considered, the larynx is not essentially an organ of voice. Rather, it was developed primarily to serve certain basic biological functions important to the survival and development of the individual and the species. As evidence of this we find many instances in the animal kingdom of certain species rarely, if ever, making use of voice, such as members of the deer family, giraffes, and rabbits, but not because they lack the means of producing voice. In their case the employment of sound is neither necessary nor advantageous, yet they have a larynx. On the other hand, many animals make free use of sound, but only in the most simple and primitive way. The anthropoid apes, for example, have an efficient laryngeal structure probably capable of producing a relatively high type of speech; what is lacking is the ability to use it.

Man, then, simply has been able to make use of the most effective and convenient mechanism suitable for the production of certain tones and noises out of which speech could be built. The factors which contribute to make the larynx the structure best suited for voice have resulted from a long series of evolutionary developments too intricate and involved to be discussed here. It is enough to say that the primary biological function of the larynx is to act as a closure mechanism or valve in the respiratory tract to prevent foreign matter from entering the trachea when we swallow and to shut air into or out of the lungs, as happens when we hold our breath in preparation for strenuous physical activity.

Speech as an Overlaid Function. Voice, therefore, can be thought of as a by-product of the larynx, an 'overlaid function,' resulting from this specialized use which man has made of the best mechanism available for the purpose. As a matter of fact, as was pointed out earlier, the entire speech mechanism can be explained and accounted for wholly on the basis of biological function and need. All of which simply means that man has been able to take several biological structures—the lungs, the larynx, the throat, mouth, and nose—and integrate them into an organized mechanism capable of producing voice and speech, a feat made possible, and necessary, by man's complicated nervous system, his superior intelligence, and his highly developed social structure.

Voice Training as a Cultivation of Function. Any study of voice and the voice-producing mechanism, when considered from the point of view of biology, must emphasize the importance of function as opposed to structure in any sound program of voice training. That is, within the limits of the normal, the important thing is not the mechanism itself, but rather the use which is made of it. This factor, more than any other, accounts for the superiority of the voice of man over that of the lower animals, as well as for the superiority of one voice over another.

So far as voice training is concerned, therefore, provided the vocal mechanism is normal, as it is in the majority of instances, the improvement in voice resulting therefrom is almost wholly neuro-muscular—in other words, a matter of habit. No observable structural changes are wrought in the larynx as a result of vocal training; there is virtually no development of muscle, in the sense that there is any change in size or shape, and no changes take place in the size, weight, or texture of the vocal folds themselves. This view is expressed by the eminent English biologist and surgeon, V. E. Negus, who probably knows more than anyone else about the laryngeal anatomy of virtually every creature that swims, flies, crawls, or walks. Negus states: 'You cannot tell, by any anatomical means, the larynx of a prima-donna from that of a woman who had the voice of a raven.' * There is little or no discoverable difference between the vocal mechanism of the savage and that of the most accomplished singer or speaker. The secret of effective voice production, therefore, must be sought for in the use that is made of the voice-producing mechanism rather than in its structure. All of the drills and exercises which are included in this chapter are presented from this point of view, their purpose being to enable the student of voice to develop more complete control over a responsive and adequate mechanism. And remember that it is not what you do *to* your voice that counts, for you can do but little, but rather what you do *with* it.

If the student is to understand how the larynx functions to produce tone and just what is involved in the management

* Negus, V. E., *The Mechanism of the Larynx,* xxix, The C. V. Mosby Company, St. Louis, 1929.

of the voice-producing mechanism, he should have some notion of what this structure looks like and how it operates.
An attempt will be made in the following pages to present
a highly condensed but, it is hoped, lucid explanation of the
basic parts of the laryngeal structure.

THE CARTILAGES OF THE LARYNX

The skeletal framework of the larynx, unlike that of the
body, is composed of cartilages rather than bones. Inciden-

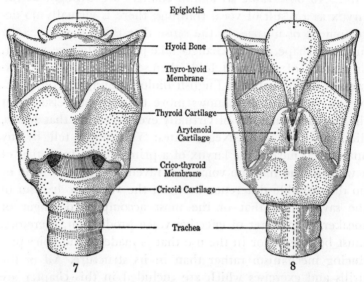

FIG. 7. Front view of the laryngeal cartilages and ligaments.

FIG. 8. Back view of the laryngeal cartilages and ligaments.

tally, it is the gradual hardening, or ossification, of these
cartilages rendering them stiff and inflexible which, more
than any other factor, accounts for the progressive change in
the quality and pitch of the voice in old age.

The Cricoid Cartilage. The base of the larynx is the cricoid cartilage (Figures 7 and 8), which in reality also forms

the first ring of the trachea. It is called cricoid (Gr. *Krikas,* ring) because it resembles a signet ring, being wide at the back but narrow in front.

The Thyroid Cartilage. The second of the two larger structures of the larynx is the thyroid, or shield-shaped, cartilage, which is joined to the sides of the cricoid by two arms, or horns. A flexible hinge-like attachment where the horns of the thyroid rest against the sides of the cricoid provides for a rotation or tilting of one upon the other. The thyroid cartilage owes its shape to the fusion of two flat plates at the front in such a way that they form a wedge-like structure known as the Adam's apple. This can easily be felt by placing the finger on the front of the neck just under the chin.* The V-shaped notch, resulting from the union of the two upper edges of the thyroid (Figure 7), can be readily located. This is known as the notch of the thyroid and should be definitely identified by the student, as future reference will be made to it.

The Arytenoid Cartilages. Of more direct importance to the vocal fold movements involved in phonation, but more difficult to describe, are the two paired arytenoid cartilages, which provide for the posterior attachment of the vocal folds. The cartilages are pyramid-shaped structures with frontal projections (vocal processes) to which the folds are attached (Figure 9). The arytenoids rest upon the slanted posterior rim of the cricoid (Figures 8 and 9), to which they are attached by a joint loose enough to permit both a rotation and a sliding motion which separates the folds in breathing but brings them back together in phonation. In fact, the chief function of the arytenoids is to provide a lever whereby the opening, closing, and tensing of the vocal folds can be effected (Figure 10). For this reason most of the muscles of the larynx are in some way concerned with the movement of these cartilages.

* With the thumb and forefinger explore the two smooth plates of your own thyroid cartilage at the front and sides. Compare what you feel with the view of the larynx in Figure 7.

The Epiglottis. The only other cartilage of particular importance in voice production is the epiglottis, a leaf-shaped structure attached to the inner side of the anterior wall of the thyroid cartilage and assuming during breathing and phonation an upright position resting against the base of the

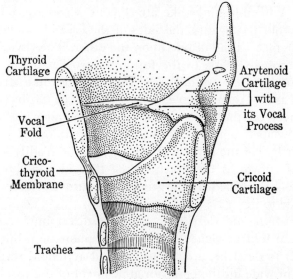

(After Allen Thomson, from Quain's *Anatomy*.)

Fɪɢ. 9. Interior of the larynx (right half), showing the relationship of the arytenoid cartilage to the cricoid cartilage and to the vocal fold.

tongue (Figure 1). No special attention need be given the epiglottis, provided it is normal in structure.

THE MUSCLES OF THE LARYNX

The most convenient division of the muscles of the larynx is into the two groups, intrinsic and extrinsic. The intrinsic muscles are those responsible for the movement of the various cartilages of the larynx and of the vocal folds themselves, while the extrinsic muscles are concerned with movements of the larynx as a whole.

Intrinsic Muscles. The sole purpose and end-result of stimulation of the intrinsic muscles of the larynx is to effect certain changes in the tension and relative positions of the vocal folds. This is accomplished as a result of delicate, reciprocal adjustments of a group of relatively tiny muscles, the exact functions and interrelationships of which have never been fully determined. Various positions which the vocal folds assume are illustrated in Figure 10, which shows them drawn together as in phonation, partially separated as in whispering, and widely separated as in deep breathing. The space between the folds is known as the glottis.

Although it is very difficult for the student to visualize from a mere description, careful study of the laryngeal mechanism reveals that the arytenoid cartilages execute a complicated movement which involves both a rotating and a sliding action. These adjustments are accomplished through the contraction and relaxation of two opposed groups of muscles—those which open the glottis and those which draw the folds together. Another group of muscles operates to tense the folds when they have been brought together by slightly tilting the arytenoid cartilages backward or at least stabilizing their position while the thyroid cartilage is also tilted forward in relation to the cricoid.

The important points to be observed with respect to these muscles are that their use requires but little energy, since they are all quite small; their action is highly integrated; and they are not under individual control. That is, one cannot deliberately relax certain of these muscles and tense others, except in connection with some activity involving basic adjustments of the vocal folds themselves, such as normally occurs in phonating, coughing, or holding the breath.

At least one important implication for voice training is suggested at this point: If undesirable conditions for vocalization exist, proper adjustment within the larynx for efficient voice production must be accomplished *indirectly* as a result of vocal drills and exercises. The resulting quality of tone will determine how well the vocal mechanism is performing. Ear training, therefore, becomes an important preliminary step and adjunct to voice training. The voice student must learn to listen for and to identify certain qualities in the vocal tone which indicate that proper conditions for voice production have been established.

Extrinsic Muscles. The two most important extrinsic muscles of the larynx function to pull the whole larynx downward or to elevate it toward the base of the tongue. These gross movements of the larynx as a whole are more directly related to certain biological functions, such as swallowing, than to the process of phonation, though they probably serve to change the position of the larynx with respect to the pharynx, thus altering the size and shape of the pharyngeal resonator to conform to different pitch levels.

THE VOCAL FOLDS

The vocal folds, or vocal cords as they are sometimes called, are in reality one pair of the intrinsic muscles of the larynx, the thyro-arytenoids. These muscles are attached in front to a point almost directly behind the notch of the thyroid cartilage and at the back to the movable arytenoid cartilages. This explains the triangular shape of the glottis when the vocal folds are open (Figure 10). The free borders of the folds are overlaid with a pearly white, tough, fibrous tissue (Figure 10). To call them cords is misleading, for they are not cords, or even bands, but rather folds or lips that project from the inner walls of the larynx in a manner shown in Figure 12. This frontal, or coronal, section should be compared with the mirror view of the larynx from above (Figures 10 and 11).

Study of these illustrations discloses that the folds are not thin and sharp, but rather wedge-shaped and inclined to be rounded on the edges, which rounding gives a mellow rich-

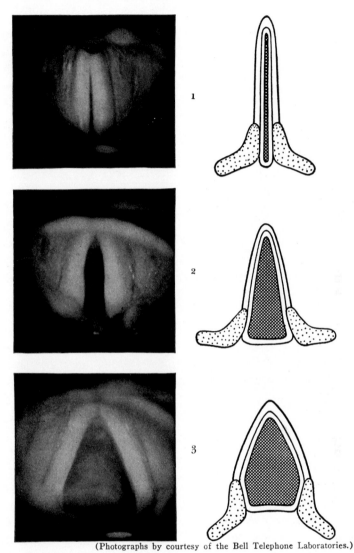

(Photographs by courtesy of the Bell Telephone Laboratories.)

FIG. 10. Three views of the larynx, illustrating the shape of the glottis and the position assumed by the vocal folds during: (1) Phonation; (2) Whispering (although this picture was not taken during actual whispering, it shows the folds partially drawn together in a manner similar to their position in whispering); (3) Deep breathing. The corresponding diagrams at the right illustrate the movements and positions of the arytenoid cartilages.

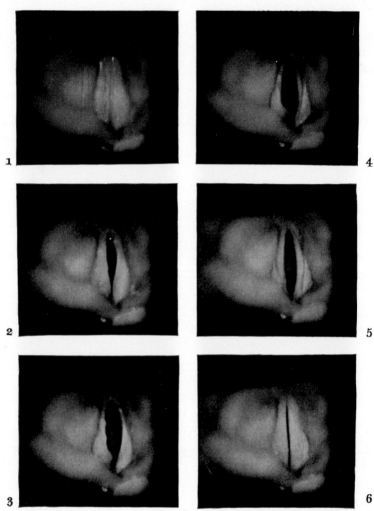

(Courtesy of the Bell Telephone Laboratories.)

Fig. 11. Frames from a high-speed motion picture of the vocal folds, showing six successive stages in one complete cycle of vibration. The first frame shows the folds drawn together at the beginning of the cycle. Breath pressure, accumulating below the larynx, blows the folds apart, and a puff of air escapes in the process. The pressure thus momentarily relieved, the elasticity of the folds causes them to snap back together, and the cycle is repeated. At the frequency of Middle C this action would take place 256 times during each second of phonation. (Note the globule of mucus on one of the folds.)

ness to vocal tones. In structure as well as in the manner of producing tone the vocal folds more closely resemble the lips of the trumpet player than the mechanism of any other musi-

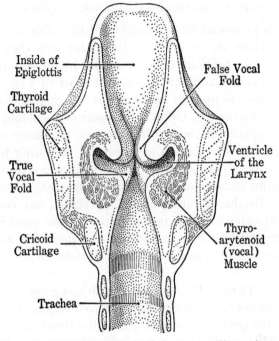

Inside of Epiglottis

False Vocal Fold

Thyroid Cartilage

Ventricle of the Larynx

True Vocal Fold

Thyro-arytenoid (vocal) Muscle

Cricoid Cartilage

Trachea

FIG. 12. Coronal, or frontal, section of the larynx illustrating somewhat diagrammatically the front half as seen from the back. This view presents a cross-section of both true and false vocal folds, as well as the thyro-arytenoid (vocal) muscles, indicating their general structure.

cal instrument. Most decidedly they are not strings, as the term vocal cords would imply.

The false vocal folds (Figure 12) apparently have no important function in phonation, but during swallowing they tend to pull together and thus aid in closing off the entrance into the trachea. It is possible that during certain types of vocalization in which there is considerable strain in the throat, these false vocal folds tend to be drawn together as they are in swallowing, thus muffling or damping the tone issuing from the true vocal folds by interfering with their free vibration and by constricting the outlet of the larynx.

THE ADJUSTMENT OF THE VOCAL FOLDS

Tone is produced by a vibration of the folds as they are drawn together and as breath is forced between them. More specifically, the folds are drawn together by the action of the laryngeal muscles and are then blown apart in a rhythmical fashion, allowing puffs of air to escape, which puffs form the vocal tone (Figure 11). Upon the manner of vocal-fold adjustment the quality of the resulting tone is to a large measure dependent. As is explained in Appendix A dealing with the physics of sound, purity of tone, that is, freedom from noise, results from the evenness and regularity of the vibrations produced by the vibrating agent. Therefore, any condition which interferes with the free vibration of the vocal folds or allows unused breath to escape between them will add various unpleasant qualities in the form of noise elements to the tone.

Pinched Throat. One of the conditions most frequently responsible for interference with the free action of the vocal folds results from excessive strain in the throat during phonation. This condition is sometimes referred to as 'pinched throat.' To test for pinched throat, place your finger in the notch of the thyroid cartilage. Keeping it there, pronounce in a sharp, loud tone, as if to a company of men some distance away, the commands, 'Ready! Aim! Fire!' If the thyroid rises appreciably during this vocalization, and especially if it disappears up under the hyoid bone at the base of the tongue as it does in swallowing, there is excessive strain in your throat and you are not using your voice properly.

The most common vocal evidences of this strain are a high pitch, and a strident, metallic quality. Pinched throat involves stimulation of the extrinsic muscles of the larynx and the larger muscles of the throat and neck involved in swallowing. These are automatically brought into play during vocalization whenever there is excessive tension in the throat. These larger muscles contract and crowd in on the laryngeal structure, thereby interfering with its proper activity. Such constrictions also tend to obstruct the laryngeal opening through which the tone must pass.

The direct effect of this added effort upon the vocal folds is to cause them to be brought too tightly together. In this position they interfere with each other and clash together as they vibrate during the production of tone. If this condition is allowed to persist in those who use their voices a great deal, serious damage to the vocal folds may result. Either they may become roughened and inflamed, or the constant friction between them may produce nodules or 'singers' nodes,' which are small calluses or corns projecting from the inner edges of the folds. Any of these conditions will result in a chronic hoarseness and breathiness of tone.

Bear in mind that tone production requires but little effort in the throat. While it is true, of course, that tone is really initiated in the larynx, the student of voice will be greatly aided if he thinks of the effort involved as coming from the lower thorax and upper abdomen, the place where the breathing activity is centered. After all, the breath does furnish the motive power of voice; tone is supported and sustained by and from the breathing muscles, and the throat should be regarded as a more passive agent where tone is megaphoned, shaped, and built up. This concept is particularly helpful in the development of loudness and projection of tone without the high pitch and evidences of strain which so often accompany increase in loudness.

PITCH CHANGES IN THE VOCAL TONE

Pitch changes in the voice result directly from the action of the larynx. Five factors are involved, namely, (1) the length, (2) weight or mass, and (3) tension of the vocal folds, (4) their elasticity, and (5) the sub-glottal breath pressure. The first three of these are essentially the properties of a vibrating string. The longer and heavier the string, the lower the resulting pitch will be; but the tighter the string, the higher the pitch will be. These facts can easily be demonstrated with any stringed instrument. Note that the short strings produce the higher pitches and that one tightens the string to raise the pitch. Also the strings producing the lower pitches are much heavier and larger than those whose frequency is higher. Observe, however, that as either the length or tension of the string is changed, the other factors remain relatively constant.

The vocal folds present a much more complicated picture, for, being elastic, their thickness and length tend to change with each change in tension. For example, if the vocal folds are tensed, that is, stretched, the pitch should rise as a result of this factor, for the folds have also tended to thin out a bit with a consequent reduction of mass per unit of length. However, the increase of tension has also caused some lengthening of the vibrating edges which, taken alone, would operate to lower the pitch. As an additional factor of complexity, the thyro-arytenoid (vocal) muscles have contracted, with a consequent further change in the elasticity of the vibrating edges. The truth is that the pitch resulting from the simultaneous operation of these several factors, some of which appear to be opposed, is undoubtedly determined by a balance attained between and among these varying forces. The exact nature of this balance or the part played by the individual factors involved in it has not been fully determined.

Pitch and Loudness. Complicating the picture still further, but of more direct importance for voice training, is the relationship which exists in the voice between loudness and pitch. Other factors being equal, an increase in loudness, which results principally from an increase of breath pressure,

05576

means a resulting rise in the pitch of the laryngeal tone. Consider the complexity of the adjustment required therefore when the loudness of a tone is increased while the pitch is held constant. With each step in the rise of breath pressure and its accompanying increase in loudness must go a proportionate readjustment of the intricate pitch-changing mechanism, if the pitch is to be maintained on a constant level. Thus, a change in either pitch or loudness necessitates a balancing, compensating change in the other mechanism.

This relationship between loudness and pitch offers at least a partial explanation of the tendency so often observed for the pitch of the voice to rise when the loudness is increased. Ask a person to speak in a loud tone, and he automatically raises the pitch of his voice; the pitch-changing mechanism has not fully compensated for the increase in breath pressure.

Another factor further complicates the situation. The increased strain accompanying the louder tone also has a direct effect in raising the pitch, especially if the breathing activity is centered too high in the chest. The throat muscles become tense, the vocal folds are crowded and their free action is hampered. The resulting tone not only becomes high in pitch, but it is also likely to take on a strained, strident, unpleasant quality. These facts explain why yells, calls, and cries are seldom very pleasant or musical in quality, and it also explains why one often develops hoarseness or sore throat after such use of the voice.

Increase of loudness results principally from increase of breath pressure, an activity concerned largely with the muscles of breathing. While it is true that some slight added effort is required to maintain the vocal folds in alignment against the increased breath pressure, this is by no means great and should result in no material alteration of the tone, either in pitch or in quality. The ability to increase loudness without a consequent rise in pitch or change in quality is one of the indications of a proper use of the voice.

FAULTS OF TONE PRODUCTION *

So far as voice and speech are concerned, the chief purpose of the larynx is to provide a fundamental tone, and in all likelihood a great many overtones as well, to give 'body' and quality to speech. Laryngeal tone is, in a large sense, the stuff out of which speech is made. It furnishes not only carrying power and quality, but also inflection, melody, and other pitch changes, which add greatly to the expressive powers of the voice. Bear in mind that speech, generally speaking, is no better than the tone out of which it is made, and that tone owes its quality partly to the manner of its initiation in the larynx.

Inasmuch as this book is devoted primarily to the training of the normal voice, no more than a passing mention can be made of those voice defects arising from some structural abnormality or pathological condition of the vocal apparatus. Therefore, unless it is otherwise indicated, it will be assumed in each case that the vocal mechanism with which we are dealing is a 'normal' one.

PROBLEMS RELATED TO VOICE QUALITY

Breathiness. The breathy, or aspirate, quality characteristic of some voices results from the escape of unvocalized air passing between vocal folds which are too loosely drawn together or which are prevented from approximating closely by the interference of some obstruction on the edges of the folds or between them. Various growths on the cords and so-called singers' nodes, or nodules, are among the most com-

* The first portion of this section will deal with those quality disorders in the voice directly traceable to faulty tone production at the larynx. Since nasality is a problem of resonance and articulation primarily, discussion of this quality disorder will be reserved for the following chapter. Some mention of it will also be made in Part II in connection with the articulation of the nasal consonants and certain of the vowels.

mon causes of obstruction to their proper alignment and free vibration. Or there may be other irregularities along the edges or the two folds may not match perfectly.

Failure of approximation of the folds may also be traceable in some instances to a weakness or paralysis of the vocal muscles or a general condition of physical weakness and debility. Naturally, if the muscles of the body generally have lost their proper tonus, the muscles of the larynx can hardly be expected to perform their functions efficiently. In case any of these conditions is suspected, the advice of a physician should be sought before any voice training is attempted.

Much more common, however, is the purely functional type of breathiness in which there is no demonstrable cause other than improper breathing and inefficient use of the larynx, both resulting from poor vocal habits. In such cases the breathing should be thoroughly checked to insure that there is proper balance and co-ordination between breathing and vocalization. The careful control of the outgoing breath is especially important, since much breath may be allowed to escape unused without the restraining influence of the breathing muscles or the efficient closure of the glottis. An excessive amount of breath is very often used in sounding the voiceless consonants or during the transition from one speech sound to another when there is no stoppage of the breath stream either at the larynx or in the mouth by the velum, tongue, or lips. The restraining control of the breathing muscles in regulating the flow of breath in exhalation becomes particularly important in these cases.

Breathiness, referred to as 'assimilation breathiness,' is especially likely to affect the quality of a vowel sound following an *h* approach or after a voiceless consonant, either a plosive or a fricative, as in such words as *he, hit, who, home, tap, sob, five,* and *thin*. Breath wastage may also occur in the form of audible breathiness and unpleasant noise in words like *sister, popcorn, seizure, statistics,* and *assistance*. Of

course, the use of a considerable amount of breath in words
such as these is unavoidable in normal speech because of the
preponderance of voiceless plosives and fricatives. These
speech sounds consume a great deal of breath. However, despite this fact, or possibly because of it, care should be taken
to insure that as little breath is used for the production of
these consonants as is consistent with clearness and naturalness; and the vowels should be carefully kept free from the
unpleasant quality which results from the escape of unvocalized breath. Avoid giving undue stress to voiceless consonants
or allowing a long delay between the release of the consonant
and the beginning of voicing of the following vowel; begin
the voicing soon after the consonant has been sounded.

A problem of timing between the articulatory and phona-
tory mechanisms is involved here. If, after the release of the
[t] in a word such as *tone*, for example, the vocal folds are
too slow in coming together or if their approximation is incomplete or inadequate, the beginning or possibly all of the
[o] will be likely to exhibit breathiness. After all, aside from
the part played by the breathing muscles in controlling exhalation, discussed in the previous chapter, there is nothing
to stop the outpouring of the breath after it has been released
in the mouth and before it is stopped by the approximation
of the vocal folds at the beginning of the vowel.

While both methods of breath control are important,
neither one should be depended upon to the exclusion of the
other; the problem of breathiness involves both breathing
and phonation. Of course, some delay between voiceless consonants in certain positions in the word and the following
vowel is inherent in the natural pattern of English speech
and this should not be eliminated altogether.* On the other
hand, an exaggeration of this factor is very likely to prove
injurious to vowel quality. Only good judgment can determine the proper balance between these two extremes.

* See the discussion of plosives in Part II.

However, breathiness may also occur under other conditions when none of these factors is present. In these cases diligent search should be instituted to find the underlying cause. It may be that strain in the throat accompanied by stimulation of the larger muscles of the neck and throat has interfered with the action of the larynx and has made an efficient adjustment of the folds impossible. This condition is often found to be associated with breathiness, but whether as a causal factor or as a result of the individual's attempt to produce an adequate tone with a defective mechanism cannot always be readily determined. In any case, the strain is a definite hindrance to voice production, and prompt steps should be taken to insure openness of throat and adequate relaxation of the muscles not actively employed in phonation. After these conditions have been established, an easy, effortless production of the vowels should be practiced.

Breathiness can more commonly be traced to an excessive laxness of the muscles of the larynx, which prevents an efficient adjustment of the vocal folds; there is not sufficient muscular activity to bring them close together into the midline, and unvocalized breath escapes between them. This fault may result merely from poor speech habits, or it may be traceable to a general physical condition of poor health, excessive fatigue, or glandular dysfunction. If a physical cause is suspected, it should be promptly investigated and treated. In the absence of any such indication, vocal training should be productive of tangible results in the majority of cases.

No simple program of treatment can be prescribed, however; training must be adjusted to fit the needs of the individual case. In general, ear training should precede voice training. The student must be made aware of this quality in his voice and he must be taught to recognize the difference between a breathy tone and a clear tone. For, inasmuch as adjustments within the larynx are accomplished only indirectly as a result of the individual's attempt to achieve a certain vocal quality, his only measure of progress will be the improvement in the quality of the tone which he is able to effect. Many valuable suggestions will be found among the drills and exercises included at the end of this chapter, especially those which deal with openness and relaxation of the throat and the development of pure tone.

Research studies of vocal-fold activity through the medium of high-speed motion-picture photography reveal that in the production of loud tones the folds close together more firmly and remain in close contact during a larger portion of the vibration cycle than when weaker tones are phonated. This fact explains why breathiness tends to become less noticeable as loudness is increased. In those cases where the technique of relaxation and quiet phonation proves unfruitful, the individual's louder tones and hence very likely his best tones may be used as a basis from which to begin the program of training to eliminate breathiness. When the quality of the louder tones has been improved, quieter types of vocalization can be practiced.

A modification of this approach involves the beginning of tone from the glottal-stop position, as will be explained in a subsequent exercise. This technique should be used very discriminatingly, however, because of its tendency to produce constrictions in the throat with accompanying qualities of voice which may be as unpleasant as the breathiness. Great care must be exercised to avoid carrying this procedure too far.

Hoarseness. Since hoarseness is sufficiently common to be readily identified by the student, no detailed description of it will be given at this point. Hoarseness always suggests the presence of physiological causes, a possibility that should in every instance be carefully investigated. Temporary hoarseness may indicate temporary conditions in the larynx, such as acute laryngitis resulting from a cold or similar infections of the respiratory tract or from misuse of the voice as in yelling or shouting. Complete vocal rest is recommended in all of these cases.

Of more interest to the student of voice are those cases of chronic hoarseness, because of the possibility of employing vocal therapy in certain instances. Here again, of course, there is always the chance that the vocal defect may have its basis in some pathology or abnormality of structure. Chronic laryngitis, characterized by inflamed or swollen vocal folds, is often at the basis of the trouble. This condition may arise from many possible causes, among the more common being sinusitis, influenza, allergies, nasal infections, dust and other irritants in the air. In fact, almost any infectious disease of the mouth or the respiratory tract may leave the edges of the vocal folds roughened, inflamed, or swollen. These laryngeal conditions are not always easy to detect, however, because the folds may not always show evidence of actual inflammation. In any case their function may be impaired.

Prolonged misuse, or abuse, of the voice such as can often be found among public speakers, teachers who use their voices a great deal under conditions of nervous tension, and others who strain the voice by forcing it from the throat or using a pitch that is too high or too low, may result in serious injury to the laryngeal structure. While in many instances there may be no readily observable indication of inflammation or even structural changes, the resulting weakness and malfunctioning of the larynx is evidenced by the hoarse or aspirate quality of the tone, the tiring of the throat after prolonged vocalization, and the susceptibility of the larynx to colds and other respiratory infections with their consequent discomfort and, in some instances, temporary loss of voice.

Thus far it has been assumed that the laryngeal mechanism was essentially normal to begin with. In reality there are many forms of structural abnormalities, many of which appear to be congenital, that make vocalization unpleasant or difficult. These structural deviations may take the form of poorly matched vocal folds, folds with irregular edges, and similar departures from an efficient laryngeal mechanism.

In all of those cases that show no evidence of active pathology, however, voice training should be undertaken in the assurance that no harm will result and in the hope that even in the worst cases, through proper re-education, more efficient use can be made of an inadequate mechanism. Voice training is definitely indicated and the outlook is quite hopeful for those individuals in whom the vocal defect is traceable to poor voice habits. In all such cases the bad habit must be broken and the proper use of the vocal mechanism developed in its place. This is necessary not only to undo whatever harm may have already been done, but also to prevent further damage.

Vocal training for hoarseness involves the following procedures: (1) in all cases where the hoarseness persists beyond a reasonable time the individual should consult a physician; (2) if voice training is indicated, proper breathing should be established as a basis for more effortless, efficient vocalization; (3) discovering and establishing the correct (optimum) basic pitch level for the individual is extremely important in all cases of hoarseness; (4) easy production of tone with controlled relaxation of the throat region should be stressed as the basic approach to training. Ear training is, of course, essential.

In general, vocalization should be made as easy and effortless as possible, for even that effort which has arisen as a product of attempted vocalization under adverse conditions only serves to constrict the throat further and thus make phonation that much more difficult, with a consequent increase of effort. Thus, vocal strain may become both an effect and a cause and may operate to maintain a vicious cycle of forced and effortful utterance.

Strained, Strident Quality. Although these qualities may also be associated with defects of resonance, there are many cases in which a strident or metallic quality in the voice is traceable to the manner in which the tone is produced in the larynx. The physiological mechanism underlying these defects is in general the opposite of that responsible for breathiness. Whereas breathiness results from an adjustment of the vocal folds that is too lax or where closure is otherwise incomplete, allowing unvocalized breath to escape through the glottis, stridency results from the vocal folds' being crowded too tightly together during phonation. Their free, even vibration is interfered with and noise elements are added to the vocal tone.

There are a number of contributing causes underlying this condition, all of which operate to constrict the muscles of the throat. An emotional disturbance or any condition associated with general tension may manifest itself in this vocal fault. Individuals who are inclined to be nervous, restless, and high-strung are more likely to have tense, strident voices than individuals of the opposite temperament. This vocal quality is also often identified, in the mind of the layman at least and probably rightly so, with a cold, unimaginative, unsympathetic type of personality. The typical villain of the radio serial or television thriller is likely to have such a voice, as is the harassing, scolding wife of the hen-pecked husband. Certain physiological conditions may also cause excessive tension in the laryngeal structures, as may any condition in the throat that interferes with phonation or makes tone production difficult.

There is little doubt that the most common cause of stridency, however, is the old, familiar pinched throat resulting from the attempt to achieve loudness and carrying power by forcing the tone from the throat. It is difficult for individuals in either public or conversational situations to disassociate the concept of earnestness, vitality, or forcefulness from that of strain and effort in the throat. The constant use of the voice under such conditions may well lead to chronic laryngitis, sometimes referred to as 'clergyman's sore throat,' or it may do other serious damage to the vocal mechanism.

An adequate program of voice training to overcome stridency should include first of all the development of proper breathing habits. If attention is centered in the breathing rather than in the voice-producing mechanism, both the extrinsic and intrinsic muscles of the larynx can be relieved of unnecessary strain. The speaker must remember that vocal force results primarily from increased pressure exerted upon the outgoing breath by the muscles of exhalation and not by forcing the tone from the throat. The effort required to adjust vocal-fold tension to balance the increased breath pressure should not result in any discomfort nor should it have any adverse effect upon vocal quality when the voice is being used properly.

Possibly it is unnecessary to remind the student of voice training that he must at all times maintain a degree of bodily poise and ease as well as emotional composure and tranquility if he would have effortless, expressive, and pleasing speech. Excessive tension in any part of the body is likely to affect the quality of the voice, since it is very difficult to relax certain muscle groups and at the same time maintain others under high tension. This fact can easily be demonstrated by contracting the muscles of one arm vigorously, as in thrusting forward, while attempting at the same time to keep the other arm relaxed.

In overcoming stridency, practice should be undertaken in the easy initiation of tone without the glottal shock * so often accompanying a tense, forced utterance. The voicing should begin so easily and smoothly that the muscles involved in swallowing are not brought into activity. During practice

---

* A momentary 'catch' or raspy explosion of the voice observable when a vowel is begun with the throat in a tense, strained condition.

the loudness should be built up only very gradually by increasing the pressure exerted upon the outgoing breath. Muscular activity in speech should at all times be kept to a minimum. Controlled relaxation and maintained openness of the vocal passages of the throat and mouth will go far toward removing all traces of strain and stridency from the tone.

In addition to proper breathing, easy initiation of tone, and relaxation, finding the best pitch level for the individual may be one of the most important factors. Stridency, tenseness, and a metallic quality are customarily associated with a pitch that is too high for the individual voice. Many helpful suggestions will be found in a later discussion of pitch, as well as in the drills and exercise material at the end of the chapter.

Harshness, Throatiness. The term throatiness is included here largely for want of a more exact one and also because the vocal fault which it designates is characterized by a throaty, guttural quality. The term harshness is probably coming into more general use to describe this quality. While harshness, or throatiness, is constantly present in the vocalization of some individuals, it is more likely to occur as the voice falls in pitch, perhaps on the last word of a phrase or sentence. Then, unless the tone is carefully managed, the voice gives the impression of 'falling back into the throat' and a harsh or raspy quality is clearly audible.

In many cases this fault is associated with inadequate breathing, the fall of the voice at the end of the phrase being coincident with an exhaustion of the breath supply. Harshness may well result from some disturbance in the delicate balance between vocal-fold tension and sub-glottic breath pressure. A general physiological cause appears to be either some interference with the free action of the vocal folds or some other factor which produces an abnormal vibration pattern of the folds. In any case, as one proceeds down the scale toward the lower limits of his range, or as loudness decreases, he arrives at a place where his tone easily breaks over into harshness unless he manages breath pressure and laryngeal adjustments very carefully.

Practice should be directed toward establishing free, easy initiation of tone on a pitch slightly higher than that at which the harshness appears. Care must be taken to insure that the tone is at all times well supported with an adequate breath supply. The concept of 'forward placement,' to be explained in a subsequent chapter, may also offer a means of avoiding this vocal fault.

Absence of Vibrato. Every pleasant and effective voice is marked by a warm, vibrant quality which may be identified as a very slight vibrato. Vibrato results from a periodic, continuous shift, or waver, in the pitch and/or loudness of a tone. Research studies indicate that the normal adult voice exhibits a vibrato of both pitch and loudness, with the possibility of a vibrato of quality as well. While vibrato is not an obviously distinguishable characteristic of the speaking voice, in singing it is consciously cultivated and often becomes a very noticeable factor, enhancing and enriching the tone. In the speaking voice it contributes to what has been designated as a sympathetic or 'resonant' quality, usually specified as one of the desirable characteristics of the superior speaking voice.

In its essential nature, vibrato in the voice can be compared to the effect produced by a violin player when he causes minute variations in the length of the string by rhythmical pulsations of his wrist communicated to the finger which presses upon the string. This vibrant quality is a characteristic of all living tissue, which instead of being static and fixed, is responding constantly and sensitively to changes in stimulation. A lack of vibrato in the voice results in a flat, metallic quality. The difference between a voice possessing this slight vibrato and one lacking it is comparable to the difference in violin playing between that of the virtuoso and the beginner.

Absence of vibrato suggests an unimaginative or cold, unresponsive type of personality or a general condition of tension and strain. Exaggerated or uneven vibrato, on the other hand, which produces a quaver or tremor in the voice, is sometimes found in certain types of paralysis, in the very old, and in the querulous, emotionally disturbed, or hysterically inclined personality.

Normal vibrato in the speaking voice is ordinarily not the result of deliberate cultivation and conscious effort, nor should it call attention to itself as an obvious aspect of tone quality. Rather, it results more or less unconsciously when a sincere, sympathetic individual has something to say, says it with a real desire to communicate, and has a vocal mechanism that is relaxed, well co-ordinated, and under good control. Thus, the approach to the development of effective vibrato in the speaking voice is indirect—a dividend, so to speak, of a good voice well used.

PROBLEMS RELATED TO VOCAL PITCH

While there is no general basic level of pitch that is best for all voices, there is within the range of each one a pitch at which that voice performs with greatest effectiveness for speech purposes, maximum loudness being attained with a minimum of effort, and the tone at that point being most rich, full, and resonant. This level, which is often referred to as the 'optimum pitch,' will be found to vary in different individuals because, it is believed, it results from a number of anatomical factors, one of them being the structure of the larynx itself, which, as we have already seen, is instrumental in determining the pitch possibilities of the individual voice. It is probable that optimum pitch is also importantly related to resonance, being the pitch at which the resonators of the voice function with maximum effectiveness.

Faulty Pitch Level. Unfortunately, in many instances an individual fails to use the basic pitch level that is best for his particular voice. Imitation of others, a poor sense of pitch, various adverse personality characteristics, emotional disturbances, strain, and nervous tension are among the factors that may contribute to the use of a faulty pitch level. Once such a level becomes established, the persistence of the habit pattern coupled with one's tendency not to hear the pitch and quality of his own voice objectively make it difficult for him to detect pitch faults without special help.

Among the vocal evidences that the general pitch level of a voice is too low we find: lack of range, especially on the downward side; harsh, guttural quality; inadequate loudness; and a tendency for the speech sounds spoken with a falling pitch to 'fade out' into throaty unintelligibility. Certain of the quality disorders already discussed, especially harshness and throatiness, may also be present. Furthermore, the tempo of speech may be too slow. Such a voice frequently gives the impression that it is 'scraping the bottom.' Prolonged or strenuous use of the voice on a pitch level that is too low may produce a condition known medically as contact ulcer of the larynx, the chief symptoms of which are hoarseness and discomfort in the throat. Possible causes for such unfavorable pitch conditions include attitudes and behavior patterns of indifference or lassitude, emotional maladjustment, a lack of physical health and vitality, or merely unfortunate vocal habits acquired perhaps through imitation or the belief that an excessively low pitch enhanced the individual's voice or personality.

On the other hand, it will often be discovered that the habitual speaking level of the individual is above, rather than below, the pitch he should be using. Worry, excitement, nervous tension, social and emotional immaturity, improper breathing, and strain in the throat resulting from other causes are among the many factors which may operate to raise the pitch of the voice above its best level. Such a voice may be shrill and tense or it may be thin and weak, or it may exhibit an immature, juvenile quality and pitch pattern. Nasalization is a frequent accompaniment of a high pitch as is also a strident, metallic quality. If the high pitch results from strain and tension, the throat will probably tire easily after use of the voice, the vocal folds may become irritated, and there may be a tendency for colds to settle in the throat, producing laryngitis and possible temporary loss of voice. Habitual use of a pitch level that is too high may produce vocal nodules, mentioned earlier in this chapter. If such a condition is present, surgical removal or a prolonged period of vocal rest may be required to eliminate the nodules, followed by a program of vocal therapy to discover the individual's optimum pitch and to establish the most desirable habits of voice production generally.

Juvenile Voice. One important type of vocal problem, variously referred to as juvenile voice or falsetto voice, might be described as a developmental hazard because it arises from the changes the laryngeal structure undergoes at the time of puberty. At this time the framework of the larynx enlarges and the vocal folds become longer, heavier, and more rounded on the edges. Such changes present a real problem, especially to the male, in whom the structural transformation is more radical than in the female, because they necessitate a completely new vocal technique, as well as new auditory concepts of pitch, quality, and loudness. The pitch of the male voice during this so-called 'change of voice' normally falls approximately an octave, the quality becomes deeper and richer, and the voice 'fills out' and increases in force. In the girl the changes in pitch and quality are less radical, the voice dropping only two or three steps in pitch but taking on a more mature quality.

Two sources of possible vocal difficulty confront the boy who is passing through this phase of maturation: (1) He must learn to use a new and enlarged vocal mechanism, and (2) he also has a psychological problem to deal with; the new voice does not feel right nor does it sound right to him, and he finds it a source of embarrassment. Consequently his first reaction may be an attempt to maintain the old, familiar, pre-adolescent pitch and quality. If this tendency persists into adulthood, as it sometimes does, he will resort to the use of what is called falsetto, a type of voice characterized by a high pitch and a thin, husky, 'faraway' quality. This he may continue to use indefinitely.

Normally the voice change at puberty is negotiated without difficulty, but in some instances the individual clings to the pre-adolescent voice which eventually becomes a falsetto, or the voice change is incomplete and the individual is left with a pitch that is too high and with an unpleasant quality characterized by hoarseness, breathiness, and a tendency for the voice to 'crack' and 'break.'

Vocal training for such conditions involves, first of all, the establishment of good breathing and relaxed, easy phonation. A careful pitch study should be made to determine the individual's total range and to discover, through the use of the sung vowel, whether he has a lower 'register' down into which he can sing or hum but which he may never have used for speaking. It may also be discovered that he will laugh or cough on the lower pitch level. Once these lower tones have been explored, the individual's optimum pitch should be located and ear training instituted to make it habitual. In this process the use of voice recordings is essential so that he may hear his own voice objectively and compare what he hears with the normal voice of another person of the same age and sex, or with his own newly discovered lower tones. It may also be necessary to include basic training in pitch through simple scale and pitch recognition exercises, using a piano or some other musical instrument that will provide the musical scale.

Remembering that in the case of juvenile voice disorders, prevention may be more important than 'cure,' it should be observed that at present too little is known of the voice of the pubescent child, how it develops, how it should be used and trained, and what dangers may beset it, for any unnecessary risks to be taken. In no case should the child be encouraged or even allowed to take part in public speaking, dramatics, singing, or any other activity that makes unusual demands upon the voice without the close supervision of a well-trained speech or voice teacher. One should also remember that nothing should be said or done that will bring embarrassment to the individual or attract undue attention to his speech or voice while it is in the process of changing.

DETERMINING THE 'PITCH PROFILE'

Determining the Total Range. With the aid of an instrument that will give the musical scale, preferably a piano, determine in relation to middle C the lowest note that you can sing with some degree of comfort and good quality. Do likewise for the highest note you can sing, without going into falsetto. The interval between them will constitute your range. In the majority of cases the singing range will not greatly exceed two octaves.

Determining the Habitual Pitch Level. Choose a short selection of prose to read or speak a few sentences in a normal, conversational manner. During the course of your reading or speaking, select a word or syllable that seems to represent most faithfully the general, natural pitch level of your voice—the level you touch most often in your speaking and the one to which you habitually return from inflectional variations above and below it. Sustain the vowel in this word or syllable and locate its pitch on the musical scale. Average the results of several trials. Study the outcome of this experiment, especially in relation to the discussion which follows; the average voice will be found to perform best when the speaking level is at approximately the mid-point of the lowest octave of the total range.

Discovering the Optimum Pitch. As was explained earlier, the optimum pitch is the pitch level at which a particular voice performs with optimum quality and general effectiveness. Although it is believed that such a pitch level actually exists in each individual voice, it is not always easy to discover. The following procedure has proved to be effective, however, in assisting individuals to locate the general region of their preferred pitch.

Again using a piano if possible, sing down the musical scale with a sustained [ɑ] (*father*) or [o], beginning with a tone that is easy for you, until you reach the lowest note that you can sing comfortably and with some degree of true quality. As was mentioned previously, this can be accepted as the lowest limit of your range. Now, beginning with this lowest note, sing back up the scale until you reach a point some three or four full steps (whole notes) above this lowest limit. This should be close to your optimum pitch.

As an example, if you are a man and find that the lowest note you can sustain effectively is F below low C, then your theoretical optimum pitch would be at about B or C—three to four notes above your lowest note. Similarly, if you are a woman and can sing down to E below middle C, then your calculated optimum pitch would be at A or B, possibly B flat, below middle C. Final results are purposely stated in approximate terms to stress the fact that this is only a method of estimating a recommended basic pitch level. Study of the basic pitch level of a large number of effective voices, however, would in all probability disclose results not far different from those which the 'pitch profile' technique will provide.

The average speaking level for women's voices has been found to be slightly below middle C, possibly close to A or A sharp; the average level for men is approximately an octave lower, or slightly less—close to low C. It is obvious that there will be variations above and below these averages in individual instances. Men may be natural tenors, or baritones (nearer to the average), or they may fall into the bass range. Women's voices may be soprano, or contralto, or they may fall somewhere in between. Although a high pitch is rarely effective or pleasant in the speaking voice, there is a limit in each voice below which it is impractical and unwise to attempt to force the pitch. As a matter of fact, it is unwise to attempt to *force* the pitch at all, either up or down; such a practice can result only in strain and unpleasant vocal quality. Optimum pitch should result from optimum conditions for general vocalization—proper breathing, relaxed, efficient phonation, and the best use of resonance. When these conditions obtain, the pitch to which the voice naturally falls should be close to the best pitch level for that voice. As was pointed out earlier, this may well be either above or below the habitual pitch the individual has been using.

Experiment with the new-found pitch by singing various vowel sounds on that level and chanting on a monotone. Proceed above and below it to discover whether an adjacent pitch might not give better results, since the method just described is not absolute but only approximate. Try a few inflectional pitch changes up and down the scale to insure that there is ample available range both ways. All this should be done, however, in accordance with the principles of good voice production previously set forth. If the newly discovered optimum pitch does not permit of relaxation of the throat and relatively effortless vocalization or if it does not feel right after it has been given a fair trial, there should be further testing and practice until more favorable results are obtained. When a suitable pitch is finally settled upon, it should be cultivated through practice in speaking and reading. The drills and exercises included in this chapter will be found useful for this purpose. And, remember that the establishment and cultivation of the best pitch level and range for each individual may be the most important single step toward the development of a generally effective speaking voice.

FAULTS OF VOCAL INTENSITY

A voice that is too loud is relatively rare in comparison with the number of thin, weak, listless voices we find in both public speaking and conversational situations. Whether justifiably or not, we are very likely to associate marked departures from a normal degree of loudness in the voice with certain personality characteristics as well as the individual's general physical condition. Omitting, of course, the possibility of hearing loss, we are inclined to think of a loud voice in connection with physical vitality and 'drive,' self-assurance, aggressiveness, and, when more extreme, arrogance, dominance, or relatively violent and uncontrolled types of emotional activity. The weak voice, on the other hand, we are likely to associate with physical weakness and lassitude, shyness, and attitudes of submissiveness, inferiority, or repression. As a matter of fact, careful study often reveals that there is a significant connection between personality characteristics such as these and corresponding degrees of intensity in the speaking voice.

In the case of a weak voice a search for possible causes should take two main directions: (1) An examination into the general physical condition of the individual. There are many physiological factors which could be related to a weak voice, among which the possibility of an endocrine imbalance or a dietary deficiency must be considered. (2) If the health study yields no clue, personality factors should be scrutinized. In case there is any evidence of feelings and attitudes of negativism, inferiority, repression, or indifference, therapeutic measures involving a mental-health program should be undertaken to build up the individual's self-confidence, establish better emotional balance, and develop a more adequate social adjustment and response.

There are many instances, of course, in which a faulty intensity level can be traced only to unfortunate speech habits acquired as a result of imitation or other environmental influences. As was found to be true in the case of pitch, the impression which one has of the loudness level of his own voice is often very misleading. If one has acquired the habit of speaking in a tone of voice that is naturally weak and soft, for example, any marked departure from this intensity level will appear to him as exaggeration. And when the individual is induced to speak up in a voice that is audible and effective, it will most likely appear to him that he is shouting. This subjective impression of one's own voice must be broken down and a more objective appraisal substituted for it before much can be accomplished in the way of developing a more adequate vocal response.

Strictly speaking, most faults of intensity are not directly related to problems of phonation. Usually if the lack of intensity results from malfunctioning of the laryngeal mechanism, there will be other vocal evidences of the condition probably even more obvious than the inadequate loudness. These include breathiness, hoarseness, throatiness, and other similar defects discussed in this chapter. Inadequate loudness of the voice unaccompanied by other vocal deficiencies, if not directly related to some physiological or psychological cause, can often be traced to improper breathing or faulty resonance. Therefore the suggested program of retraining, to establish an effective intensity level in the speaking voice, is based on the drills and exercises dealing with Support of Tone in Chapter II and Strength of Tone in Chapter IV.

Drills and Exercises for Phonation

RELAXATION OF THE ORGANS OF PHONATION AND ARTICULATION

1. To relax the throat and neck, drop the head forward, chin toward the chest, the muscles of the neck thoroughly re-

laxed. Gradually lift the head to its original position. Repeat a number of times.

2. Drop the head forward as before, rotating the head from the shoulders from left to right. Note that when the jaw is fully relaxed, the mouth falls open as the head is rotated backward.

3. Vary the above exercise by keeping the neck relaxed, but rotating the head by moving the shoulders in such a way that the head more or less falls around in a circle.

4. To relax the jaw, practice vocalizing words and syllables ending in [ɑ], allowing the jaw to fall open and remain relaxed following the final sound. Repeat, *yah, fah, pah, po-pah, bo-bah,* etc.

5. Repeat *fah* moderately rapidly by a gross movement of the jaw, keeping the tongue relaxed and motionless and moving the jaw up and down in a loose, lazy fashion: *fah-fah-fah-fah,* etc.

6. Keeping the jaw motionless but relaxed, repeat the following in a smooth, easy rhythm with a gross movement of the tongue:

   a. Yah-yah-yah-yah-yah, etc.
   b. Yuh [jʌ]-yuh-yuh-yuh, etc.
   c. Yaw-yaw-yaw-yaw-yaw, etc.
   d. Yo-yo-yo-yo-yo-yo, etc.

7. Take a deep breath and sigh. Be sure that you fully relax on the sigh; 'give up' to it. Take a deep breath and sigh audibly.

8. Read the following selections very quietly with open and relaxed throat. Be sure there is ample breath support, but do not strain. These exercises will provide a good oppor-

tunity to apply the techniques of breathing and phrasing explained in the preceding chapter.

a. I stood on the bridge at midnight,
   As the clocks were striking the hour,
And the moon rose o'er the city,
   Behind the dark church-tower.
                              H. W. LONGFELLOW, 'The Bridge'

b. At midnight when the cattle are sleeping
   On my saddle I pillow my head,
   And up at the heavens lie peeping
   From out of my cold, grassy bed,—
   Often and often I wondered
   At night when lying alone
   If every bright star up yonder
   Is a big peopled world like our own.
                         UNKNOWN, 'The Cowboy's Meditation'

c. Often I think of the beautiful town
      That is seated by the sea;
   Often in thought go up and down
   The pleasant streets of that dear old town,
      And my youth comes back to me.
         And a verse of Lapland song
         Is haunting my memory still:
   'A boy's will is the wind's will,
   And the thoughts of youth are long, long thoughts.'
                            H. W. LONGFELLOW, 'My Lost Youth'

d. The curfew tolls the knell of parting day,
      The lowing herd winds slowly o'er the lea,
   The plowman homeward plods his weary way,
      And leaves the world to darkness and to me.
        THOMAS GRAY, 'Elegy Written in a Country Churchyard'

e. Though I speak with the tongues of men and of angels, and have not charity, I am become as sounding brass or a tinkling cymbal. And though I have the gift of prophecy, and understand all mysteries, and all knowledge; and though I have all faith, so that I could remove mountains, and have not charity, I am nothing. And though I bestow all my goods to feed the poor, and though I give my body to be burned, and have not charity, it profiteth me nothing.

I Corinthians 13:1-4

EASY INITIATION OF TONE

As we have observed earlier in this chapter, most if not all of those defects of phonation arising from a normal speech mechanism result from some type of interference with the free, natural action of the vocal folds. Furthermore we have seen that interference is usually in the form of tensions and constrictions of the larger muscles of the neck and throat. In practicing the following drills and exercises, and as a matter of fact in all vocalization, attention should be centered upon the throat to accomplish two results: (1) Openness of throat to provide for free and easy passage of the tone; and (2) relaxation of all muscles not directly and actively concerned with phonation. This means the removal of virtually all traces of strain and effort in voice production. Bear in mind that the motive power of voice is related to the action of the muscles of breathing, not to the mechanism of tone production.

The purpose of the following exercises is to establish quiet, effortless initiation of tone. Voice should be produced so easily that the muscles which hinder its production will not be brought into play.

1. Yawn to relax and open the throat. Feel the cool air on the walls of the pharynx. Become conscious of the rise of the soft palate and the depression of the back of the tongue. This basic position should be assumed as a preliminary step to all of the vocal exercises.

2. Take an easy breath, always from the middle of the body, of course; open the throat and very quietly and carefully pronounce *one*, relaxing on the count. Be careful that the tone does not become breathy. Hold the vowel for approxi-

mately a second. Count in this manner from one to five at the rate of one count each three or four seconds.

3. Vary Exercise 2 by giving the counts a prolonged upward inflection.

4. Take an easy breath and with open, relaxed throat quietly whisper *no*. Relax. Take a new breath and just as quietly vocalize the *no* without changing the conditions in the throat. Note the low pitch and the relaxed quality of the tone. Do the same for *yes, how, how now, oh, who, who are you, one, two,* etc.

5. Apply the same technique to the following selection, pausing for a new breath at each place indicated by the dash. Keep the throat open in a position resembling that for the beginning of a yawn. Round out the vowel tones and prolong them.

> Above the clouds—the moon was slowly drifting—
> The river sang below—
> The dim Sierras far beyond—
> Uplifting their minarets of snow.

6. Starting from the yawn position repeat very lightly *ho-ho-ho-ho*, holding each vowel two or three seconds. Pay careful attention to the way in which the tone is begun. Avoid breathiness on the one hand, and harshness on the other. Select a pitch that is easy for you. Continue this drill until the quality of the tone is entirely satisfactory. Prolong one of the vowels from time to time.

7. Repeat Exercise 6, using [hu] instead of [ho]. Likewise substitute [hɑ] for [ho].

8. Begin [hu] as above, holding it for two or three seconds. Then very carefully and gradually merge the [u] into [o], with continuous phonation, keeping the throat open as before. Maintain a constant pitch.

9. Begin [hu] as above, then gradually merge it into [o] and then into the vowel [ɑ], all on one breath and on one pitch and with a steady flow of tone. Watch the quality of the [ɑ] very carefully; guard against flatness, breathiness, and throatiness. The chief purpose of this exercise is to carry over into the [ɑ] some of the open feeling in the back of the throat associated with the formation of [u] and [o]. It will sound like [hu-u-u-o-o-o-ɑ-ɑ-ɑ].

10. Sing [hu-ɑ], merging the two vowels together, and also [ho-ɑ]. Continue these drills until the quality of the [ɑ] becomes entirely satisfactory. Then try forming [hɑ] several times very lightly. Remember always to begin vocalization with the throat feeling as if it were in the yawn position.

11. Practice initiating the vowel [ɑ] a number of times, touching it very lightly and holding it for only a second or so. Strive for a 'velvet-edge' quality; avoid breathiness and glottal shock.

12. Take a comfortable breath and with open throat begin the whispered vowel [ɑ] so quietly that only you can hear it. After two or three seconds, very gradually begin to vocalize the [ɑ] without disturbing the relaxed, open condition of the throat. Continue the vowel until it builds up to a full, resonant tone of good volume. Practice this drill until the transition from whispered to vocalized [ɑ] is accomplished smoothly and without harshness or breathiness.

13. Begin the vowel [ɑ] very easily and quietly, but as a pure tone. Then gradually produce a crescendo effect by building up the volume until the tone becomes quite strong. Make sure that increase of loudness results merely from increased pressure exerted upon the outgoing breath and not from strain in the throat. Take care that the pitch of the tone remains constant as the volume rises and that the throat remains open and relaxed throughout. Repeat, using other vowels.

14. Repeat Exercise 13 except with crescendo-diminuendo effect, allowing the tone to fade away very gradually at the end. Again be sure that pitch and quality remain constant as volume changes. Experiment with other vowel sounds.

15. Count from one to six, speaking each count more or less separately, at the rate of about one count each two seconds. Begin very softly and gradually increase the loudness level with each count until you are speaking very loudly when you reach six. Do not allow the pitch to rise as loudness is increased and check to make sure that your throat does not tighten up. The quality at the end should remain full and resonant; not become tight and pinched.

OVERCOMING BREATHINESS

1. If breathiness is still present after very quiet initiation of tone as recommended in the previous section of drills, try the expedient of beginning the tone with a glottal shock. The theory underlying this recommendation is that for the glottal shock, or glottal plosive as it is also called, the vocal folds are drawn well together, and if the tone is begun from this position, there is more likelihood that the folds will remain in sufficiently close approximation to prevent the escape of unvocalized breath between them. Use the glottal shock approach to [ɑ], [u], and [o], and various other vowel sounds.

2. The action of the vocal folds in the production of loud tones makes breathiness less likely than when a softer tone is used. Keeping this principle in mind, try the following exercises:

   a. Prolong [o] for a few seconds on a distinctly loud tone. Try it on a tone of medium loudness. Reduce the loudness until it is a soft tone. Is there any increase of breathiness with decrease in loudness? If so, try the sequence again, trying to maintain the same efficient use of breath for the softer tones as characterized the louder tones.

b. Repeat Exercise a, using [ho], [a], [hɑ], [no] and the phrase, 'Who are you?'

c. Count from one to five, taking a new breath supply for each count, first in a loud voice and then much more softly. Practice this exercise until the soft tone is free from breathiness and is otherwise satisfactory in quality.

3. Guard against 'assimilation breathiness'; practice very carefully vowel sounds following [h] or any voiceless consonant. The sound, or rather sounds, represented by the symbol [h] do not constitute a specific sound entity. The [h] is merely a voiceless approach to the voiced sound which follows it. The articulatory mechanism is shaped for the vowel sound, air is blown through partially closed vocal folds, and then the voicing is begun. Too often an excess of breath is blown out on the [h]; the voicing is too long delayed and the beginning of the vowel becomes breathy and 'ragged.' Practice the following drills until the initiation of tone following a short aspiration becomes smooth, easy, and free from unpleasant breathiness.

a. In the following pairs of words sound the [h] with as much economy of breath as is consistent with a clearly audible sound, but with no breathy effect upon the following vowel. The vowel in the second member of each pair should be as free from breathiness as the vowel in the first member.

eat	heat	all	hall
it	hit	old	hold
ate	hate	[u]	who
at	hat	eye	high
arm	harm	air	hair

b. Form the vowel tones very carefully in the following syllables, prolonging the vowel for a time on a comfortable pitch: *who, ho, ha, haw, how, home, hunt, hum, him, hem.*

c. Hence! home, you idle creatures, get you home.

d. Heavy, heavy hangs over thy head.

e. O hark, O hear! how thin and clear!

4. Much of what has been said with respect to the management of [h] also applies to any voiceless fricative preceding a vowel or other voiced sound. The aspiration should not be unduly prolonged nor should the breathy quality be allowed to extend noticeably into the beginning of the vowel. The same care must also be employed when a word begins with a voiceless plosive; the voicing of the following sound should be started as soon after the explosion of breath on the consonant as is consistent with the normal pattern of English speech. An excessive expulsion of breath on these sounds is not only unpleasant and wasteful of breath, but the following sound is likely to become breathy. With the foregoing points in mind, practice these drills:

a. Pronounce the following pairs of words, taking care that the vowel in the second member of each pair is as free from breathiness and as carefully initiated as the vowel in the first member:

own	tone	ill	pill	in	kin
aim	tame	odd	pod	old	cold
aisle	tile	Ann	pan	up	cup
all	tall	out	pout	aim	came
E	tea	ah	pa	all	call

b. Count from one to twenty on one breath. Pay particular attention to those digits beginning with voiceless fricatives and plosives, such as [t], [f], and [s].

c. Pronounce the following words, carefully guarding

against using an excessive amount of breath: *thistle, sister, photograph, freshen, statistics, sixty-six, pamphlet, philosophy, thick and thin, time and tide, tit for tat.*

4. Read the following, avoiding noticeable breathiness:

a. Peter Piper picked a peck of pickled peppers.
b. Fe, fi, fo, fum!

c. O holy Hope! and high Humility;
   High as the heavens above!
These are your walks, and you have show'd them me,
   To kindle my cold love.

d. Blow, blow, thou winter wind,
   Thou art not so unkind
   As man's ingratitude;
   Thy tooth is not so keen
   Because thou art not seen,
   Although thy breath be rude.

   Freeze, freeze, thou bitter sky,
   Thou dost not bite so nigh
   As benefits forgot;
   Though thou the waters warp,
   Thy sting is not so sharp
   As friend remembered not.

SHAKESPEARE, *As You Like It,* II. vii

e. Force compelled the signature of unwilling royalty to the great Magna Charta; force put life into the Declaration of Independence and made effective the Emancipation Proclamation; force beat with naked hands upon the iron gateway of the Bastille and made reprisal in one awful hour for centuries of kingly crime; force waved the flag of revolution over Bunker Hill and marked the snows of Valley Forge with blood-stained feet.

JOHN M. THURSTON

DEVELOPING PURITY OF TONE

In this connection the term 'purity' is used to designate a tone free from breathiness, harshness, and all other unpleasant components of noise. It will be noted that in a previous section the sung, or prolonged, vowel was used almost exclusively as a basis for the various exercises. A number of reasons make this procedure necessary and desirable, the most important of which is that only as the vowel is held for a certain length of time can its quality and the manner of its production be studied and adjusted to produce the desired results.

At this point the objection may well be raised that one cannot very well go about singing constantly in place of speaking and that it is with voice for speech that we are primarily concerned. It is the purpose of this section of exercises to establish the carry-over from the sung vowel to the spoken vowel, by means of reading and speaking words, phrases, sentences, and finally selections of poetry and prose. Bear in mind that essential conditions remain the same for the following drills as they were for the previous ones. There is no real difference between the manner of producing good quality in the prolonged vowel of the exercise in which [hu] is sung, for example, and the manner of speaking the word *who* with equally good quality of vowel tone. The only important difference which concerns us at this point is one of duration and pitch change. Therefore, conditions of breathing and tone production should be as carefully controlled for the reading and speaking exercises which follow as they were for the previous drills in which the mere establishment of such conditions was the primary concern.

1. Starting from the yawn position, sing [u] on a comfortable pitch. Work for a clear tone easily initiated and free from breathiness, throatiness, and harshness. In a similar manner sing [o], then [ɑ].

2. Beginning [u] as above, gradually merge it into the vowel [ɑ], keeping the throat open and relaxed throughout. Begin [o] the same way and merge it into [ɑ].

3. Maintaining similar relaxed conditions in the throat, speak very carefully the following phrases, prolonging the vowel sounds. Avoid extreme artificiality, however; let the reading follow naturally from the meaning.

   a. How are you?
   b. Blow, bugle, blow!
   c. We are all well.
   d. Roll on, thou deep and dark blue Ocean—roll!
   e. The yellow half-moon large and low.

4. Read the following selections slowly, breathing as indicated by the dashes and prolonging and carefully molding the vowel tones. Merge each phrase into one continuous sound unit, broken only momentarily by the stop consonants.

     a. The ocean old—centuries old—
       Strong as youth and as uncontrolled—
       Paces restless to and fro—
       Up and down the sands of gold.

     b. With deep affection and recollection—
       I often think of those Shandon bells—
       Whose sound so wild would—
       In the days of childhood—
       Fling round my cradle—their magic spells.
            F. S. MAHONY, 'The Bells of Shandon'

5. Read the following selections very quietly but by no means dully, giving careful attention to breathing, openness of throat, and formation of vowel tones. Mold and form each vowel as carefully as you did when you sang [u], [o], and [ɑ] in Exercise 1. Your tone will be greatly improved if your reading reflects the real meaning and the dominant mood of each selection. Remember that quality of tone is not wholly a mechanical thing, but arises also as a result of conditions of thinking and feeling within the individual. Catch the spirit of the poems, and make a genuine effort to share the

meaning which they have for you with your hearer. Use inflection and change of pitch freely.

> a. A violet by a mossy stone,
>   Half hidden from the eye;
>   Fair as a star when only one
>   Is shining in the sky.

> b. The Night has a thousand eyes,
>   The Day but one;
>   Yet the light of the bright world dies
>   With the dying sun.

> c. Abou Ben Adhem (may his tribe increase!)
>   Awoke one night from a deep dream of peace,
>   And saw, within the moonlight in his room,
>   Making it rich, and like a lily in bloom,
>   An angel writing in a book of gold:
>   Exceeding peace had made Ben Adhem bold,
>   And to the Presence in the room he said,
>   'What writest thou?'—The vision raised its head,
>   And, with a look made of all sweet accord,
>   Answered, 'The names of those who love the Lord.'
>   'And is mine one?' said Abou. 'Nay, not so,'
>   Replied the angel. Abou spoke more low,
>   But cheerily still; and said, 'I pray thee, then,
>   Write me as one that loves his fellow-men.'
>
>   The angel wrote, and vanished. The next night
>   It came again, with a great awakening light,
>   And showed the names whom love of God had blessed,—
>   And lo! Ben Adhem's name led all the rest!
>   LEIGH HUNT, 'Abou Ben Adhem'

> d. Under the wide and starry sky,
>   Dig the grave and let me lie.
>   Glad did I live and gladly die,
>   And I laid me down with a will.
>   This be the verse you grave for me:
>   *Here he lies where he longed to be;*
>   *Home is the sailor, home from the sea,*
>   *And the hunter home from the hill.*
>   R. L. STEVENSON, 'Requiem'

e. The sea is calm tonight.
   The tide is full, the moon lies fair
   Upon the straits;—on the French coast the light
   Gleams and is gone; the cliffs of England stand,
   Glimmering and vast, out in the tranquil bay.
   Come to the window, sweet is the night-air!
   Only, from the long line of spray
   Where the sea meets the moon-blanch'd land,
   Listen! you hear the grating roar
   Of pebbles which the waves draw back, and fling,
   At their return, up the high strand,
   Begin, and cease, and then again begin,
   With tremulous cadence slow, and bring
   The eternal note of sadness in.

   The Sea of Faith
   Was once, too, at the full, and round earth's shore
   Lay like the folds of a bright girdle furl'd.
   But now I only hear
   Its melancholy, long, withdrawing roar,
   Retreating, to the breath
   Of the night-wind, down the vast edges drear
   And naked shingles of the world.

   Ah, love, let us be true
   To one another! for the world, which seems
   To lie before us like a land of dreams,
   So various, so beautiful, so new,
   Hath really neither joy, nor love, nor light,
   Nor certitude, nor peace, nor help for pain;
   And we are here as on a darkling plain
   Swept with confused alarms of struggle and flight,
   Where ignorant armies clash by night.

                          MATTHEW ARNOLD, 'Dover Beach'

   f. A lonely lake, a lonely shore,
      A lone pine leaning on the moon;
      All night the water-beating wings
      Of a solitary loon.

      With mournful wail from dusk to dawn
      He gibbered at the taunting stars—

A hermit soul gone raving mad,
And beating at his bars.

LEW SARETT, 'The Loon'

g. Sweet and low, sweet and low,
    Wind of the western sea,
  Low, low, breathe and blow,
    Wind of the western sea!
  Over the rolling waters go,
  Come from the dying moon, and blow,
    Blow him again to me;
  While my little one, while my pretty one sleeps.

ALFRED TENNYSON, 'The Princess'

h. As a fond mother, when the day is o'er
    Leads by the hand her little child to bed,
    Half willing, half reluctant to be led,
  And leaves his broken playthings on the floor,
  Still gazing at them through the open door,
    Nor wholly reassured and comforted
    By promises of others in their stead,
  Which, though more splendid, may not please him more;
  So Nature deals with us, and takes away
    Our playthings one by one, and by the hand
    Leads us to rest so gently, that we go
  Scarce knowing if we wish to go or stay,
    Being too full of sleep to understand
    How far the unknown transcends the what we know.

H. W. LONGFELLOW, 'Nature'

i. The Arctic moon hangs overhead;
    The wide white silence lies below.
  A starveling pine stands lone and gaunt,
    Black-penciled on the snow.

  Weird as the moan of sobbing winds,
    A long, lone call floats up from the trail,
  And the naked soul of the frozen North
    Trembles in that wail.

LEW SARETT, 'The Wolf Cry'

j. There's a barrel-organ caroling across a golden street
    In the City as the sun sinks low;

And the music's not immortal; but the world has made it sweet
  And fulfilled it with the sunset glow;
And it pulses through the pleasures of the City and the pain
  That surround the singing organ like a large eternal light;
And they've given it a glory and a part to play again
  In the Symphony that rules the day and night.

And now it's marching onward through the realms of old romance,
  And trolling out a fond familiar tune,
And now it's roaring cannon down to fight the King of France,
  And now it's prattling softly to the moon.
And all around the organ there's a sea without a shore
  Of human joys and wonders and regrets;
To remember and to recompense the music evermore
  For what the cold machinery forgets.

ALFRED NOYES, 'The Barrel-Organ'

ESTABLISHING A DESIRABLE BASIC PITCH LEVEL

As was discussed previously in this chapter, it is probably true that many individuals habitually employ a conversational pitch level that is either too high or too low for the particular voice concerned. The principal reasons for these deviations have also been explained in some detail in earlier sections. When vocal conditions are right for proper tone production, pitch will tend to take care of itself. That is, the level to which your voice falls when effective breathing conditions are observed and when the throat is open and properly relaxed is likely to be close to the pitch you should cultivate and use for all normal conversational speech. Disagreeable qualities of tone in the form of throatiness, harshness, or stridency may result if the voice is habitually forced below or above this natural level.

No arbitrary rules can be laid down regarding a desirable basic pitch for all voices; such a procedure would be impossible. Individual voices differ markedly in the pitch to which they most easily and naturally respond, the natural pitch being determined by the essential structure of the voice mechanism itself, principally the length and weight of the vocal folds. As a matter of fact, within reasonable limits, the pitch of the individual voice is not the most important factor in determining its excellence; many good speakers have voices that are naturally high, for example. The important consideration is that the pitch should be right for that particular voice.

1. Following the instructions presented earlier in this chapter, locate your habitual speaking level, or key. Where does it fall with respect to your total pitch range? How does it compare with your calculated optimum pitch as determined by the 'pitch profile' technique?

2. Take your calculated optimum pitch and experiment with it, singing the vowels [ɑ], [o], [u] on a range of two or three notes above and below the theoretical level. Which sounds and feels best?

3. Some ear training may well need to precede the habitual establishment of your newly found basic pitch level. You need to become conscious of the pitch of your voice; learn to recognize when it becomes too high or goes too low for comfort and best effect. Using a piano, sing [ɑ] or [o] up and down the scale through your lowest octave. Does it sound and feel better as you approach the middle of the octave?

4. Without using the piano at first, count from one to five on a monotone attempting to estimate 'by ear' as closely as possible your optimum pitch level as discovered from the 'pitch profile.' Hold one of the counts long enough for you to locate it on the piano. How close did you come to your optimum pitch? Practice this drill until you have firmly established the 'feel' and the sound of your optimum pitch level.

5. Count very quietly from one to five, taking an easy breath before each count and completely relaxing as you sound each vowel tone. Guard against breathiness or throatiness. Take careful note of the pitch of your voice; how close is it to your optimum level? Do not be too surprised if it comes out a bit lower. If it does, try raising it up to the optimum pitch, but still retaining much of the same feeling of easy relaxation you had before.

6. In attempting to establish the optimum speaking level for your voice, avoid falling into a monotone. After all, this is merely the general, or basic, level which characterizes your voice as a whole and to which you return most often as you vary the pitch both above and below this level during the natural intonations and inflections of expressive speech. Speak the following sentences on what you now consider to be your best pitch level, as determined by the 'pitch profile' results and your own experimentation to achieve the best results. Speak them in a natural way, however, allowing your voice to vary in pitch in accordance with the meaning you are attempting to convey.

a. When do you expect to return?
b. I expect to be home on Monday.
c. What do you suppose made him do it?
d. One doesn't have time to take all the courses he would like to while going to school.
e. A liberal education can be helpful in many ways.
f. One's 'ear for music' can be greatly improved through training.

7. In reading the following selections, note how the feeling and mood are conducive to deep, full tones, relaxed throat, and lower pitch. Avoid any feeling of forcing the pitch down, however; strive rather to give an understanding, warm, and sympathetic interpretation of the selection itself. While the

vocal techniques and general style of speech employed in interpreting these poems will probably not be typical of ordinary conversational speech, observe carefully the pitch level which you employ. If you appear to achieve a deeper, richer quality and greater ease and flexibility at this level than you customarily observe in your voice, work for a carry-over of this lower pitch and more relaxed quality into your everyday speaking. These exercises should aid you in avoiding the tense throat and strained quality so often characteristic of conversational speech.

a. Glooms of the live-oaks, beautiful-braided and woven
   With intricate shades of the vines that myriad-cloven
      Clamber the forks of the multiform boughs,—
         Emerald twilights,—
         Virginal shy lights,
  Wrought of the leaves to allure to the whisper of vows,
 When lovers pace timidly down through the green colonnades
   Of the dim sweet woods, of the dear dark woods,
   Of the heavenly woods and glades,
 That run to the radiant marginal sand-beach within
    The wide sea-marshes of Glynn.
            SIDNEY LANIER, 'The Marshes of Glynn'

b. Once upon a midnight dreary, while I pondered, weak and
    weary,
  Over many a quaint and curious volume of forgotten lore,—
  While I nodded, nearly napping, suddenly there came a tapping,
  As of someone gently rapping, rapping at my chamber door.
 ' 'Tis some visitor,' I muttered, 'tapping at my chamber door:
    Only this and nothing more!'
       . . . . .
  Deep into that darkness peering, long I stood there, wondering, fearing,
  Doubting, dreaming dreams no mortal ever dared to dream before;
  But the silence was unbroken, and the stillness gave no token,
  And the only word there spoken was the whispered word 'Lenore!'

This I whispered, and an echo murmured back the word
   'Lenore!'
        Merely this and nothing more.

                EDGAR ALLAN POE, 'The Raven'

c. As toilsome I wander'd Virginia's woods,
  To the music of rustling leaves kick'd by my feet, (for 'twas
    autumn,)
  I mark'd at the foot of a tree the grave of a soldier;
  Mortally wounded he and buried on the retreat, (easily all
    could I understand,)
  The halt of a mid-day hour, when up! no time to lose—yet
    this sign left,
  On a tablet scrawl'd and nail'd on the tree by the grave,
  Bold, cautious, true, and my loving comrade.

  Long, long I muse, then on my way go wandering,
  Many a changeful season to follow, and many a scene of life,
  Yet at times through changeful season and scene, abrupt, alone,
    or in the crowded street,
  Comes before me the unknown soldier's grave, comes the in-
    scription rude in Virginia's woods,
  Bold, cautious, true, and my loving comrade.

          WALT WHITMAN, 'As Toilsome I Wandered
          Virginia's Woods'

    d. Lead out the pageant: sad and slow,
      As fits a universal woe,
      Let the long, long procession go,
      And let the sorrowing crowd about it grow,
      And let the mournful martial music blow,
      The last great Englishman is low.

          ALFRED TENNYSON, 'Ode on the Death of the
          Duke of Wellington'

e. Beautiful was the night. Behind the black wall of the forest,
  Tipping its summit with silver, arose the moon. On the river
  Fell here and there through the branches a tremulous gleam
    of the moonlight,
  Like the sweet thoughts of love on a darkened and devious
    spirit.

Nearer and round about her, the manifold flowers of the garden

Poured out their souls in odors, that were their prayers and confessions

Unto the night, as it went its way, like a silent Carthusian.

Fuller of fragrance than they, and as heavy with shadows and night-dews,

Hung the heart of the maiden. The calm and the magical moonlight

Seemed to inundate her soul with indefinable longings,

As, through the garden gate, and beneath the shade of the oak-trees,

Passed she along the path to the edge of the measureless prairie.

Loud and sudden and near the note of a whippoorwill sounded

Like a flute in the woods; and anon, through the neighboring thickets,

Farther and farther away it floated and dropped into silence.

'Patience!' whispered the oaks from oracular caverns of darkness;

And, from the moonlit meadow, a sigh responded, 'Tomorrow!'

H. W. LONGFELLOW, Evangeline

f. How dear to this heart are the scenes of my childhood,
  When fond recollection presents them to view!
The orchard, the meadow, the deep-tangled wildwood,
  And every loved spot that my infancy knew;—
The wide-spreading pond, and the mill which stood by it,
  The bridge, and the rock where the cataract fell;
The cot of my father, the dairy-house nigh it,
  And e'en the rude bucket which hung in the well.
The old oaken bucket, the iron-bound bucket,
  The moss-covered bucket which hung in the well.

SAMUEL WOODWORTH, 'The Old Oaken Bucket'

MAKING YOUR NEW PITCH LEVEL HABITUAL

Obviously superior vocal habits are of little practical value if they are exhibited only when you are demonstrating some exercise or when you are in a public performance of some sort or are otherwise consciously controlling your voice. If good voice is going to work for us, it must do so all of the time—in the classroom, at the office, and in other everyday situations, not just when we happen to think about it.

Many of the drills and exercises in a book of this sort are for practice primarily and are designed to accomplish a certain specific result. Consequently they may not, in and of themselves, always bear a close or direct relationship to everyday uses of the voice. But just as the golfer may need to study his putting techniques on the practice green, and the music student must spend long hours working on musical scales before he is ready to play Beethoven, so an individual wishing to improve his speaking voice must first concentrate on certain techniques that will eventually enable him to gain better control over his voice production generally. In the end, however, these techniques must be integrated into a total pattern of speaking that will become natural and habitual.

This final carry-over is often not easy to accomplish, and for a time you may need to apply your mind consciously to the task of incorporating the newly learned techniques into your ordinary speaking. If you do this faithfully, after a while good voice production will become unconscious and automatic. Do not become discouraged if this does not happen immediately; bear in mind that your present vocal habits did not develop overnight either. Some time will be required to break down old vocal patterns and build up new ones in their place.

The following exercises were designed to assist you in this process of carry-over:

1. Record your voice while you are reading some factual or conversational material or just talking naturally, but at your best pitch level as you have discovered it to be. Play back the

sample and listen to it carefully. Does your voice sound higher or lower than you thought it would, or about the same?

2. Repeat Exercise 1 for practice until you learn to hear yourself as others hear you. The recorded version should begin to sound familiar and natural to you as you come to identify it with what your voice sounds like and feels like as you talk.

3. Without checking first, read some material at what you think is your optimum pitch. Avoid falling into a monotone; read it naturally with some expression. Using the method described earlier in this chapter, check the pitch level you were using with a piano or other musical instrument. How close were you to your optimum pitch? Are you developing a 'feel' for this pitch?

4. Continue Exercise 3 until you can pitch your voice where you want it and be sure of your 'ear' without having to check each time.

5. Practice the following selections, using your optimum-pitch level and making your 'rendition' sound as natural and as conversational as possible. Check your pitch level from time to time to make sure you are maintaining it faithfully.

a. If you wish to describe a flame flickering away, a tree on a plain, sit down before the flame or the tree till it no longer resembles, for you, any other flame or any other tree. That is the way men become original.

b. No man can accomplish that which benefits the ages and not suffer. Discoverers do not reap the fruit of what they discover. Reformers are pelted and beaten. Men who think in advance of their time are persecuted. They who lead the flock must fight the wolf.

c. The maxim that no people ought to be free till they are fit to use their freedom, is worthy of the fool in the old story who resolved not to go into the water till he had learned to swim. If men are to wait for liberty till they become wise and good in slavery, they may indeed wait forever.

d. Once when the snow of the year was beginning to fall,
We stopped by a mountain pasture to say 'Whose colt?'
A little Morgan had one forefoot on the wall,
The other curled at his breast. He dipped his head
And snorted at us. And then he had to bolt.
We heard the miniature thunder where he fled,
And we saw him, or thought we saw him, dim and grey,
Like a shadow against the curtain of falling flakes.
'I think the little fellow's afraid of the snow.
He isn't winter-broken. It isn't play
With the little fellow at all. He's running away.
I doubt if even his mother could tell him, "Sakes,
It's only weather." He'd think she didn't know!
Where is his mother? He can't be out alone.'
And now he comes again with a clatter of stone
And mounts the wall again with whited eyes
And all his tail that isn't hair up straight.
He shudders his coat as if to throw off flies.
'Whoever it is that leaves him out so late,
When other creatures have gone to stall and bin,
Ought to be told to come and take him in.'
                    ROBERT FROST, 'The Runaway'

e. He said to his friend, 'If the British march
By land or sea from the town tonight,
Hang a lantern aloft in the belfry arch
Of the North Church tower as a signal light—
One, if by land, and two, if by sea;
And I on the opposite shore will be,
Ready to ride and spread the alarm
Through every Middlesex village and farm,
For the country-folk to be up and to arm.'
                    H. W. LONGFELLOW, 'Paul Revere's Ride'

f. A foolish consistency is the hobgoblin of little minds, adored by little statesmen and philosophers and divines. With consistency a great soul has simply nothing to do. He may as well concern himself with his shadow on the wall. Speak what you think now in hard words and to-morrow speak what to-morrow thinks in hard words again, though it contradict everything you said to-day—'Ah, so you shall be sure to be misunderstood.'—Is it so bad, then, to be misunderstood? Pythagoras was misunderstood, and Socrates, and Jesus, and Luther, and Copernicus, and Galileo, and Newton, and every pure and wise spirit that ever took flesh. To be great is to be misunderstood. . . .

RALPH WALDO EMERSON

g. Now blessings light on him that first invented sleep. It covers a man all over, thoughts and all, like a cloak; 'tis meat for the hungry, drink for the thirsty, heat for the cold, and cold for the hot. 'Tis the current coin that purchases all the pleasures of the world cheap; and the balance that sets the king and the shepherd, the fool and the wise man even.

CERVANTES

ILLUSTRATING GOOD VOICE PRODUCTION

1. Prepare a short, informal talk on a subject familiar to you, for example, your home town, your favorite hobby, an interesting trip you have taken, demonstrating all you have learned about good voice production thus far. Put your mind to this and watch your breathing, be sure your throat is open and relaxed, get a nice, easy tone free of breathiness and other unpleasant qualities, and keep your voice pitched at its best level.

2. Listen to your voice carefully during the next few days and weeks as you use it in everyday speech situations. Make a conscious effort to apply all of the things you have studied and practiced thus far. Do not become too concerned if this practice makes you a bit self-conscious about your speech; this feeling won't last long, and it is the price you must pay to get new, desirable habits established in the place of old, undesirable ones. And remember—the more conscientious you are in applying the new habits, the sooner they will become automatic and 'natural.'

IV

Resonance in the Voice

It is resonance * which is chiefly responsible for building up the weak, indifferent sounds emitted by the vocal folds into the full, vibrant tones that we associate with a good voice. It is also resonance which, in large measure, determines the basic quality of the individual voice. We must not mistake its function, however; resonance adds nothing to the original sound. It simply develops the potentialities present in some degree in the laryngeal tone. Let us consider for a moment how and through what agencies this seeming magic is accomplished.

The three principal resonators of the voice are the pharynx, the mouth, and the nasal passages. Very probably the chest also contributes materially to the finished tone, though there is considerable uncertainty about the specific way in which it functions.

CHEST RESONANCE

That there is true resonance of the cavity type in the chest itself appears quite improbable. Bear in mind that the chest cavity, as was pointed out in the chapter on breathing, is almost wholly filled with the soft, spongy mass of the lung tissue. It seems highly probable that the only effect of such an arrangement would be to absorb and damp out sound waves rather than resonate them. The effectiveness of such a set-up has been compared with that of a resonator filled with wet sponges.

* The material on the acoustics of voice and speech included in Appendix A forms a logical introduction to the discussion of resonance in this chapter.

112

The trachea and bronchi, however, present a quite different situation. They are open, free cavities of sufficient size and proper shape to provide resonance. The fact that they are below rather than above the larynx does not materially affect the situation. There is one factor, however, that does definitely restrict infra-glottal resonance—the size and shape of the cavities provided by the trachea and bronchi remain relatively fixed. This lack of adjustability limits the range of frequencies to which these resonators can respond to those pitches most closely approximating the natural frequency of the cavities.* With respect to their effect upon the voice, this means that only at certain pitch levels are the infra-glottal resonators functioning with maximum efficiency, while at other frequencies they can have little or no effect upon the vocal tone because they cannot be tuned to those pitches. This condition may in part explain a characteristic of voice production known as optimum pitch, discussed in the previous chapter.

The Chest as a Sounding Board. The reality of vibrations on the bony walls of the chest cannot be doubted. They can actually be felt if the hand is placed upon the sternum during phonation, and they can readily be heard if one explores the surface of the chest with a stethoscope, or even places his unaided ear against it. Vibrations from the vocal folds, conducted through the cartilages to the vertebrae and thence to the ribs and through the ribs to the sternum, could easily accomplish the forced vibration of the entire bony framework of the thorax. From this we may conclude that not only the chest but in all probability the entire body, particularly the trunk and the bony structures of the head, function to some extent as a sounding board to reinforce the laryngeal tone or to damp out certain frequencies and in this way affect vocal quality.

No particular drills, exercises, or techniques of voice pro-

---

* See Appendix A for an explanation of tuned resonators.

duction are of much avail, however, in increasing chest resonance or in making better use of whatever benefit may come
from it, except that it seems to function more actively in the
production of low tones than it does in the case of tones of
higher pitch. Also it is reasonable to assume that the chest
will be more effective as a sounding board if good posture is
maintained and if an adequate supply of air is available at
all times.

PHARYNGEAL RESONANCE

The pharynx, or throat (Figure 1), is one of the most important resonators of the voice, although its specific role in
the resonation of the vocal tone is perhaps less clearly understood than the functions of either the mouth or nasal passages. However, it is generally agreed that it plays an important part in forming what has been termed the vocal megaphone, and that it is particularly responsible for providing
resonance for the fundamental and the lower overtones.
Amplification of these frequencies gives to the finished tone
a quality described as mellow, rich, or full. Selective resonation of the lower overtones is also instrumental in giving to
the various vowel sounds their characteristic quality.

In order to be responsive as a resonator over any appreciable range of frequencies, the size and shape of the pharynx
must be capable of modification, since it functions as a tuned
resonator. Within limits this is possible. Let us see briefly
how this adaptation is accomplished (Figure 1). The entire
posterior wall of the pharynx is lined with muscular tissue,
which, when it contracts, constricts the walls and reduces the
size of the pharyngeal cavity. The size of the pharynx can be
modified further by the action of the back of the tongue and
by the shape and position of the epiglottis, as well as by the
action of the velum, or soft palate. All of these adjustments
are important not only in providing for the characteristic differences in resonance of the various vowel sounds but also in

making possible more subtle changes in the general quality of the vocal tone.

The Effect of Surface Texture upon Quality. There is, however, another way, in addition to changes in its size and shape, in which the pharynx may operate to effect modifications of tone quality, and this is accomplished through changes in the texture of the pharyngeal walls. It has been demonstrated that in addition to the size and shape of a resonator and the size of its opening or openings, the texture of the material out of which it is made is also operative in modifying the quality of the tone which it resonates. This principle is involved in an explanation of the differences in quality between the tone produced by a flute or clarinet made of wood and the tone of one made of metal.

One effect of a soft surface, for example, is to broaden a resonator's tuning (increase its range of response) and decrease its efficiency. This decrease of efficiency is associated with a damping effect which such a resonator has upon the higher overtones, with a consequent proportionate increase in the relative prominence of the lower partials and the fundamental. As was mentioned previously, this arrangement of overtones has the effect of imparting to the tone-complex a mellow richness and fullness. The open, relaxed pharynx has such an effect upon the voice. Conversely, a hard-surface resonator has the effect of giving prominence to the higher partials with the result that the tone takes on a quality which has been described as a metallic brilliance. Therefore, when the muscles of the pharynx are contracted with a consequent hardening of the surfaces of the resonator, the vocal tone may become metallic and strident.

Thus we may have in the physics of resonance a definite basis upon which to recommend openness and relaxation of the pharyngeal passageway as an aid to better tone quality. A tight, constricted throat means a harsh, tense voice; a relaxed throat contributes to mellowness and richness of tone.

an effect partially traceable at least to the influence of pharyngeal resonance.

NASAL RESONANCE

The nasal passages are the least adaptable of the chief resonators of the voice, and it is probably for this reason that their function in voice production is the most restricted. In the English language there are only three sounds which are resonated primarily in the nasal cavities: the consonants [m], [n], and [ŋ] (as in *sing*); and even these sounds owe their characteristic quality not to changes in the nasal cavities themselves, but rather to articulatory adjustments in the mouth.

Whether the nasal passages play any part in the resonation of speech sounds other than in the nasal consonants just mentioned has long been a subject of active controversy in the field of voice training. Opinion has ranged all the way from a flat denial of any nasal resonance in the vowel sounds to the opposite extreme of extravagant claims for the importance of such resonance in all tone production. Research studies support the conclusion that in the majority of speakers, both good and bad, the vowel sounds may have some degree of nasal resonance, the actual amount depending upon a number of factors.

It has been found, for one thing, that vowel sounds following or preceding nasal consonants will show more nasal resonance than vowels associated with oral consonants. That is, the vowel in the word *man* is much more likely to be nasalized than the same vowel in *bad*. This is known as assimilation nasality. It has also been observed that individuals whose voices exhibit nasality are more inclined to speak with tight jaws and consequently insufficient mouth opening than are those people with superior voices. Simply stated, the principle in this instance appears to be that if the sound can't get out through the mouth, it will come out through the nose. In this fact we have a strong argument for relaxation of the jaw muscles and careful rounding out of all speech tones if good quality is to be attained.

Nasality. Voices judged to be badly nasal have been found to show more nasal resonance on all vowels than superior voices. The amount of nasal resonance, however, which the individual speaker will use is partly determined by prevailing practice in the particular section of the country in which he has learned to speak. In sections of the Middle West and the South and in parts of New England, for example, much more nasal resonance is commonly heard than in certain other localities of the East. It is also worth some notice in passing that our attitude toward nasality, whether we find it pleasant or unpleasant, is influenced to a large extent by our linguistic background and training. If we come from localities where much nasal resonance is commonly heard, we do not find it unpleasant or think of it as being a fault of voice production. All of which suggests the conclusion that the term nasality is, within limits, a relative one, having a rather pronounced subjective basis.

The Physical Basis of Nasality. There is, however, a definite physical basis underlying nasality. In the first place, it might be well to make some distinction between the terms *nasal resonance* and *nasality,* inasmuch as both have been used in discussing this problem. Nasal resonance can be defined as a normal amount of resonance in the nasal passages during the production of vowels and nasal consonants as found in the speech of a majority of individuals whose voices would be judged to be of average or superior quality. Nasality, as the word is commonly used, is a relative term denoting a departure from normal nasal resonance in the direction of either too much or too little. Hence it follows that there are two kinds of nasality, a positive nasality (too much nasal resonance or nasal emission on non-nasal sounds), also called nasalization, and a negative nasality (too little), sometimes referred to as denasalization. The speech of one exhibiting the positve type is characterized by a sharp, 'twangy' quality on the vowel sounds, or a hollow, 'nosey' sound with obvious evidence of excessive nasal leakage on both the vowels and oral consonants, characteristic of cleft palate speech. Denasalization, on the other hand, is associated with a lack of resonance and nasal emission on the nasal consonants and a definite impression of a stuffiness or dullness of the vowel tones. This type has sometimes been called 'adenoid speech' or 'cold-in-the-head speech.'

The Relation of Nasal Resonance to Oral Resonance. In order to understand clearly the various aspects of the problem of nasal resonance, the part that it plays in voice production, and its relation to nasality, a more complete explanation is needed of the essential mechanism involved. First of all it must be understood that the relationship between the nasal cavities and the mouth cavity is governed by a rather complicated valvular mechanism composed principally of the velum, or soft palate, the walls of the pharynx, and the pillars that form the sides of the opening between the pharynx and the mouth. When the velum is elevated (Figure 13), the other structures pull in to meet it to form a sphincter-like closure between the mouth and the nasal passages. But when the velum is relaxed and open, tone is allowed to pass up into the nasal chambers (Figure 14).

Consider for a moment the mechanism involved in the production of a vowel sound. Assuming that the velum remains closed, the speech 'megaphone' consists of the throat and the mouth (Figure 13). But suppose that during the production of a vowel sound the velum should be allowed to relax and open slightly, then the nasal chambers will be called into play as accessory or supplementary resonators opening off the main resonator tube (Figure 14). The effect upon the vocal tone will be beneficial so long as the size of the posterior opening into the nasal resonator, regulated by the action of the velum and other structures, remains smaller than the anterior opening, determined by the size of the nostrils and the space between the turbinates and the septum. When, however, the velum is allowed to relax to the point at which the opening into the nasal cavities is larger than the anterior opening out of the nasal passages, then the

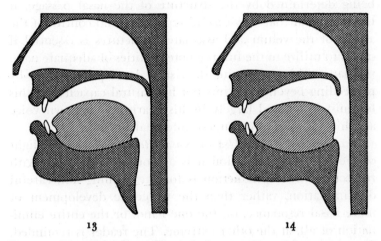

13   14

FIG. 13. Diagrammatic outline of the mouth, nasal passage, and pharynx, with the velum raised as in the production of an oral sound.

FIG. 14. Same as Figure 13 except with velum lowered, creating an opening into the posterior nasal passageway.

tone becomes dammed up in the resonator, as it were, and a type of resonance known as *cul-de-sac,* or 'blind alley,' resonance results. It is this type of resonance that has the effect of changing the quality of the tone to that which we recognize and identify as nasality. Thus, *cul-de-sac* resonance is responsible for nasality, particularly as the term is used to indicate so-called 'nasal twang.'

From this explanation it can be seen that the degree of opening of the velum and hence the amount of nasal resonance desirable in the production of a vowel tone may vary from individual to individual, depending upon the structure of the nasal passages. A person with a great deal of freedom through the anterior nasal passages can stand much more nasal resonance than the person with thin nostrils, enlarged turbinates, or deviated septum. Therefore, since the anterior opening out of the nasal resonator remains relatively fixed, being determined by the structure of the nasal passage, it becomes clear that very careful regulation and control of the action of the velum and associated structures is essential if one is to utilize to the full the potentialities of adequate nasal resonance without running the risk of developing nasality by proceeding beyond the limits of his natural capacity. In this he must be guided largely by his hearing of his own voice and his recognition of undesirable qualities in it.

Developing Proper Use of Nasal Resonance. In the light of the foregoing discussion it is obvious that the need with respect to vowel production is for ear training and careful discrimination, rather than the wholesale development of more nasal resonance, on the one hand, or the entire elimination of all, at the other extreme. The reader is reminded, however, that the velum functions as an integral part of a complicated articulatory and resonance mechanism, and it is not easy, and may not even be desirable, to attempt to gain individual control over its movements. Instead of striving merely for control of the velum, it is often more advantageous to approach the problem of nasality and nasal resonance by giving attention to good, clear articulation, adequate mouth opening, and a relaxed openness of the pharynx.

In conclusion, it might be well to point out that the average untrained voice is more likely to suffer from too much nasal resonance rather than from too little. Careful control of nasal resonance requires some effort; the muscles of the palate and the pharynx must be energized if the port into the posterior nasal chambers is to be discriminatingly regulated. Mere relaxation of these muscles is all that is required to keep it open, and the path of least effort leads to a sluggish and inactive palate with a consequent nasalization of sounds which should be predominantly oral. While relaxation as a principle is highly desirable in most of the activities involved in tone production, it should never be carried to the point at which articulation becomes disorganized and the clearness and precision which should characterize the various speech sounds are destroyed. More nasal resonance on [m], [n], and [ŋ], but more oral and pharyngeal resonance on the vowel tones should generally be the aim of voice training.

The Sinuses and Nasal Resonance. It is not now generally believed that the sinuses play any important part in resonation, except perhaps in an indirect and somewhat negative way. They do serve to make the bones of the face and the nasal passages lighter and hence more vibrantly responsive as a sounding board. Therefore, when they become inflamed and filled with mucus, they have the effect of deadening the sounding-board function of the facial bones. Furthermore, the inflammation may spread from the sinuses themselves to adjacent areas of the mucous membrane lining the nasal cavities, causing excessive discharge and swelling of the tissues, and thereby seriously interfering with nasal resonance. There is also the further danger that discharge from the sinuses may drop down on the vocal folds, setting up a secondary inflammation or laryngitis, which may become chronic if the condition is allowed to persist. The result may be huskiness or hoarseness in the voice. Aside from other possible factors involved in this malady, sinusitis should be regarded as a serious menace to voice production.

Obstructions in the Nasal Passageway. There are in reality many conditions besides sinusitis which operate to obstruct the nasal passageway, producing more or less distortion of the vowel sounds and a reduction of the normal resonance on the nasal consonants [m], [n], and [ŋ]—a condition referred to as denasalization. One of the most common causes of this stuffy, cold-in-the-head speech, particularly among children, is the enlargement of the pharyngeal tonsil (Figure 1), a condition known as adenoids. A broken or deviated septum, enlarged turbinates, nasal polypi and other growths in the nose, and irritations and swelling of the tissues resulting from 'hay fever' or colds are also prominent among the causes of negative nasality.

These conditions are, of course, not to be alleviated through vocal training, nor is such training of much avail in improving the voice as long as the physiological basis of the denasality is present, if it is at all serious. When, however, the cause has been removed through medication, surgery, or some other means, vocal training is usually necessary to adjust the voice to a somewhat altered resonance mechanism. Such training will be directed mainly toward the development of adequate nasal resonance on the nasal consonants, the elimination of leakage through the nasal passages on the non-nasal consonants, and the establishment of a proper balance between nasal and oral resonance on the vowel sounds. Such a program involves training the ear to identify both the desirable qualities in the voice that are to be developed and the undesirable ones that are to be avoided.

ORAL RESONANCE

Of all the resonators of the voice, the mouth is the most important single one, largely by virtue of its variability in shape and size and in its relationship to the other resonators. Its remarkable versatility results principally from the mobility and adaptability of the chief organ of articulation, the tongue. There are indeed few sounds in the English language that are not in part at least normally dependent upon some adjustment of tongue position. In addition to the tongue, virtually all of the other structures that go to make up the boundaries of the mouth are likewise readily adjustable—the velum, the walls of the pharynx, the lower jaw, and the lips. Each contributes its part to the intricate and precise adjustments necessary to the production of even the simpler speech sounds. In the formation of the vowel tones, the function of the mouth as a resonator really assumes its greatest importance. As a result of alterations in size and shape, it acts in a selective capacity as a tuned resonator to amplify certain partials in the complex laryngeal tone, thereby giving the tone a characteristic quality which we identify as a vowel sound.

Vowel Sounds as Resonance Tones. In order that this process may be more clearly understood, let us consider for a moment just how vowel sounds are formed. Examine carefully the approximate position of the tongue with respect to the pharynx and mouth in the production of the vowel [u] (as in *moon*), for example (Figure 15). Note that the tongue is low in front and high at the back and that it serves to divide the mouth into two cavities or chambers, a rather large one at the back and a somewhat smaller one in front. The large cavity forms a resonator which will respond to low pitches and hence will amplify the fundamental and the lower overtones, while the resonator in the front of the mouth will amplify the overtones of medium pitch. This particular combination of amplified overtones in their relation to each other and to the fundamental gives us a quality of tone which we recognize and identify as the vowel [u]. Recall, furthermore, that the pitch to which a resonator will respond is also determined by the size of its opening. For [u] we have a very small opening effected by the pursing of the lips. This operates to lower the pitch to which the resonator in the front of the mouth will respond. Thus, the vowel [u] has one of the lowest resonance frequencies of any of the vowel sounds.

Back Vowels and Front Vowels. Change either the position of the tongue or the shape of the lips and the quality of the tone is likewise changed, and we no longer have [u] but some other vowel sound. If the back of the tongue is lowered through progressive stages from the position shown in Figure 15, with an accompanying unrounding and widening of the lips, until it reaches a position where it is more or less flat in the mouth, it will have assumed the characteristic positions for the so-called back vowels, [u], [ʊ], [o],

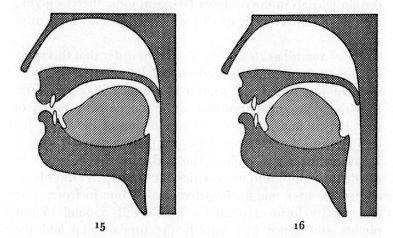

15   16

FIG. 15. Illustrating the position of the tongue in the formation of the high back vowel [u] (as in *moon*).

FIG. 16. Illustrating the position of the tongue in the formation of the high front vowel [i] (as in *eat*).

[ɔ], [ɒ], and [ɑ].* Their name is derived from the fact that they result from movements of the back of the tongue.

Figure 16 represents the opposite of the situation observed in the formation of [u]. Instead of being humped up in the back, the tongue is now raised high in front. This illustrates the typical formation of the mouth in the production of the vowel [i] (as in *eat*). Pronounce first [u] and then [i] and this shift of tongue position can be clearly felt. Note also that for [i] the lips are drawn back to a wide, open position. Pro-

* For a more detailed description of these sounds, as well as those which follow, consult Chapter IX, especially the vowel diagram near the beginning of the chapter.

gressive lowering of the front of the tongue to a position in the floor of the mouth, with accompanying changes in the shape and size of the lip opening, produces the so-called front vowels, [i], [ɪ], [e], [ɛ], [æ], and [a]. For the front vowels the higher overtones are more prominent and the front resonator is more important in determining the quality of the tone than in the case of the back vowels; in their production the lower frequencies and the back of the mouth are primarily involved. This fact is also supported by the 'feel' or kines-thetic impression of the two types of sounds: [i] appears to be associated with the front of the mouth, [u] with the back of the mouth and the throat.

By way of summary it should be emphasized once more that the vowel tones are purely resonance phenomena— changes in quality resulting from variations in the size and shape of the oral and pharyngeal cavities, possibly associated also with certain modifications of the epiglottis and the lar-ynx itself. The characteristic frequencies resonated in the case of each vowel are overtones found in the complex tone produced by the vocal folds. Observe that, within normal limits, the vowels are independent of the fundamental pitch of the voice; all of the different vowel sounds can be sung or spoken on the same pitch. Likewise, any one of the vowel sounds can be produced on a wide variety of pitch levels.

Molding Tone into Speech Sounds. What are the implica-tions in this process of oral resonance and vowel formation with respect to the actual problems of voice training? The most important observation to be made is that for each speech sound, though we have considered the problem pri-marily from the point of view of the vowels only, there is a more or less definite, characteristic adjustment of the organs of articulation and of the resonators of the mouth and throat. It is this adjustment which gives to the sound its recognizable quality; and the clearness and fidelity of the finished product depend directly upon the care and precision with which that adjustment has been made. Thus the laryngeal tone and the unvocalized breath stream become the raw materials out of which speech sounds and words are molded and shaped.

We might compare this process, by way of analogy, with that by which formless clay becomes a finished piece of art in the hands of the sculptor. By skillful shaping, molding, and modeling, a definite organic configuration is fashioned out of the shapeless raw material. But suppose that the artist proceeded in a manner similar to the way in which many individuals form their speech sounds into words. A careless slap here, a twist there, and a jab somewhere else, with a movement always loose, vague, and approximate, would result in a figure misshapen, ugly, and unrecognizable. This analogy illustrates very well the difference between clear, pleasant, well-modulated speech, and the opposite variety— indistinct, unco-ordinated, mumbling speech.

One important factor, aside from that of mere carelessness, responsible for the deterioration of speech sounds is the fact that the adjustments responsible for their formation into words and phrases are not static and isolated ones. Rather, speech is a moving, dynamic process; one cannot stop to adjust the articulatory mechanism carefully for each separate sound. The adjustments must be made 'on the run,' as it were, and unless we are ever alert and careful, we are likely to miss the mark and mutilate the sound as a result. Of course, we should also avoid the other extreme, of overprecise, labored, and artificial diction. In the speech of the average individual, however, there is little danger of such conditions developing. The attainment of clearness and precision of speech consistent with ease, informality, and naturalness should be the objective of training in articulation.

Relaxation and openness of the throat, flexibility and ready response of the tongue, jaw, and lips, and discriminating control of oral and nasal resonance are prime essentials of careful, pleasant, well-modulated speech.

TONE PLACEMENT

The term 'tone placement' can be found in much of the literature written on the subject of voice training for speech or for song. However, modern research has shown that the term, as it is most commonly used, is almost wholly figurative and psychological, having very little basis in scientific fact.

Despite the absence of scientific confirmation, however, there is some value in the use of the term, purely as a figurative concept to secure various desirable effects in tone production. The student of voice, in attempting to establish certain conditions which suggest to him that he is actually 'placing' his tone in various ways, for example against his teeth, is often able to modify more or less indirectly his oral and pharyngeal resonance in such a way as to achieve a desirable quality of voice. The use of the term in this way becomes merely a trick or device in voice training and as such it is sometimes efficacious.

As a demonstration of tone placement, try the following experiment: Pronounce the vowel [ɑ] (as in *father*) several times in such a way that it appears to be made far back in the throat, suggesting some of the characteristics of the vowel [ɔ] (as in *awe*). Note the muffled, 'dark' quality of the tone. Now think of placing the [ɑ] in the front of the mouth, against the teeth, if you wish, so that the manner of its production vaguely suggests the 'feel' of the vowel [i] (as in *eat*). If your experiment was successful, the quality should have changed to a more vibrant, brilliant tone. Thus the often-used term 'frontal placement' may be employed to concentrate particular attention on the part which the resonator in the front of the mouth plays in the formation of certain sounds. The result is undoubtedly some modification of oral resonance. Caution must be exercised, however, not to carry this process too far, lest an actual change of vowel occur and cause one's speech to sound distorted.

In general, speech is improved by giving attention to frontal placement, since a large proportion of the consonants and many of the vowels are directly dependent upon activity of the front of the tongue. If speech is to be made clear and easy and is to be spoken as Shakespeare advised, 'trippingly on the tongue,' it must be taken, figuratively speaking, out of the back of the mouth and out of the throat and brought to the front of the mouth where the principal activity of articulation is centered.

DRILLS AND EXERCISES FOR RESONANCE

OPENNESS AND RELAXATION OF THE PHARYNX

One of the practices most disastrous to good voice quality is the habit of elevating or 'humping up' the back of the tongue too high in the mouth during phonation. The effect is a considerable narrowing of the vocal outlet, or speech 'megaphone,' with a consequent likelihood of a resulting nasal twang and a serious loss of volume and fullness of tone. The following drills are designed as an aid in guarding against this difficulty.

1. Continue practicing the yawn. Feel the tongue as it is depressed in the back, and the velum as it rises. Your throat is now fully open.

2. With the aid of a hand mirror and a good source of light, explore as much as can be seen of the mouth and throat during the process of yawning. Note the position of the tongue and the velum and observe how the pharynx opens. Still using the mirror, but without actually yawning, duplicate these same conditions. Practice until you are able to do this readily.

3. Observing with a mirror again, pronounce [ɑ] with the throat open as it was in Exercise 2.

4. Duplicate the feeling of the yawn as nearly as you can and sing [o], keeping the throat as open as possible. Do not allow it to close up with the beginning of phonation. Of course, there will be some movement of the tongue; it is the feeling of openness that is important.

5. Repeat Exercise 4, using the vowel [u].

6. Assume the open throat position once more and, as in the previous exercise, sing [u] for a short time. Then carefully merge this vowel into [ɑ], keeping the feeling all the while of the open, relaxed throat. The transition from the one vowel to the other should be gradual and continuous with no break in the flow of tone.

7. Repeat Exercise 6, substituting the vowel [o] for [u].

8. Apply the same technique to the three vowels [u], [o], and [ɑ], beginning with [u], changing to [o], and then to [ɑ].

9. With the throat open as in the previous exercises, read the following sentences and selections; prolong all of the vowel tones, forming them very carefully and building them up with pharyngeal resonance.

   a. Who are you? (Compare this sentence with Exercise 6.)
   b. Over the rolling waters go.
   c. Round and red as the harvest moon through the mist of the marshes.
   d. Life knocked with its hundred hands at the golden gate of the morning.

       e. O for boyhood's time of June,
          Crowding years in one brief moon.

   f. From the church no Angelus sounded,
      Rose no smoke from the roofs, and gleamed no lights from the windows.

   g. And lo! with a summons sonorous
      Sounded the bell from its tower, and over the meadows a drum beat.

h. She left the web, she left the loom,
   She made three paces through the room,
   She saw the water-lily bloom,
   She saw the helmet and the plume.

i. O Thou vast Ocean! ever sounding Sea!
   Thou vast symbol of a drear immensity!
   Thou thing that windest round the solid world,
   Like a huge animal, which downward hurled
   From the black clouds, lies weltering alone,
   Lashing and writhing till its strength be gone.
   Thy voice is like the thunder, and thy sleep
   Is as a giant's slumber, loud and deep.
                    BRYAN W. PROCTOR, 'Address to the Ocean'

j. To-morrow, and to-morrow, and to-morrow
   Creeps in this petty pace from day to day
   To the last syllable of recorded time;
   And all our yesterdays have lighted fools
   The way to dusty death. Out, out, brief candle!
   Life's but a walking shadow, a poor player
   That struts and frets his hour upon the stage
   And then is heard no more; it is a tale
   Told by an idiot, full of sound and fury,
   Signifying nothing.
                    SHAKESPEARE, *Macbeth*, V. v

k. So live, that when thy summons comes to join
   The innumerable caravan, which moves
   To that mysterious realm, where each shall take
   His chamber in the silent halls of death,
   Thou go not like the quarry-slave at night,
   Scourged to his dungeon, but, sustained and soothed
   By an unfaltering trust, approach thy grave
   Like one who wraps the drapery of his couch
   About him, and lies down to pleasant dreams.
                    W. C. BRYANT, 'Thanatopsis'

l. *Ghost.* I am thy father's spirit;
   Doom'd for a certain term to walk the night,
   And for the day confined to fast in fires,
   Till the foul crimes done in my days of nature
   Are burnt and purg'd away. But that I am forbid

To tell the secrets of my prison-house,
I could a tale unfold whose lightest word
Would harrow up thy soul, freeze thy young blood,
Make thy two eyes, like stars, start from their spheres,
Thy knotted and combined locks to part
And each particular hair to stand on end,
Like quills upon the fretful porpentine:
But this eternal blazon must not be
To ears of flesh and blood. List, list, O, list!
If thou didst ever thy dear father love . . .
Revenge his foul and most unnatural murder.

SHAKESPEARE, Hamlet, I. V

m. And then I pressed the shell
    Close to my ear
    And listened well,
    And straightway like a bell
    Came low and clear
    The slow, sad murmur of the distant seas,
    Whipped by an icy breeze
    Upon a shore
    Wind-swept and desolate.
    It was a sunless strand that never bore
    The footprint of a man,
    Nor felt the weight
    Since time began
    Of any human quality or stir
    Save what the dreary winds and waves incur.
    And in the hush of waters was the sound
    Of pebbles rolling round,
    Forever rolling with a hollow sound.
    And bubbling sea-weeds as the waters go
    Swish to and fro
    Their long, cold tentacles of slimy gray.
    There was no day,
    Nor ever came a night
    Setting the stars alight
    To wonder at the moon;
    Was twilight only and the frightened croon,
    Smitten to whispers, of the dreary wind
    And waves that journeyed blind—

And then I loosed my ear. . . . O, it was sweet
To hear a cart go jolting down the street.

JAMES STEPHENS, 'The Shell'

MOUTH OPENING AND RELAXATION OF THE JAW

The mouth forms the final unit of the speech megaphone, as well as its chief outlet. And just as no megaphone can function efficiently with its edges closed in or with its opening stuffed with paper, so one cannot hope to have a resonant voice or clear speech if he is lip-lazy or if a tight jaw forces him to talk between closed teeth. Vocal evidences of such conditions are muffled speech sounds, nasal twang, and a general flatness and dullness of tone.

The student of voice should not forget, therefore, that the function of the mouth is not only to articulate recognizable speech sounds, but also to round out and build up the speech tone by giving it 'body' and resonance. Obviously, if the mouth is to function in this capacity, it, like the throat, must provide free and open passage for the tone.

1. Review the exercises for relaxation included in Chapter III.

2. Relax the jaw, allowing the mouth to fall open. To facilitate this process, pull down on the jaw with the thumb and fingers as if stroking the beard. Does the jaw remain open and relaxed or do tight muscles pull it back to the closed position?

3. Keeping the jaw relaxed and passive, move it around and from side to side by grasping it with the thumb and fingers. If your jaw resists these movements, it is not properly relaxed.

4. Under its own 'power' this time, move the jaw around in a rotary movement from left to right. Reverse the direction of movement.

5. Repeat *ouch* a number of times, opening the mouth wide.

6. Pronounce the following words, exaggerating the mouth opening for the initial vowels: *open, almond, army, oddly, habit, action, offer, outfit, alder, oxen, Oxford.*

7. Repeat rapidly the two vowels [u] and [ɑ], merging them together until a [w] is clearly distinguishable between them. Exaggerate the lip action as well as the jaw opening. Repeat a number of times.

8. Repeat the vowels [i], [ɑ] and [u], exaggerating the lip and jaw action for each; lips wide for [i], mouth open for [ɑ], lips pursed and rounded for [u].

9. Pronounce the following sentences and selections clearly, opening the mouth and forming the vowel tones very carefully.

    a. Where are you going and what do you wish?
    b. Humpty Dumpty sat on a wall.
    c. Round and round flew each sweet sound.
    d. April showers bring May flowers.
    e. About, about and in and out.
    f. O Thou vast Ocean! ever sounding Sea!
    g. He laughs best who laughs last.
    h. Bob's watch stopped when it fell in the water.
    i. Around the rough and rugged rock the ragged rascal ran.

    j. 'Good speed!' cried the watch, as the gate-bolts undrew;
       'Speed!' echoed the wall to us galloping through;
       Behind shut the postern, the lights sank to rest,
       And into the midnight we galloped abreast.

      k. He wandered east, he wandered west,
         And heard no human sound;
       For months and years, in grief and tears,
         He wandered round and round.

      l. All in a hot and copper sky,
         The bloody Sun at noon,
         Right up above the mast did stand,
         No bigger than the Moon.

m. I wandered lonely as a cloud
    That floats on high o'er vales and hills,
    When all at once I saw a crowd,
    A host, of golden daffodils;
    Beside the lake, beneath the trees,
    Fluttering and dancing in the breeze.
        WORDSWORTH, 'I Wandered Lonely as a Cloud'

NASAL AND ORAL RESONANCE

As was explained earlier in this chapter, the chief objective with respect to this particular problem is not the wholesale development of more nasal resonance on all sounds, nor the total elimination of it from the vowels. Rather, the objective is full nasal resonance on the [m], [n], and [ŋ], and discriminating control of nasal resonance on the vowel sounds with the major emphasis upon pharyngeal and oral resonance. Careful ear training is an indispensable complement to voice training at this point; one must educate his ear to distinguish between full nasal resonance for the nasal consonants, but unpleasant nasality in the vowel tones.

In those voices where a stuffy denasalization is present, properly directed vocal training can often effect a considerable improvement in quality unless serious organic conditions are present. This improvement is accomplished by placing more emphasis on the three nasal sounds. They are stressed and prolonged a bit more when they occur in speech. Exercises involving prolongation of the nasals, such as humming, serve to stress the nasal sounds and make one aware of the pronounced vibrations in and around the nasal passages.

Development of Nasal Resonance.

1. Hum [m] on various pitch levels up and down the scale. Feel the tingling on the lips and the resonance throughout the nasal passages.

2. Hum [n] similarly, without, of course, the lip sensation referred to above.

3. Sing or read the following, emphasizing and sustaining the [ŋ] for increased nasal resonance: *

   a. Running; coming; going; ting-a-ling; ding-dong.
   b. Ring and swing. (Repeat, singing on a monotone)
   c. Ringing and swinging. (Repeat, singing on a monotone)
   d. On wings of song.
   e. Rejoice, you men of Angiers, ring your bells!
   f. What conquest brings he home?

     g. Blow, bugle, blow, set the wild echoes flying.
       Blow, bugle; answer, echoes, dying, dying, dying.

4. Read the following carefully, giving particular prominence to all nasal consonants:

   a. Eenie, meenie, minie, mo.
   b. Mumbo Jumbo, god of the Congo.
   c. The moon never beams without bringing me dreams.
   d. The moan of doves in immemorial elms and the hum of innumerable bees.
   e. O Wind, if winter comes, can spring be far behind?

     f. O wind, a-blowing all day long,
       O wind, that sings so loud a song!

    g. That orbèd maiden, with white fire laden,
      Whom mortals call the Moon,
     Glides glimmering o'er my fleece-like floor
     By the midnight breezes strewn.

h. And the Raven, never flitting, still is sitting, still is sitting
   On the pallid bust of Pallas, just above my chamber door.
   And his eyes have all the seeming of a demon's that is dream-
      ing
   And the lamplight o'er him streaming throws his shadow on
     the floor:

* See also the practice material accompanying the discussion of [m], [n], and [ŋ] in Chapter VIII.

And my soul from out that shadow that lies streaming on the
    floor
  Shall be lifted—never more!

EDGAR ALLAN POE, 'The Raven'

> i. The king was in the counting house,
> Counting out his money.
> The queen was in the parlor,
> Eating bread and honey.
> The maid was in the garden,
> Hanging out her clothes;
> Along came a bumblebee
> And stung her on the nose.

Mother Goose

> j. The Moving Finger writes; and, having writ,
> Moves on: nor all your Piety nor Wit
>   Shall lure it back to cancel half a line,
> Nor all your Tears wash out a word of it.

k. Nothing stirred in the drawing-room or in the dining-room
or on the staircase. Only through the rusty hinges and swollen
sea-moistened wood-work certain airs, detached from the body
of the wind crept around corners and ventured indoors. Almost
one might imagine them, as they entered the drawing-room,
questioning and wondering, toying with the flap of hanging
wallpaper, asking, would it hang much longer, when would it
fall?

VIRGINIA WOOLF

> l. Moon on the field and the foam,
> Moon on the mount and the wold
> Moon, bring him home! bring him home!

Distinguishing Between Nasal and Oral Resonance. The
aims are to develop auditory discrimination and to become
aware of the acoustic and kinesthetic distinction between a
necessary and proper amount of nasal resonance and nasal
emission on the nasal consonants, on the one hand, and oral
resonance and oral emission of the vowels and oral consonants, on the other. An important corollary involves the

recognition of excess nasalization in the production of the vowels.

In the final analysis, your ear is your best guide in the development of proper nasal and oral resonance. In the following exercises try to hear the difference between the two.

1. As in a previous exercise, with the aid of a small mirror study the action of the velum under a number of different conditions. Observe its position in yawning, its relaxation in nasal breathing, and its activity in the production of the vowel [ɑ]. Note carefully how it operates, in conjunction with the pharyngeal wall, to close off and to adjust the opening into the posterior nasal chambers.

2. Using the mirror once more, allow the velum to remain relaxed as in nasal breathing while the vowel [ɑ] is produced. Observe the distinctly nasal quality and with the fingers held lightly against the nostrils, note the considerable amount of nasal resonance as evidenced by the easily felt vibrations. Pinch the nostrils completely shut and observe the marked decrease in volume. Now let us reverse the process. With the velum held high, as for the yawn, again produce [ɑ]. Note the distinctly altered quality of this sound and also the relative absence of nasal resonance. This time vibrations can hardly be detected in the nostrils. This latter [ɑ] is a good example of an oral vowel and it possesses a quality that should be the dominant characteristic of all of the vowel sounds.

3. Alternate the two conditions described in Exercise 2, pronouncing first the nasal [ɑ] followed by the oral [ɑ]. Associate the kinesthetic feel of the two sounds with the distinct difference in quality. Repeat several times.

4. Practice reproducing silently the two conditions described in Exercise 2, by first relaxing and then raising the velum. Check your success with a mirror. Associate the feeling of

openness in the throat with the good oral quality of the second vowel produced in Exercise 2.

5. Alternate the sounds [ŋ] and [ɑ] a number of times. Observe carefully the difference in resonance between the two and feel the difference in the back of the throat. Test the difference in nasal resonance by the method suggested in Exercise 2.

6. Sing [mo] with a continuous tone, prolonging both the nasal [m] and the oral [o]. Make a sharp distinction between the feel of the two sounds when the transition is made from the consonant to the vowel. Try this with the other vowels, [e], [ɔ], [ɑ], and so on.

7. Reverse the process suggested in Exercise 5. Sing the vowel first with oral resonance and then relax the velum for the nasal consonant.

8. Sing on a monotone the phrase, 'O king,' repeating it a number of times. Distinguish clearly between the oral and the nasal sounds.

9. Pronounce the following pairs of sounds, sustaining the vowel tones for a short time. There should be no perceptible difference between the quality of the vowel following the nasal consonant and the quality of the vowel following the oral consonant. Practice this drill until the vowels in each pair sound exactly the same.

[bo]–[mo]	[do]–[no]	[go]–[ŋo]
[bu]–[mu]	[du]–[nu]	[gu]–[ŋu]
[bɑ]–[mɑ]	[dɑ]–[nɑ]	[gɑ]–[ŋɑ]
[be]–[me]	[de]–[ne]	[ge]–[ŋe]

10. While great care should be exercised in pronouncing all vowels when they precede or follow nasal consonants to avoid what has been termed 'assimilation nasality' (an excess of

nasal resonance on the vowel influenced by the proximity of the nasal sound), there are a few vowels that should receive special attention because of their particular susceptibility to unpleasant 'nasal twang.' The front vowels are most likely to be affected, among the worst offenders in this respect being [e], [æ], and the diphthong [ɑʊ]. Practice words and phrases containing these sounds, of which a few are suggested here, exercising special care to insure ample oral resonance on the vowels and to guard against assimilation nasality.*

a. name   man   thank   mouse
   came   stand   sank   sound
   main   span   bank   now
   mate   camp   manx   noun
   nation   lamb   mangle   down town

b. But who hath seen her wave her hand?
   Or at the casement seen her stand?
   Or is she known in all the land,
       The Lady of Shalott?

c. Far in the northern land,
   By the wide Baltic strand,
   I with my childish hand,
       Tamed the ger-falcon.

11. In reading the following selections, distinguish carefully between the nasal and the oral sounds. Give full nasal resonance to [m], [n], and [ŋ]; careful lip rounding and oral resonance to all of the vowel sounds.

a. Alone, alone, all, all alone,
   Alone on a wide, wide sea.

b. Lead out the pageant: sad and slow,
   As fits an universal woe,
   Let the long, long procession go,
   And let the sorrowing crowd about it grow,

* See also the practice material accompanying the discussion of [e] and [æ] in Chapter IX.

And let the mournful martial music blow;
The last great Englishman is low.

TENNYSON, 'Ode on the Death of the
Duke of Wellington'

c. Come from the hills where your hirsels are grazing,
   Come from the glen of the buck and the roe;
Come to the crag where the beacon is blazing,
   Come with the buckler, the lance, and the bow.
     Trumpets are sounding,
     War-steeds are bounding,
Stand to your arms, and march in good order,
     England shall many a day
     Tell of the bloody fray,
When the Blue Bonnets came over the Border.

SCOTT, *Border Ballad*

d. A Snow Man stands in the moonlight gold
   Smoking his pipe serenely,
For what cares he that the night is cold,
Though his coat is thin and his hat is old
   And the blustering winds blow keenly.

UNKNOWN

Development of Oral Resonance. As was stated previously, the two chief objectives relating to oral resonance are concerned with (1) the careful adjustment of the articulators to insure proper molding and shaping of the tone, and (2) openness and freedom of the oral and pharyngeal passageways to provide for amplification. Of course, the two are very closely related; it is always helpful to think of the mouth as a part of the speech 'megaphone.'

1. The lips play a very important part in the modulation of tone into speech sounds. Study the shape and position of the lips in the production of the vowels [u], [ɔ], [ɑ], [æ], and [i].

2. Repeat the phrase, 'we are, too,' a number of times, noting the position of the lips in the careful formation of the three different vowels. Repeat it rapidly as a drill, exaggerating the action of the lips.

3. Repeat *we-we-we-we-we-we-we* rapidly a number of times to facilitate agility of lip movement.

4. Sing [ho] several times on a comfortable pitch, prolonging the vowel. Observe that [o] is a round vowel; note the position of the lips. Think of shaping the tone into the vowel sound. Work to project the tone out of the mouth, keeping the throat open. Try the same technique with the words *home* and *who*.

5. Repeat Exercise 4, using a number of different vowels with several oral consonants, such as [p], [b], and [d].

6. Working at the piano if possible, sing the vowel [ɑ] on various pitch levels up and down the scale. Get the mouth and throat open, keep the tone out of the nose, and strive to concentrate it in the front of the mouth. Work with your tone until it assumes something of the full, resonant quality of the piano tone. In 'placing' the tone in the front of the mouth, avoid flatness as the one extreme, and a muffled, hollow quality as the other.

7. For achieving 'frontal placement,' sing the vowels [i]–[ɑ] a number of times, merging the first carefully into the second. Vary this drill, using [mi]–[ɑ].

8. The following sentences and selections contain no nasal sounds. Check carefully to guard against nasalization on any of the sounds. Open your mouth well and work for oral resonance.

    a. Who are you? (Vary the emphasis on each word)
    b. How are you? (Vary the emphasis as above)
    c. How do you do? (Vary the emphasis as above)
    d. This is the house that Jack built.
    e. This is a beautiful day.
    f. We are all very well.

        g. Hard by the shores of far Brazil,
           We rode for pleasure, years ago;

Led forward ever by the will
To brave each risk, to fight each foe.

h. The little boy sat at the table with the little girl. They refused to say a word as they ate their breakfast. I asked why they were so quiet. They replied that they were sad because their dog had died. I assured these little tots that I would buy a bigger, prettier dog at the store. I thought that this would cause the sparkle to creep back to their eyes, but I had utterly failed because I could scarcely replace the pet that they had loved.

9. Read the following, rounding out the vowel tones very carefully with a relaxed and open throat. Pay careful attention to lip action to insure ample oral resonance.

a. Heigh ho! heigh ho! it's home from work we go!
b. This was the noblest Roman of them all.

c. So all day long the noise of battle rolled
Among the mountains by the winter sea.

d. Those evening bells! Those evening bells!
How many a tale their music tells
Of youth, and home, and that sweet time
When last I heard their soothing chime!

e. Loud from its rocky caverns, the deep-voiced neighboring ocean
Speaks, and in accents disconsolate answers the wail of the forest.

f. Who has seen the wind?
Neither I nor you:
But when the leaves hang trembling,
The wind is passing through.
Who has seen the wind?
Neither you nor I:
But when the trees bow down their heads,
The wind is passing by.

CHRISTINA ROSSETTI, 'The Wind'

g. The splendor falls on castle walls
And snowy summits old in story;

The long light shakes across the lakes,
  And the wild cataract leaps in glory.
Blow, bugle, blow, set the wild echoes flying,
Blow, bugle; answer, echoes, dying, dying, dying.

O hark, O hear! how thin and clear,
  And thinner, clearer, farther going!
O, sweet and far from cliff and scar
  The horns of Elfland faintly blowing!
Blow, let us hear the purple glens replying;
Blow, bugle; answer, echoes, dying, dying, dying.

TENNYSON, 'The Bugle Song'

h. The moon above the eastern wood
    Shone at its full; the hill-range stood
    Transfigured in the silver flood,
    Its blown snows flashing cold and keen,
    Dead white, save where some sharp ravine
    Took shadow, or the sombre green
    Of hemlocks turned to pitchy black
    Against the whiteness at their back.

WHITTIER, *Snow-Bound*

i. There is sweet music here that softer falls
Than petals from blown roses on the grass,
Or night-dews on still waters between walls
Of shadowy granite, in a gleaming pass;
Music that gentlier on the spirit lies
Than tired eyelids upon tired eyes;
Music that brings sweet sleep down from the blissful skies.
Here are cool mosses deep,
And thro' the moss the ivies creep,
And in the stream the long-leaved flowers weep,
And from the craggy ledge the poppy hangs in sleep.

TENNYSON, 'The Lotus-Eaters'

j. Roll on, thou deep and dark blue Ocean—roll!
    Ten thousand fleets sweep over thee in vain;
    Man marks the earth with ruin—his control
    Stops with the shore;—upon the watery plain
    The wrecks are all thy deed,

BYRON, *Childe Harold's Pilgrimage*

k. Surely, whoever speaks to me in the right voice, him or her I
    shall follow,
  As the water follows the moon, silently, with fluid steps any-
    where around the globe.
  All wait for the right voices;
  Where is the practised and perfect organ? Where is the de-
    veloped soul?

WALT WHITMAN

PROJECTION AND STRENGTH OF TONE

Inasmuch as the problem of projection and support of
tone is very closely related to breathing as well as to resonance, reference should be made to the discussion and exercises under the last section of the second chapter. In this
section it was pointed out that support and strength of tone
are to a large extent dependent upon proper management
of the breath. In no case should strength of tone be associated with marked increase of muscular effort in the throat.

For purposes of ordinary conversation no great demands
are made upon the voice by way of volume and carrying
power. A quiet, easy tone that can be produced and maintained with but little effort is usually sufficient, provided the
speaker can readily make himself heard and understood and
also provided the tones are full and resonant. However, there
are times when unusual situations will make greater demands upon us, and for those occasions we need a voice that
has the power and endurance to stand up under strenuous
use and one that will carry over longer distances and to larger
groups without thinning out and losing its effectiveness. For
such purposes a voice should possess a degree of what may
be called projection, which is in effect at least just ordinary
carrying power.

If one is to achieve carrying power, however, without at
the same time developing as a by-product therefrom such
undesirable qualities as harshness, shrillness, and a high
pitch, careful attention must be given to certain fundamen-

tals involved in this problem of projection. In the first place, projection is chiefly dependent upon three factors: (1) increase of breath pressure, (2) full use of resonance and some prolongation of vowel tones, and (3) free, unhampered vibration of the vocal folds. The management of the breath to increase volume, involving greater activity of the muscles governing exhalation, was explained in Chapter II. Full use of resonance, as we have seen, necessitates in addition to an adequate breath supply an open pharynx and careful molding of the tone in the mouth and by the lips. With respect to the vocal folds, it is self-evident that any condition which interferes with their free vibration will operate to decrease their efficiency as tone-producing agents. An increase in the amount of time given to the vowel tones produces some change in the tempo or rhythm of speech; the tempo must be slower if speech is to be made to carry. The vowel tones must not only be held for a longer time but they must also be 'filled out' to a greater extent than in quiet speaking.

This last step involves maintaining the stress throughout more of the accented vowel rather than placing all of it on the beginning of the tone as is done in brisk, staccato speech. When stress is distributed in this way, the vowel tone is better supported throughout its entire duration; it is not allowed to 'fade out' after being given a vigorous stroke at the beginning. Carrying power is thereby greatly increased, since it is largely dependent upon the amount of vocal tone present. All of this is, of course, assuming that articulation is adequate; it goes without saying that if speech is to be *understood* as well as heard, articulation must be clear.

Keep the foregoing principles in mind as you practice the exercises which follow. Get the feeling of projecting your voice; make it sound 'big.' Fill the room with it or try the exercises out in the open. Pay special attention to breathing and to building up the vowel tones, supporting them well from the breathing muscles. Think of the throat and mouth as being a megaphone through which the tone is molded and amplified. Watch very carefully for evidence of 'cracking' or stridency in the tone, an excessive rise in pitch, or an increase of tension in the throat. Avoid yelling; all that is wanted is a full, round, resonant tone that will carry well.

1. Count from one to five, breathing with each count and filling out the middle of the vowel tones. Concentrate on making the tone carry.

2. Call as if to someone at a distance, prolonging the vowel tones. Watch your breathing and guard against shrillness in the tone.

   a. Yoo hoo! Ho there!
   b. Wait for me!
   c. Hey! Hie! Come on!
   d. Who goes there?

3. To fix in your mind more clearly the relationship of loudness to the speaking situation as well as to establish more objectively the difference between a quiet tone and a well-supported, 'projected' one, read the following selection, using three different degrees of loudness and projection:

   a. Quite conversationally to two or three persons.
   b. As if to a room full of people.
   c. As if addressing a large audience from the speaker's platform. With no public-address system!

Much has been given to us, and much will rightfully be expected from us. We have duties to others and duties to ourselves; and we can shirk neither. We have become a great nation, forced by the fact of its greatness into relations with other nations of the earth; and we must behave as beseems a people with such responsibilities. Toward all other nations, large and small, our attitude must be one of cordial and sincere friendship. We must show not only in our words but in our deeds that we are earnestly desirous of securing their good will by acting toward them in a spirit of just and generous recognition of all their rights . . . No weak nation that acts manfully and justly should ever have cause to fear us, and no strong power should ever be able to single us out as a subject for insolent aggression.

THEODORE ROOSEVELT

4. Read the following selections for strength of tone and projection:

> a. And lo! from the assembled crowd
> There rose a shout, prolonged and loud.

> b. A good old negro in the slums of the town
> Preached at a sister for her velvet gown.
> Howled at a brother for his low-down ways,
> His prowling, gussling, sneak-thief days.
> Beat on the Bible till he wore it out,
> Starting the jubilee revival shout.
> And some had visions, as they stood on chairs,
> And sang of Jacob, and the golden stairs.
> And they all repented, a thousand strong,
> From their stupor and savagery and sin and wrong
> And slammed their hymn books till they shook the room
> With 'Glory, glory, glory,'
> And 'Boom, boom, BOOM.'

VACHEL LINDSAY, 'The Congo'

> c. He clasps the crag with crooked hands;
> Close to the sun in lonely lands,
> Ringed with the azure world, he stands.
>
> The wrinkled sea beneath him crawls;
> He watches from his mountain walls,
> And like a thunderbolt he falls.

TENNYSON, 'The Eagle'

> d. Bowed by the weight of centuries he leans
> Upon his hoe and gazes on the ground,
> The emptiness of ages in his face,
> And on his back the burden of the world.

> e. Ye crags and peaks, I'm with you once again!
> I hold to you the hands you first beheld,

To show they still are free. Methinks I hear
A spirit in your echoes answer me,
And bid your tenant welcome home again!
Hail! Hail! Oh sacred forms, how proud you look!
How high you lift your heads into the sky!
How huge you are! how mighty, and how free!

JAMES KNOWLES, *William Tell*, I. ii

f. I say to the House as I said to the Ministers who have joined
this government, I have nothing to offer but blood, toil, tears,
and sweat. We have before us an ordeal of the most grievous
kind. We have before us many, many months of struggle and suffering.

You ask, what is our policy? I say it is to wage war by land, sea
and air. War with all our might and with all the strength God
has given us, and to wage war against a monstrous tyranny never
surpassed in the dark and lamentable catalogue of human crime.
That is our policy.

You ask, what is our aim? I can answer in one word. It is victory. Victory at all costs—victory in spite of all terrors—victory,
however long and hard the road may be, for without victory
there is no survival. Let that be realized. No survival for the British Empire, no survival for all that the British Empire has stood
for, no survival for the urge, the impulse of the ages, that mankind shall move forward toward his goal.

I take up my task in buoyancy and hope. I feel sure that our
cause will not be suffered to fail among men.

I feel entitled at this juncture, at this time, to claim the aid
of all and to say, 'Come then, let us go forward together with our
united strength.'

WINSTON CHURCHILL

g. *Tribune:* Hence! home, you idle creatures, get you home.
Is this a holiday? What! know you not,
Being mechanical, you ought not walk
Upon a laboring day without the sign
Of your profession? Speak, what trade art thou?

First Commoner: Why, sir, a carpenter.

Tribune: Why dost thou lead these men about the streets?

Second Commoner: Indeed, sir, we make holiday, to see
Caesar and to rejoice in his triumph.

Tribune: Wherefore rejoice? What conquest brings he home?
What tributaries follow him to Rome,
To grace in captive bonds his chariot-wheels?
You blocks, you stones, you worse than senseless things!
O you hard hearts, you cruel men of Rome,
Knew you not Pompey? Many a time and oft
Have you climb'd up to walls and battlements,
To towers and windows, yea, to chimney-tops,
Your infants in your arms, and there have sat
The live-long day, with patient expectation,
To see great Pompey pass the streets of Rome;
And when you saw his chariot but appear,
Have you not made an universal shout,
That Tiber trembled underneath her banks,
To hear the replication of your sounds
Made in her concave shores?
And do you now put on your best attire?
And do you now cull out a holiday?
And do you now strew flowers in his way
That comes in triumph over Pompey's blood?
Be gone!
Run to your houses, fall upon your knees,
Pray to the gods to intermit the plague
That needs must light on this ingratitude.

Adapted from SHAKESPEARE, *Julius Caesar,* I. i

h. They tell us, sir, that we are weak—unable to cope with so
formidable an adversary. But when shall we be stronger? Will
it be the next week, or the next year? Will it be when we are
totally disarmed, and when a British guard shall be stationed in
every house? Shall we gather strength by irresolution and inac-
tion? Shall we acquire the means of effectual resistance by lying
supinely on our backs, and hugging the delusive phantom of hope,
until our enemies shall have bound us hand and foot? Sir, we
are not weak, if we make a proper use of those means which the
God of nature hath placed in our power . . . The battle, sir,
is not to the strong alone; it is to the vigilant, the active, the
brave. Besides, sir, we have no election. If we were base enough
to desire it, it is now too late to retire from the contest. There is
no retreat, but in submission and slavery! Our chains are forged,

their clanking may be heard on the plains of Boston! The war is inevitable—and let it come!! I repeat it, sir, let it come!!!

It is in vain to extenuate the matter. Gentlemen may cry, Peace, Peace—but there is no peace. The war is actually begun! The next gale that sweeps from the north will bring to our ears the clash of resounding arms! Our brethren are already in the field! Why stand we here idle? What is it that gentlemen wish? What would they have? Is life so dear, or peace so sweet, as to be purchased at the price of chains and slavery? Forbid it, Almighty God! I know not what course others may take; but as for me, give me liberty, or give me death!

PATRICK HENRY, Conclusion of *Speech in the Virginia Convention,* 1775

GENERAL EXERCISES FOR RESONANCE

1. Lying, robed in snowy white
   That loosely flew to left and right—
   The leaves upon her falling light—
   Thro' the noises of the night
       She floated down to Camelot;
   And as the boat-head wound along
   The willowy hills and fields among,
   They heard her singing her last song,
       The Lady of Shalott.

   Heard a carol, mournful, holy,
   Chanted loudly, chanted lowly,
   Till her blood was frozen slowly,
   And her eyes were darken'd wholly,
       Turned to tower'd Camelot.
   For ere she reach'd upon the tide
   The first house by the water-side
   Singing in her song she died,
       The Lady of Shalott.

   TENNYSON, 'The Lady of Shalott'

2. We are the music-makers,
       And we are the dreamers of dreams,
   Wandering by lone sea-breakers,
       And sitting by desolate streams;—
   World-losers and world-forsakers,
       On whom the pale moon gleams:

Yet we are the movers and shakers
Of the world for ever, it seems.

With wonderful deathless ditties
We build up the world's great cities,
   And out of a fabulous story
   We fashion an empire's glory:
One man with a dream, at pleasure,
   Shall go forth and conquer a crown;
And three with a new song's measure
   Can trample a kingdom down.

We, in the ages lying
   In the buried past of the earth,
Built Nineveh with our sighing,
   And Babel itself with our mirth;
And o'erthrew them with prophesying
   To the old of the new world's worth;
For each age is a dream that is dying,
   Or one that is coming to birth.

O'SHAUGHNESSY, 'Ode'

3. I saw you toss the kites on high
And blow the birds about the sky;
And all around I heard you pass,
Like ladies' skirts across the grass—
   O wind, a-blowing all day long,
   O wind, that sings so loud a song!

I saw the different things you did,
But always you yourself you hid.
I felt you push, I heard you call,
I could not see yourself at all—
   O wind, a-blowing all day long,
   O wind, that sings so loud a song!

O you that are so strong and cold,
O blower, are you young or old?
Are you a beast of field and tree,
Or just a stronger child than me?
   O wind, a-blowing all day long,
   O wind, that sings so loud a song!

R. L. STEVENSON, 'The Wind'

4. I was born an American; I live an American; I shall die an American; and I intend to perform the duties incumbent upon me in that character to the end of my career. I mean to do this with absolute disregard of personal consequences. What are the personal consequences? What is the individual man, with all the good or evil that may betide him, in comparison with the good or evil which may befall a great country, and in the midst of great transactions which concern that country's fate? Let the consequences be what they will, I am careless. No man can suffer too much, and no man can fall too soon, if he suffer or if he fall in the defense of the liberties and constitution of his country.

DANIEL WEBSTER

5. You may measure the heights and sound the depths; you may gain the rewards of power and renown; you may quiver under the electric current of applause—the time will come when these will fall from you like the rags that cover your body. The robes of power and the husks of pretense will alike be stripped away, and you must stand at the end as you stood at the beginning—revealed.

Under such a test Abraham Lincoln might stand erect, for no man loved the humbler, nobler traits more earnestly than he. What he pretended to be he was; genuine and sincere, he did not need embellishment.

HENRY WATTERSON

6. Away to the woods on the wings of the wind!
   All nature is calling, my feet must obey.
   The clouds in their swift scurry thither are beckoning
   Away to the woods,
         Come Away!

   The voice of the west wind is wooing my footsteps,
   The clouds scamper onward to show me the way:
   The grasses are mocking the high, swaying treetops;
   I'm off at their bidding—
         Away!

UNKNOWN

V

Variety and Expressiveness

THE speech of every individual engaged in earnest and animated conversation is normally characterized by a degree of variety and emphasis. And the more lively and absorbing the talk, the more diversity and change there is likely to be in the various qualities and aspects of the voice. All of which bears testimony to the fact that in the interplay of ideas constituting social intercourse mere words can accomplish but little. While a simple mathematical problem or directions for getting to the post office can be explained simply with words spoken mechanically and without expression, shades of meaning, attitudes, and feelings of the speaker—the aspects of spoken language which have been referred to as intellectual and emotional connotations—can be conveyed only through the so-called expressive qualities of the voice.

Almost two thousand years ago Quintilian wrote, 'It is not of so much importance what sort of thoughts we conceive within ourselves, as it is in what manner we express them; since those whom we address are moved only as they hear.'

MEANING AS DETERMINED BY EXPRESSION

As a matter of fact, it is frequently the expressional connotations of words rather than their purely symbolical value that we refer to when we use the term 'meaning' to designate our reactions to what has been spoken. For example, how often have you thought, or said to yourself, in response to a cryptic remark overheard, 'Now, I wonder what he meant by that?' In all probability you were thinking not of the words themselves, which you understood readily enough, but rather of the manner in which the words were spoken—some queer inflectional twist given to them, or an unusual quality which you detected, or thought you detected, in the voice. This very common experience is without doubt at the basis of such well-known expressions as, 'It isn't so much what you say as how you say it' and 'Your voice will give you away.' Even the familiar practice of 'reading between the lines' may often be nothing more than your attempted interpretation of an imagined expressional pattern according to which the words in question might have been spoken.

To demonstrate the role which such expression plays in the determination of meaning, experiment with a plain statement of fact, such as 'She saw me.' By alternately stressing 'she,' 'saw,' and 'me,' one may give direct, simple answers to the questions, 'Who saw you?' 'What did she do?' and 'Whom did she see?' Further, by the use of more subtle combinations of the various forms of emphasis, many really complex and involved meanings may be conveyed in these three simple words. For example, one may say them in such a way as to express surprise and astonishment that she saw him. A slight change of expression and the obvious meaning becomes surprise and pleasure. In like manner, it is comparatively easy to imply such feelings and attitudes as disgust, fear, indifference, sorrow, perplexity, amusement, and sarcasm. As a matter of fact, virtually these same meanings can be expressed through the medium of the simple exclamation, 'oh.' Thus we see that, in speech, meaning involves much more than merely choice of words, important as that aspect of communication often is. Much also depends upon how the words are spoken.

So important is this identification between the intent, or meaning, of the speaker and the accompanying expressional patterns of his voice in influencing our behavior that we often respond more naturally and readily to the expression than we do to the actual words addressed to us. Thus a cheery greeting, a reference to the weather, or an inquiry regarding our health and well-being may affect us out of all proportion to the stimulus value of the words themselves merely as words. We are responding to the warm, friendly feeling behind them conveyed to us by the manner in which they were spoken. While domestic animals may have a 'vocabulary' in the sense that they know the meanings of certain words, their response to their verbal environment is often not so much to the words themselves, as to such non-verbal cues as actions, facial expressions, and voice quality and inflection.

The classical example of the power of expression is found in the oft-repeated story told of the great Polish actress, Helena Modjeska, who was asked quite unexpectedly to appear on a benefit program in a short dramatic sketch. She complied with the request and, speaking in her native language, she held her English-speaking audience breathless with the power of her dramatic reading at the conclusion of which all were deeply moved. Subsequently it was disclosed that the content of her sketch had been merely the letters of the Polish alphabet repeated over and over.

In the light of the foregoing observations it becomes obvious that variety and expressiveness must be one of the essential characteristics of an effective voice and that a tendency toward monotony is a distinct vocal fault. Since the function of speech is to convey meanings, or, more properly, to stir up meanings in the mind of the auditor, the most effective voice is one that is completely responsive to the attitudes, moods, and purposes of the speaker.

FORMS OF VARIETY AND EMPHASIS

In the discussion of the physics of sound (Appendix A) it is pointed out that sound can be described only in terms of its chief characteristics—duration, loudness, pitch, and quality. Since voice, acoustically, is only a complex of sound waves, vocal variety must be described as a variation in one or more of these four basic factors. Therefore a voice may vary in duration, which is usually considered in terms of the rate or tempo of speaking, and in loudness, pitch, and quality. In the human voice all of these are variable factors, the physiological mechanisms responsible for the changes in each case having been discussed in previous chapters. It must not be supposed, however, that these are isolated factors operating independently of each other. On the contrary, they are often very closely interrelated, as was shown previously in the case of pitch and loudness; one seldom finds a variation in any one of them unaccompanied by a variation in one or more of the other three. For example, an increase in force on a word for purposes of emphasis is very frequently accompanied by a rise in pitch. Say 'I won't!' or 'I did not!' forcefully with marked emphasis upon the last word in each case and observe the tendency for both the force and the pitch to rise together. Thus, emphasis is usually a very complicated function, involving not one but several forms.

Variety of Time or Rate. The characteristic of sound known as time is usually applied to speech as rate or tempo, with respect to which speech may be described as slow, average, or rapid. Any marked deviation from an average rate of speaking may be interpreted to reflect either one or both of the following conditions:

1. *General Temperamental and Personality Characteristics of the Individual.* Because of factors not wholly understood at present, individuals differ greatly in the rapidity of their motor activities such as walking, as well as in the alacrity with which they think, come to conclusions, arrive at decisions, and express themselves. We are all familiar with individuals who think slowly, move ponderously, and speak with a deliberate, even tempo. At the other extreme is the quick, active person, described as 'high strung' or nervous, in whom all of the normal processes seem to be accelerated.

The speech of such a person is likely to be hurried, lively, and forceful, and possibly indistinct because of a rapid, broken rhythm. Between these two extremes we find the majority of speakers whose rate of speaking more nearly corresponds to what we identify as average. Of course, it must be understood that these tempos are normal, or at least habitual, for these particular individuals. For purposes of emphasis, speakers can and should vary considerably from these norms. One should not consider himself bound by his temperamental type and think that simply because he is naturally a slow, or fast, talker, nothing can be done about it. Rate is, within limits, a distinctly variable factor and, as we shall see, it is a valuable form of emphasis. For that reason the speaker should learn to control it and vary it to suit his purposes.

2. *The Speaker's Attitude Toward What He Is Saying and His Purpose with Respect to His Hearers.* There is a startling difference in tempo between a small boy's account of a fight or an accident and that same boy's 'oral report' in the classroom. The general rate of a political speech is likely to be quite different from that of a sermon, and a 'pep talk' at a football rally sounds distinctly different in tempo from a commencement address.

In general it can be said that a slow rate is characteristic of such mental states as wonder, doubt, indecision, perplexity, reverence, sorrow, and deep thought, while a rapid tempo is associated with joy, excitement, anger, humor, and a feeling of confidence and well-being. Variation in rate can be used, therefore, as a general form of emphasis to elicit desired responses from the hearer. The slow, dignified tempo of scripture reading and the rapid, lively rate of the soapbox harangue arise from basically different purposes. Conversation, since it is the reflection of more or less spontaneous thoughts and feelings, is normally characterized by marked and often abrupt changes in rate. The voice should be sufficiently flexible and sensitive to respond to such changes of mood and purpose.

Duration and Pause. From a physical point of view, the rate of speaking is a product of two factors: (1) The length of time spent on the individual speech sounds, particularly the vowels, which is called the duration of the sound, and (2) the length of the pauses between words and phrases. Usually, though not always, these two factors operate together. That is, when vowel tones are prolonged, pauses are also likely to be longer, while in rapid utterance both speech sounds and pauses become greatly shortened. In general it is desirable to preserve some sort of balance between these two factors for the sake of the rhythm and melody of speech. Often a naturally rapid speaker, when asked to speak more slowly, responds by merely increasing the length of his pauses, meanwhile speaking the syllables and words as rapidly as before. The result is a choppy, disjointed rhythm.

Both duration and pause are common forms of emphasis. Note in the sentence, 'Are we all going?' how the vowel in 'all' is prolonged when that word is emphasized. As a matter of fact, duration is often found to be associated with other forms of emphasis, particularly inflection and increase of force. Conversely, an increase of rate is employed to indicate subordination of relatively unimportant ideas so that the important points may stand out in contrast. In a sentence such as, 'The prisoner, seeing that further struggle was useless, settled himself for a long and disagreeable ride,' the speaker hurries over the less important explanatory or qualifying material, in this example contained in the participial phrase, with an increase of rate, a decrease of force, and often a lowering of the general pitch level. These examples provide further evidence of the complicated and involved nature of emphasis.

Pause, used as a form of emphasis, is somewhat more formalized and less spontaneous than duration. And while it is sometimes found in conversational speech, it is more familiar as a device frequently used in repartee and humor involving an element of surprise or irony, in formal public speaking, and in acting and public reading. A familiar example of the pause in conversation is its use to create suspense and 'build-up' in some such situation as that in which the speaker says, 'Do you know what I think?' or 'And what do you think I saw?' The usual pattern is for such a question to terminate abruptly at the end in a 'dramatic pause,' during which some-one may breathlessly ask, 'What?' But whether or not a verbal response is elicited from an eager listener, the pause has served its purpose, which is, in this instance, to focus attention on what is to follow. In serious or involved speak-ing and reading, the pause also provides an opportunity for the hearers to digest what has just been spoken. In this case the speaker pauses to give time for his ideas to 'sink in.' In-cidentally, the pause also provides the speaker with an oppor-tunity to collect his thoughts and to prepare for what is to follow.

Variety of Force. Force, often combined with inflection and prolongation of the accented vowel, is the most obvious as well as the most crude and elementary form of emphasis. Ask an individual to read or speak a sentence with particu-lar emphasis upon a certain word, and the probabilities are that he will accent it largely by increasing the force with which it is uttered. Force is very closely related to pitch, as was explained previously, and, because more time is neces-sary in which to apply the force, it is also likely to involve duration. Variety of force is associated with an expression of more or less obvious or mechanical relationships among ideas or facts. It is the form of emphasis one most naturally and readily uses in explaining a problem, giving directions, issuing orders, and in similar matter-of-fact types of commu-nication. Partly because of the frequency with which it is used and also because it is not adaptable to the expression of fine shades of meaning and purpose, force alone is among the least effective of the four forms of variety.

In addition to these rather limited intellectual values, force is also associated with the expression of certain of the more basic, elementary emotional states, such as anger, defiance, disgust, and pain. Listen to the child's vociferous 'ouch!' when he pricks his thumb, or his equally forceful 'I won't!' of stubbornness, or his 'You did, too!' of accusation. While it is true that other forms of emphasis are often found in such expressions, it is marked increase of force that chiefly characterizes these utterances, which can hardly be said to reflect a very high level of intellectual or emotional response.

As a form of emphasis, force needs but little cultivation in the conversational speech of the average individual; it is probable that he already uses it to excess. That is, he is too prone to use force, which accomplishes little more than the mere gaining of attention, when another form of variety might have proved much more effective in expressing a specific attitude, point of view, or differentiation of thought. Bear in mind that precise meanings are conveyed by precise expression, and that in this connection primary dependence upon a variation of force is hardly adequate.

Variety of Pitch. Animated, lively conversation is ordinarily marked by constant and often wide variations of pitch, which reflect the meaning of what is spoken. This very common and highly conventionalized form of emphasis is more closely related to the intellectual than to the emotional, reflecting the mental states and purposes of the speaker with respect to what he is saying as well as the response which he desires to elicit from his hearers. Variations in pitch indicate whether the speaker is asking for information or giving it, whether he is doubtful or certain, hesitant or confident, interested or indifferent, ironical or sincere. In fact, pitch change offers the only effective method of making fine and delicate distinctions among ideas, of indicating precise and intricate relationships, and of conveying the exact purpose and point of view of the speaker.

Pitch changes in speech may occur in either of two ways: (1) The change may take place *during* the production of tone with continuous voicing, in which case there will be a pitch *glide* in the voice, or (2) the change may occur *between* tones, constituting a vocal *leap* from one pitch level to another. The first of these, illustrated in such musical instruments as the trombone or Hawaiian guitar, is also known as *inflection* or slide and would be heard if a person responded to an interesting or startling statement with 'oh?' indicating surprise with an upward rise of pitch. The second type of pitch change, illustrated in the piano, is sometimes called *change of pitch* or *interval,* which would characterize the expression 'oh-oh!' with which we often respond when a child falls down or stubs his toe.

Inflection. One of the basic differences between singing and speaking is that while in singing the tone is held relatively constant during the production of each note represented on the musical score, in speaking there is an almost continual variation of pitch up and down the scale. And since much of this variation takes place during the production of voiced speech sounds, a variety of inflections result. They are often so complicated and so varied, or possibly so subtle, that in listening to voices we may not be aware of them as separate and distinct changes of pitch. When an attempt is made to isolate and study them, however, they will be found to fall into one of the following three types:

1. *The Downward Slide, or Falling Inflection.* This is the pitch change identified with dropping the voice at the end of a phrase or sentence expressing a complete thought unit. If someone asks you where you live and you reply, 'I live at home,' in all probability your answer will be given with a falling inflection on the word, 'home.' This inflection

is, in general, expressive of such mental states as certainty, positiveness, command and defiance, and the giving of information rather than the requesting of it. The end of every complete thought should ordinarily be indicated by the use of a downward inflection, though there is danger of monotony if the inflection becomes unduly pronounced or prolonged or if it is used for phrases that are not truly independent thought units.

2. *The Upward Slide, or Rising Inflection.* This form of inflection is in general the antithesis of the downward slide, being expressive of doubt, hesitancy, uncertainty, and surprise. It is associated with a request for information and it is often heard at the end of incomplete, dependent thoughts to indicate their relationship to the main thought which is to follow. Note, for example, the use of the rising inflection in the following sentence: 'Four score and seven years ago our fathers brought forth upon this continent a new nation.' Ordinarily this would be spoken with a rising inflection on 'ago' and on 'continent' and a falling inflection on 'nation' to indicate the completion of the thought.

Excessive or indiscriminate use of the upward slide is to be avoided, for such use will lend an air of doubt, hesitancy, and uncertainty to one's speech, and will suggest the presence of such qualities as timidity and indecision in one's whole personality. Especially to be avoided is the disturbing practice, common among some public speakers, of using the rising inflection at the end of phrases and sentences that should normally express a complete thought unit. The effect contributes to a monotonous, sing-song quality suggestive of 'oratorical' artificiality.

3. *The Double Inflection, or Circumflex.* When the two types of inflection just discussed are fused into a simple or multiple combination and are used together, we have a form of inflection that is much more complex than either of the other two and less obvious and direct in its implications. It

is associated with the expression of doubt, surprise, irony, and so-called 'double meanings.' Say 'well' slowly and in a doubtful mood as if considering an answer to a difficult problem and note how the inflectional pattern is inclined to follow the general form of a 'ʋ,' beginning on a relatively high pitch, sliding down, and then rising to a higher level again all on the one sound. Or pronounce the exclamation 'oh' to convey the meaning of 'I told you so' and you are likely to have the opposite of the 'ʋ' pattern. In general the circumflex is expressive of the more subtle relationships among ideas, and the more complex and obscure attitudes and purposes of the speaker.

The Interval, or Step. While inflection, as was pointed out, is a continuous pitch change during the utterance of sound, the interval is a vocal leap, as it were, executed between tones. The three syllables of such a word as 'contentment,' for example, may be spoken on three different pitch levels, one for each syllable, with the change being made between syllables. Or, as was pointed out previously, take the commonly heard expression 'oh-oh!' meaning 'I told you so' or 'that's too bad' and you have a good example of the interval, the first 'oh' being spoken on a higher level, the second 'oh' on a lower, with a complete break of the tone between them.

Along with inflection, the interval is a common form of emphasis. Important words or phrases are made more prominent when they are spoken on a higher pitch level than the rest of the sentence. Conversely, relatively unimportant ideas are subordinated by being spoken on a lower general level of pitch. In speaking the sentence, 'Comment, I suppose, is superfluous,' a natural tendency would be to speak the qualifying 'I suppose' on a lower pitch level, thereby emphasizing the main thought by contrast. The accented syllables of a polysyllabic word are often given a higher pitch than the rest of the word for the same reason—to secure emphasis.

Key. Key is a term sometimes used to designate the normal or habitual pitch level of an individual's speech or the general pitch level on which a certain selection is read or spoken. As was pointed out in Chapter III, there are a number of anatomical and physiological factors which cause individual voices to differ markedly in this respect. The chief physiological influence in the determination of key is the basic muscle tonus of the individual, a factor that is often related to the various personality types discussed earlier in connection with rate. Thus the high-strung individual talks in a higher key usually than the naturally slow, phlegmatic person, because of the increased tension placed upon the vocal folds. The emotional tone or mood of the speaker, operating largely through changes in body tensions, is also important in determining variations in the key that he will use at any particular time, because even within the natural compass of the voice the flexibility of the mechanism is such as to allow considerable latitude in the pitch level that may be employed in specific instances. For example, when one is happy, eager, or generally light-hearted, the pitch of his voice will likely be higher than it is when he feels stupid, depressed, or sorrowful.

Range. The limits within which the speaker's voice is confined as he varies the pitch from the lowest to the highest tones that he will use in speaking determine his range, or compass. The same procedure applied to singing gives the singing range. Many speakers give the effect of monotony simply because their range is too limited. Their speech may be marked by a certain variety of pitch, but the variations are so slight as hardly to be noticeable. The possibilities of the vocal mechanism in producing pitch changes have already been discussed. Man possesses in his larynx a remarkable instrument potentially capable of a range of three octaves or better, and responsive to a subtlety and flexibility of pitch change hardly equaled among musical instruments, yet too often he is content to conduct his speech activities almost on a monotone, varying only a very few tones above and below his basic pitch level. With a few exceptions, man's speech needs could be served by a larynx of relatively simple design, in contrast to the wonderfully intricate and efficient instrument which is at his disposal. The plain truth is that in the ordinary use of the voice we are failing to take advantage of the possibilities for expressive speech which the vocal mechanism affords.

Determining One's Speaking Range. Consult Chapter III for the procedure to be followed in determining your 'pitch profile,' which includes your singing range, your habitual speaking level, and your recommended speaking level, or optimum pitch. To this information should be added your speaking range, or an approximation of it. There is no reliable way of determining this precisely without elaborate instrumentation, but it can be estimated with some degree of success. Proceed as follows:

Speak a fairly complicated sentence or read a short prose passage in what you regard as your normal conversational manner. Practice it several times until you are satisfied that it is representative of your ordinary, natural speaking. While you are going over it aloud, listen for the particular place in it where in your estimation the pitch of your voice drops the lowest and then find another place where it seems to rise the highest. These points may consist of mere fleeting words or syllables, but 'catch' yourself and prolong the tone long enough for you to locate it on a piano or other musical instrument that will give you the musical scale. Make several trials at both high and low points and average the results of each series of trials to establish an estimated low and an estimated high. The number of notes between these two points will constitute your estimated speaking range.

Compare your results with the following data: The best actors and others whose voices are highly trained have a useful range in speaking which approaches in some instances as much as two octaves. Good speakers whose voices would be judged as especially effective employ a range of an octave or more, while poor speakers inclined to monotony confine their range within very narrow limits. While extremes of pitch range are to be avoided except in particularly vivid and expressive speech, the habitual range of the average voice is likely to be too narrow.

Therefore, we must add to our concept of variety and direction of pitch change, the concept of extent of the change, because it is well known that marked changes within any of the forms of emphasis are more effective than minor changes. Emphasis is effective solely to the extent that it serves to attract and direct the attention of the listener, and attention is gained only by that which is changing. Therefore, there must be a variety of change, and the extent of the change must be sufficient to provide a stimulus strong enough to command and hold attention.

While the use of an excessively high pitch level is a common fault in the speaking voice, some speakers go to the other extreme and make the mistake of pitching their voices too near the lower limits of their effective range and fail to use the higher levels for inflection and pitch change. The result is likely to be a low, rumbling type of voice with a monotonous falling inflection and possible harshness at the end of each phrase and sentence. The speaker should not lose sight of the fact that the possibilities for pitch change are always greater above the basic pitch of the voice than below it, for the reason that in the properly pitched speaking voice the most effective level will be found well within the lowest octave of the range. This means that a falling inflection is definitely limited in extent unless it is begun at a pitch somewhat above the general level of the voice.

In the cultivation of a more effective variety of pitch, do not hesitate to give emphatic words and phrases something of a 'lift'; get the voice up and out of a dull, monotonous pitch level, and give it sparkle, life, and color. No feature of voice production contributes more substantially to the speaker's interestingness, to his power of commanding and holding attention, and to his ability to make his personality felt than the gracefulness, ease, and appropriateness with which he is able to use variation of pitch in the expression of thought and feeling.

Variety of Quality or Timbre. A variation of quality is the one form of emphasis most effective in revealing the *emotional* states of the speaker, and because it is largely an emotional manifestation, it is also one of the most subtle forms of emphasis and the most difficult to control. Quality of voice is also most revealing of the prevailing temperament of the individual as well as his changing moods. We have learned from experience that even though we are not able to see a person, we can often tell when we hear his voice whether he is angry, sad, fearful, happy, or in pain. Unlike vocal force, however, which is also closely related to these cruder basic emotional states, quality is also indicative of more highly organized attitudes and feelings. Thus, the cynical, suspicious, jealous, or discontented person is likely to have a distinctly different quality of voice from the happy, optimistic, friendly, or sympathetic individual. When we say that the voice 'gives one away' or when we consciously or unconsciously judge a person by his voice, it is the quality primarily that we have in mind. Animals especially, as was mentioned earlier in this chapter, are very sensitive to shadings of vocal tone, often depending upon such clues for the true meaning of what is spoken to them.

Emotion and Vocal Quality. Emotional states operate to influence vocal quality largely as a result of changes in muscle tonus. These changes are brought about primarily through the functioning of the sympathetic division of the autonomic nervous system, and they differ for the various forms of emotional behavior. For example, such states, or attitudes, as contentment, happiness, love, and a feeling of general well-being are conducive to relaxation, repose, and neuro-muscular co-ordination, while such attitudes as jealousy, fear, anger, anxiety, and unhappiness operate to increase basic muscle tonus, induce restlessness, and break down learned patterns of response. This explains why a relatively superficial and transitory emotional experience such as stage fright may be capable in extreme cases of profoundly affecting vocal utterance even to the extent of making speech virtually impossible for the time being.

As was explained in Chapter IV, quality is an aspect of sound heavily dependent upon overtones, their number and relative intensities. Changes in the tonicity of the muscles governing the resonators of the voice, particularly the pharynx, effect certain alterations in the size, shape, and surface-texture of these resonators, with the result that they respond differently to the overtones in the voice. This change in the composition of the complex vocal tone we recognize as a change in the quality of the voice. It can be seen from this brief explanation and from a more detailed discussion of the nature of sound in Appendix A that quality is a highly complex factor of voice and that its control is dependent upon a delicate and intricate co-ordination and adjustment of virtually the entire mechanism involved in speech.

The Subjective Nature of Quality as a Form of Emphasis. To complicate the problem still further, when we speak of kinds of quality or changes in quality as an aspect of voice, we are almost wholly in the realm of the subjective. The scientific analysis of quality is a difficult and intricate process demanding elaborate apparatus; and even after the results are obtained, there are no objective standards or norms upon which comparisons or evaluations can be made, nor are there exact terms available to describe what has been observed. There is little standardization in the vocabulary of vocal quality and for this reason confusion has frequently arisen because the terms may not mean the same thing to the reader or hearer as they did to the one who used them. The terminology has been borrowed almost entirely from sense modalities other than the auditory and it constitutes an arbitrary, floating nomenclature.

Consider, for example, some of the words which have at various times been employed to describe different kinds of sounds, most of which have been applied to the voice. They are all more or less familiar terms, but how many of them have any direct relationship to sound as such and how many of them can be accurately and specifically defined? For instance, a tone can be either smooth or rough, thin or full, light or dark, light or heavy, soft or hard, round or flat, brilliant or dull, harsh or tender, warm or cold, sweet or sour; and tones have even been described as golden, blue, or dark brown. There is no doubt that these words had a more or less definite meaning for those who used them, but all they can convey to another person is merely an impression, a feeling, and such a reaction is difficult to identify with accuracy. Possibly this nondescript list of terms, a list which could be amplified many-fold, is evidence not only of the subtlety and elusiveness of quality as a form of emphasis but of its effectiveness and versatility as well. In any case, it is clear that quality does not easily lend itself, as pitch does, to ready classification and to deliberate and conscious employment for purposes of emphasis. Its inherently subjective nature and its close connection with emotional behavior make it difficult to control and difficult to study objectively.*

The Use of Quality as a Form of Emphasis. As a matter of fact, despite attempts of the student to approach the problem

---

* Inasmuch as the individual is rarely aware of the quality of his own voice or of changes in its quality, the technique of studying it through the medium of recordings, outlined in Chapter I, can be used with considerable success in this connection. Such an attempt at objective study of vocal quality presents by far the best method by which an individual can gain some measure of control over this most important aspect of voice production.

of vocal quality objectively, the bulk of his efforts in the end will follow predominantly subjective lines. That is, he should make sure that his thinking is vivid and discriminating, that his emotional response is true and genuine, and that fundamentally his 'disposition' and his outlook upon life are essentially sound and wholesome. Then, if his speech mechanism is responsive and his emotional expression uninhibited, the evidence of his thinking and feeling will unconsciously be reflected in the quality of his voice. Training should be directed primarily, therefore, toward the stimulation of mental and emotional response, and toward the development of a sensitive, well-co-ordinated vocal mechanism.

As an individual interested in improving your voice, form the habit of reading aloud a great deal. Choose your material carefully so that a variety of definite attitudes and purposes are represented and further that it is material to which you can and do react in a positive and vigorous manner. Awaken your responses; make an effort to get the author's purpose and point of view, and allow these to dominate completely your interpretation. If these requirements are conscientiously met, oral reading will be found to be of inestimable value in the development of desirable vocal quality and the ability to use and control vocal quality as a means of emphasis.

Aside from the employment of quality as a form of emphasis, the individual should also be sensitive to the basic characteristic quality of his voice to the end that it may truly reflect his personality as he desires others to know it. All undesirable qualities such as nasality, flatness, harshness, or shrillness should be carefully eliminated by giving attention not only to the mechanical and physical aspects of the problem as set forth in detail in the various chapters of this book, but also to the more intangible aspects of personality so intricately bound up with all uses of the voice. There is, for example, a distinct and highly desirable characteristic of an expressive voice, sometimes referred to as a warm or sympathetic quality, that is not merely a result of proper resonance and tone production, but which is also associated with such mental attitudes as optimism, friendliness, and magnanimity, and an awareness of and a sympathetic response to other individuals and things generally as we find them around us. After all, dullness or disagreeableness in the voice may reflect simply dullness or disagreeableness in the personality.

MONOTONY IN RELATION TO VARIETY

Monotony can be defined as an absence of change, a sameness; and while variety and monotony at first glance appear to be truly antithetical, a moment's reflection will disclose that one can have variety in his vocal utterance but still be monotonous. For example, a repetition of the same expressional pattern over and over again, a pattern which in itself might be sufficiently varied, would produce a true monotony if continued over a period of time. We have all heard speakers who illustrated this vocal fault, allowing the voice to rise here and fall there in the same manner from phrase to phrase, until the final and total effect was one of complete monotony. One of the worst offenders in this respect is the public speaker, referred to previously, who habitually allows the pitch of his voice to rise at the ends of phrases and sentences in a kind of sing-song cadence. Such a speaker is said to lack 'conversational quality.'

Thus we see that there is such a thing as a monotony of variation, paradoxical as that may seem. This fault, more likely to be heard in public and formal speech than in conversational and informal speaking, is usually traceable to bad speech habits. An individual guilty of such a fault is more concerned with the mechanics of his speaking than he is with the ideas which he is expressing, his attitude toward those ideas, or his purpose in speaking. What is needed is a ready and true vocal response to vivid thinking and spontaneous feeling. Such a response must be unstudied and sincere, following naturally the 'meaning' of what is spoken.

Causes of Monotony. When proper variety and emphasis in speech are lacking, the cause can usually be traced to one or more of the following conditions:

1. *An Unresponsive Vocal Mechanism.* The physiology underlying muscular response is much too complex to be fully explained at this point, but it should be noted that muscular activity involving comparatively rapid movements, especially of complicated muscle groups, demands a rapid shift of inhibition and stimulation from one muscle group to another. With respect to this ability, which might be termed neuro-muscular flexibility, individuals differ markedly. Some persons are able to perform acts involving intricate and rapid motor adjustments with ease, while others perform them slowly and deliberately. Rapid changes of pitch, loudness, tempo, and quality, such as one finds in lively, animated speech, demand a high degree of co-ordinated, flexible neuro-muscular activity, which some individuals seem to possess to a much greater extent than others.

This skill is partly, though not entirely, dependent upon control of muscular tension and relaxation. A certain degree of relaxation is essential to co-ordinated muscular activity. The cat, for example, is a creature traditionally noted for the speed and precision of its motor responses, and it is also argued that the cat owes its gracefulness to its perfect command of relaxation. Conversely, a high degree of uncontrolled muscular tension makes co-ordinated motor activity difficult if not impossible. In such cases inhibition and stimulation are shifted from one muscle group to another only with considerable difficulty and delay, and when the response does occur it is likely to be extreme, spasmodic, or ill-timed. Thus the dancing or handwriting of an individual who finds it difficult to relax properly is either stiff and inflexible or marked by extreme, uncontrolled, angular movements. And the voice is no exception, the most common vocal evidences of neuro-muscular inflexibility being either a hard monotony of tone, tempo, and pitch, or a broken, spasmodic speech pattern.

Vocal training, therefore, to the extent that it is directed toward this particular problem, involves (1) the achievement of a proper degree of relaxation, especially of the muscles directly involved in speech, including breathing, tone production, and articulation; and (2) the development through carefully planned practice and drill of a co-ordinated control of the speech mechanism. There is no question that in the majority of normal individuals adequate relaxation can be achieved, without which it is very doubtful whether the second objective can be attained. With respect to motor skill, there is some evidence to indicate that to a degree it may be the result of native ability; however, experience has clearly shown that within fairly broad limits, at least, training and practice can accomplish much.

The student should give particular attention to drills and exercises involving wide variations of pitch, tempo, loudness, and quality. Exaggerate the degree of change and variety in these vocal 'gymnastics' merely for the liberating effect which such exaggeration affords. Just as one cannot effectively train for the shot-put by pitching a tennis ball, so there is but very limited value to be derived from vocal drills executed in a listless, routine fashion, which consequently make no special demands upon the vocal mechanism. Oral reading is again recommended, especially material of a lively, spirited nature. As you read, fall naturally into the mood and tempo of the selection and exaggerate the forms of variety which you use in the hope that at least some of the training will carry over into your habitual speech patterns.

2. *Lack of Sensory Discrimination.* It has been well established that before an individual can introduce meaningful changes of loudness, tempo, pitch, or quality into his

voice, he must first be able to *hear* those differences, or he must in some other way be made aware of them. A person who cannot distinguish one pitch from another is said to be suffering from tone-deafness, a condition in some respects comparable to color-blindness. However, actual tone-deafness is rare, as is total insensitivity to the other aspects of sound; most individuals are able to discriminate between tones provided they differ sufficiently in pitch, loudness, duration, or quality. The degree of actual difference required, however, has been found to vary widely among individuals, some being able to recognize very small differences while others are insensible to anything but wide variations.*

In addition to being able to hear and discriminate differences between tones, however, the individual must have sufficient neuro-muscular co-ordination and control to enable him to reproduce those heard differences in his own voice. In other words, while tone production is basically dependent upon sensory perception and discrimination, it is also a motor process and involves doing as well as hearing. That is, after a person has become aware of certain tone differences or pitch changes, there still remains the problem of reproducing those changes in the voice. While there is little question that motor skills can be acquired and developed through practice and training, there is evidence that sensory discrimination depends to a greater extent upon native ability, or native endowment, so to speak. However, it has been amply established that, within the limits of that native ability, sensory discrimination can be greatly improved.

One should school himself to listen to tones and to become aware of differences among them. Discrimination is first of all a matter of paying close attention to differences. Listen to the voices you hear—those of your friends, public speakers, radio and television performers. Observe their use of em-

* Refer to Appendix B for data relating to the testing of various sensory abilities involved in voice production.

phasis and the presence or absence of variations in time, pitch, loudness, and quality. In the same way develop a consciousness of your own voice; note how it sounds as well as how it 'feels' when the pitch rises or falls. In training for pitch discrimination the study of a musical instrument may be of value, particularly if it is an instrument in which the pitch intervals can be determined and varied at will, such as one finds in the violin, Hawaiian guitar, or the trombone. Work with intervals much smaller than a semitone, and through constant practice and attention learn to recognize and identify these narrow variations of pitch. A long step toward the acquisition of a more expressive voice will have been taken when you have made yourself aware of those variations of pitch, loudness, time, and quality which constitute what we call emphasis and expressiveness in speaking.

3. *Lack of Discrimination in Thinking.* In no aspect of voice and speech training can the close relationship between speech and the intellectual and emotional processes be ignored. In the final analysis, as we think and feel, so do we speak. As we have stressed so often thus far in this book and shall continue to stress, monotony of voice and speech may reflect simply a monotony of intellectual response, or a lack of adequate response. We are not likely to speak or read with careful emphasis and variety indicating certain relationships between and among the various ideas we are expressing if we are not aware of those relationships. Words are likely to be spoken with significant emphasis only if they have significance for the speaker. This simple fact is important in explaining much of the dull, monotonous speech of the classroom in contrast to the lively, more natural speech of the playground. For the same reason the 'canned' radio or television speech and the formal address often lack the directness, vividness, and simple appeal of the fisherman's story or the gossip's account of the latest scandal. In the one case the speaker is concerned largely with mere words, which may

or may not mean a great deal to him, while in the other situation he is deeply conscious not only of his purpose in speaking but also of the real meaning of what he is saying in terms of ideas, concepts, and impressions.

Thus it can be seen that the problem of expressing oneself adequately, which in most contexts means communicating effectively, involves not merely an intellectual grasp of what is being spoken, but also a sensitive awareness of its deeper significance. With respect to this awareness, individuals differ markedly. Some people, for example, possessing sensitive, imaginative natures, participate much more fully and completely in all experiences with which they come in contact than other types of individuals who are often described as cold, unresponsive, and stolid. The sensitive person is much more likely to respond sympathetically to people and to situations than the stolid type, because, being imaginative, he more readily sees the other side, places himself in the other person's situation, and identifies himself with the experience. Such an individual may have a rather highly developed sense of humor and may be changeable and relatively unstable emotionally. The speech of this type of person is much more likely to be varied and expressive than is the speech of the opposite type, because it reflects his sensitive reaction to the various aspects of his environment.

It must not be thought, of course, that these more or less typical categories constitute mutually exclusive classes of individuals into the one or the other of which all persons must fall. Rather they represent at the most merely personality stereotypes or tendencies based upon the presence or absence of certain more or less specific characteristics. The extent to which these individual characteristics can be developed or changed through training has not at present been definitely determined. Regardless of whether individual traits are alterable, however, it has been conclusively dem-

onstrated many times that the personality as a whole is amenable to training.

4. *Emotional Repression.* Very often stolidity of manner and lack of expression are traceable not to a total absence
of emotional response within the individual, but rather to
an attitude or pattern of behavior which makes it difficult
if not impossible for him to allow any expression of that
response. It is not to be supposed, for example, that the
Indian owed his traditional stolidity and 'poker face' to a
total lack of feeling and of emotional reaction to his environment. Instead he had developed the habit of inhibiting the
expression of any such reactions, a behavior pattern which
was the product of his culture. However, the Indian does
not stand alone in this respect; there are many people who,
either because of a natural timidity and self-consciousness or
because of a conviction that to give expression to emotion
and feeling is *prima facie* evidence of weakness and lack of
self-control, exhibit a dull, expressionless speech and personality.

Such individuals, and indeed all who would make their
personalities felt through superior use of the voice, must
realize that speech, besides being a medium for the control
of behavior through the communication of purely intellectual concepts from one person to another, is most effective
when it also reflects feelings, attitudes, intentions, and points
of view. Don't suppress your feelings; let them 'shine
through' your voice.

Two Approaches in Vocal Training. The causes of monotony which have just been discussed suggest two avenues of
approach in training to develop variety and expressiveness
in the voice.

1. *Develop a Flexible, Responsive Vocal Mechanism.*
This is, of course, the first and most fundamental step in
any sound program of voice training. The voice must be
brought under control and must be made capable of doing

what we want it to do. This is accomplished through an awareness of vocal effectiveness, through ear training in discrimination, and through vocal drills and exercises to achieve freedom, flexibility, and control of the entire vocal mechanism. The possibilities are virtually unlimited for the development of variety, melody, and emphasis in the voice as a result of training pursued along these lines. Suggestions for such a program are outlined in the exercises at the end of this chapter and elsewhere throughout this book.

2. *Develop an Alert, Discriminating Mind and a Sensitive, Sympathetic Outlook on Life.* As has been pointed out, this aspect of the problem is of necessity intricately bound up with the first. The individual attempting to improve his vocal communication should banish repressions and self-conscious timidity and learn to think in terms of ideas, feelings, and concepts instead of mere words. Not only should he be acutely conscious of his immediate and ultimate purpose in speaking, but he must think discriminatingly and actively while he is speaking with respect to the true significance of what he is saying and its impact upon the hearer. And finally, he must quicken his imagination and enlist the aid of emotional responses to give to his speech that elusive yet very real quality of vitality, impressiveness, and 'personality.'

Exercises for Variety and Emphasis

DEVELOPING FLEXIBILITY AND AGILITY OF VOICE

1. Count from one to ten, taking a breath before each count and prolonging the vowel tone in each word to three or four times its normal length. Vary the pitch in the following ways:

a. Give each of the counts a quiet, prolonged upward inflection as if asking a question.

b. Use a stronger upward inflection expressing marked surprise.

c. Use a prolonged downward inflection, suggesting a quiet finality.

d. Increase the strength and abruptness of the downward inflection to suggest a more positive conviction.

e. Pronounce them once more, this time varying the inflectional pattern from one to the other, including some examples of the circumflex. Be sure that all of the pitch changes are clearly exaggerated.

2. Count from one to five on a breath as if speaking a phrase, giving the whole a decided upward inflection in the form of a question. Emphasize one of the digits. For example, 'One, two, *three,* four, five?' In this case, the question centers around the word 'three.' Repeat, stressing the other digits in turn. Again exaggerate all pitch changes. Note to what extent pitch, force, quality, and prolongation of the vowel in the word are involved as forms of emphasis in this exercise.

3. Repeat Exercise 2, using a downward inflection all the way through, stressing first one digit and then another. In effect these drills will take the form of answers to the drills in Exercise 2. That is, the implied question, 'One, *two,* three, four, five?' should be answered by the statement, 'One, *two,* three, four, five.'

4. Pronounce the exclamation *oh* in such a way that it will suggest each of the meanings listed below. Make the meaning very clear through exaggeration. What particular forms of emphasis are used?

a. Mild surprise
b. Great surprise
c. Polite interest
d. Marked indifference
e. Disappointment
f. Pity (The poor thing!)
g. Disgust

   h. Sarcasm (I told you so!)
   i. Pleased surprise

5. Pronounce the sentence, 'She saw me,' suggesting the following different meanings:

   a. Asking a question. (Emphasize alternately 'she,' 'saw,' and 'me.')
   b. Pleased surprise
   c. Horrified surprise
   d. Stout affirmation (She did, too!)
   e. Sarcasm (She wouldn't look at me!)

6. Vary the expressional pattern with which you read the sentence, 'Why did you do that?' Suggest a number of different meanings, such as surprise, accusation, anger, and despair. Note what forms of emphasis are used.

7. Portray the following meanings:

   a. 'Oh, he did?' (Surprise)
   b. 'Oh, he did!' (A threat; you'll see about that!)
   c. 'Oh, he did!' (Fear)
   d. 'Oh, he did!' (Jeering)
   e. 'You won't mind, will you?' (Fearful that he will mind)
   f. 'You won't mind, will you?' (Of course he won't)
   g. 'You are going, aren't you?' (You want to know)
   h. 'You are going, aren't you?' (Of course he's going)
   i. 'Why did you do that?' (Mere request for information)
   j. 'Why did you do that?' (Accusingly)
   k. 'He was pretty good.' (He was really very good.)
   l. 'He was pretty good.' (He was only fair.)

8. Read the sentence, 'We are all going,' suggesting such meanings as surprise, defiance, disappointment, disgust, and sarcasm. In how many different ways can this short statement be spoken?

9. How many different meanings can you read into the expression, 'You were wonderful'? A few are suggested below:

   a. Warmly (From an enthusiastic admirer)
   b. Statement (He was good; the others were bad.)
   c. Statement (He used to be good but he isn't any more.)
   d. You are surprised that he wasn't pretty bad.
   e. Question (You are pleased to learn that he was a success.)
   f. Forced politeness (He was really pretty bad.)
   g. Sarcasm (In how many different ways can this expression be read so that the real meaning will be just the opposite of what the words themselves ostensibly mean?)

10. Say *Hello* in a number of different ways, as in greeting an old friend, as an exclamation of surprise, a teacher greeting one of her pupils, a crusty old boss to his employee, and as a call to attract attention.

11. A complete dramatic sketch was once written in which the chief character spoke just two words, 'Come here,' varying the expression in each case to make the words fit each different situation as it arose. The following are some situations in which these words might be used, expressing a distinctly different meaning in each case. Try them. Note in this exercise what a comparatively important part variation in quality plays in determining the true meaning. For each situation speak just the two words, 'Come here.'

   a. Your child, a small boy, has just been very exasperating. You call him to you so that you may scold him.
   b. Now it is a neighbor's child whom you do not especially like.
   c. You call to your dog in a friendly fashion.
   d. You find in a crowd an old school chum whom you haven't seen for years. You call to him to attract his attention.

e. You are swimming out beyond your depth; you suddenly become frightened and call out.

f. You excitedly read in the paper the news that you have won an important contest. You want to show it to your roommate.

g. You are walking along the seashore and you suddenly discover something very interesting and curious; you have never seen anything like it before. You call to your companion.

h. You discover just in time a trick that was about to be played on you. Your roommate has a guilty look; you command in mock seriousness.

i. You are a teacher in a small country school. The school 'bully' has gone one step too far; you determine to have it out with him. Very sternly you command him to come to the front of the room.

j. You are awakened by a faint noise that appears to come from outside. Cautiously and quietly you creep to the window and look out. In the yard below you see in the dim light the dark figure of a man attempting to force open a window. Frightened, you call in a 'stage whisper' to your roommate.

VARIETY OF TIME OR TEMPO

Observe how emphasis can be secured in the following passages by a variation of tempo and by a judicious use of pause. In some of the selections the meaning can be expressed more effectively and more appropriately by a slow tempo; others are more suited to a faster rate.

1. We should have a great many fewer disputes in the world if words were taken for what they are—the signs of our ideas only, and not for things themselves.

2. But yesterday the word of Caesar might
Have stood against the world; now lies he there,
And none so poor to do him reverence.

3. Reading maketh a full man; conference a ready man; histories make men wise; poets, witty; the mathematics, subtle; natural philosophy, deep; moral philosophy, grave; logic and rhetoric, able to contend.

4. And now abideth faith, hope, charity, these three; but the greatest of these is charity.

5. Our country, right or wrong. When right, to be kept right; when wrong, to be put right.

6. 'Courage!' he said, and pointed toward the land,
  'This mounting wave will roll us shoreward soon.'
  In the afternoon they came unto a land
  In which it seemed always afternoon.
  All round the coast the languid air did swoon,
  Breathing like one that hath a weary dream.
  Full-faced above the valley stood the moon;
  And, like a downward smoke, the slender stream
  Along the cliff to fall and pause and fall did seem.

  A land of streams! some, like a downward smoke,
  Slow-dropping veils of thinnest lawn, did go;
  And some thro' wavering lights and shadows broke,
  Rolling a slumbrous sheet of foam below.

                         TENNYSON, 'The Lotus-Eaters'

7. My Friends: No one not in my situation can appreciate my feeling of sadness at this parting. To this place, and the kindness of these people, I owe everything. Here I have lived a quarter of a century, and have passed from a young to an old man. Here my children have been born, and one is buried. I now leave, not knowing when or whether ever I may return, with a task before me greater than that which rested upon Washington. Without the assistance of that Divine Being who ever attended him, I cannot succeed. With that assistance, I cannot fail. Trusting in Him who can go with me, and remain with you, and be everywhere for good, let us confidently hope that all will yet be well. To His care commending you, as I hope in your prayers you will commend me, I bid you an affectionate farewell.

                    ABRAHAM LINCOLN, 'Farewell to Springfield'

VARIETY OF PITCH

Emphasis, subordination, and contrast are secured in the following selections principally as a result of variation of pitch and inflection. Study the inflection patterns represented.

1. All things I thought I knew; but now confess
   The more I know I know, I know the less.

2. There is an idea, which is not without its advocates, that a vigorous executive is inconsistent with the genius of republican government.

3. Men often oppose a thing merely because they have had no agency in planning it, or because it may have been planned by those whom they dislike.

4. Heaven is the work of the best and kindest of men and women. Hell is the work of prigs, pedants, and professional truth-tellers. The world is an attempt to make the best of both.

5. I like work; it fascinates me! I can sit and look at it for hours. I love to keep it by me; the idea of getting rid of it nearly breaks my heart.

6. Liberty is to the collective body, what health is to every individual body. Without health no pleasure can be tasted by man; without liberty, no happiness can be enjoyed by society.

7. The law of nature is that a certain quantity of work is necessary to produce a certain quantity of good of any kind whatever. If you want knowledge, you must toil for it; if food, you must toil for it; and if pleasure, you must toil for it.

8. Of all the pestilences dire,
   Including famine, flood, and fire,
   By Satan and his imps rehearsed,
   The neighbors' children are the worst.

9. When I was a child, I spake as a child, I understood as a child, I thought as a child; but when I became a man, I put away childish things.

10. He who knows, and knows he knows,—
    He is wise—follow him.
    He who knows, and knows not he knows,—
    He is asleep—wake him.
    He who knows not, and knows not he knows not,—
    He is a fool—shun him.
    He who knows not, and knows he knows not,—
    He is a child—teach him.

    Arabian Proverb

11. *Bassanio:* Sweet Portia,
    If you did know to whom I gave the ring,
    If you did know for whom I gave the ring,
    And would conceive for what I gave the ring,
    And how unwillingly I left the ring,
    When naught would be accepted but the ring,
    You would abate the strength of your displeasure.

    Portia: If you had known the virtue of the ring,
    Or half her worthiness that gave the ring,
    Or your own honor to contain the ring,
    You would not then have parted with the ring.
    SHAKESPEARE, *The Merchant of Venice,* v. i

12. Came the relief, 'What, sentry, ho!
    How passed the night through thy long waking?'
    'Cold, cheerless, dark—as may befit
    The hour before the dawn is breaking.'
    'No sight? no sound?' 'No, nothing save
    The plover from the marshes calling.
    And in yon western sky, about
    An hour ago, a star was falling.'
    'A star? There's nothing strange in that.'
    'No, nothing; but, above the thicket,
    Somehow it seemed to me that God
    Somewhere had just relieved a picket.'
    BRET HARTE, 'Relieving Guard'

13. 'Tis hard to say, if greater want of skill
    Appear in writing or in judging ill;
    But, of the two, less dangerous is the offence
    To tire our patience than mislead our sense.
    . . .

Of all the causes which conspire to blind
Man's erring judgment, and misguide the mind,
What the weak head with strongest bias rules,
Is *pride,* the never-failing vice of fools.

. . .

Avoid extremes; and shun the fault of such
Who still are pleased too little or too much.

ALEXANDER POPE, 'An Essay on Criticism'

14. *Phoebe:* Think not I love him, though I ask for him;
'Tis but a peevish boy:—yet he talks well;—
But what care I for words? Yet words do well
When he that speaks them pleases those that hear.
It is a pretty youth:—not very pretty:—
But, sure, he's proud; and yet his pride becomes him;
He'll make a proper man: the best thing in him
Is his complexion; and faster than his tongue
Did make offence, his eyes did heal it up.
He is not tall; yet for his years he's tall. . . .
There be some women, Silvius, had they mark'd him
In parcels as I did, would gone near
To fall in love with him: but, for my part,
I love him not, nor hate him not.

SHAKESPEARE, *As You Like It,* III. v

15. It is not the critic who counts; not the man who points out
how the strong man stumbled, or where the doer of deeds could
have done them better. The credit belongs to the man who is
actually in the arena; whose face is marred by dust and sweat
and blood; who strives valiantly; who errs and comes short again
and again; who knows the great enthusiasms, the great devotions,
and spends himself in a worthy cause; who at the best knows in
the end the triumph of high achievement; and who at the worst,
if he fails, at least fails while daring greatly; so that his place
shall never be with those cold and timid souls who know neither
victory nor defeat.

THEODORE ROOSEVELT

16. If you observe a really happy man you will find him building a boat, writing a symphony, educating his son, growing
double dahlias in his garden, or looking for dinosaur eggs in
the Gobi desert. He will not be searching for happiness as if it

were a collar button that has rolled under the radiator. He will not be striving for it as a goal in itself, nor will he be seeking for it among the nebulous wastes of metaphysics.

To find happiness we must seek for it in a focus outside ourselves. If you live only for yourself you are always in immediate danger of being bored to death with the repetition of your own views and interests. . . . It matters little, for psychological purposes, whether you interest yourself in making your city cleaner or enlist in the international campaign to rid the world of the illicit opium traffic, whether you go in for birth control or become a crusader against the vicious influence of Comstockery and superstition. Choose a movement that represents a distinct trend toward greater human happiness and align yourself with it. No one has learned the meaning of living until he has surrendered his ego to the service of his fellow men. . . .

W. BERAN WOLFE

VARIETY OF QUALITY

Note what an important role the factor of vocal quality plays in expressing the mood and true meaning of the selections which follow.

1. O, Mona's waters are blue and bright
   When the sun shines out like a gay young lover;
   But Mona's waves are dark as night
   When the face of heaven is clouded over.

2. Others may sing of the wine and the wealth and the mirth,
   The portly presence of potentates goodly in girth;—
   Mine be the dirt and the dross, the dust and scum of the earth!

3. Oh, but he was a tight-fisted hand at the grindstone, Scrooge! A squeezing, wrenching, grasping, scraping, clutching covetous old sinner! Hard and sharp as flint, from whom no steel had ever struck out generous fire; secret and self-contained and solitary as an oyster. The cold within him froze his old features, nipped his pointed nose, shrivelled his cheek, stiffened his gait, made his eyes red, his thin lips blue; and spoke out shrewdly in his grating voice.

CHARLES DICKENS, *A Christmas Carol*

4. Remember me when I am gone away,
    Gone far away into the silent land;
    When you can no more hold me by the hand,
Nor I half turn to go, yet turning stay.
Remember me when no more, day by day,
    You tell me of our future that you planned;
    Only remember me; you understand
It will be late to counsel then or pray.
Yet if you should forget me for a while
    And afterwards remember, do not grieve:
    For if the darkness and corruption leave
    A vestige of the thoughts that once I had,
Better by far you should forget and smile
    Than that you should remember and be sad.

                   CHRISTINA ROSSETTI, 'Remember'

5. Somewhere—in desolate wind-swept space—
    In twilight-land—in No-man's land—
Two hurrying Shapes met face to face,
    And bade each other stand.

'And who are you?' cried one agape,
    Shuddering in the gloaming light.
'I know not,' said the second Shape,
    'I only died last night!'

                   T. B. ALDRICH, 'Identity'

6. I only know that shadows flew
Across my face like falling dew.
What things were there I do not know,
But there was the leaf that rustled so.
I do not say that darker air
Had borne the ghosts that wandered there
Between the cracks of pallid fog;
I only say I heard a frog
Boom once from out the dusty stair.
I only know that silver hair
Rose lightly where the wind began,
And that the beam which hanged a man
Still seemed to creak with more than weight
When moonlight came and night grew late.
And leaves against the window pane
Shook slowly in the deadened rain,

Where wind had risen, whining low
    Among the leaves that rustled so.
                                        FREDERICK GOSHE, 'Haunted'

7. 'Is there anybody there?' said the Traveller,
        Knocking on the moonlit door;
    And his horse in the silence champed the grasses
        Of the forest's ferny floor;
    And a bird flew up out of the turret
        Above the Traveller's head;
    And he smote upon the door again a second time;
        'Is there anybody there?' he said.
    But no one descended to the Traveller;
        No head from the leaf-fringed sill
    Leaned over and looked into his grey eyes,
        Where he stood perplexed and still.
    But only a host of phantom listeners
        That dwelt in the lone house then
    Stood listening in the quiet of the moonlight
        To that voice from the world of men:
    Stood thronging the faint moonbeams on the dark stair,
        That goes down to the empty hall,
    Harkening in an air stirred and shaken
        By the lonely Traveller's call.
    And he felt in his heart their strangeness,
        Their stillness answering his cry,
    While his horse moved, cropping the dark turf,
        'Neath the starred and leafy sky;
    For he suddenly smote on the door, even
        Louder, and lifted his head:—
    'Tell them I came, and no one answered,
        That I kept my word,' he said.
    Never the least stir made the listeners,
        Though every word he spake
    Fell echoing through the shadowiness of the still house
        From the one man left awake:
    Ay, they heard his foot upon the stirrup,
        And the sound of iron on stone,
    And how the silence surged softly backward,
        When the plunging hoofs were gone.
                        WALTER DE LA MARE, 'The Listeners'

8. It was the very witching time of night that Ichabod, heavy-hearted and crestfallen, pursued his travels homewards, along the sides of the lofty hills which rise above Tarry Town. All the stories of ghosts and goblins that he had heard in the afternoon now came crowding upon his recollection. The night grew darker and darker; the stars seemed to sink deeper in the sky, and driving clouds occasionally hid them from his sight. He had never felt so lonely and dismal. He was, moreover, approaching the very place where many of the scenes of the ghost stories had been laid. In the center of the road stood an enormous tulip-tree, known by the name of Major Andre's tree.

As Ichabod approached this fearful tree, he began to whistle: he thought his whistle was answered—it was but a blast sweeping sharply through the dry branches. As he approached a little nearer, he thought he saw something white hanging in the midst of the tree—he paused and ceased whistling; but on looking more narrowly, perceived that it was a place where the tree had been scathed by lightning, and the white wood laid bare. Suddenly he heard a groan—his teeth chattered and his knees smote against the saddle: it was but the rubbing of one huge bough upon another, as they were swayed about by the breeze. He passed the tree in safety, but new perils lay before him.

About two hundred yards from the tree a small brook crossed the road, and ran into a marshy and thickly wooded glen, known by the name of Wiley's Swamp. A few rough logs, laid side by side, served for a bridge over this stream. As he approached this stream, his heart began to thump: he summoned up, however, all his resolution, gave his horse half a score of kicks in the ribs, and attempted to dash briskly across the bridge. But instead of starting forward, the perverse old animal came to a stand just by the bridge, with a suddenness that had nearly sent his rider sprawling over his head. Just at this moment a plashy tramp by the side of the bridge caught the sensitive ear of Ichabod. In the dark shadow of the grove, on the margin of the brook, he beheld something huge, misshapen, black and towering. It stirred not, but seemed gathered up in the gloom, like some gigantic monster ready to spring upon the traveler.

The hair of the affrighted pedagogue rose upon his head with terror. What was to be done? To turn and fly was now too late; and besides, what chance was there of escaping ghost or goblin, if such it was, which could ride upon the wings of the wind?

Summoning up, therefore, a show of courage, he demanded in
stammering accents, 'Who are you?' He received no reply.

Adapted from IRVING, *The Legend of Sleepy Hollow*

9. *Shylock.* How like a fawning publican he looks!
      I hate him for he is a Christian;
      But more for that in low simplicity
      He lends out money gratis, and brings down
      The rate of usance here with us in Venice.
      If I can catch him once upon the hip,
      I will feed fat the ancient grudge I bear him.
      He hates our sacred nation; and he rails,
      Even there where merchants most do congregate,
      On me, my bargains, and my well-won thrift,
      Which he calls interest. Cursed by my tribe,
      If I forgive him!

SHAKESPEARE, *The Merchant of Venice*, I. iii

10. Out rode from his wild, dark castle
       The terrible Heinz von Stein
    He came to the door of a tavern
       And gazed on its swinging sign.

    He sat himself down at a table,
       And growled for a bottle of wine;
    Up came with a flask and a corkscrew
       A maiden of beauty divine.

    Then, seized with a deep love-longing,
       He uttered, 'O damosel mine,
    Suppose you just give a few kisses
       To the valorous Ritter von Stein!'

    But she answered, 'The kissing business
       Is entirely out of my line;
    And I certainly will not begin it
       On a countenance ugly as thine!'

    Oh, then the bold knight was angry,
       And cursed both coarse and fine;
    And asked, 'How much is the swindle
       For your sour and nasty wine?'

And fiercely he rode to the castle
And sat himself down to dine;
And this is the dreadful legend
Of the terrible Heinz von Stein.

CHARLES GODFREY LELAND, 'Heinz von Stein'

GENERAL EXERCISES FOR VARIETY AND EMPHASIS

In the selections which follow, determine what forms of emphasis best express not only the meaning, but also the mood and feeling intended by the author. You will observe that a number of the poetry selections, especially those in blank verse, can be effectively read in a very conversational manner. In all of the selections do not be afraid to exaggerate the expressional pattern slightly just for practice and to emphasize the particular vocal techniques being employed. There is little danger of that exaggeration carrying over into normal speech, but hopefully, some of the desirable effects will.

1. Words are both better and worse than thoughts; they express them, and add to them; they give them power for good or evil; they start them on an endless flight, for instruction and comfort and blessing, or for injury and sorrow and ruin.

2. The rocky ledge runs far into the sea,
   And on its outer point, some miles away,
   The lighthouse lifts its massive masonry,
   A pillar of fire by night, of cloud by day.

3. I strove with none; for none was worth my strife,
   Nature I loved, and next to Nature, Art:
   I warmed both hands before the fire of life;
   It sinks, and I am ready to depart.

4. Isaac and Archibald were two old men.
   I knew them, and I may have laughed at them
   A little, but I must have honored them
   For they were old, and they were good to me.

5. God give us men. A time like this demands
   Strong minds, great hearts, true faith and ready hands!

Men whom the lust of office does not kill,
Men whom the spoils of office cannot buy,
Men who possess opinions and a will,
Men who love honor, men who cannot lie.

J. G. HOLLAND

6. Our incomes should be like our shoes; if too small, they will gall and pinch us, but if too large, they will cause us to stumble and to trip. But wealth, after all, is a relative thing, since he that has little, and wants less, is richer than he that has much, but wants more. True contentment depends not upon what we have; a tub was large enough for Diogenes, but a world was too little for Alexander.

COLTON

7. Thinking cannot be clear till it has had expression. We must write, or speak, or act our thoughts, or they will remain in half torpid form. Our feelings must have expression, or they will be as clouds, which, till they descend in rain, will never bring up fruit or flower. So it is with all the inward feelings; expression gives them development. Thought is the blossom; language the opening bud; action the fruit behind it.

HENRY WARD BEECHER

8. When all the world is young, lad,
   And all the trees are green;
And every goose a swan, lad,
   And every lass a queen;
Then hey for boot and horse, lad,
   And round the world away;
Young blood must have its course, lad
   And every dog his day.

When all the world is old, lad,
   And all the trees are brown;
And all the sport is stale, lad,
   And all the wheels run down;
Creep home and take your place there,
   The spent and maimed among;
God grant you find one face there
   You loved when all was young.

CHARLES KINGSLEY, 'Young and Old'

9. W'en you see a man in wo,
　　　Walk right up and say 'hullo!'
　　Say 'hullo' an' 'how d'ye do?
　　　How's the world a-usin' you?'
　　Slap the fellow on his back,
　　Bring yer han' down with a whack;
　　Waltz right up, and don't go slow,
　　Grin an' shake an' say 'hullo!'

　　　　　　　　　　　　　　s. w. foss, 'Hullo'

10. The fault, dear Brutus, is not in our stars,
　　But in ourselves, that we are underlings.
　　Brutus and Caesar: what should be in that 'Caesar'?
　　Why should that name be sounded more than yours?
　　Write them together, yours is as fair a name;
　　Sound them, it doth become the mouth as well;
　　Weigh them, it is as heavy; conjure with them,
　　'Brutus' will start a spirit as soon as 'Caesar.'
　　Now, in the names of all the gods at once,
　　Upon what meat doth this our Caesar feed,
　　That he is grown so great?

　　　　　　　　　　SHAKESPEARE, *Julius Caesar*, i. ii

11. When, in disgrace with fortune and men's eyes,
　　I all alone beweep my outcast state,
　　And trouble deaf heaven with my bootless cries,
　　And look upon myself, and curse my fate,
　　Wishing me like to one more rich in hope,
　　Featured like him, like him with friends possessed,
　　Desiring this man's art, and that man's scope,
　　With what I most enjoy contented least;
　　Yet in these thoughts myself almost despising,
　　Haply I think on thee; and then my state,
　　Like to the lark at break of day arising
　　From sullen earth, sings hymns at heaven's gate;
　　　For thy sweet love remembered such wealth brings
　　　That then I scorn to change my state with kings.

　　　　　　　　　　　SHAKESPEARE, *Sonnet* XXIX

12. The microbe is so very small
　　You cannot make him out at all,

But many sanguine people hope
To see him through a microscope.
His joined tongue that lies beneath
A hundred curious rows of teeth;
His seven tufted tails with lots
Of lovely pink and purple spots,
On each of which a pattern stands,
Composed of forty separate bands;
His eyebrows of a tender green;
All these have never yet been seen—
But Scientists, who ought to know,
Assure us that they must be so. . . .
Oh! let us never, never doubt
What nobody is sure about!

HILAIRE BELLOC, 'The Microbe'

13. When the sun goes down and the world is still,
    Then Jock o' Dreams comes over the hill;
    Over the hill he quietly slips,
    Holding his finger to his lips.

    His golden hair is pale as the moon,
    He has two bright stars on his velvet shoon;
    Soft his step as an elfin dance,
    His sea-blue eyes have an elfin glance.

    The dreams he carries are light as air,
    He tosses them here, he tosses them there,
    In at the windows, under the doors,
    All the way up to the attic floors.

    Through the silent streets he goes walking about
    Till the moon drops down and the stars go out;
    Then lightly swinging his empty sack,
    Softly, softly, he wanders back.

    A cold little wind runs over the ground,
    A sleepy bird makes a tiny sound,
    The sky in the East grows rosily red,
    The children murmur and turn in bed.
    Over the world the sunlight streams—
    But what has become of Jock o' Dreams?

ROSE FYLEMAN, 'Jock o' Dreams'

14. There was an old preacher once who told some boys of the
Bible lesson he was going to read in the morning. The boys, finding the place, glued together the connecting pages. The next
morning he read on the bottom of one page: 'When Noah was
one hundred and twenty years old he took unto himself a wife,
who was'—then turning the page—'one hundred and forty cubits
long, forty cubits wide, built of gopher-wood, and covered with
pitch inside and out.' He was naturally puzzled at this. He read
it again, verified it, and then said: 'My friends, this is the first
time I ever met this in the Bible, but I accept it as an evidence
of the assertion that we are fearfully and wonderfully made.'

HENRY W. GRADY

15. Ho, for the Pirate Don Durke of Dowdee!
    He was as wicked as wicked could be,
    But oh, he was perfectly gorgeous to see!
    The Pirate Don Durke of Dowdee.

    His conscience, of course, was as black as a bat,
    But he had a floppety plume on his hat,
    And when he went walking it jiggled—like that!
    The plume of the Pirate Dowdee.

    His coat it was crimson and cut with a slash,
    And often as ever he twirled his mustache,
    Deep down in the ocean the mermaids went splash,
    Because of Don Durke of Dowdee.

    Moreover, Dowdee had a purple tattoo,
    And stuck in his belt where he buckled it through
    Were a dagger, a dirk and a squizzamaroo,
    For fierce was the Pirate Dowdee.

    So fearful he was he would shoot at a puff,
    And always at sea when the weather grew rough,
    He drank from a bottle and wrote on his cuff,
    Did Pirate Don Durke of Dowdee.

    Oh, he had a cutlass that swung at his thigh,
    And he had a parrot called Pepperkin Pye,
    And a zigzaggy scar at the end of his eye,
    Had the Pirate Don Durke of Dowdee.

He kept in a cavern, this buccaneer bold,
A curious chest that was covered with mould,
And all of his pockets were jingly with gold!
Oh jing! went the gold of Dowdee.

His conscience, of course, it was crook'd like a squash,
But both of his boots made a slickery slosh
And he went through the world with a wonderful swash,
Did Pirate Don Durke of Dowdee.

It's true he was wicked as wicked could be,
His sins they outnumbered a hundred and three,
But oh, he was perfectly gorgeous to see,
The Pirate Don Durke of Dowdee.

MILDRED PLEW MEIGS, 'The Pirate Don Durke
of Dowdee'

16. Something there is that doesn't love a wall,
That sends the frozen-ground-swell under it,
And spills the upper boulders in the sun;
And makes gaps even two can pass abreast.
The work of hunters is another thing:
I have come after them and made repair
Where they have left not one stone on a stone,
But they would have the rabbit out of hiding,
To please the yelping dogs. The gaps I mean,
No one has seen them made or heard them made,
But at spring mending-time we find them there.
I let my neighbor know beyond the hill;
And on a day we meet to walk the line
And set the wall between us once again.
We keep the wall between us as we go.
To each the boulders that have fallen to each.
And some are loaves and some so nearly balls
We have to use a spell to make them balance:
'Stay where you are until our backs are turned!'
We wear our fingers rough with handling them.
Oh, just another kind of out-door game,
One on a side. It comes to little more:
There where it is we do not need the wall:
He is all pine and I am apple orchard.
My apple trees will never get across
And eat the cones under his pines, I tell him.

He only says, 'Good fences make good neighbors.'
Spring is the mischief in me, and I wonder
If I could put a notion in his head:
'*Why* do they make good neighbors? Isn't it
Where there are cows? But here there are no cows.
Before I built a wall I'd ask to know
What I was walling in or walling out,
And to whom I was like to give offence.
Something there is that doesn't love a wall,
That wants it down.' I could say 'Elves' to him,
But it's not elves exactly, and I'd rather
He said it for himself. I see him there
Bringing a stone grasped firmly by the top
In each hand, like an old-stone savage armed.
He moves in darkness as it seems to me,
Not of woods only and the shade of trees.
He will not go behind his father's saying,
And he likes having thought of it so well
He says again, 'Good fences make good neighbors.'

ROBERT FROST, 'Mending Wall'

17. Whose woods these are I think I know.
His house is in the village though;
He will not see me stopping here
To watch his woods fill up with snow.

My little horse must think it queer
To stop without a farmhouse near
Between the woods and frozen lake
The darkest evening of the year.

He gives his harness bells a shake
To ask if there is some mistake.
The only other sound's the sweep
Of easy wind and downy flake.

The woods are lovely, dark and deep,
But I have promises to keep,
And miles to go before I sleep,
And miles to go before I sleep.

ROBERT FROST, 'Stopping by Woods
on a Snowy Evening'

18. It is impossible to say how first the idea entered my brain; but once conceived, it haunted me day and night. Object there was none. Passion there was none. I loved the old man. He had never wronged me. He had never given me insult. For his gold I had no desire. I think it was his eye! yes, it was this! He had the eye of a vulture—a pale blue eye, with a film over it. Whenever it fell upon me, my blood ran cold; and so by degrees—very gradually—I made up my mind to take the life of the old man, and thus rid myself of the eye forever.

Now this is the point. You fancy me mad. Madmen know nothing. But you should have seen *me*. You should have seen how wisely I proceeded—with what caution—with what foresight—with what dissimulation I went to work! I was never kinder to the old man than during the whole week before I killed him. And every night, about midnight, I turned the latch of his door and opened it so gently! And then, when I had made an opening sufficient for my head, I put in a dark lantern, all closed, closed, so that no light shone out, and then I thrust in my head. Oh, you would have laughed to see how cunningly I thrust it in! I moved slowly—very, very slowly, so that I might not disturb the old man's sleep. It took me an hour to place my whole head within the opening so far that I could see him as he lay upon his bed. Ha—would a madman have been so wise as this? And then, when my head was well in the room, I undid the lantern cautiously—oh, so cautiously—cautiously (for the hinges creaked) —I undid it just so much that a single thin ray fell upon the vulture eye. And this I did for seven long nights—every night just at midnight—but I found the eye always closed; and so it was impossible to do the work; for it was not the old man who vexed me, but his Evil Eye.

Upon the eighth night I was more than usually cautious in opening the door. A watch's minute hand moves more quickly than did mine. Never before that night, had I *felt* the extent of my own powers—of my sagacity. I could scarcely contain my feelings of triumph. To think that there I was, opening the door, little by little, and he not even to dream of my secret deeds or thoughts. I fairly chuckled at the idea; and perhaps he heard me; for he moved on the bed suddenly, as if startled. Now you may think that I drew back—but no. His room was as black as pitch with the thick darkness (for the shutters were close fastened, through fear of robbers), and so I knew that he could not see the

opening of the door, and I kept pushing it on steadily, steadily.
I had my head in, and was about to open the lantern, when
my thumb slipped upon the tin fastening, and the old man
sprang up in bed, crying out—'Who's there?'

EDGAR ALLAN POE, 'The Tell-Tale Heart'

19. *Pooh-Bah.* I am, in point of fact, a particularly haughty and
exclusive person, of pre-Adamic ancestral descent. You will understand this when I tell you that I can trace my ancestry back
to a protoplasmal primordial atomic globule. Consequently, my
family pride is something inconceivable. I can't help it. I was
born sneering. But I struggle hard to overcome this defect. I
mortify my pride constantly. When all the great Officers of State
resigned in a body, because they were too proud to serve under
an ex-tailor, did I not unhesitatingly accept all their posts at once?

Pish-Tush. And the salaries attached to them? You did.

Pooh-Bah. It is consequently my degrading duty to serve this
upstart as First Lord of the Treasury, Lord Chief Justice, Com-
mander-in-Chief, Lord High Admiral, Master of the Buckhounds,
Groom of the Back Stairs, Archbishop of Titipu, and Lord
Mayor, both acting and elect, all rolled into one. And at a salary!
A Pooh-Bah paid for his services! I a salaried minion! But I do
it! It revolts me, but I do it.

Nanki-Poo. And it does you credit.

Pooh-Bah. But I don't stop at that. I go and dine with middle-
class people on reasonable terms. I dance at cheap suburban
parties for a moderate fee. I accept refreshments at any hands,
however lowly. I also retail State secrets at a very low figure . . .

*Ko-Ko (the ex-tailor, now Lord High Executioner of Titipu,
entering).* Pooh-Bah, it seems that the festivities in connection
with my approaching marriage must last a week. I should like
to do it handsomely, and I want to consult you as to the amount
I ought to spend upon them.

Pooh-Bah. Certainly. In which of my capacities? As First Lord
of the Treasury, Lord Chamberlain, Attorney-General, Chancellor of the Exchequer, Privy Purse, or Private Secretary?

Ko-Ko. Suppose we say as Private Secretary.

Pooh-Bah. Speaking as your Private Secretary, I should say
that as the city will have to pay for it, don't stint yourself, do
it well.

Ko-Ko. Exactly—as the city will have to pay for it. That is your advice.

Pooh-Bah. As Private Secretary. Of course you will understand that, as Chancellor of the Exchequer, I am bound to see that due economy is observed.

Ko-Ko. Oh. But you said just now 'don't stint yourself, do it well.'

Pooh-Bah. As Private Secretary.

Ko-Ko. And now you say that due economy must be observed.

Pooh-Bah. As Chancellor of the Exchequer.

Ko-Ko. I see. Come over here, where the Chancellor can't hear us. (*They cross stage.*) Now, as my Solicitor, how do you advise me to deal with this difficulty?

Pooh-Bah. Oh, as your Solicitor, I should have no hesitation in saying, 'Chance it—'

Ko-Ko. Thank you. (*Shaking his hand.*) I will.

Pooh-Bah. If it were not that, as Lord Chief Justice, I am bound to see that the law isn't violated.

Ko-Ko. I see. Come over here where the Chief Justice can't hear us. (*They cross again.*) Now, then, as First Lord of the Treasury?

Pooh-Bah. Of course, as First Lord of the Treasury, I could propose a special vote that would cover all expenses, if it were not that, as Leader of the Opposition, it would be my duty to resist it, tooth and nail. Or, as Paymaster-General, I could so cook the accounts, that as Lord High Auditor I should never discover the fraud. But then, as Archbishop of Titipu, it would be my duty to denounce my dishonesty and give myself into my own custody as First Commissioner of Police.

Ko-Ko. That is extremely awkward.

Pooh-Bah. I don't say that all these people couldn't be squared; but it is right to tell you that I shouldn't be sufficiently degraded in my own estimation unless I was insulted with a very considerable bribe.

Ko-Ko. The matter shall have my careful consideration.

w. s. GILBERT, from The Mikado

20.   All the world's a stage,
   And all the men and women merely players;
   They have their exits and their entrances;
   And one man in his time plays many parts,

His acts being seven ages. At first the infant,
Mewling and puking in the nurse's arms;
Then the whining school-boy, with his satchel
And shining morning face, creeping like snail
Unwillingly to school. And then the lover,
Sighing like furnace, with a woeful ballad
Made to his mistress' eyebrow. Then a soldier,
Full of strange oaths, and bearded like the pard,
Jealous in honour, sudden and quick in quarrel,
Seeking the bubble reputation
Even in the cannon's mouth. And then the justice,
In fair round belly with good capon lin'd,
With eyes severe and beard of formal cut,
Full of wise saws and modern instances;
And so he plays his part. The sixth age shifts
Into the lean and slipper'd pantaloon,
With spectacles on nose and pouch on side;
His youthful hose, well sav'd, a world too wide
For his shrunk shank; and his big manly voice
Turning again toward childish treble, pipes
And whistles in his sound. Last scene of all,
That ends this strange eventful history,
Is second childishness and mere oblivion;
Sans teeth, sans eyes, sans taste, sans everything.

SHAKESPEARE, As You Like It, II. vii

21. Say that she rail; why then I'll tell her plain,
She sings as sweetly as a nightingale;
Say that she frown, I'll say she looks as clear
As morning roses, newly wash'd with dew;
Say she be mute and will not speak a word,
Then I'll commend her volubility
And say she uttereth piercing eloquence.

SHAKESPEARE, Taming of the Shrew, II. i

DEVELOPING AN EXPRESSIVE VOICE FOR EVERYDAY SPEAKING

Having studied the expressive qualities of the voice in this chapter and having gained some experience in their use through specialized exercises and the reading of selected passages, we now face the final, and most important, step—the carry-over of these vocal skills into everyday communicative speech. Let us remind ourselves once more that these vocal abilities will hardly be worth the effort of acquiring unless we put them to work—unless we use them naturally in our speaking to make our ideas clear to our hearer, impress him with our attitudes and intentions regarding those ideas, and stimulate him to some sort of appropriate response. When we have accomplished this, we have done about all that can be expected of spoken communication.

Following are a few suggested assignments to help you take advantage of the training this chapter has afforded by assisting you to incorporate a desirable pattern of variety and expressiveness into your everyday speaking.

1. The following excerpt from the Report of the Harvard Committee entitled *General Education in a Free Society* discusses a topic of general interest to everyone—conversation. Prepare this selection for reading aloud, making it as effective and conversational in style as possible. Study the passage first for its content—What are the main ideas? What points are to be made? What explanations are there? What sort of response is wanted from the hearer? What forms of emphasis will you use and where?

Conversation is a lost art. The question is, where was it lost? If we carry on less, or less good, conversation than our ancestors did, is it because we have lost the art, or because, having become technicians, we have little to say that is suitable for general conversation, or because we are much more interested in doing things—driving, for example, or playing bridge? Learned persons are apt to disparage conversation as trivial or frivolous, but unjustly so. If you are looking for the uncovering of important truths during a dinner party, you will be looking for the wrong thing. The contribution of general conversation is the revelation of personality. While nothings are being bandied about and trivial words, like the lightest balloons, are launched into the air, contact with personalities is being achieved through characteristic inflections and emphases, through readiness or shyness of response. In conversation the idea is inseparable from the man; conversation is useful because it is the most unforced and natural means of bringing persons together into a society. Beyond its social function, conversation is a delight in itself. It is an art, yet it loses its value if it becomes artificial. Its essence is spontaneity, impetus, movement; the words of a conversation are evanescent, things of the moment, while written words are formalized, rigid, and fixed. Starting with simple things like the weather and minor personal happenings, it proceeds to weave a pattern of sentiments and ideas, and through these of persons, which is fugitive just because it is alive.

2. Prepare a short talk summarizing the excerpt included above in Exercise 1. What do they say about conversation, its present status, its essential nature, etc.? Make this as vivid and effective as you attempted to make your reading of the passage.

3. Now let us react in some constructive way to the passage in Exercise 1. You may, or may not, agree with all of the points included in it. If you do not agree, you will think of arguments on the other side; if you do agree, there will be additional points you will want to bring out.

Prepare a short talk or prepare to participate in an informal group discussion, presenting your reactions to this discussion of conversation. Following are some points that might be considered:

a. Is conversation really a lost art, as they say?
b. Is it true, as they imply, that we have less to talk about today that is suitable for general conversation than our ancestors had?
c. What are some ways by which we could improve our conversation ability?
d. Is 'shop talk' a suitable form of conversation?

As you give your talk or participate in the discussion, listen to your voice; is it sufficiently expressive and 'dynamic' to 'put across' your ideas effectively? Apply what you have learned in this chapter.

4. Prepare a short talk explaining something. This is a form of speaking or writing called exposition. What forms of emphasis and variety are most useful when you are explaining something? Pitch change? Use of force as a form of emphasis? As your subject, you could explain how something works, how something is done, or how something is made. Your main purpose is clearness; your hearers must understand and be able to 'follow' you. Make a real effort to help them do this.

5. Now, let us try a simple narrative. This form of speaking is somewhat more versatile and varied than the explanation and consequently may require more complex patterns of emphasis and expressiveness. Here your chief purpose is to make your 'story' interesting, colorful, and vivid. Do not be afraid to let yourself 'go' a bit in this assignment; let your voice express something of the excitement, fear, interest, or whatever you feel the dominant attitude is. Share this experience with your hearers; try to make them experience it as you did. Some suggested topics:

a. A childhood experience I remember.
b. My most embarrassing moment.
c. My most thrilling experience.

VI

Voice and Personality

I⊤ has been said so often as to be almost a commonplace that voice expresses or reflects personality. Let us examine for a moment what such a statement may mean. While no one knows exactly what personality is, most people find the subject interesting, not to say fascinating, and many definitions and explanations have been proposed. One popular concept among laymen is to equate personality with social skill or adroitness—the ability to elicit positive reactions from others under a variety of circumstances.

Another popular concept, related to the one mentioned above, is to interpret personality in terms of the salient impression which an individual creates in others. From this point of view we may have an individual described as an aggressive personality, for example, or a fearful personality. It will be noted that there is a strong element of evaluation in both of these concepts, in relation to which a given individual's personality is likely to be thought of as being either good or bad. Moreover, the average individual is very likely to think of personality in terms of certain fairly widely accepted stereotypes.

Consider as an example of the application of these popular concepts the way in which different individuals react to the kind of social stimulation presented by a party or a reception. One type of person will fairly 'shine' in such a situation. He will be active, bright and sparkling in his manner, talkative, smiling and friendly to all he meets. He shows by his behavior that he is having a good time. People like him; he

is said to have 'lots of personality.' Consider another type of
individual. He is ill at ease and restless, meets as few people
as possible, and, since he finds it difficult to express himself,
avoids conversation, preferring to sit back by himself and
watch the others. Emotionally he may be in a turmoil inside.
Such a person is likely to be the one spoken of as having 'no
personality.' Yet a moment's reflection makes clear that he
has reacted to this common situation just as violently and
just as completely as the other type of individual; the difference lies in the kind of reaction. In the last case it has been
largely negative as far as the social situation is concerned,
and a large part of the reaction may have been subjective in
the form of emotional disturbances. In the other case the
behavior was objective, easily observed, and all the more
impressive because the reactions were predominantly positive with respect to the social situation.

Serious consideration of the subject makes it obvious, however, that the term personality is much more fundamental
and embracing in its scope than would be implied from the
popular points of view mentioned above. In its broadest
sense personality can be thought of as the organization of
the needs, abilities, and potentialities of the individual. It
includes the habits, sets, traits, values, motivations, that go
to make up the person. These characteristics, it must be
stressed, are not directly observable as overt behavior; they
must be inferred from such behavior. To complicate the picture still further, it must be remembered that this behavior
results from more than merely the forces within the individual. Rather, it is the product of the interaction of these
forces with various situational factors arising from the environment.

Since the environment is subject to constant change, it can
be appreciated why the various attempts to pigeonhole or
classify personality scientifically have been generally unsuc-
cessful. Within normal limits, there is, for example, no pure

aggressive type or submissive type, or introverted type. Man is a remarkably unpredictable creature and his conduct in one situation offers no positive guarantee that he will behave similarly in a different situation. The picture has become proverbial of the 'tinhorn tyrant' who rules his office with an iron hand, but who becomes putty in the hands of his family who know how to 'manage' him. How could such an individual be classified with respect to the trait of dominance, for example? However, the results of personality study, as well as common observation, have established that in relation to their general behavior given individuals do possess certain traits or characteristics to a much greater degree than do other individuals. Furthermore, it is often true that the characteristics that happen to be strongly represented in the personality are also disclosed in the voice, since voice and speech constitute man's chief means of social adjustment and control. The voice, therefore, which is the natural medium of emotional expression, may be the chief aspect of an individual's behavior that gives us a clue, real or fancied, as to what is taking place within him—his real personality.

Consider, as an example, the suspicious, hypercritical, unfriendly person, distrustful of his fellows. One expects such a person to possess a voice exhibiting harsh, disagreeable qualities, producing an unpleasant effect upon the hearer. The morose, inhibited, or generally unresponsive individual is likely to have a dull, monotonous voice, lacking most of the qualities of warmth, friendliness, and expressiveness. Lethargic, negative, indifferent attitudes contribute to poor tone quality and imperfect, muffled articulation. States of excitement, worry, or high nervous tension are likely to manifest themselves in a tight, harsh, high-pitched voice and usually a fast and broken rhythm of utterance. On the other hand, one is always surprised and shocked when the warm, friendly, sympathetic individual fails to reflect any of those engaging qualities in his voice and speech.

Of course, it cannot be contended that these close relationships between personality characteristics and corresponding qualities of vocal utterance invariably exist. However, the important point is that they have existed frequently enough in the experience of the average person to lead him to associate the two together and base certain conclusions upon that association. That this entire process of inference is often a purely unconscious one is only further evidence of the general validity of the experience upon which it is based. One has little difficulty in identifying the qualities and traits of the various characters in the more popular forms of radio and television drama, for example. Unless the element of surprise is involved in the characterization, there is never any doubt that the villain is a villain, even before his nefarious deeds are brought to light, because he sounds like a villain. The actor takes great care to make sure that every quality and characteristic of his voice and speech literally shout villainy. He is merely taking advantage of the common tendency to judge a person by his voice.

Our discussion of personality characteristics has thus far been confined pretty largely to the popular conception of personality types and traits. Much of the testing and experimental work in that field of psychology devoted to a study of personality has likewise been concerned with traits, which can be defined as generalized patterns or types of responses. Among the traits that have claimed the greatest amount of interest and attention from psychologist and layman alike are those known as introversion and extroversion—the subjective and the objective personality. Broadly speaking, these two categories of individuals differ principally in the obviousness of their reactions to the social environment.

The introverted person's reactions are often within himself and hence he may give the outward impression of not reacting at all. Such an individual is likely to reject the company of his fellows for quiet and seclusion. He is inclined to be shy and ill at ease among others, finds it difficult to express himself orally, and gives the impression of being 'shut in' and inhibited. In such individuals feeling and emotion are likely to be intense and easily stimulated, and imagination may be very active, though any overt expression will tend to be inhibited. Pronounced introversion is reflected in a 'drying up' of all forms of vocal expression. The speech of the introvert tends to be meager, and the voice may be lacking in expressive qualities, not because of any want of inner activity to express, but because any verbalization of thinking and feeling tends to be repressed. The general impression created on others is often one of dullness and apathy or shyness, or the individual may be thought of as being queer and 'touchy.'

The extroverted person, on the other hand, represents more nearly what we have come to think of, more or less superficially, as the 'normal' or desirable type of personality. He is the typical 'good fellow,' inclined to be pleasant, friendly, and well poised socially. He enjoys social intercourse as well as physical activity and creates an impression of vitality and alertness. He is often inclined to aggressiveness. His speech is likely to be ready and lively, its expressive qualities being limited only by the depth, or lack of depth, of his thinking and feeling.

Of course, it must be understood that these two opposite characterizations are purely typical and for that reason are, to a large degree, stereotyped. In reality, there is no sharp line of demarcation between these personality types—if we can generalize sufficiently to refer to them as types. In other words, they do not represent two mutually exclusive groups, although the division becomes more apparent as we approach the two extremes. Rather, they represent opposed tendencies or patterns of behavior; two ends of a continuous scale, at a certain point on which a given individual can, with varying degrees of accuracy, be located. That is, each normal person presents a picture combining certain specific qualities belonging to each type. In certain respects and in relation to certain situations he may exhibit introversion; in some other respects he may incline toward extroversion. His position on the scale is determined by the degree to which he inclines toward the one general type or the other.

Contrary to some popular thinking, the characteristics of introversion, if not represented in an extreme form, are by no means wholly detrimental. The power of imagination and the other intellectual qualities which may be associated with this type of personality, together with the accompanying depth of emotional experience and sensitivity to emotional stimulation, often combine to produce great artists, writers, actors, scientists, and philosophers. To speech and voice, introversion offers the possibility of great beauty and power of expression, because deep down within the personality, as it were, there may be much to express. Before this can happen, of course, the repression and inhibition resulting from the individual's complex emotional organization must be overcome. This step is often difficult of accomplishment and there may be limits beyond which progress appears impossible. The important contributions which speech and voice training may make to such personality changes are discussed in later sections of this chapter.

EMOTION AND SPEECH

In what respects does emotional behavior differ from so-called intellectual behavior? To the extent that the two can be distinguished, the most important objective difference is that emotional behavior tends to become diffuse, general, all-over behavior. When a person is angry, he is literally as well as figuratively 'mad all over,' and his responses, instead of being organized and carefully directed toward the accomplishment of a definite goal, as they would be if he were acting intelligently, become gross, excessive, and ill directed. Consider, for illustration, the familiar picture of an individual discovering a knot in the lace as he is about to put on his shoe. He restrains his first impulse to break the lace and sets himself patiently to the task of untying the knot. This is directed, intellectual behavior. But suppose that the longer he works at it, the tighter the knot becomes; time is growing short and he becomes more and more exasperated. Finally he loses all restraint, suddenly jerks at the lace, breaks it, throws the shoe on the floor, and stamps on it. His behavior has now become emotionally directed primarily and as such it is random, disorganized, and pointless.

The fundamental explanation for this difference between the two types of response is to be found in a physiological mechanism originally designed by nature for the protection of the organism when danger threatened. Under primitive conditions such protection necessitated an immediate, automatic, total physical response in the form of either meeting the danger and overcoming it or escaping from it as quickly as possible. In either case, basic emotional activity was involved. This particular mechanism has its seat in a division of the nervous system referred to as the sympathetic division of the autonomic nervous system. Man still has such a mechanism in his make-up and it functions today very much as it did in his primitive ancestors ages ago. Ample evidence of such functioning can be seen in the behavior of anyone under the influence of such emotional states as excitement, anger, or fear. All emotional activity is accompanied by certain typical physiological responses, and the stronger the emotional stimulus, the more pronounced will be these bodily reactions and the more they tend to become identical for all types of emotions. From experience, most individuals have become familiar with the more common accompaniments of such a typical emotional response as stage fright presents, for example. The pounding heart, the gasping breath, the trembling knees, and the cold sweat are all recognized components of an all-too-familiar picture, though the experience which gave rise to these symptoms may have been a public performance, a football game, a piece of bad news, or an interview with a prospective employer.

One of the most important ways in which strong emotion operates to manifest itself in speech and voice characteristics is through an alteration in the functioning of the breathing mechanism. Under stress of emotional stimulation, breathing is taken under automatic control as a part of nature's method of preparing the organism to meet the projected emergency. Breathing becomes deeper and the rate is markedly increased. The effect upon speech is to disrupt the smooth flow of the phrases, producing an effect as if the speaker were gasping for breath; and there is likely to be no reserve of breath when the speaker needs it most. Tone quality may also suffer, becoming breathy and muffled.

Another way in which emotion shows itself in speech is through a breakdown in the fine co-ordinations so necessary to good speech. Common experience has shown how difficult it is to perform any complicated activity such as writing, typing, or piano playing when one is disturbed by excitement, anxiety, or self-consciousness; and speech, being a still more complex activity, is readily affected. Such vocal disturbance may produce breathiness, resulting from the breakdown of co-ordinations either within the larynx or between the breathing and the voice-producing mechanisms. The trembling which so often accompanies emotional activity manifests itself in vocal tremors. In more extreme cases, abnormal hesitations, broken speech rhythms, and cluttered articulation may all result from this emotion-motivated failure of the speech mechanism to function smoothly as an integrated unit.

However, it is through changes in muscle tonus that the more subtle expressive qualities of the voice, particularly those associated with variations in quality and pitch, are linked with emotional stimulation. Most types of emotional activity, even though relatively slight, are accompanied by some degree of alteration in basic muscle tonus including the muscles involved in phonation. The effects upon voice of such a condition have been explained in previous chapters. It has been shown, for instance, how tension of the muscles lining the walls of the resonators can give the voice a strained, strident quality. In fact, any such tenseness in the resonators will so alter their size, shape, and surface texture as to affect the resulting quality of the tone. It is interesting to note in this connection that one of the effects, or symptoms, of personality maladjustment is a general increase in muscle tonus. This is pretty much in line with common experience; everyone finds it difficult to relax when in a state of excitement, anxiety, or frustration. Relaxation is always associated with poise, calmness, and a feeling of well-being. We find herein further evidence substantiating the close dependence of a good voice upon sound physical health and a constructive, wholesome mental outlook.

In this connection we must not lose sight of the fact that such emotional states as we have been discussing, which are merely transitory experiences in the life of the average person, represent more nearly the habitual reaction patterns of those individuals whose personalities are inclined to be somewhat maladjusted. The unhappy, socially inadequate person, for example, goes about among his fellows in a state of continual tension, resembling a mild case of chronic stage fright. And in all such instances the voice is likely to reflect in some manner the kind of personality behind it, or, more correctly, of which it is a part. Therefore, suspicion, worry, apathy, moroseness, discontent, and feelings of inferiority are states of mind most difficult to reconcile with a well-modulated, pleasant, effective voice. Voice training and emotional training must go hand in hand.

STAGE FRIGHT

Some consideration of the characteristic type of emotional response popularly known as stage fright has an important place in any discussion of speech and personality, since it is closely related to problems of voice production as well as to certain personality characteristics. Stage fright manifests itself usually in situations involving speech in which one individual addresses a group in a more or less formal setting, though it may occur under many other circumstances as well. Athletes, for example, have been observed to exhibit a reaction essentially the same as stage fright just before an important contest. The disturbances of speech associated with stage fright are essentially those discussed earlier in this chapter, namely, lack of co-ordination between breathing and speaking, the weak, breathy tone, the tremorous, thin quality, and the faulty articulation often aggravated by numerous hesitations and a broken rhythm.

A number of theories have been advanced to explain the cause of stage fright, among them being that it has its basis in some deep, underlying fear or feeling of inferiority on the part of the individual afflicted. Another theory holds that this reaction is a learned response, arising as a result of an unpleasant emotional experience in a situation similar to that in which the speaker later exhibits the symptoms of stage fright. It was hinted in a preceding paragraph that this behavior may be related to certain aspects of personality. As an illustration, it is generally believed that introverts and individuals predominantly weak in such characteristics as aggressiveness and self-sufficiency are more likely to exhibit symptoms of stage fright than is the well-poised, dominant, aggressive person.

Stage Fright as a Fear Response. The most tenable theory is that the behavior pattern known as stage fright is in reality correctly named because it does represent a form of fear reaction in which all of the symptoms can be traced directly to the typical 'fight or flight' activity controlled by the autonomic nervous system and arising from physiological changes taking place within the body.

What, however, stimulates the fear response into activity? Of what is the speaker afraid? As a matter of fact, there is probably no one thing or no one aspect of the experience to which the fear can be definitely attached. Rather, it is the whole speech situation that furnishes the stimulus; the speaker is not sure that he can cope with it successfully. Since every speech situation is unique and presents new problems, it can be appreciated why experience alone, while being of decided advantage to the speaker, is not always successful in enabling him to overcome stage fright completely.

Undoubtedly the basic attitude most responsible for the appearance of the symptoms is the speaker's feeling that the audience represents a crisis situation, a life-or-death matter, as it were, with everything at stake and with a definite possibility of failure. So long as the performer allows his mind to dwell upon such thoughts, he is almost certain to have trouble. His plight then becomes essentially the same as that which confronted our remote ancestor when, with knotted club, he met his enemy upon a narrow path and must choose to fight it out or take to his heels. In either case nature equipped him for the emergency by preparing him for some sort of violent physical activity. However, when nature does as much for the public speaker today, virtually all of the changes which take place within his body are a distinct hindrance to him rather than a help.

Overcoming Stage Fright. Since there is no successful way of preventing this automatic mechanism from functioning, once it has been set into operation, the most sensible procedure is to prevent it from becoming stimulated into activity in the first place. In other words, prevent the emotion of fear from developing. This demands a predominantly psychological approach to the problem of the control of stage fright in that it concerns the speaker's attitude toward the speech situation. The feeling that it presents anything like a crisis must carefully be avoided and a much more positive attitude substituted. The speaker should recall his past successes rather than his failures and should look upon himself as being perfectly capable of meeting the present situation adequately. No suggestion that he is inferior, that he is on trial, that it is a life-or-death matter, or that he is in danger of failing should be allowed to enter his head. He should be content to do his best and should realize that no more will be expected of him. His hearers he should think of as being people like himself, neither inferior nor superior but helpful and friendly in their feeling toward him and interested in what he may have to say, not just because he is saying it but because the subject-matter appeals to them. He should remember that they are not expecting him to exhibit symptoms of stage fright and that in all likelihood they will not be aware of it if he does have a mild attack. The speaker should find comfort in the thought that stage fright always feels much worse than it looks.

There is also a further approach to this problem through an application of the well-known James-Lange theory of emotional behavior. According to this theory the mere assumption of the outward form or posture of an emotional state tends to induce the corresponding feeling within. In other words, the way to feel brave is to act brave. However sound or unsound this may be as psychological theory, common experience has taught that there is much of practical value in such a technique in dealing with stage fright. Accordingly, the public speaker is advised to assume the outward appearance of calm, poise, and self-possession. He should breathe deeply and smoothly, avoid awkward, slouchy positions, speak in a firm, resonant voice, and in general keep himself well under control. There is no question that such a procedure will do much to dissipate any feelings of fear or inadequacy.

Finally, it should be remembered that the speaker's difficulties are likely to be increased to the extent that he thinks about himself; too great a preoccupation with self lies at the very root of his fear. From such thoughts may very easily arise doubts, feelings of inadequacy, and self-consciousness. Let him forget about himself and concentrate upon what he is to say, which of course should be very carefully prepared. He should lose himself in his subject; the urge to speak should be strong and the desire to communicate must become a compelling force. When the speaker has achieved this state, he will have little time or concern for stage fright.

SUGGESTIONS FOR THE IMPROVEMENT OF VOICE AND PERSONALITY

What are the implications for voice training in the picture of speech and personality thus far set forth in this chapter? If the two are so closely related, will training in one improve the other? Can anything constructive be done about one's personality? At least partial answers can be given to these important questions.

In the first place, the individual should make sure that his voice is at all times expressive and responsive to thought and feeling. Even the most gifted musician must have a good instrument if he is to perform successfully. An untrained, defective, or unresponsive voice cannot be expected to do justice to whatever favorable qualities of personality the individual may possess. This is particularly true of the voice exhibiting some special defect, such as nasality, flatness, or an excessively high pitch, which will create an unpleasant, unfavorable impression despite other possible good qualities of voice or personality.

As was pointed out in the first chapter, the possibilities for improving the vocal mechanism are very favorable in virtually all cases. It has been the primary aim of this book to present a complete program of training to effect such improvement. In fact, it can safely be said that any individual not presenting serious disorders of voice, speech, or hearing can with proper training materially improve his vocal performance.

Improvement of Voice as Conditioned by Personality. The close identification of voice with personality necessitates that training in voice and training in personality must often proceed simultaneously. As a matter of fact, improvement in the one may be largely determined by the possibility of development in the other. Of the two, personality is the stronger influence and unfortunately is less amenable to change and is also much more difficult to deal with directly. All of which means that progress in voice will be slow, difficult, and generally unsatisfactory so long as any one or more of the following conditions obtains:

1. *If the Individual Has Nothing to Express.* Discrimination in the use of voice and in speech always depends upon discrimination in thinking and feeling. If the individual's reactions to his environment are so dull or his mental processes so impotent as to awaken no inward responses, then he can hardly be expected to exhibit an expressive voice, no matter how well trained his vocal mechanism may be. Even the finest violin produces but raucous noise in the hands of one who has no talent for music.

As can readily be seen, this problem takes one considerably beyond the limitations of what is ordinarily defined as voice training proper; yet the two cannot be separated. The obvious solution is to make voice and speech training a fundamental and integral part of the individual's total development. He must be stimulated to think and feel and discriminate; he must be taught to react to his environment. In other words, effective use of the voice cannot be thought of as being merely a grace or manner to be assumed only on special occasions and then to be laid aside and forgotten. If a superior voice is to be of material benefit to one, it must work for him *on the job,* all the time. Whatever the individual has to say must be said with as much clearness and meaning and with as much purpose and motivation as he is capable of mustering. His realization of the importance of good speech as a tool with which he can adjust himself happily and effectively to his social environment, as well as a tool with which he can control that environment more nearly to his own desires and purposes, will furnish the impelling motive needed to achieve real and lasting success in voice and speech training.

2. *If Unfavorable, Negative, or Antisocial Qualities Are Present to Any Degree in the Individual's Personality.* The student of voice should take stock of himself and appraise himself objectively with respect to desirable and undesirable personality characteristics. Any tendencies toward such attitudes as excessive fear, timidity, moroseness, lassitude, indifference, arrogance, intolerance, and bitterness must be studiously eradicated, and in their place desirable, positive mental states of optimism, sympathy, friendliness, alertness, and self-reliance should be cultivated. Every individual, of course, represents something of a balance between the negative and the positive characteristics, but he inclines toward a general dominance of the one or the other.

So-called personality adjustment or integration, however, implies a certain degree of objective-mindedness with respect to desirable and undesirable characteristics—the ability to recognize weaknesses, and the disposition to improve the personality by cultivating the good qualities and eradicating the detrimental ones. The individual will be aided in this process if he gives consideration to such aspects of his social relationships and his mental health as are indicated by the following questions:

1. Are you inclined to be tolerant of others' opinions and points of view?
2. Are you interested in people or do they generally bore you?
3. Are you inclined to be at ease with people?
4. Are you usually successful in controlling your temper or do you 'flare up' easily?
5. Can you take honest criticism without having your feelings hurt?
6. Are you reasonably free from worries?
7. Can you admit your own mistakes and laugh at yourself, or must you resort frequently to self-pity?
8. Do you make an effort to find new friends and cause people to like you?
9. Do you have a number of interests that make life seem worth while and that provide you with enjoyable relaxation?
10. Do you have a reasonable amount of confidence in yourself and in what you are doing?
11. Are you able to make up your mind and come to decisions with reasonable facility and freedom from strain?
12. Do you meet responsibility and face reality for the most part in good spirit and do you feel that you are doing the best you can?
13. Do you have some goal, or goals, which you are trying to reach in terms of a philosophy of life?
14. Are you reasonably happy and do you find enjoyment and satisfaction in your work?
15. Do you try to keep yourself physically fit?

Of course, one cannot always give simple, unqualified answers to questions such as these. However, they do serve to focus attention upon important indications of strength and weakness in one's basic attitudes and in his characteristic reactions to his environment—a behavior pattern that is known as personality. If in this process of appraisal, one finds too many of these items entered against him on the negative side of the ledger, he should take warning and embark upon an honest and sincere program of self-improvement.

3. *If Inhibitions and Repressions Rob the Voice of Its Expressive Qualities.* Many individuals appear dull, negative, or uninteresting not because they are that way, but because excessive timidity, self-consciousness, or habitual repression of feeling makes it very difficult if not impossible for them to express what is taking place within themselves. Often such attitudes are deeply rooted in childhood experiences and training, or possibly the individual is simply too self-conscious to speak out with feeling and conviction, or he may believe that such expression is a mark of affectation.

Whatever the fundamental causes, repressive tendencies must be broken down if the possibilities for either a good voice or an effective personality are to be fully realized. This development must be kept within reasonable bounds, of course; no one admires the impulsive, unpredictable, completely uninhibited person who, though he may be the 'life of the party,' is rash and extravagant in his speech and behavior generally. Such behavior suggests insincerity and instability. For the average person, however, this is more a theoretical than an actual danger; what his speech is most likely to need is more spontaneity and versatility of expression. Inhibitions and repressions must usually be reduced. There is little danger of his becoming 'temperamental.'

Voice Training as Personality Development. As a final word on the subject of speech and personality, let us consider how voice training may contribute to personality development and an improved social adjustment. In the first place, it has been pretty well established that individuals tend to become what they believe other people think them to be. When people react more favorably toward us because our voice conveys the impression that we are friendly, competent, and interesting, there is a strong tendency for us to develop those qualities in our personality. If we are treated with respect by others, we soon come to have more respect for ourselves. Then, too, one's own consciousness of having a pleasant, effective voice of which he does not need to be ashamed contributes materially to a feeling of poise, self-confidence, and a just pride in himself. A good voice, like good clothes, can do much for an ego that otherwise might be inclined to droop.

On the other hand, many individuals develop feelings of inadequacy and inferiority because of the presence of a voice or speech defect which has been a source of worry or embarrassment to them. Nor is this true only of serious speech disorders such as stuttering. Lesser vocal deficiencies in the form of a faulty pitch level, a disagreeable voice quality such as stridency or nasality, or mumbling articulation may so trouble the individual by his acute awareness of them as to handicap him seriously in his social relationships. In these cases voice and speech training may do much to promote desirable personality qualities of confidence, ease, and poise in dealing with others.

EXERCISES AND PRACTICE MATERIAL

The practice material which follows has been chosen primarily to illustrate the close relationship between speech and personality, especially as vocal expression is influenced by mental attitudes, moods, and characteristic emotional states.

More specifically, the exercises for this chapter have been designed to accomplish three objectives:

1. To give the student experience in reacting to various emotional states, purposes, and points of view. As was pointed out previously in this chapter, if the voice is to become expressive, the individual must have something to express; he must be sensitive and responsive to his environment and particularly to emotional stimulation. The exercises are designed to test and develop the readiness and versatility of that response.

2. To show how certain concepts, moods, and affective states are manifested in voice and speech. In this connection the student is asked to observe closely to what extent his voice naturally responds to the various speech purposes and situations represented in the practice material and to study the manner in which this response takes place. Thus, the exercises also constitute a test of the responsiveness and flexibility of the student's vocal equipment, and hence function as a review and culmination of what he has covered in previous chapters.

3. To aid the student in removing inhibitions and self-consciousness which may constitute serious hindrances to the expressive use of his voice.

The student is urged to study each selection carefully to determine its mood and feeling-tone and the point of view from which it was written. Try to catch the essential spirit of the selection; imagine that you really are the character or person speaking. Then study to discover how this interpretation can best be manifested through the expressive qualities of the voice. As you practice the exercises and drill material, note how the voice *naturally* responds to vivid thinking and genuine feeling. Finally, do not hesitate to 'step out' and demonstrate those qualities in your interpretation; exaggerate the expression somewhat merely for the sake of the practice value you will receive from it. But bear in mind that any deviation from your accustomed manner of speaking will appear to you as definite exaggeration because it will sound strange and new at first. As a matter of fact, such feeling should be hailed by the student as a reassuring sign of progress.

1. Listen to a radio or television drama and write a short analysis of the way in which the personality of each of the principal characters was revealed through the various expressive qualities of the voice.

2. How many different personality types can be suggested by the various ways in which 'hello' can be spoken? The grouchy person; the cold, indifferent personality; the hearty, friendly individual; et cetera. Proceed similarly with 'good morning.'

3. Practice the expression, 'come in,' as it might be heard in various situations. Suggest the busy, efficient secretary; the cordial hostess; the Dean to a student about to be reprimanded; the 'big boss' in various moods; the professional man; et cetera.

4. In the following selection, an adaptation in dialogue form of a scene from Charles Dickens's *A Christmas Carol*, distinguish sharply between the crabbed, bitter personality of Scrooge and the youthful enthusiasm and friendliness of the nephew. Note particularly the difference in the quality of voice which may be used to suggest the contrasting characters. Don't think only of the vocal differences, however; remember that they are merely reflections of opposed attitudes and points of view.

NEPHEW (*bursting into the room*): A merry Christmas, uncle! God save you!

SCROOGE (*startled at first*): Bah! Humbug!

NEPHEW: Christmas a humbug, uncle! You don't mean that, I am sure.

SCROOGE: I do. Merry Christmas! What right have you to be merry? What reason have you to be merry? You're poor enough.

NEPHEW: Come then, what right have you to be dismal? What reason have you to be morose? You're rich enough.

SCROOGE (*can think of no better reply*): Bah! Humbug!

NEPHEW: Don't be cross, uncle.

SCROOGE: What else can I be, when I live in such a world of fools as this? Merry Christmas! Out upon merry Christmas! If I could work my will, every idiot who goes about with 'Merry Christmas' on his lips should be boiled with his own pudding, and buried with a stake of holly through his heart. He should!

NEPHEW (*pleading*): Uncle!

SCROOGE: Nephew, keep Christmas in your own way, and let me keep it in mine.

NEPHEW: Keep it! But you don't keep it.

SCROOGE: Let me leave it alone, then. Much good may it do you! Much good it has ever done you!

NEPHEW: There are many things from which I might have derived good by which I have not profited, I dare say, Christmas among the rest. But I am sure that I have always thought of Christmas-time, when it has come round, as a good time; a kind, forgiving, charitable, pleasant time. And therefore, uncle, though it has never put a scrap of gold or silver in my pockets, I believe that it *has* done me good, and *will* do me good; and I say, God bless it!

SCROOGE (*to his clerk in another room who has involuntarily applauded this speech*): Let me hear another sound from *you,* and you'll keep Christmas by losing your situation! (*To his nephew*) You're quite a powerful speaker, sir; I wonder you don't go into Parliament.

NEPHEW: Don't be angry, uncle. Come, dine with us tomorrow.

SCROOGE (*defiantly*): No! I'll be bound if I will!

NEPHEW: But why? Why?

SCROOGE (*not able to think of anything better to reply*): Why did you get married?

NEPHEW: Because I fell in love.

SCROOGE (*growling*): Because you fell in love! Good-afternoon!

NEPHEW: I want nothing from you; I ask nothing of you; why cannot we be friends?

SCROOGE: Good-afternoon!

NEPHEW: I'm sorry with all my heart to find you so resolute. But I have made the trial in homage to Christmas, and I'll keep my Christmas humor to the last. So A Merry Christmas, uncle!

SCROOGE: Good-afternoon!
NEPHEW: And A Happy New Year!
SCROOGE: Good-afternoon!! (*As the nephew leaves*)

SELECTIONS ILLUSTRATING THE FANCIFUL, PLAYFUL, HUMOROUS

1. Behold the mighty Dinosaur,
   Famous in prehistoric lore,
   Not only for his weight and strength,
   But for his intellectual length.
   You will observe by these remains
   The creature had two sets of brains—
   One in his head (the usual place),
   The other at his spinal base.
   Thus he could reason *a priori*
   As well as *a posteriori*.
   No problem bothered him a bit;
   He made both head and tail of it.
   So wise he was, so wise and solemn,
   Each thought filled just a spinal column.
   If one brain found the pressure strong,
   It passed a few ideas along;
   If something slipt his forward mind,
   'Twas rescued by the one behind;
   And if in error he was caught,
   He had a saving afterthought.
   As he thought twice before he spoke,
   He had no judgments to revoke;
   For he could think, without congestion,
   Upon both sides of every question.
   Oh, gaze upon this model beast,
   Defunct ten million years at least!

                           BERT LESTON TAYLOR, 'The Dinosaur'

2. The night was thick and hazy
   When the 'Piccadilly Daisy'
   Carried down the crew and captain in the sea;
   And I think the water drowned 'em;
   For they never, never found 'em
   And I know they didn't come ashore with me.

Oh! 'twas very sad and lonely
When I found myself the only
Population on this cultivated shore;
But I've made a little tavern
In a rocky little cavern,
And I sit and watch for people at the door.

I spent no time in looking
For a girl to do my cooking,
As I'm quite a clever hand at making stews;
But I had that fellow Friday,
Just to keep the tavern tidy,
And to put a Sunday polish on my shoes.

I have a little garden
That I'm cultivating lard in,
As the things I eat are rather tough and dry;
For I live on toasted lizards,
Prickly pears, and parrot gizzards,
And I'm really very fond of beetle-pie.

I sometimes seek diversion
In a family excursion
With the few domestic animals you see;
And we take along a carrot
As refreshment for the parrot,
And a little can of jungleberry tea.

If the roads are wet and muddy
We remain at home and study—
For the goat is very clever at a sum,—
And the dog, instead of fighting,
Studies ornamental writing,
While the cat is taking lessons on the drum.

We retire at eleven,
And we rise again at seven;
And I wish to call attention, as I close,
To the fact that all the scholars,
Are correct about their collars,
And particular in turning out their toes.

                                    C. E. CARRYL, 'Robinson Crusoe's Story'

3. In this by-place of nature there abode, in a remote period of American history, that is to say, some thirty years since, a worthy wight of the name of Ichabod Crane, who sojourned, or, as he expressed it, 'tarried,' in Sleepy Hollow, for the purpose of instructing the children of the vicinity. The cognomen of Crane was not inapplicable to his person. He was tall, but exceedingly lank, with narrow shoulders, long arms and legs, hands that dangled a mile out of his sleeves, feet that might have served for shovels, and his whole frame most loosely hung together. His head was small, and flat at top, with huge ears, large green glassy eyes, and a long snipe nose, so that it looked like a weather-cock perched upon his spindle neck, to tell which way the wind blew. To see him striding along the profile of a hill on a windy day, with his clothes bagging and fluttering about him, one might have mistaken him for the genius of famine descended upon the earth, or some scarecrow eloped from a cornfield.

IRVING, *The Legend of Sleepy Hollow*

4. Who, or why, or which, or *what*
Is the Ahkond of Swat?

Is he tall or short, or dark or fair?
Does he sit on a stool or sofa or chair,
or Squat,
The Ahkond of Swat?

Is he wise or foolish, young or old?
Does he drink his soup and his coffee cold
or Hot,
The Ahkond of Swat?

Does he wear a turban, a fez, or a hat?
Does he sleep on a mattress, a bed or a mat,
or a Cot,
The Ahkond of Swat?

Does he like to lie on his back in a boat
Like the lady who lived in that isle remote,
Shalott,
The Ahkond of Swat?

Does he beat his wife with a gold-topped pipe,
When she lets the gooseberries grow too ripe,
                              or Rot,
            The Ahkond of Swat?

Does he like new cream, and hate mince-pies?
When he looks at the sun does he wink his eyes,
                              or Not,
            The Ahkond of Swat?

Someone, or nobody knows I wot
Who or which or why or what
                    Is the Ahkond of Swat!
                    EDWARD LEAR, 'The Ahkond of Swat'

5. There was once a Neolithic Man
        An enterprising wight,
    Who made his chopping implements
        Unusually bright.

                        .   .   .

    To his Neolithic neighbors,
        Who were startled and surprised,
    Said he, 'My friends, in course of time,
        We shall be civilized!
    We are going to live in cities!
        We are going to fight in wars!
    We are going to eat three times a day
        Without the natural cause!
    We are going to turn life upside down
        About a thing called gold!
    We are going to want the earth, and take
        As much as we can hold!
    We are going to wear great piles of stuff
        Outside our proper skins!
    We are going to have diseases!
        And Accomplishments!! And Sins!!!'
                    CHARLOTTE PERKINS GILMAN, 'Similar Cases'

6. When I, good friends, was called to the Bar,
        I'd an appetite fresh and hearty,
    But I was, as many young barristers are,
        An impecunious party.

I'd a swallow-tail coat of a beautiful blue—
　　A brief which was brought by a booby—
A couple of shirts and a collar or two,
　　And a ring that looked like a ruby!

In Westminster Hall I danced a dance,
　　Like a semi-despondent fury;
For I thought I should never hit on a chance
　　Of addressing a British Jury—
But I soon got tired of third-class journeys,
　　And dinners of bread and water;
So I fell in love with a rich attorney's
　　Elderly, ugly daughter.

The rich attorney, he wiped his eyes,
　　And replied to my fond professions:
'You shall reap the reward of your enterprise,
　　At the Bailey and Middlesex Sessions.
You'll soon get used to her looks,' said he,—
　　'And a very nice girl you'll find her—
She may very well pass for forty-three
　　In the dusk, with a light behind her!'

W. S. GILBERT, from Trial by Jury

SELECTIONS ILLUSTRATING OR SUGGESTING CHARACTER TYPES

1. I've loops o' string in the place of buttons, I've mostly holes
　　for a shirt;
　My boots are bust and my hat's a goner, I'm gritty with dust
　　and dirt;
　An' I'm sitting here on a bollard watchin' the China ships go
　　forth,
　Seein' the black little tugs come slidin' with timber booms
　　from the North,
　Sittin' and seein' the broad Pacific break at my feet in foam. . . .
　Me that was born with a taste for travel in a back alley at
　　home.

　They put me to school when I was a nipper at the Board
　　School down in the slums,
　An' some of the kids was good at spellin' and some at figures
　　and sums;

And whether I went or whether I didn't they learned me
nothin' at all,
Only I'd watch the flies go walkin' over the maps on the wall,
Strollin' over the lakes an' mountains, over the plains an'
sea,—
As if they was born with a taste for travel . . . somethin' the
same as me!

If I'd been born a rich man's youngster with lots o' money to
burn,
It wouldn't ha' gone in marble mansions and statues at every
turn,
It wouldn't ha' gone in wine and women, or dogs an' horses
an' play,
Nor yet in collectin' bricks an' bracks in a harmless kind of
a way;
I'd ha' paid my fare where I've beat my way (but I couldn't
ha' liked it more!),
Me that was born with a taste for travel—the same if you're
rich or poor.

I'd ha' gone bowlin' in yachts and rollin' in plush-padded
Pullman cars,—
The same as I've seen 'em when I lay restin' at night-time
under the stars,
Me that have beat the ties and rode the bumpers from sea to
sea,
Me that have sweated in stokeholds and dined of mouldy salt-
horse and tea,
Me that have melted like grease at Perim and froze like boards
off the Horn,
All along of a taste for travel that was in me when I was born.

I ain't got folks an' I ain't got money, I ain't got nothin' at all,
But a sort of a queer old thirst that keeps me movin' on till
I fall,
And many a time I've been short o' shelter and many a time
o' grub,
But I've got away from the rows o' houses, the streets, an' the
corner pub—
And here by the side of a sea that's shinin' under a sky like
flame.

Me that was born with a taste for travel, give thanks because
o' the same.

CICELY FOX SMITH, 'The Traveller'

2. When Susan's work was done, she'd sit
   With one fat guttering candle lit,
   And window opened wide to win
   The sweet night air to enter in;
   There, with a thumb to keep her place
   She'd read, with stern and wrinkled face.
   Her mild eyes gliding very slow
   Across the letters to and fro,
   While wagged the guttering candle flame
   In the wind that through the window came.
   And sometimes in the silence she
   Would mumble a sentence audibly,
   Or shake her head as if to say,
   'You silly souls, to act this way!'
   And never a sound from night I'd hear,
   Unless some far-off cock crowed clear;
   Or her old shuffling thumb should turn
   Another page; and rapt and stern,
   Through her great glasses bent on me
   She'd glance into reality;
   And shake her round old silvery head,
   With—'You!—I thought you was in bed!'—
   Only to tilt her book again,
   And rooted in Romance remain.

WALTER DE LA MARE, 'Old Susan'

3. I must go down to the seas again, to the lonely sea and the sky,
   And all I ask is a tall ship and a star to steer her by,
   And the wheel's kick and the wind's song and the white sail's
   shaking,
   And a grey mist on the sea's face, and a grey dawn breaking.

   I must go down to the seas again, for the call of the running
   tide
   Is a wild call and a clear call that may not be denied;
   And all I ask is a windy day with the white clouds flying,
   And the flung spray and the blown spume, and the sea-gulls
   crying.

I must go down to the seas again, to the vagrant gypsy life,
To the gull's way and the whale's way where the wind's like
    a whetted knife;
And all I ask is a merry yarn from a laughing fellow-rover,
And quiet sleep and a sweet dream when the long trick's over.

JOHN MASEFIELD, 'Sea-Fever'

4. 'I know what you're going to say,' she said,
    And she stood up looking uncommonly tall;
    'You are going to speak of the hectic Fall,
And say you're sorry the summer's dead.
    And no other summer was like it, you know,
    And can I imagine what made it so?
Now aren't you, honestly?' 'Yes,' I said.

'I know what you're going to say,' she said;
    'You are going to ask if I forget
    That day in June when the woods were wet,
And you carried me'—here she dropped her head—
    'Over the creek; you are going to say,
    Do I remember that horrid day.
Now aren't you, honestly?' 'Yes,' I said.

'I know what you're going to say,' she said;
    'You are going to say that since that time
    You have rather tended to run to rhyme,
And'—her clear glance fell and her cheek grew red—
    'And have I noticed your tone was queer?—
    Why, everybody has seen it here!—
Now aren't you, honestly?' 'Yes,' I said.

'I know what you're going to say,' I said;
    'You're going to say you've been much annoyed,
    And I'm short of tact—you will say devoid—
And I'm clumsy and awkward, and call me Ted,
    And I bear abuse like a dear old lamb,
    And you'll have me, anyway, just as I am,
Now aren't you, honestly?' 'Ye-es,' she said.

H. C. BUNNER

5. 'I am an old friend of Dr. Jekyll's—Mr. Utterson of Gaunt Street—you must have heard my name; and meeting you so conveniently, I thought you might admit me.'

'You will not find Dr. Jekyll; he is from home,' replied Mr.
Hyde, blowing in the key. And then suddenly, but still without
looking up, 'How did you know me?' he asked. . . .

'By description,' was the reply.

'Whose description?'

'We have common friends,' said Mr. Utterson.

'Common friends?' echoed Mr. Hyde a little hoarsely. 'Who
are they?'

'Jekyll, for instance,' said the lawyer.

'He never told you,' cried Mr. Hyde, with a flush of anger.
'I did not think you would have lied.'

'Come,' said Mr. Utterson, 'that is not fitting language.'

The other snarled aloud into a savage laugh; and the next
moment, with extraordinary quickness, he had unlocked the
door and disappeared into the house.

R. L. STEVENSON, *Dr. Jekyll and Mr. Hyde*

SELECTIONS INVOLVING IMAGINATION, FEELING, INSPIRATION

1. When I heard the learn'd astronomer;
   When the proofs, the figures, were ranged in columns before
      me;
   When I was shown the charts and the diagrams, to add,
      divide, and measure them;
   When I, sitting, heard the astronomer, where he lectured with
      much applause in the lecture-room,   ·
   How soon, unaccountable, I became tired and sick;
   Till rising and gliding out, I wander'd off by myself,
   In the mystical moist night-air, and from time to time,
   Look'd up in perfect silence at the stars.

WHITMAN, 'When I Heard the Learn'd Astronomer'

2. Night is a dead, monotonous period under a roof; but in
the open world it passes lightly, with its stars and dews and per-
fumes, and the hours are marked by changes in the face of Nature. What seems a kind of temporal death to people choked
between walls and curtains, is only a light and living slumber
to the man who sleeps afield. All night long he can hear Nature
breathing deeply and freely; even as she takes her rest, she turns
and smiles; and there is one stirring hour unknown to those
who dwell in houses, when a wakeful influence goes abroad over
the sleeping hemisphere, and all the outdoor world are on their

feet. It is then that the cock first crows, not this time to announce the dawn, but like a cheerful watchman speeding the course of night. Cattle awake on the meadows; sheep break their fast on dewy hillsides, and change to a new lair among the ferns; and houseless men, who have lain down with the fowls, open their dim eyes and behold the beauty of the night.

R. L. STEVENSON, *Travels with a Donkey*

3. I met a traveler from an antique land
   Who said: Two vast and trunkless legs of stone
   Stand in the desert. Near them, on the sand,
   Half sunk, a shattered visage lies, whose frown,
   And wrinkled lip, and sneer of cold command,
   Tell that its sculptor well those passions read
   Which yet survive, stamped on these lifeless things,
   The hand that mocked them and the heart that fed;
   And on the pedestal these words appear:
   'My name is Ozymandias, king of kings;
   Look on my works, ye Mighty, and despair!'
   Nothing beside remains. Round the decay
   Of that colossal wreck, boundless and bare
   The lone and level sands stretch far away.

P. B. SHELLEY, 'Ozymandias'

4. Bowed by the weight of centuries, he leans
   Upon his hoe and gazes on the ground,
   The emptiness of ages in his face,
   And on his back the burden of the world.
   Who made him dead to rapture and despair,
   A thing that grieves not and that never hopes,
   Stolid and stunned, a brother to the ox?
   Who loosened and let down this brutal jaw?
   Whose was the hand that slanted back this brow?
   Whose breath blew out the light within this brain?

   Is this the Thing the Lord God made and gave
   To have dominion over sea and land;
   To trace the stars and search the heavens for power;
   To feel the passion of Eternity?
   Is this the dream He dreamed who shaped the suns
   And marked their ways upon the ancient deep?
   Down all the caverns of Hell to their last gulf

There is no shape more terrible than this—
More tongued with censure of the world's blind greed—
More filled with signs and portents for the soul—
More packed with danger to the universe.

                EDWIN MARKHAM, 'The Man with the Hoe'

5. What is a minority? The chosen heroes of this earth have been in the minority. There is not a social, political, or religious privilege that you enjoy today that was not bought for you by the blood and tears and patient sufferings of the minority. It is the minority that have vindicated humanity in every struggle. It is the minority that have come out as iconoclasts to beat down the Dagons their fathers have worshiped—the old abuses of society. It is the minority that have stood in the van of every moral conflict, and achieved all that is noble in the history of the world. You will find that each generation has been always busy in gathering up the scattered ashes of the martyred heroes of the past, to deposit them in the golden urn of a nation's history.

                                        JOHN B. GOUGH

6. With malice toward none; with charity for all; with firmness in the right, as God gives us to see the right, let us strive on to finish the work we are in; to bind up the nation's wounds; to care for him who shall have borne the battle, and for his widow, and his orphan—to do all which may achieve and cherish a just and lasting peace among ourselves, and with all nations.

                                        ABRAHAM LINCOLN

7. Like to the falling of a star,
    Or as the flights of eagles are,
    Or like the fresh spring's gaudy hue,
    Or silver drops of morning dew,
    Or like a wind that chafes the flood,
    Or bubbles which on water stood:
    Even such is man, whose borrowed light
    Is straight called in and paid to night.
    The wind blows out, the bubble dies,
    The spring intombed in autumn lies;
    The dew's dried up, the star is shot,
    The flight is past, and man forgot.

                                        FRANCIS BEAUMONT

8. Wynken, Blynken, and Nod one night
   Sailed off in a wooden shoe—
Sailed on a river of crystal light,
   Into a sea of dew.
'Where are you going, and what do you wish?'
   The old moon asked the three.
'We have come to fish for the herring fish
   That live in this beautiful sea;
Nets of silver and gold have we!'
            Said Wynken,
            Blynken,
            And Nod.

The old moon laughed and sang a song
   As they rocked in the wooden shoe;
And the wind that sped them all night long
   Ruffled the waves of dew.
The little stars were the herring fish
   That lived in the beautiful sea—
'Now cast your nets wherever you wish—
   Never afeard are we';
So cried the stars to the fishermen three:
            Wynken,
            Blynken,
            And Nod.

EUGENE FIELD

9. I went to Washington the other day and I stood on the
Capitol Hill; my heart beat quick as I looked at the towering
marble of my country's Capitol, and the mist gathered in my
eyes as I thought of its tremendous significance, and the armies
and the Treasury, and the judges and the President, and the
Congress and the courts, and all that was gathered there. And I
felt that the sun in all its course could not look down on a better
sight than that majestic home of a republic that had taught the
world its best lessons of liberty. And I felt that if honor and
wisdom and justice abided therein, the world would at last owe
that great house in which the ark of the covenant of my country
is lodged, its final uplifting and its regeneration.

HENRY W. GRADY

PART II
DICTION FOR SPEECH

PHONETIC SYMBOLS USED IN THIS BOOK

Consonants

SYMBOL	KEY WORD	REPRESENTATIVE SPELLINGS
[p]	*p*ea [pi]	a*pp*le, hiccou*gh*
[b]	*b*ee [bi]	e*bb*, tri*b*e
[t]	*t*ea [ti]	a*tt*end, *Th*omas
[d]	*d*ay [de]	la*dd*er, bla*d*e
[k]	*k*ey [ki]	li*qu*or, *ch*aracter, *c*an, a*cc*oun*t*
[g]	*g*un [gʌn]	*gu*est, *gh*ost, e*gg*
[h]	*h*at [hæt]	*wh*o
[f]	*f*ee [fi]	rou*gh*, *ph*onetic, ru*ff*le
[v]	*v*ine [vaɪn]	o*f*, dro*v*e, Ste*ph*en
[θ]	*th*in [θɪn]	(spelled only with *th*)
[ð]	*th*en [ðɛn]	(spelled only with *th*)
[s]	*s*ent [sɛnt]	*s*cent, *c*ent, les*s*on
[z]	*z*oo [zu]	hi*s*, bu*zz*
[ʃ]	*sh*ip [ʃɪp]	*s*ure, na*ti*on, fi*ss*ure
[ʒ]	a*z*ure [æʒɚ]	mea*s*ure, gara*g*e
[tʃ]	*ch*ip [tʃɪp]	crea*t*ure, wa*tch*
[dʒ]	*j*oy [dʒɔɪ]	*g*entle, sol*di*er, he*dg*e
[m]	*m*e [mi]	gram*m*ar, sole*m*n, li*mb*
[n]	*n*ap [næp]	*kn*ee, *gn*aw, pen*n*y

241

SYMBOL	KEY WORD	REPRESENTATIVE SPELLINGS
[ŋ]	si*ng* [sɪŋ]	si*nk*
[l]	*l*ea [li]	E*ll*a, who*l*e
[r]	*r*un [rʌn]	a*rr*ive, *wr*eck
[j]	*y*ou [ju]	*u*nite, on*i*on
[w]	*w*on [wʌn]	ang*u*ish, *o*ne
[hw] *	*wh*en [hwen]	(always spelled with *wh*)

VOWELS

SYMBOL	KEY WORD	REPRESENTATIVE SPELLINGS
[i]	*see* [si]	*sea,* rec*ei*ve, bel*ie*ve, rav*i*ne, th*ese*
[ɪ]	*sit* [sɪt]	b*u*sy, pr*e*tty, c*i*ty, h*y*mn
[e]	*gate* [get]	br*ea*k, th*ey*, h*ai*l, s*ay*
[ɛ]	m*et* [mɛt]	br*ea*d, f*ai*r, *a*ny
[æ]	*c*ash [kæʃ]	(customarily spelled with *a*)
[a]	*a*sk [ask]	c*a*lf, l*au*gh

(As sometimes pronounced in American speech. These words and similar ones are also often pronounced with [æ], occasionally with [ɑ])

[ɑ]	f*a*ther [fɑðɚ]	h*o*nest (as pronounced in certain areas)
[ɒ]	cl*o*th [klɒθ]	w*a*tch

(As frequently pronounced in American speech, although [ɔ] is also often heard as the vowel in certain words belonging to

---

* This is listed merely for purposes of reference. It is treated in this book not as a separate sound unit, but merely as a glottal fricative or *h* approach to the *w*. It is thus comparable to the *h* approach to [j], as we find in the word *hue*. (Compare *hue* with *you*.)

this group, and [ɑ] will be heard in others. The vowel [ɒ] is likely to be heard in the British pronunciation of *not*)

[ɔ]	all [ɔl]	*ough*t, *taugh*t, *law*, *tal*k, *broa*d
[o]	go [go]	*boa*t, *sou*l, *low*, *hoe*, *thoug*h
[ʊ]	look [lʊk]	*fu*ll, *shou*ld, *woma*n
[u]	moon [mun]	*grou*p, *grew*, *move*, *true*, *rude*
[ʌ]	cut [kʌt]	*love*, *trou*ble, *floo*d
[ə]	above [əbʌv]	connect, acid, suppose
	ever [ɛvə]	actor, liar, murmur

(The latter examples as pronounced in the Eastern and Southern American dialects)

[ɝ]	bird [bɝd]	her, word, fur, heard

(General American pronunciation)

[ɜ]	bird [bɜd]	her, word, fur, heard

(Eastern and Southern American pronunciation)

[ɚ]	ever [ɛvɚ]	actor, liar, murmur

(General American pronunciation)

DIPHTHONGS

SYMBOL	KEY WORD	REPRESENTATIVE SPELLINGS
[aɪ]	ride [raɪd]	*lie*, *buy*, *dye*, *right*
[aʊ]	how [haʊ]	*flour*, *bough*
[ɔɪ]	voice [vɔɪs]	*boy*
[ju]	cute [kjut]	*union*, *few*, *view*, *beauty*
[eɪ]	gate [geɪt]	*break*, *they*, *hail*, *say*

(As sometimes transcribed. Refer to the discussion of the
vowel [e] in Chapter IX)

[ou]   *go* [gou]   *boat, soul, low, hoe, though*

(As sometimes transcribed. Refer to the discussion of the
vowel [o] in Chapter IX)

ː   Indicates prolongation of the vowel which it follows.

ˌ   When placed beneath [m̩], [n̩], or [l̩], indicates that
the consonant is used syllabically, i.e. to form a
syllable without an accompanying vowel.

ˈ   When placed above and to the left of a syllable indicates this syllable is to receive primary accent.

ˌ   Same symbol placed to the left and below the syllable indicates secondary accent.

[ʔ]   Symbol for the glottal stop.

VII

Developing Clearness and 'Correctness' of Speech

THUS far in this book Part I has dealt with the development of a pleasing and effective speaking *voice,* with little said about *speech* as such. Attention was directed to such aspects of the voice as pitch, loudness, quality, and general expressiveness. It is obvious that the total picture is as yet incomplete, for it is pretty futile to have a beautiful and charming voice if the hearer cannot understand what is being said or if peculiarities or 'mistakes' in pronunciation call attention to themselves and interfere with communication. Part II, therefore, will be devoted to the task of helping you learn to speak more clearly so that people can understand you more readily and of making you aware of any peculiarities or bad habits of pronunciation you may have in your speech.

DEVELOPING CLEARNESS OF SPEECH: ARTICULATION

You have often heard the request, 'What was that again; I didn't hear what you said.' What the person usually meant was, 'I *heard* you all right, but I didn't *understand* you.' As we know when we stop to think about it, communication involves the production of a set of symbols—words and phrases —that are sufficiently distinct as to be heard and recognized by the person to whom we are talking. These are in effect signals that are sent by the speaker and received and understood by the hearer.

These signals are composed of sound, or, more properly, sounds, that are distinguished by certain characteristics of pitch, quality, and energy distribution which give to each

245

speech sound or word a distinct individuality. That man is capable of producing and interpreting these signals according to a conventionalized pattern called language accounts for his ability to communicate orally—to talk. As we have partially seen from Part I, these sound patterns result from certain modifications in the resonance and articulatory mechanisms, and possibly in the breathing as well, involving in addition to the resonators already discussed, the articulatory organs consisting of the lips, teeth and jaws, tongue, palate, velum or soft palate, and, in the case of one sound, [h], the vocal folds themselves. These articulators supply the explosions and friction sounds characteristic of the consonants, while the vowels, as we have seen, are produced by the resonators. The two—vowels and consonants—put together, form syllables, words, and phrases that 'make sense' to a hearer—when he can understand them.

Clear-cut, easily understood speech, therefore, is the product of molding and shaping vowel tones with good quality and resonance and of pronouncing the consonants carefully. In general, clearness of articulation depends upon (1) the care and exactness with which the resonance and articulatory adjustments for the various speech sounds are made, and (2) the ease and precision with which the speech organs are changed from the position required for one sound to the position for the sound immediately following. Since speech is a moving, dynamic process, these adjustments must be made 'on the run,' as it were, and in the rapid shift from one sound to another we frequently fall far short of the mark and only roughly approximate the correct positions of the several articulatory organs, as well as the proper movements of those organs, in the pronunciation of successive speech sounds. The result too often is mumbling, indistinct speech that fails in its function of communication.

To correct this fault we must either move the lips, tongue, velum, and jaw more rapidly and precisely, or we must slow down the tempo of our speaking to a pace that will allow a more careful formation of the speech sounds and of the transition movements that connect them. Exercises may need to be undertaken to develop flexibility of the articulators and a relaxed, co-ordinated control over them. It is just as important for clear speech that we have good control over the speech organs as it is for the expert typist to have 'educated' fingers.

One of the first steps in the achievement of good speech has been taken when an individual becomes aware of good speech. One easily falls into a way of talking, which, though it may be careless or ineffective, appears perfectly satisfactory to him until in some way its shortcomings are brought to his attention. Even then it is not easy to change long-established speech habits because, for one thing, any departure from an accustomed style of speaking is likely to appear strange and unnatural to the speaker at first. The result is a degree of self-consciousness. The individual must recognize this feeling for what it is, however, and learn to discount it until the new method of speaking has become well established. For example, if a person is in the habit of speaking with a minimum of lip and jaw movement, he can expect at first to feel as if he were producing a series of facial contortions whenever he attempts to speak distinctly. He should comfort himself with the thoughts that the feeling will soon disappear and that what may appear to him as rank exaggeration may very well appear to others as perfectly normal speech.

The foregoing observations are based upon two assumptions regarding the speech of the average individual, for whom these remarks are intended: (1) The speech of the average individual would be improved if attention were given to overcoming the effects of carelessness and to eliminating certain mannerisms which may at times call adverse attention to themselves. (2) In this process of retraining, the average individual is not likely to go to the extreme of developing over-precise, artificial, pedantic articulation. This latter eventuality should not be wholly ignored, however. Reason and good judgment must never be cast aside, else one may acquire a type of unnatural, 'cultivated' speech which may be as objectionable in the one direction as carelessness is in the other. Speech must at all times be kept natural, easy, and unaffected.

FAULTS OF ARTICULATION

Although faulty articulation may take any number of forms, when it is carefully analyzed it will usually be found to result (1) from general sluggishness of the speech organs, producing mumbling, careless speech, or (2) from a rapid, jerky, broken rhythm of speaking in which only certain stressed syllables are pronounced with any degree of clearness, the unstressed sounds being badly muffled or omitted altogether. Of course, in addition to these types of general faults, there are more restricted defects confined to specific sounds, such as we find in lisping, or foreign dialect.

Why does the individual speak the way he does? What accounts for the presence of inadequate speech or speech that falls short of what it could be? Assuming that the mechanism itself is essentially normal in structure, one or more of the following causes will usually be found:

Imitation. Imitation is a powerful factor in the development of speech in the individual, and our speech patterns often reflect the influence of our parents and other members of our family, our teachers, our friends, and, of course, the general speech style of the community or area where we grew up. We are fortunate if the models to which we have been exposed were good ones. Too often some of them at least were not good, and it also appears to be true, unfortunately, that in too many instances the poor models seem to have exerted a greater influence on us than the good ones!

Habits of Carelessness and Indifference. It is true that good speech generally requires more effort and attention than poor speech. In speech, as in many other learned motor activities, the lazy way is hardly to be recommended. This deterioration is facilitated if the individual is unaware of how his speech sounds or how it affects others, or if he does not care. In all fairness, it must be said that habits of carelessness in speech can develop very easily, even though the individual may be making an honest effort to speak well.

Basic Personality Characteristics. There are many ways in which an individual's personality may have an effect on his speech. The generally slow-moving, phlegmatic person may exhibit some of those characteristics in his speech, resulting in a slow tempo and 'mushy,' poorly formed sounds and words, referred to as oral inactivity. Such people are inclined to be lip-lazy and tongue-lazy, and the final result in extreme cases is a sort of mumbling drawl. The opposite temperament also produces its special brand of speech pattern. The nervous, high-strung, hyperactive person is likely to talk fast and, if he is not able to negotiate the proper articulatory adjustments so rapidly, many sounds are dropped out or are distorted. Such a person tends to 'hit the high spots' only and his speech rhythm may be jerky and broken. Then, there is the shy, bashful person who is literally afraid to open his mouth. While it may be difficult or impossible to alter such basic personality traits as these, speech training can be aimed at compensating for the adverse personality factors. The phlegmatic individual must learn to speak more precisely, the high-strung person can learn to speak more slowly and carefully, and the timid individual can be encouraged to speak up with more emphasis and force.

Deficiencies of Hearing. It is a recognized fact that, under normal conditions, the ability to produce a certain speech sound is contingent upon the individual's ability to **hear** that sound, which implies more than merely being aware that some sort of sound is being produced. Hearing, so far as speech production is concerned, involves the ability to discriminate one sound from another—the ability to perceive the fine distinctions that make one particular speech sound different from all others. If the individual's hearing is deficient, it is likely that his speech will reflect this, for he will tend to speak as he hears speech, omitting or distorting those portions that he does not perceive clearly.

Undeveloped or Inferior Motor Skill. Individuals differ considerably at all age levels with respect to motor ability and the application of that ability to a specific learned activity. We do not expect all people to become experts at golfing, swimming, or typing, for example, but we are convinced that, even despite a lack of specific aptitude, almost anyone can improve through careful study and practice. It is not surprising that speech, which is basically a motor process, should behave in many respects like any other learned activity. It can be poorly learned, one can be clumsy at it, but with attention and effort one's skill can be materially improved.

When articulation lacks clearness and easy intelligibility, attention should be directed toward the following conditions, one or more of which may be contributing to the difficulty:

1. *Immobile, flaccid lips.* The lips are among the most important speech organs, not only in shaping the resonators of the mouth in the formation of the vowel sounds, but also in the production of the labial consonants, [p], [b], [m], [w], [f], and [v]. These sounds, as well as those vowels which depend in part upon lip rounding for their quality, chiefly [u], [ʊ], [o], and [ɔ], all suffer a serious loss of quality and distinctness when lip activity is deficient.

2. *Sluggish, inactive tongue.* The tongue is without doubt the most important single organ of articulation, since in normal speech a majority of the sounds including both vow-

els and consonants are in some manner dependent upon its functioning. Vowels will tend to lose their characteristic quality, and such consonants as [t], [d], [l], [r], and [s] will become blurred and indistinct if the tongue fails in its essential activity. The familiar 'mush-mouth' type of speech will be the result.

3. *Tight jaw.* A tight jaw interferes with the speech 'megaphone,' of which the mouth opening is a part, contributing to nasality and flatness of tone and seriously impairing the quality of all vowel sounds. No individual can talk between closed teeth and hope to have clear diction or a full, resonant voice.

4. *Inactive velum.** When the velum is allowed to hang in a passive, relaxed position, it fails in its function of closing off the nasal chambers from the throat and mouth. The result is a distinct nasalization of the vowels and all other oral sounds, while many of the consonants that depend for their production upon an accumulation of air pressure within the mouth, as for example [p], [t], and [s], may be emitted as faint puffs of air through the nose.

Exercises for Flexibility and Control of the Articulators

Despite the skepticism with which articulation drills and exercises have been viewed by some authorities, there are still worthwhile benefits for the student who pursues them conscientiously and applies them with understanding. Such exercises can:

1. Through a stimulation of the kinesthetic sense, make the individual aware of what it feels like to open his mouth, control his lips, and manipulate his tongue. As was mentioned previously, part of the explanation for poor articulation can be traced to a lack of awareness on the part of the

* See also the discussion of nasality and nasal resonance in Chapter IV.

speaker. He is not conscious of what his speech sounds like to others, and he is even less aware of what he is doing, or not doing, with his articulators when he talks. The visual sense can be brought into play very easily to supplement the kinesthetic if those exercises which are visible are practiced in front of a mirror.

2. Through a process of exaggeration of position and movement, help the individual overcome a feeling of strangeness and self-consciousness which might otherwise accompany an increase in articulatory activity during speech. Through practice the individual gets used to opening his mouth and moving his lips and tongue more vigorously, with the result that it is easier for him to incorporate a desirable amount of this activity into speech without feeling that his speech is exaggerated or unnatural.

3. Assist the individual in the production of specific speech sounds, words, and phrases through direct carry-over of those exercises that most closely resemble actual articulatory movements in speech. Achievement of this transfer will be in direct proportion to the individual's awareness of the purpose of the exercise and its ultimate application to speech production.

In practicing the following exercises,* keep the above-mentioned values in mind. Also take care that the rhythm of repetitive drills is smooth and even. Do not 'tie up'; keep muscular tension at a level consistent with easy, relaxed control. In many of the exercises it is well to begin more slowly, keeping the above points in mind, only gradually increasing the speed as better control is developed. Additional drill material can be chosen from later sections of the book where individual speech sounds are presented in more detail.

* For an explanation of the phonetic symbols used in some of the drills, consult the key to the phonetic alphabet included at the beginning of Part II.

EXERCISES FOR THE TONGUE

1. Try lapping like a cat; run the tongue in and out as rapidly as possible.

2. Extend the tongue as far as possible and try to touch the chin.

3. Try to touch the tip of your nose with the end of your tongue.

4. Extend the tongue and move it rapidly from side to side.

5. Explore the roof of the mouth with the tip of the tongue as far back as possible, beginning on the upper gum ridge. Can you touch your soft palate?

6. Repeat the nonsense word *tucka* [tʌkə] ten or fifteen times, as rapidly as possible.

7. Repeat Exercise 6, substituting the word *tucker* [tʌkɚ]. (General American.)

8. Repeat rapidly, but clearly, [li], [li], [li], etc.

9. Substitute [lɑ], [lɑ], [lɑ], etc.

10. Substitute [ti–li], [ti–li], [ti–li], etc.

11. Repeat Exercise 10, using [li–ri].

12. Repeat the word *giggle* rapidly seven or eight times.

13. Develop various rhythm patterns, using the syllable [lɑ]. A few are suggested below. The underlined syllables are to be stressed and prolonged slightly, the others are given a quick, light touch. No sounds should be lost; all must be clearly audible. La is sounded as [lɑ].

    a. la, la la, la la, la la, etc.
    b. la la la la la, la la la la la, etc.
    c. la la la la la la, la la la la la la, etc.

14. Repeat Exercise 13, using [tɑ], [dɑ], [kɑ], and [gɑ].

15. Repeat clearly the following sequences, at first slowly and then more rapidly, stressing each syllable equally:

    a. [lɑ–le–li–lɑ], [lɑ–le–li–lɑ], etc.
    b. [tɑ–te–ti–tɑ], [tɑ–te–ti–tɑ], etc.
    c. [kɑ–ke–ki–kɑ], [kɑ–ke–ki–kɑ], etc.

16. With an easy motion of the tongue repeat the following syllables, allowing no 'break' in the tone between them:

    a. ya [jɑ]–ya–ya–ya–ya–ya, etc.
    b. yaw [jɔ]–yaw–yaw–yaw–yaw, etc.
    c. yo [jo]–yo–yo–yo–yo–yo, etc.
    d. you [ju]–you–you–you–you, etc.

17. Practice the 'locomotive yell,' using only the tongue and keeping the jaw and lips motionless. Begin slowly, gradually increasing the tempo: rah, rah, rah, rah, rah, etc.

18. Pronounce carefully [θri], [θre], [θraɪ], [θro], [θru].

19. Pronounce the following sentences carefully, paying special attention to the action of the tongue:

    a. Truly rural.
    b. The rat ran over the roof of the house.
    c. Lovely lilies grew along the lake.
    d. Alone, alone, all, all alone.

EXERCISES FOR THE LIPS

1. Repeat rapidly: me [mi]–me–me–me–me–me, etc.

2. Substitute [wi], [maɪ], [mo], and [me] in the above exercise.

3. Pronounce the following rapidly and clearly:

    a. [i–u], [i–u], [i–u], [i–u], etc.
    b. [mi–me–maɪ–mo–mu]. Repeat several times.
    c. [wi–we–waɪ–wo–wu]. Repeat several times.

4. Repeat and exaggerate [i–ɑ–u]. Lips should be drawn back tightly for [i], mouth open for [ɑ], lips rounded for [u].

5. Exaggerate the lip movement in pronouncing the following exercises and sentences:

    a. [wi–wo–wi–wu]. Repeat several times.
    b. [pri–pre–praɪ–pro–pru]. Repeat several times.
    c. Peter Piper picked a peck of pickled peppers.
    d. We went away for a while.
    e. We will wait for Will.
    f. The wire was wound round the wheel.
    g. Bubble, bubble boiled the pot.

EXERCISES FOR THE JAW

1. Drop the jaw lazily and allow the mouth to fall open.

2. Move the relaxed jaw from side to side with the hand.

3. Move the jaw around in a circle.

4. Pronounce *ouch*. Open the mouth wide; repeat a number of times.

5. Repeat *ah–ger* [ɑgɚ] a number of times, opening the mouth wide on [ɑ] and stressing the first syllable.

6. Repeat Exercise 5, substituting [ɑwɑ], [ɑ – i], and [ɑ – u].

7. Repeat *gobble* [gɑbl̩] rapidly, opening the mouth wide on [ɑ].

8. Pronounce the following sentences, exaggerating the mouth opening for all of the stressed vowels:

    a. Humpty Dumpty sat on a wall.
    b. The wagon wobbled wildly.
    c. Around the rough and rugged rock the ragged rascal ran.

'Correctness' of Speech: Pronunciation

There are two chief aspects of pronunciation: (1) placing the accent or stress on the proper syllable within the word—that is, whether one says 'DE tail' ['ditel] or 'de TAIL' [dɪ'tel] for *detail*—and (2) choosing the particular vowel or consonant that is to be used in a given instance. For example, the word *data* may be heard as 'DAY ta' [detə], 'DA ta' [dætə], or even 'DAH ta' [dɑtə], depending on which vowel the speaker chooses to use in the first syllable. Similarly, although *garage* is more properly pronounced as 'ga razh' [gəraʒ], one also hears 'ga raj' [gəradʒ], the pronunciation being determined by the choice of consonant used in the final syllable.

The question immediately arises, 'Well, what should it be —['ditel] or [dɪ'tel], [detə] or [dætə], [gəraʒ] or [gəradʒ]?' Which is 'correct'? Since this question is not nearly as simple as it sounds, the answer is not always easy to determine. The seemingly obvious admonition to 'look it up in the dictionary' is not always the final answer to the problem for a number of reasons, some of which are discussed in more detail in Chapter X, where problems and standards of pronunciation are dealt with at greater length than in the present brief discussion. There is little question that a good dictionary does provide a valuable guide to general preferences in pronunciation, and it is also true that the average individual could make more frequent and profitable use of it than he does.

In using the dictionary, the student should keep the following suggestions in mind:

1. Choose a dictionary of recent date and of a size no smaller than the popular 'college' or 'collegiate' editions. Generally, the more complete the edition, the better.

2. Learn to interpret the symbols used by your dictionary as a guide to pronunciation. Unfortunately, there is not uni-

form agreement among dictionary makers at present regarding the symbols used to indicate how a word is to be pronounced. Each dictionary, however, does include a full explanation of its own system in a section of the introductory material under some such heading as 'Key' or 'Guide' to pronunciation. Generally a combination of respelling and diacritical marks is used to indicate the phonetic values of letters, with the addition of a phonetic symbol or two in one instance. Only one English dictionary published thus far in this country uses phonetic symbols exclusively.*

3. Keep in mind the limitations of a dictionary as a determiner of 'correct' pronunciation. The chief limitations, as well as some of the broader considerations to be kept in mind when deciding what is 'correct' or 'proper,' are discussed in Chapter X.

In addition to dictionaries there are a number of handbooks of pronunciation and textbooks on phonetics, some of which are included in the Bibliography at the end of this book, which contain valuable information and supply answers to many knotty problems relating to usage and standards of pronunciation.

In general, the individual should be governed by a principle which applies to other aspects of voice and speech as well, namely, that the best speech is that which does not call specific attention to itself for what it is. In line with this point of view, a concept of regional or area standards of pronunciation has grown up and is meeting with increasing acceptance over the country as a whole. According to this concept, speech, including pronunciation, which is 'proper,' 'correct,' or recommended for Boston or New York, for example, may not be recommended for Chicago, San Francisco, or Charleston. This principle recognizes that people do not talk or pronounce the same way in all sections of the country

* Kenyon, John S., and Knott, Thomas A., *A Pronouncing Dictionary of American English,* G. and C. Merriam Company, Springfield, Mass., 1944.

and perhaps may not have to in order to be 'correct' for the area in which they live.

Regional standards may not always be easy to determine in certain instances, however. In these cases the best guide is what appears to be the accepted speech of the particular area—the speech most often heard and considered 'correct' by the leaders of the community, the individuals most influential because of cultural or educational background or who have risen to positions of leadership because of other qualifications. It must be recognized that at best this is only a general guide and much must be left to the good taste, judgment, and discrimination of the individual.

In connection with the problems related to pronunciation, it is indeed unfortunate that the spelling of a word offers so little indication of how that word will, or should, sound when spoken aloud. One of the first concepts, therefore, that the individual must grasp if he is to be successful in improving his pronunciation, or articulation, involves the distinction between a speech sound and a letter of the alphabet; the two are often quite different. While written language is recorded in alphabet symbols which we call letters, spoken language consists of words made up of combinations of phonetic units, or speech sounds, more exactly labeled phonemes. If the spelling of modern English were phonetic, as it was during the early period of its development, there would be a close correspondence between letters and sounds, each letter representing only one sound and always the same sound. If this were the situation, we could tell by looking at a word how to pronounce it.

A few examples will demonstrate how far modern English spelling has departed from the actual sounds it is supposed to represent. The written word *ought* consists of five letters, but the spoken word has only two sounds—the vowel sound as in *ball* and a *t* [ɔt]. Moreover, the same spelling, *ough,* produces six different sounds and combinations of sounds in *through* [θru], *though* [ðo], *trough* [trɔf], *bought* [bɔt], *bough* [baʊ], and *enough* [ɪnʌf]. On the other hand, the sound *ee* [i] is spelled in nine different ways in the words *feet, feat, be, people, receive, key, believe, quay,* and *machine.* Consider the different ways in which the letter *a* is pronounced in *man* [mæn], *say* [se], *barn* [bɑrn], *hall* [hɔl], *human* [hjumən], and *any* [ɛnɪ]. It is thus futile and misleading to talk about the *a* sound, for example, unless some key word is used to identify it, for if it is the *a* sound in *ball* that is referred to, it isn't *a* [e] at all, but rather *aw* [ɔ].

One of the reasons for such confusion becomes plain when we realize that we have some 45 sounds in English speech but only 26 letters with which to represent them. Furthermore, of these 26 letters, three—*q, c,* and *x*—are useless, since they always duplicate sounds also represented by other letters; for example, *q* is usually *kw,* as in *quick* [kwɪk]. The vowels present a particularly knotty problem, since we have only six letters, including *y,* with which to represent some 17 identifiable vowel sounds in American speech.

It can be seen immediately that at least an elementary knowledge of phonetics—a study of the sounds of a spoken language—is a most valuable asset to the individual attempting to improve his speech. The most important tool of phonetics is the phonetic alphabet, in which one symbol is used to represent one sound that is always the same. The phonetic alphabet is the easiest and surest method of recording speech as it is actually spoken, and heard, as well as the most effective means of becoming conscious of speech sounds as separate and distinct entities. For these reasons it is employed in this book whenever it becomes necessary to talk about speech sounds—articulation and pronunciation.

A simplified form of the phonetic alphabet, as used in this book, has been included at the beginning of Part II. In addition to the phonetic symbols and key words illustrating the use of each sound, additional words illustrating several other spellings for the same sound have been added. As we have already noticed, some of the sounds are regularly spelled in as many as eight or ten different ways, but only the most representative examples are included in this list.

It is urged that the student study the phonetic alphabet and gain sufficient familiarity with it to enable him not only to interpret the symbols used in this book to illustrate speech sounds, but also to record, with some degree of accuracy, spoken language as he hears it, both his own and that of others. This valuable ear training is a necessary and important prelude to speech training. Exercises to facilitate acquaintance with the phonetic symbols and to promote ear training are included later in this chapter.

VOWELS AND CONSONANTS

All speech sounds can be classified roughly as either vowels or consonants, depending upon their acoustic characteristics as determined by the manner in which they are formed in the mouth. Vowels are defined as sonorous speech sounds produced by relatively open and unobstructed throat and mouth passageways. As has been explained, they are resonance phenomena, resulting from changes in the shape and size of the various resonance chambers. Consonants, as a class, are made up of less sonority and more noise elements than vowels—the result of a greater degree of obstruction imposed upon the outgoing tone, or, as in the case of the voiceless consonants, upon merely the unvocalized breath. To illustrate, compare the open passageway and the degree of sonority, or tone, in the vowel [ɑ], with that found in the consonant [v]. In the vowel the 'vocal megaphone' is relatively open, while in the consonant considerable resistance is offered to the outgoing tone as it is forced through the restricted passageway formed, in this case, between the lower lip and the upper teeth.

It is obvious that these are relative conditions, however,

and therefore there is no sharp dividing line between these two classifications of speech sounds, as far as their physical properties are concerned. That is, some of the consonants, such as [m], [l], and [r], resemble vowels in that they are produced through a relatively open passageway and hence have almost as much sonority and freedom from noise elements as certain of the more obstructed vowels, as for example, [i]. Some of the weakest consonants, on the other hand, from the point of view of phonetic power are [θ], [f], [p], [t] and [k].

The point to be noted here is simply that the vowels give quality and carrying power to the voice, while the consonants are chiefly responsible for clearness of articulation. Therefore, the vowels should be formed carefully with due regard to their quality, and the consonants should be sounded clearly. Neither one should be emphasized at the expense of the other, although those consonants that are particularly weak are in danger of being lost from one's speech unless special care is taken to articulate them clearly.

Ear training becomes of supreme importance in the production of vowels of good quality, since in their formation the shape and position of the speech organs are much less fixed and invariable than in the case of the consonants. To cite an example, the typical position of the tongue in relation to the teeth in the formation of the consonant [θ] is relatively definite and hence describable and demonstrable; but it is much more difficult to determine with accuracy the position of the articulatory mechanism in the production of the vowel [ɔ]. Furthermore, it has been demonstrated that the adjustment for any given vowel is inclined to vary from individual to individual and it may even be different at different times for the same individual.

Vowels depend for their identity upon duration of tone and upon certain pitch and resonance characteristics as determined by adjustments of the mouth and throat cavities.

There appear to be a number of other factors involved as well, some of which are obscure and not clearly understood at present. The consonants, on the other hand, are produced by the contact, or near-contact, of the various articulatory organs, a process that can be observed and studied with some degree of accuracy. For these reasons we must form a clear auditory image of what the vowel tones sound like and we must learn to identify that sound and reproduce it accurately; but in the case of the consonants some study of the manner of their formation should help us to analyze and correct many of our most noticeable faults of speech. All of the speech sounds will be discussed in detail in succeeding chapters, and attention will be called to the chief problems involved in their production and use.

Exercises for Ear Training and Use of the Phonetic Alphabet

Your first step toward improvement of your speech will have been taken when you have become aware of how speech actually sounds, both your own and that of others. We have been using speech unconsciously for so long that we no longer really listen to it unless we are learning a foreign language, preparing for a dialect part in a play, or in some other way we are taught how to listen and what to listen for.

Partly for reasons which have already been discussed, there are many differences between what a word looks like when we see it written or printed and what it sounds like when it is put into the actual stream of speech. Since we are so used to dealing with written or printed language symbols and thinking in terms of letters, we need to keep reminding ourselves that we must concentrate on what a word actually sounds like, not what it looks like or what we think it should sound like. Thus, the simple statement, 'I see the cat,' *looks* merely like four separate words put together—[aɪ si ði kæt]—

which is the way a second-grader might read it. We know
that is not the way it really sounds in normal speech, which
is more like [aɪ si ðə kæt]. In this example the expressional
pattern of the thought-unit has materially altered the pronunciation of one of the words. These differences we must
learn to detect, and the phonetic alphabet teaches us to listen
for them and makes it possible to record them graphically.

Your first step is to become sufficiently familiar with phonetic symbols so that you will come to think in terms of
speech sounds, rather than written alphabet letters. Remember that the two are often deceptively different. For example,
although the word *suns* ends with the letter *s,* in speech this
final sound is actually a *z*—[sʌnz]. Try it aloud; do you hear
it? The same is true of *his* [hɪz] and *is* [ɪz]. Try these aloud
too and you will hear the [z] at the end. However, *this,* which
looks similar to *his,* does actually end with [s]. Compare the
two and you will see. The words *ripped* and *rigged* both end
with the letter *d,* but it is obvious that the final sound is not
the same when they are pronounced. Try it.

Likewise we need to become aware of what we know when
we stop to think about it—that there is no [k] in *knot* [nɑt],
no [g] in *sing* [sɪŋ], no [p] in *diphthong* [dɪfθɔŋ], no [t] or [h]
in *then* [ðɛn], and, of course, no [b] in *thumb* [θʌm]. We
need to remember also that *bought,* which has six letters,
has only three sounds—[bɔt]—and that the *eigh* in *height,* the
ie in *lie,* the *ye* in *lye,* the *y* in *by,* and the *uy* in *buy* all
spell the same sound—the diphthong [aɪ]. Furthermore, we
do not pronounce two *s's* in *miss* or two *t's* in *bottle* simply
because they happen to be spelled that way.

1. Study carefully the examples included below. Look at the
printed word, pronounce it carefully aloud to see whether
you can hear each of the sounds in it. Then compare what
you hear with the phonetic transcription of that word. Do
you see the correspondence between the sound and the sym-

bol in each case? Compare with the key to the phonetic alphabet included at the beginning of Part II.

heat	[hit]	true	[tru]
long	[lɔŋ]	should	[ʃʊd]
think	[θɪŋk]	beauty	[bjutɪ]
around	[əraʊnd]	measure	[mɛʒɚ]
where	[hwɛr]	call	[kɔl]
city	[sɪtɪ]	jump	[dʒʌmp]
heard	[hɝd]	are	[ɑr]
Salem	[seləm]	quote	[kwot]
fleece	[flis]	mother	[mʌðɚ]
she	[ʃi]	honor	[ɑnɚ]
house	[haʊs]	freshman	[frɛʃmən]
they	[ðe]	advertise	['ædvɚ,taɪz]
chimes	[tʃaɪmz]	university	[junəvɝsətɪ]
can't	[kænt]		

2. Transcribe the following simple words, using phonetic symbols.* Refer freely to the key included earlier, as well as to the examples just given. Pronounce each word aloud several times slowly and carefully, although you must avoid distorting any of the sounds in doing so. Listen for the sounds and put down each one as you hear it. Ignore the conventional spelling.

hill	school	money	books
get	bag	piece	calm
stop	salt	rug	agree
lazy	point	around	right
booth	these	vista	better
nurse	wish	yarn	chest
white	June	long	dance

* To facilitate the writing of phonetic symbols, the script form differs slightly from the printed form in the case of a few of the symbols. Although it would be quite acceptable in these assignments to follow the printed form as closely as possible, for information on the script symbols consult one of

3. Most of the words in Exercise 2 were made up of single syllables. Incidentally, can you pick out those with more than one syllable? The words in the following list contain two or more syllables. You may find these more difficult to analyze for their component sounds because the problem of stress or accent is involved in the pronunciation of most polysyllabic words, and a change of stress may produce a change of sound. Proceed as you did above, listening carefully as you pronounce the word aloud, trying to catch each separate sound. Try to pronounce the word naturally in relation to individual sounds, even though you put it into 'slow motion' to make analysis easier. Remember that every *unstressed* vowel that sounds like a short, weak form of the vowel in *up* [ʌp] is transcribed as [ə], regardless of how it is spelled. The weak form of [ɝ] as in the final syllable of *better* [bɛtɚ] is transcribed as [ɚ] if your pronunciation pattern conforms to General American, [ə] if your speech is Eastern or Southern American, in which case the word would be [bɛtə]. Do you hear the difference?

suppose	supper	football	autocrat
gasoline	isolate	special	feature
meadow	evoke	dictate	dogmatic
enough	phonetics	friendly	surpass
further	kingdom	qualify	occasion
frequently	similar	actor	cabbage

4. Now, let us try some phrases and simple sentences similar to the following examples: *around the block* [əraʊnd ðə blak], *out of luck* [aʊt əv lʌk], *from time to time* [frəm taɪm tə taɪm], *around and around* [əraʊnd ənd əraʊnd], *The boy went to see a circus* [ðə bɔɪ wɛnt tə si ə sɝkəs]. You will note that the weak, unstressed [ə] occurs very frequently in these

the phonetics workbooks listed in the Bibliography, such as *An Introduction to General American Phonetics* by Van Riper and Smith or *The Phonetic Alphabet* by Cartier.

examples. It is likely to appear in many of the unstressed syllables of polysyllabic words and in unstressed words within phrases and sentences. Thus, connectives, auxiliary verb forms, and prepositions, such as *the, from, of, an, and, have, but,* and *was,* are very likely to take this weak vowel [ə] as these words appear in the natural flow of speech. This unstressed vowel and related sounds will be discussed in more detail in later sections; do not be too concerned about it now. Just listen for the individual sounds as you hear them spoken naturally in the following examples:

> a. bread and butter   sink or swim
>   down the street   from here and there
>   for better or for worse   on top of the world

> b. The boy stood on the burning deck
> c. Birds of a feather flock together
> d. He was trying to catch a fish
> e. This is the house that Jack built
> f. What was that you brought from the store?

> g. Mary had a little lamb,
>   Its fleece was white as snow.
>   And everywhere that Mary went,
>   The lamb was sure to go.

> h. Twinkle, twinkle, little star,
>   How I wonder what you are;
>   Up, above the world so high,
>   Like a diamond in the sky.

5. [nɑu lɛt ʌs traɪ sʌmθɪŋ ə lɪtḷ mor dɪfəkʌlt]. Can you 'translate' this sentence? Take a look at the list of words below. Following each word in phonetic transcription are several different pronunciations which you doubtless have heard, some common ones and some not so common. Pronounce each example, 'translating' the phonetic symbols as faithfully

as you can. Which one is the pronunciation you commonly
use? Which one does the dictionary recommend?

Harry	[hærɪ]	[hɛrɪ]	
poor	[pʊr]	[por]	
hurry	[hɜ˞ɪ]	[hʌrɪ]	
data	[detə]	[dætə]	[dɑtə]
ration	[ræʃən]	[reʃən]	
Mary	[mɛrɪ]	[merɪ]	
ask	[æsk]	[ask]	[ɑsk]
fellow	[fɛlo]	[fɛlə]	[fɛlə˞]
fog	[fɑg]	[fɔg]	[fɒg]
door	[dor]	[dɔr]	
stomach	[stʌmək]	[stʌmɪk]	
finance	[fɪ'næns]	['faɪnæns]	
new	[nju]	[nu]	
because	[bɪkɔz]	[bɪkʌz]	
debate	[dɪbet]	[dəbet]	
when	[hwɛn]	[wɛn]	
house	[haʊs]	[haʊs]	[hæʊs]
issue	[ɪʃʊ]	[ɪsju]	
luxury	[lʌkʃərɪ]	[lʌgʒərɪ]	
adult	[ə'dʌlt]	['ædʌlt]	
room	[rum]	[rʊm]	
soot	[sʊt]	[sut]	[sʌt]
huge	[hjudʒ]	[judʒ]	

VIII

The Articulation of Consonants

VARIOUS classifications of consonant sounds have been devised, based on their acoustic characteristics as well as on the manner of their articulation. One of the simplest classifications divides consonants into the two groups, voiced and voiceless. That is, for each separate adjustment of the articulators we have in many instances not just one sound but two, one being produced merely by forcing the breath out through the constricted passageway of the mouth, as in the case of [s], the other being formed by emitting the *vocalized* breath in the same manner, as in the production of [z]. Therefore, [z] theoretically is merely [s] with a voice element added to it.

To demonstrate this relationship, begin the sound of [s], holding it for a few seconds, thus [s-s-s-s]. Then without interrupting the steady flow of the breath stream, start the vocal folds vibrating and thus change the [s] into [z], which will result in [s-s-s-z-z-z]. In a similar manner compare [f] with [v], and [ʃ] with [ʒ]. Place your finger on your larynx during this experiment and note the absence of any vibration during the production of voiceless consonants, but observe how clearly the vibrations can be felt when any voiced consonant is sounded. Refer to the table of phonetic symbols at the beginning of Part II and observe how the consonants can be divided on the basis of the presence or absence of voice. The voiceless member of each pair is given first, followed by its voiced analogue. Note that not all of the consonants can be paired thus.

With respect to the manner in which consonants are

268

formed in the mouth as well as their resulting acoustic characteristics, they can be further classified into four groups: (1) Plosives, (2) Fricatives, (3) Nasals, and (4) Glides. The *plosives,* so named because their formation involves a release or explosion of impounded breath, include the sounds [p] and [b], [t] and [d], [k] and [g], and [tʃ] and [dʒ]. These latter two are sometimes also referred to as affricates, because each one is a combination of a plosive and a fricative, as we shall see in a later section. The *fricatives,* so named because the manner of their production results in a friction-like noise, comprise the sounds [f] and [v], [θ] and [ð], [s] and [z], [ʃ] and [ʒ], and [h]. There are only three *nasal* sounds, [m], [n], and [ŋ]. The four sounds known as *glides,* [l], [r], [w], and [j], are the result of a movement or a gliding of either the tongue or the lips or both during the production of the sound.

A third type of classification is based upon the place of articulation as determined by the organs which happen to be involved. In each case the name designates the point of contact or the point of obstruction in the mouth. Following is a table listing the consonants according to such a classification:

1. Bilabial *   [p], [b], [m], [w]
2. Labio-dental   [f], [v]
3. Lingua-dental   [θ], [ð]
4. Lingua-alveolar   [t], [d], [n], [l], [s], [z]
5. Lingua-palatal   [ʃ], [ʒ], [r], [j]
6. Lingua-velar   [k], [g], [ŋ]
7. Glottal   [h]

The student must not allow himself to become confused by these different classifications. When he considers the basis

---

* There is no need to be confused by what may sound like strange terms. 'Labial' and 'labio' refer to the lips, 'dental,' of course, to the teeth, 'lingua' to the tongue, 'alveolar' the gum ridge, 'palatal' the palate, 'velar' the velum or soft palate, and 'glottal,' of course, the glottis.

upon which each one rests, he will see that instead of constituting mutually exclusive groups, the classifications refer
simply to important identifying characteristics by means of
which certain sounds can be differentiated from others. In
this way the terms serve as an aid in studying and identifying individual sounds. For example, when it is stated that
[p] is a voiceless, bilabial plosive, one has gone a long way
toward describing not only the nature of the sound but also
the manner and place of its formation in the mouth.

The following chart lists all of the consonant sounds in
their proper relationship to the three methods of classification explained in the preceding paragraphs:

	Bilabial	Labio-dental	Lingua-dental	Lingua-alveolar	Lingua-palatal	Lingua-velar	Glottal
Plosives	p b			t d		k g	ʔ
Fricatives		f v	θ ð	s z	ʃ ʒ		h
Nasals	m			n		ŋ	
Glides	w			l	r j		

FIG. 17. Classification of the consonant sounds upon the basis of (1)
manner of formation and acoustic characteristics (left-hand column),
(2) place of articulation (across the top), and (3) presence or absence
of voicing (sounds listed at the left of each column are voiceless; those
on the right are voiced).

THE PLOSIVES

Clearness and precision in the articulation of the plosive
consonants depend upon (1) the firmness of the closure in
the mouth, (2) sufficient breath pressure, and (3) a quick,
clean-cut release of the impounded air. In English speech all
of the voiceless plosives, when they occur initially, are defi-

nitely aspirated. That is, there is a noticeable puff or explosion of air when the sound is released. Some degree of aspiration is given these sounds under certain other conditions also, the actual amount depending upon the position and use of the sound within the word. A marked aspiration in the form of a puff of air can easily be felt if the hand is held close to the lips while the word *top* is pronounced, as an example. While this aspiration is an integral part of our speech pattern, it should never be allowed to become objectionable or to become so extreme that it calls adverse attention to itself. This is not only wasteful of breath, but, as was pointed out in a previous chapter, such a practice may easily affect the quality of the following vowel, producing breathiness.

THE CONSONANTS [p] AS IN [pɪg] *pig* AND [b] AS IN [bɪg] *big*

These two bilabial plosives are formed by bringing the lips together, building up pressure in the mouth, and suddenly releasing it. The mechanics are similar for the two sounds except that the vocal folds are in vibration for [b]—it is a voiced sound—while [p] results merely from the escape of unvocalized breath. [p] is aspirated and is ordinarily more vigorously exploded than [b]. Hold your hand close to your lips as you pronounce the word *pay;* compare this with *bay* and you will notice a considerable reduction in the puff of air that escapes following the initial sound. Both [p] and [b] are often combined with other consonants to form blends, as we find in such words as *please, pride, speech, spring, split, blow,* and *brown.*

[p] and [b] are not considered difficult sounds and ordinarily cause little trouble. Any condition that interferes with a good contact between the two lips, however, will contribute to a distortion of the sounds, probably the most common cause being poor speech habits in the form of immobile or

flaccid lip action. Structural irregularities of the jaw or lips can also interfere with the production of good bilabials, the most common of which is a receding lower jaw, protruding upper teeth, or both. An unusually short or inactive upper lip can also contribute to poor articulation of the labial plosives. In such cases of structural irregularities there is a tendency for the lower lip to make contact with the upper teeth instead of the upper lip, resulting in a sound resembling [f] or [v]. In the speech of such an individual, *berry* sounds like 'very,' *robe* like 'rove,' *pay* like 'fay,' and *pail* like 'fail.'

Unless the structural deviation is extreme, a perfectly acceptable [p] and [b] can usually be achieved through practice and attention directed to the problem. And, of course, the effects of carelessness and indifference should be studiously guarded against here, as in all speech production. In the exercises which follow, work for a light, but precise, closure of the two lips during the first phase of these two sounds, and a quick, simultaneous release for the plosive phase. Be sure that [p] and [b] are clearly differentiated in the following words:

INITIAL		MEDIAL		FINAL	
pig	big	rapid	rabid	rope	robe
pen	Ben	ripping	ribbing	cap	cab
peach	beach	ample	amble	nap	nab
pun	bun	maple	Mabel	pup	pub
park	bark	Harper	harbor	tripe	tribe
push	bush	loppy	lobby	rip	rib

BLENDS WITH [l]		BLENDS WITH [r]	
plot	blot	pride	bride
plead	bleed	prick	brick
plume	bloom	preach	breach
plank	blank	prim	brim
plaque	black	price	Bryce

1. Her pupils brought her a basket of apples and pears.
2. Barbara's favorite book is *Pride and Prejudice*.
3. The boys played ping pong an hour before supper.
4. The bear and her cubs ambled off among the bushes.
5. Private Baxter hurt his elbow and broke a rib.
6. Everywhere they observed the bright broom blossoms.
7. A blinding blizzard blew over the brown prairies.
8. This roundabout business was like robbing Peter to pay Paul.
9. Painting is silent poetry, and poetry is a speaking picture.
10. A compliment is usually accompanied with a bow as if to beg pardon for paying it.

11. A public speaker is a person who will sit up all night writing a speech that will put an audience to sleep the next day.

12. Oscar Wilde, after attending a first performance of a play which was a complete failure, was greeted by his friends. 'How did your play go last night, Oscar?' asked one. 'Oh,' replied the playwright, 'the play was a great success, but the audience was a failure.'

13. Perverseness is one of the primitive impulses of the human heart—one of the indivisible, primary faculties of sentiments which give direction to man.

14. Sensual pleasures are like soap bubbles, sparkling, evanescent. The pleasures of intellect are calm, beautiful, sublime, ever-enduring and climbing upward to the borders of the unseen world.

15. Little black beetle said one day,
    'Little bug, you're in my way!
    Little bug, don't bother me,
    I'm a big bug, don't you see?'
    Little bug said, 'I can do
    Quite as many things as you!'

16. Over the ripening peach
    Buzzes the bee,
    Splash on the billowy beach
    Tumbles the sea.

But the peach
And the beach
They are each
Nothing to me,

THE CONSONANTS [t] AS IN [tim] *team* AND [d] AS IN [dim] *deem*

These two sounds are known as post-dentals, or lingua-alveolar plosives. In their production the tip of the tongue makes contact with the gum ridge just above the upper teeth in front. There is the same difference in voicing and in aspiration between [t] and [d] as was explained in the previous section between [p] and [b]. As in the case of [p], one should avoid an exaggerated, too-noisy aspiration of breath in sounding [t]. On the other hand, omission or excessive diminution of the aspiration will make [t] resemble [d], and the speech will sound 'foreign.'

One of the most common faults associated with these sounds is that of allowing the tongue-tip to fall so low that it rests against the teeth instead of the upper gum ridge. A [t] or [d] made with the tongue in this position, known as a dentalized [t] or [d], has a quality suggesting the sound of [θ] or [ð], with the result that *tide,* for example, tends to sound like [tθɑɪd], and *dime* resembles [dðɑɪm]. This fault is often associated with lisping, a speech defect which also results from the practice of keeping the front of the tongue too low in the mouth.

In careless speech [t] and [d] are often elided, or 'swallowed,' when found in the medial position. They may simply be omitted with no other sound added or the glottal stop may be substituted for them. Thus, in the speech of some individuals the word *little* sounds like [lɪl] or it may be pronounced [lɪʔl̩] The word *kitten* may become [kɪʔn̩] and *saddle* may resemble [sæʔl̩] or [sæəl].

One of the most difficult combinations of sounds to articulate occurs when [t] is both preceded and followed by [s], as in the word *tests*. In the speech of many persons the [t] is elided and *tests* becomes 'tess.' If this fault is to be corrected, the sequence of sounds must be broken down into its several steps, which should be studied and practiced more or less separately. As an example, the pronunciation of *tests* will be greatly facilitated if one thinks of the word as being pronounced [tes], the [s] being held, or rather suspended, for an instant, and the [ts], a sound resembling the German *z*, added as the final step.

A more exact explanation is that the *sts* of such combinations is in reality just one prolonged [s], interrupted by the plosive [t]. After the tongue has moved from the [s] position to make tight contact with the gum ridge so that pressure can be built up for the [t], the breath stream is stopped. The result is that the first [s] becomes suspended momentarily. Then the [t] is released very suddenly into the final [s], as it were, and the two sounds merge into a closely integrated unit.

This articulatory sequence produces the effect of a transition or slight break between the first *s* and the *t*, so that the word which we have used as an example appears to be pronounced *tes-ts*, though the break, as has been explained, is not complete, but only apparent. There should be no lapse of breath pressure at any time. The same is true of all of the *sts* words. To gain facility in the articulation of these words, practice the following carefully:

> insis–ts (not *insiss*)
> wris–ts (not *wriss*)
> crus–ts (not *cruss*)
> lis–ts (not *liss*)
> mas–ts (not *mass*)
> boos–ts (not *booss*)

When [t] and [d] occur at the ends of words, they are in constant danger of being dropped out in the speech of the careless. This fact accounts for the so often heard *kep* for *kept, tole* for *told,* and *pass* for *past.* Final *t*'s and *d*'s should be sounded, though not stressed.

In accordance with a principle of connected speech which we shall discuss in a later chapter under *assimilation,* there is some tendency for [t] to be pronounced as [d] when it occurs between two vowels or other voiced sounds. Thus, *little* is often 'liddle,' *notice* becomes 'nodice,' and *Saturday* may be pronounced as 'Saderday.' This practice should be carefully avoided.

It might be well to call attention in passing to the fact that when *ed* forms the past tense of verbs, it is sounded as [d] after voiced sounds, but it is pronounced as [t] following voiceless sounds. Thus, *ripped* becomes [rɪpt], but *ribbed* is pronounced [rɪbd]. Similarly, we have *banked* [bæŋkt] and *banged* [bæŋd], *tossed* [tɒst] and *teased* [tizd], *roughed* [rʌft] and *loved* [lʌvd]. Care should be taken that the *d* does not become unvoiced when it should remain [d]. When the *ed* ending is preceded by either [t] or [d] it is pronounced as a separate syllable and the *d* remains [d], as in *wanted* [wɒntəd].

In the following exercises distinguish between the voiceless [t] and the voiced [d] and observe carefully the placement of the tongue-tip on the gum ridge just back of the upper teeth.

INITIAL		MEDIAL		FINAL	
team	deem	writing	riding	moot	mood
tin	din	latter	ladder	grit	grid
toes	doze	metal	medal	cot	cod
tub	dub	waiter	wader	coat	code
town	down	Sutton	sudden	seat	seed
tune	dune	bleating	bleeding	bet	bed

BLENDS WITH [r]		MISCELLANEOUS BLENDS		
try	dry	stripe	dream	string
trip	drip	twist	dwarf	drank
train	drain	stop	robbed	twice
trunk	drunk	slept	tugged	Dwight
true	drew	talked	loved	felt
troll	droll	test	teased	felled

1. Tom had wanted to buy a tan coat.
2. Dan put the ladder back in the shed.
3. Timothy walked into his room and packed his trunk for the trip.
4. Can you touch your teeth with the tip of your tongue?
5. Donald's party bagged two deer on their recent hunting trip.
6. Dorothy tried to teach Tom to dance the tango.
7. Ten trains went over the trestle each day.
8. The road led past the dark wood and on down into the little town.
9. Thomas counted out the money in ten and twenty dollar bills.
10. Dwight tried to hold the bottle steady while he poured out two drops of the medicine.

11. Tomorrow, and tomorrow, and tomorrow,
    Creeps in this petty pace from day to day,
    To the last syllable of recorded time;
    And all our yesterdays have lighted fools
    The way to dusty death.

SHAKESPEARE, Macbeth, v. v

12. Amidst the mists and coldest frosts,
    With barest wrists and stoutest boasts,
    He thrusts his fists against the posts
    And still insists he sees the ghosts.

13. A philosopher once uttered a prayer: 'Deliver us from the deadly danger of denying to those who disagree with us the propensities of rightness and reasonableness that we so easily appropriate to ourselves.'

14. There is the same difference between the tongues of some, as between the hour and the minute hand; one goes ten times as fast, and the other signifies ten times as much.

15. There is a tide in the affairs of men,
Which, taken at the flood, leads on to fortune.

16. The devil was sick, the devil a saint would be;
The devil was well, the devil a saint was he.

17. It is as easy to deceive one's self without perceiving it as it is difficult to deceive others without their finding it out.

18. Night's candles are burnt out, and jocund day
Stands tiptoe on the misty mountain-tops.

19. A tutor who tooted the flute
Tried to tutor two tooters to toot;
Said the two to the tutor,
'Is it easier to toot or
To tutor two tooters to toot?'

20. A man of words and not of deeds,
Is like a garden full of weeds;
For when the weeds begin to grow,
Then doth the garden overflow.

21. A daughter of the gods, divinely tall,
And most divinely fair.

THE CONSONANTS [k] AS IN [kot] *coat* AND [g] AS IN [got] *goat*

These sounds are called lingua-velar plosives, since the point of contact occurs between the back of the tongue and the soft palate or velum. [g] is voiced and [k] is the voiceless, aspirated sound, although the explosive release of air is less noticeable here than in the case of [p] and [t]. No special difficulties are ordinarily encountered in the production of [k] and [g], although there is some danger of a slight distortion of the sounds if the explosive release is allowed to become sluggish. These two sounds should be kept light and clear. Too much breath pressure may result in a heavy, guttural quality.

Practice the following exercises, pronouncing the words naturally, but striving for a clear, easily heard [k] and [g]:

INITIAL		MEDIAL		FINAL	
Kate	gate	ankle	angle	buck	bug
cot	got	backing	bagging	cock	cog
come	gum	Becker	beggar	lack	lag
cap	gap	bicker	bigger	pick	pig
could	good	broken	brogan	Beck	beg
curl	girl	anchor	anger	snack	snag

BLENDS WITH [r]		BLENDS WITH [l]	
crime	grime	clue	glue
creed	greed	clad	glad
crow	grow	Clyde	glide
crab	grab	clean	glean
crew	grew	class	glass
craft	graft	clamor	glamor

1. The dog began to growl when he caught sight of the cat.
2. Can you count how many ducks are out in the garden?
3. On coronation day the king was crowned in the cathedral.
4. Many crimes are committed by pick-pockets.
5. Kate packed her crystal carefully in the big crate.
6. With care you can keep your grass clean and green like a carpet.

7. Hark! hark! the dogs do bark,
    The beggars have come to town;
  Some in rags, some in tags,
    And some in velvet gowns.

8. There was a crooked man,
    And he went a crooked mile,
  And he found a crooked sixpence
    Against a crooked stile;

He bought a crooked cat,
    Which caught a crooked mouse,
And they all lived together
    In a little crooked house.

9. He clasps the crag with crooked hands;
   Close to the sun in lonely lands,
   Ring'd with the azure world, he stands.

10. True hope is swift, and flies with swallow's wings;
    Kings it makes gods, and meaner creatures kings.

11. There is beauty in the bellow of the blast,
    There is grandeur in the growling of the gale,
       There is eloquent out-pouring
       When the lion is a-roaring
    And the tiger is a-lashing of his tail!

                      W. S. GILBERT, *The Mikado*

THE CONSONANT COMBINATIONS [tʃ] AS IN [tʃɛst] *chest* AND [dʒ] AS IN [dʒɛst] *jest*

Each of these sounds is roughly described as a combination of a plosive and a fricative, as can be seen in the phonetic symbols used to represent them. Actually they are fricative sounds begun plosively from positions approximately indicated by the [t] and the [d], and are referred to by phoneticians as affricates. While the two elements of each combination are not formed exactly as they would be if pronounced separately, the two merging together into a closely knit unit, serious faults in the production of either element will manifest themselves in the finished sound. Two of the most common problems involve the dentalized [t] and [d], explained in a previous section, and lisping—to be discussed later in this chapter—especially when it involves the formation of [ʃ] and [ʒ], as it often does. For the proper production of [tʃ] and [dʒ], therefore, attention should be directed toward perfecting the four component sounds out of which the combinations are formed. After this is accomplished, a slight amount of attention and practice should take care of any deviations in these two affricates.

For individuals with a foreign language background, [tʃ] and [dʒ] may present some special problems. Although two phonetic symbols are used to represent each of these combinations, [dʒ], for example, is often spelled with only one alphabet letter—*j* in the case of such words as *jump* [dʒʌmp] or *g* as in *gem* [dʒɛm] or *age* [edʒ]. Such spelling is hardly a fair representation of the complex nature of this sound. Furthermore, not only is this sound missing from many foreign languages, but there is an additional complicating factor—the letter *j* in most foreign languages is used to represent the spoken sound [j], which we usually spell with the letter *y*, as in *yet* [jɛt]. Therefore, it is to be expected that [dʒ] will be improperly pronounced by individuals whose speech reflects a foreign language influence and that the most common substitution for it will be [j], in which case *jump* will become 'yump' [jʌmp] and *joke* will sound like 'yoke' [jok]. Paired words will be found useful in teaching the distinction between [j] and [dʒ]. Not only the acoustic difference, but the difference in mechanics of production, should be stressed, especially the fact that [dʒ] begins from a closed position:

| Yale—jail | yam—jam | use—juice | yet—jet |
| yoke—joke | year—jeer | yes—Jess | yell—jell |

In addition to the substitution of [j], other foreign dialect variations in the pronunciation of [dʒ] include the substitution of [ʒ], especially among those who have spoken French, and the tendency to unvoice [dʒ], particularly when it occurs in the final position, a practice that results in changing [dʒ] to [tʃ], in which case *age* [edʒ] becomes 'aitch' [etʃ] and *ridge* sounds like 'rich' [rɪtʃ].

Difficulties may also arise in the pronunciation of [tʃ], spelled typically with *ch* as in *chin* [tʃɪn], although they are likely to be somewhat less common than in the case of its voiced correlative [dʒ]. Again, various substitutions may occur for this combination, a common one being [ʃ], making *chin* sound like 'shin' [ʃɪn] and *chip* like 'ship' [ʃɪp]. As in the case of [dʒ], it should again be pointed out that [tʃ] begins from a closed position, approximately that for [t]. Consequently [tʃ] resembles a plosive in many respects, while [ʃ], of course, is a continuant. Pairs containing these two sounds are readily available for use in teaching the difference between them:

ship—chip	shoe—chew	shin—chin	wish—witch
share—chair	sheet—cheat	sheep—cheap	cash—catch
shop—chop	shows—chose	shan't—chant	hush—hutch

The exercises which follow are designed (1) to teach the distinction between the voiceless [tʃ] and the voiced [dʒ] and (2) to facilitate their proper positioning in the mouth. This will be done through the use of the paired word technique by comparing the two combination-sounds with the consonants which begin them.

INITIAL		MEDIAL		FINAL	
chill	Jill	lunching	lunging	match	Madge
chump	jump	riches	ridges	search	surge
char	jar	nature	major	rich	ridge
choke	joke	batches	badges	lunch	lunge
cheap	jeep	etches	edges	H	age
chain	Jane	breeches	bridges	larch	large

COMPARING [t] AND [tʃ]		COMPARING [d] AND [dʒ]	
tip	chip	dab	jab
time	chime	don	John
tub	chub	Dale	jail
tore	chore	dear	jeer
tin	chin	daunt	jaunt
tier	cheer	dust	just
too	chew	dot	jot
top	chop	debt	jet

1. Jack chased the pigeon back into its cage.
2. The teacher asked Charles to watch his speech.

3. The child stood on tiptoe to reach the pitcher.

4. Rachel sat on the edge of her chair fidgeting with her hand-kerchief.

5. John and Jerry studied geology until lunch time.

6. The judge questioned the jury as to whether it had reached a verdict.

7. John stood with his chest up and his chin in, just like a soldier.

8. At lunch time the men sat munching their sandwiches in the shade of the old church.

9. It is with our judgments as with our watches: no two go just alike, yet each believes his own.

    10. The stormy March is come at last,
        With wind, and cloud and changing skies;
    I hear the charging of the blast,
        That through the snowy valley flies.

11. Cheerfulness charms us with a spell that reaches into eternity; and we would not exchange it for all the soulless beauty that ever graced the fairest form on earth.

12. If a little knowledge is dangerous, where is the man who has so much as to be out of danger?

13. If to do were as easy as to know what were good to do, chapels had been churches, and poor men's cottages princes' palaces.

14. When I was a child, I spake as a child, I understood as a child, I thought as a child; but when I became a man, I put away childish things.

15. Imagination is that faculty which arouses the passions by the impression of exterior objects; it is influenced by these objects; its fear or courage flies from imagination to imagination.

PROBLEMS IN THE ARTICULATION OF PLOSIVES

1. When two plosives occur together, either in the same word or as the final and initial sounds of adjacent words, the first one is not completely released, but is merely held and joined with the second one. Thus, in *wept* [wɛpt], for ex-

ample, the [p] is not released separately; some pressure is built up but it is simply merged with the explosion which occurs for [t]. The same is true when there are two words, as in *sit down* [sɪt daʊn]. These are not pronounced as two distinct words in the sense that the [t] of the first one is completed before the [d] of the second one is begun; rather there is just the closure for [t], which is held while there is a silent 'shift' to [d], which is exploded for both of them. Study carefully the relationship between the two plosives of such combinations as are found in the following words. Pronounce the words in 'slow motion' and observe how the one plosive merges into the other:

acts	limped	can't go	street car
sagged	asked	red bird	stop gap
whisked	subdue	whisk broom	hot potato

2. When a plosive is followed directly by a nasal consonant, the plosive is released over the velum directly into the nasal chambers, with one result that the explosion is greatly lessened. Under certain circumstances when [n] follows [t] or [d], it becomes a separate syllable by itself without an intervening vowel, in which case it is said to be syllabic. This happens in such words as *beaten* [bitṇ] and *laden* [ledṇ], a pronunciation that will be discussed in more detail in a later section. Study the transition between the plosive and the adjacent nasal in the following words. Can you tell which ones take the syllabic [n]?

topmast	snub nose	hit me
sudden	quagmire	submit
catnip	button	kitten

3. When [t] or [d] is followed by [l] in an unstressed position, as in the words *battle* or *saddle,* the tip of the tongue remains in contact with the gum ridge, and the plosive is exploded into the [l] around the sides of the tongue. Pro-

nounce *battle* [bætl̩] and *saddle* [sædl̩] carefully, slowing down the transition from the [t] to the [l] but otherwise maintaining a natural formation of the sounds. The plosives are formed quite differently from the way they are pronounced in *bat* and *sad*. In the examples cited and similar cases, the [l] is said to be syllabic, somewhat similar in function to the syllabic [n] just noted.

4. When a plosive is followed by a fricative, the explosion is made through the narrow outlet of the fricative, and the two sounds merge into a closely integrated unit. This is especially true of combinations in which both the plosive and the fricative have certain aspects of production in common, as in *cats, campfire, roads,* and *subversive*. However, the best examples of this phonetic principle are found in the pronunciation of the two affricates [tʃ] and [dʒ], already discussed.

5. When, because of foreign language influence or for some other reason, the voiceless plosives [p], [t], and [k] are pronounced without the rather marked aspiration customarily given them in English, the individual's speech will sound 'peculiar' and foreign. In these cases it becomes difficult to distinguish the voiceless sound from its voiced correlative with the result that *pan* tends to sound like 'ban,' *time* will resemble 'dime,' and *cap* will tend to become 'gap.' The little puff of air should always characterize the voiceless plosives when they occur initially or at the beginning of a stressed syllable.

6. On the other hand, it is possible to exaggerate the aspiration to the point at which the plosive becomes noisy and conspicuous. This tendency should be avoided.

7. It is obvious to anyone who listens to speech critically that final and post-vocalic (following a vowel) plosives are not normally pronounced with the same vigor and precision as initial plosives or those which begin stressed syllables. For example, although we have often been enjoined to sound the final consonants when we speak, it would be ridiculous and

conspicuous to pronounce the [t] of *sat,* the [p] of *cup,* or the [k] in *sack* with the same prominence we give these sounds when they begin words like *top, pan,* or *keen.* In other words, the initial and final sounds of a word like *kick* [kɪk], although they appear on the surface to be similar and employ the same symbol, are in reality produced quite differently. Pronounce such words as *tot, pup,* and *cook* carefully, comparing the beginning and final sounds. While final consonants should by no means be dropped out, they must be pronounced in a manner consistent with ease and naturalness, which means a considerable reduction in the explosive phase of the sound. Pronounce the following words and sentences several times, studying the formation of the final sounds. Try to achieve a sound that is definitely intelligible, but not unnatural or exaggerated:

gag	bob	lap	cup
toot	pop	street	hat
deed	kick	look	back

1. Out of sight, out of mind.
2. Cap in hand, he stood up straight and tall.
3. Please lend me a sheet of paper for my notebook.
4. He sat with his back to the light holding the sack on his lap.
5. Hand in hand, they went down the road.
6. Dick drove the herd of sheep through the gate.

PRACTICE MATERIAL FOR PLOSIVES

1. Success depends upon previous preparation, and without such preparation there is sure to be failure.

> 2. Double, double, toil and trouble;
> Fire burn and caldron bubble.

> 3. There was a time when meadow, grove, and stream,
> The earth, and every common sight,
>   To me did seem
> Apparelled in celestial light.

4. Humpty-Dumpty sat on a wall,
Humpty-Dumpty had a great fall;
All the king's horses and all the king's men
Couldn't put Humpty-Dumpty together again.

5. Peter, Peter, pumpkin eater,
Had a wife and couldn't keep her;
Put her in a pumpkin shell
And there he kept her very well.

6. A chubby little sister
Was rubbing at her tub;
A chubby little brother
Came up to help her rub.
The chubby little brother
Fell in with a cry;
The chubby little sister
Then hung him up to dry.

7. The ship was cheered, the harbor cleared,
Merrily did we drop
Below the kirk, below the hill,
Below the lighthouse top.

8. A silly young fellow named Hyde
In a funeral procession was spied;
When asked, 'Who is dead?'
He giggled and said,
'I don't know; I just came for the ride.'

9. There was a fat man of Bombay
Who was smoking one sunshiny day;
When a bird, called a snipe,
Flew away with his pipe,
Which vexed the fat man of Bombay.

10. To sit in solemn silence in a dull, dark dock,
In a pestilential prison, with a life-long lock,
Awaiting the sensation of a short, sharp shock,
From a cheap and chippy chopper on a big, black block.

11. A great elm-tree spread its broad branches; at the foot of
which bubbled up a spring of the softest and sweetest water, in
a little well, formed of a barrel; and then stole sparkling away

through the grass, to a neighboring brook, that babbled along among alders and dwarf willows.

WASHINGTON IRVING, *The Legend of Sleepy Hollow*

12.   Piping down the valleys wild,
        Piping songs of pleasant glee,
        On a cloud I saw a child,
        And he laughing said to me:

        'Pipe a song about a lamb!'
        So I piped with merry cheer,
        'Piper, pipe that song again.'
        So I piped: he wept to hear.

WILLIAM BLAKE, 'The Piper'

13. Teasing Tom was a very bad boy;
     A great big squirt was his favorite toy;
     He put live shrimps in his father's boots,
     And sewed up the sleeves of his Sunday suits;
     He punched his poor little sisters' heads,
     And cayenne-peppered their four-post beds;
     He plastered their hair with cobbler's wax,
     And dropped hot halfpennies down their backs.

W. S. GILBERT, *Patience*

14. Talent is something, but tact is everything. Talent is serious, sober, grave, and respectable; tact is all that, and more too. It is not a sixth sense, but is the life of all five. It is the open eye, the quick ear, the judging taste, the keen smell, and the lively touch. It is the interpreter of all riddles, the surmounter of all difficulties, the remover of all obstacles. It is useful in all places, and at all times; it is useful in solitude for it shows a man his way into the world; it is useful in society, for it shows him his way through the world.

W. P. SARGILL

THE NASALS: [m] AS IN [mæp] *map*, [n] AS IN [næp] *nap*, AND [ŋ] AS IN [sɪŋ] *sing*

The sounds listed above are the only ones in English speech to be emitted solely through the nasal chambers. These sounds are the nasal equivalents of three oral sounds described in a previous section—[b], [d], and [g]. That is, they are formed similarly. Take [m], for example; the oral articulation is the same as for [b]—the two lips are brought together to close off the vocalized breath stream. Unlike [b] and the rest of the oral consonants, for all three nasals the velar-pharyngeal port is open and the tone is nasally emitted. With the nasal port thus open, [n] is formed with the tip of the tongue against the upper gum ridge similar to [d], and [ŋ] is produced in the same general position as [g] is (with the back of the tongue humped up against the velum), in this case lowered somewhat. Pronounce each of the nasals slowly, holding it for a few seconds; listen to its quality and study the manner of its formation. Prolongation is easy, since the sounds are continuants, in contrast to the plosives, or stops, we were studying earlier.

Since the articulatory adjustments in the mouth do approximate those for the three oral consonants mentioned, it can be seen that, to a considerable degree, faults present in the formation of these oral sounds will also manifest themselves in the corresponding nasals. In the articulation of [m], for example, precise and agile lip activity is important, as it is also in the production of [b]. The primary requirement for proper formation of the nasal consonants, however, is a free and open nasal passageway to provide ample resonance and easy emission of the sounds. As was also pointed out in Chapter IV, when the nasal passages become obstructed for any reason, we have a condition that is very likely to distort these sounds or make their formation impossible. We have what could be described as 'cold-in-the-head' speech, which produces a voice quality disorder as well as an articulatory problem. In severe conditions the oral equivalents become substituted for the nasal sounds, [m] changing to [b], [n] to [d], and [ŋ] to [g]. In such speech *good morning* sounds something like 'good bawdig' [gʊd bɔdɪg].

Where remediable structural deviations and other adverse

nasal conditions exist, medical treatment should be instituted, if at all feasible, for the most satisfactory and permanent improvement in voice and speech. Where such treatment is not possible or feasible, considerable progress can still be made in many instances through a careful program of study and practice. A number of suggestions and exercises for improvement of voice quality were included in Chapter IV, and it is suggested that those be reviewed in connection with the present discussion in cases where any real problem exists in the proper formation or use of the nasal consonants. In general, improvement of articulation, as well as voice quality, in these cases depends upon a greater concentration on the nasal sounds in speech with a general intensification in the mechanics of their production. This involves greater stress on these sounds, which usually means not only forming them as carefully as possible, but increasing the emphasis given them and especially prolonging them somewhat longer than usual. In this way moderately unfavorable physical factors can be at least partially compensated for.

Aside from obscuring the [m] because of sluggish lip movement, the most common bad habit in the articulation of the nasals is probably that of substituting [n] for [ŋ] in certain words, a practice often incorrectly referred to as 'leaving off the g.' This mistaken conception is in all probability traceable to the conventional spelling of [ŋ], which is typically with *ng* as in *sing* [sɪŋ] and *singing* [sɪŋɪŋ]. A brief analysis of [ŋ] will demonstrate, however, that it is a distinct and separate sound, containing neither [g] nor [n], and bearing little, if any, relationship to the latter, except that both are nasals. Therefore, when an individual says *comin'* [kʌmən] for *coming* [kʌmɪŋ], he is actually changing the final sound of the word from [ŋ] to [n], but he is 'leaving off' nothing. In any case, the substitution is unacceptable in most instances and for this reason should be avoided. Make a list of all the *-ing* words you can think of—especially the present participle form of verbs, which is where the substitution typically occurs—and practice them until you become fully conscious of the [ŋ] ending, not only in speech exercises but in your everyday talking as well.

Does your speech exhibit any of the unacceptable pronunciations listed below? Practice these carefully:

going (not *goin'*)	walking (not *walkin'*)
morning (not *mornin'*)	living (not *livin'*)
working (not *workin'*)	nothing (not *nothin'*)
doing (not *doin'*)	sleeping (not *sleepin'*)
coming (not *comin'*)	eating (not *eatin'*)

Another problem in the use of [ŋ] may appear in the speech of individuals who exhibit some foreign language influence in their background or whose speech reflects regional dialectal variations characteristic of certain sections of the United States, particularly New York City. This fault, often referred to as the '*ng* click,' involves the addition of [g] or [k] after the [ŋ] in words where such sounds do not belong, as when *singing* is pronounced as [sɪŋgɪŋ], with or without a suggestion of [g] or [k] at the end. If you will compare the pronunciation of *singer* [sɪŋɚ] with *finger* [fɪŋgɚ], you will discover that the [g] is included in certain words and not in others, but that the spelling makes no distinction. Although there are rather detailed rules that can be applied to this problem of when to use [ŋ] and when to use [ŋg],* perhaps the speaker would be well advised to adopt the simpler procedure of learning the accepted pronunciation of each word as it appears and habituating it to his speech.

In regional dialects, as in New York City, the intrusive [g]

* Thomas, Charles K., *An Introduction to the Phonetics of American English,* rev. ed., pp. 81-2, The Ronald Press Company, New York, 1958.

is most likely to appear in phrases where the [ŋ] is followed by another word beginning with a vowel, as in the combination *Long Island* [lɔŋ-gaɪlənd], *going along* [goɪŋ-gəlɔŋ], and *calling a number* [kɔlɪŋ-gənʌmbə]. In these and similar examples, the added [g] is likely to become attached to the beginning of the syllable following the [ŋ]. The added [g] may also occur on final *ng,* as when *singing* is pronounced as [sɪŋgɪŋk] or [sɪŋgɪŋg], without a vowel following.

Ear training must be used when working with this problem so that awareness of the added plosive will be developed. Practice on the following paired words should hasten that awareness and should teach the individual when to use [ŋk] or [ŋg] and when [ŋ] alone is the proper sound:

bank—bang	sink—sing	linger—singer
kink—king	rank—rang	longer—longing
clank—clang	rink—ring	finger—wringer
hunk—hung	sunk—sung	hunger—among

Syllabic [m] *and* [n]. The consonant [m], occasionally, and the consonant [n], frequently, form syllables alone without the aid of a vowel, in which case they are said to be syllabic. Syllabic [m] may occur in such words as *chasm* [kæzm̩] or *prism* [prɪzm̩], although the pronunciations [kæzəm] and [prɪzəm] are more common. Syllabic [n] is the rule in such words as *sadden* [sædn̩] and *cotton* [katn̩], where the [n] and the preceding consonant are formed similarly. Syllabic [n] is also often heard in such words as *lesson* [lɛsn̩] and *soften* [sɒfn̩] because the transition from the preceding consonant to the [n] can be made without sounding an intervening vowel. Compare the pronunciations [lɛsn̩] and [lɛsən] and you will detect the difference; either one would be quite acceptable. In a word like *bacon* a syllabic [n] would be quite unlikely, however, and the more natural and common pronunciation would be [bekən]. Which of the words in the following list do you think should be pronounced with syllabic [m] or [n]? Would you say [mʌtn̩] or [mʌtən], [rizn̩] or [rizən], [blɑsm̩] or [blɑsəm], for example, and for which of the words in the list would either pronunciation be acceptable?

mutton	reason	blossom	realism
brighten	riddance	listen	rhythm
garden	kitten	relation	bottom
cousin	Latin	question	women

Practice Material for [m]

Comparing [m] *and* [b]

INITIAL		MEDIAL		FINAL	
bad	mad	ruby	roomy	cub	come
bean	mean	Ebbett	Emmett	rib	rim
bit	mit	carbon	Carmen	robe	roam
bite	mite	bobbing	bombing	slab	slam
boot	moot	Farber	farmer	Abe	aim
buff	muff	clabber	clamor	hub	hum

Sentences and Selections with [m]

1. Many men make much money from mines.

2. The moan of doves in immemorial elms and the murmur of innumerable bees.

3. More men are needed during the summer to work on the farm.

4. Names mean nothing if not remembered.

5. Mary came to the meeting but missed the chairman's opening remarks.

6. Some men never seem to learn from experience.

7. You will never 'find' time for anything; if you want time, you must make it.

8. The gathering dusk of evening made the printed page a mere mist before his eyes.

9. Come in the evening, or come in the morning;
Come when you're looked for, or come without warning.

> 10. We are the music-makers,
> And we are the dreamers of dreams,
> Wandering by lone sea-breakers,
> And sitting by desolate streams.

> 11. It was many and many a year ago,
> In a kingdom by the sea,
> That a maiden lived, whom you may know
> By the name of Annabel Lee.

> 12. Tell me not in mournful numbers,
> Life is but an empty dream.

> 13. I wish I could remember that first day,
> First hour, first moment of your meeting me,
> If bright or dim the season, it might be
> Summer or Winter for aught I can say;
> So unrecorded did it slip away.
>> CHRISTINA ROSSETTI, 'The First Day'

14. Washington Irving once remarked, 'Honest good humor is the oil and wine of a merry meeting, and there is no jovial companionship equal to that where the jokes are small and the laughter abundant.' But he did not mean that to have a sense of humor a person must say something funny every few minutes.

15. Man is not the creature of circumstances; circumstances are the creatures of men. We are free agents, and man is more powerful than matter.

> 16. A sonnet is a moment's monument,–
> Memorial from the Soul's eternity,
> To one dead deathless hour.

> 17. We are no other than a moving row
> Of Magic Shadow-shapes that come and go
> Round with the Sun-illumin'd Lantern held
> In Midnight by the Master of the Show.

PRACTICE MATERIAL FOR [n]

Comparing [n] *and* [d]

INITIAL		MEDIAL		FINAL	
doe	know	paddle	panel	greed	green
dip	nip	trader	trainer	bard	barn
deed	need	divine	divide	dud	done
dear	near	cider	signer	trade	train
deck	neck	padding	panning	side	sign
dock	knock	rudder	runner	plaid	plan

Sentences and Selections with [n]

1. *No, No, Nanette* was a musical that ran for many weeks in the nineteen-twenties.

2. Senator Holden's name was entered for the next nomination.

3. An enormous shipment of grain was sent to the natives.

4. Ned was presented with a handsome pen and pencil set on his graduation.

5. His uncle earned no end of money and never spent any of it.

6. Nancy enrolled for Latin and economics in her freshman year.

7. A Nicaraguan proverb says, 'One man in one day with a match can clear a hundred acres.'

8. Little wind, blow on the hilltop;
    Little wind, blow down the plain;
    Little wind, blow up the sunshine;
    Little wind, blow off the rain.

9. Who has seen the wind?
    Neither I nor you:
    But when the leaves hang trembling,
    The wind is passing through.

Who has seen the wind?
    Neither you nor I:
    But when the trees bow down their heads,
    The wind is passing by.

                       CHRISTINA ROSSETTI

10. Hunting after happiness is like hunting after a lost sheep in the wilderness—When you find it, the chances are that it is a skeleton.

11. A little nonsense now and then is relished by the wisest men.

12. All nature is but art unknown to thee
All chance direction, which thou canst not see.

13. Yet Ah, that Spring should vanish with the Rose!
That Youth's sweet-scented manuscript should close!
The Nightingale that in the branches sang,
Ah whence, and whither flown again, who knows!

14. Nothing that is can pause or stay;
The moon will wax, the moon will wane,
The mist and cloud will turn to rain,
The rain to mist and cloud again
Tomorrow be today.

H. W. LONGFELLOW

Practice Material for [ŋ]

Comparing [ŋ] *and* [g]

MEDIAL		FINAL	
rigger	wringer	tug	tongue
logging	longing	sag	sang
bagging	banging	hug	hung
wigless	wingless	sprig	spring
Briggs	brings	rug	rung
bagged	banged	rig	ring

Sentences and Selections with [ŋ]

1. I heard the mockingbirds singing as I was walking along the road.
2. People were coming and going all day long.
3. Helen's uncle was wearing a ring on his little finger.
4. Is it wrong to sing that song?
5. The young man was going along the wrong road.
6. Bring me something to eat first thing in the morning.

7. I'll sing you a song,
  Though not very long,
  Yet I think it's as pretty as any;
  Put your hand in your purse,
  You'll never do worse,
  And give the poor singer a penny.

8. The king was in the counting-house,
  Counting out his money;
  The queen was in the kitchen,
  Eating bread and honey;

  The maid was in the garden,
  Hanging out the clothes;
  Along come a bumble-bee
  And stung her on the nose.

9. There was a rustling that seemed like a bustling
  Of merry crowds justling at pitching and hustling;
  Small feet were pattering, wooden shoes clattering,
  Little hands clapping and little tongues chattering,
  And, like fowls in a farm-yard when barley is scattering,
  Out came the children running.
      ROBERT BROWNING, 'The Pied Piper of Hamelin'

10. Deep into the darkness peering, long I stood there wondering, fearing,
  Doubting, dreaming dreams no mortal ever dared to dream
   before.

11. Those who have finished by making all others think with
them, have usually been those who began by daring to think
with themselves.

12. Where there's more of singing and less of sighing,
  Where there's more of giving and less of buying,
  And a man makes friends without half trying.

13. Words are things; and a small drop of ink, falling like
dew upon a thought, produces that which makes thousands, perhaps millions, think.

14. Come in the evening, or come in the morning;
  Come when you're looked for, or come without warning.

15. Then the whining schoolboy, with his satchel
    And shining morning face, creeping like snail
    Unwillingly to school.

THE FRICATIVES

The fricatives differ from the plosives in two important ways: (1) Instead of the breath stream being completely stopped in the mouth and then exploded, there is merely a narrowing or partial obstruction produced by the articulators through which the breath stream is forced under some degree of pressure. The acoustic character of the resulting 'friction' sound is determined by the place and nature of the obstruction, the size of the opening, and whether the outgoing breath stream is vocalized or unvocalized. (2) The fricatives are continuants and hence can be prolonged, while, of course, the plosives must be produced more or less instantaneously.

Some of the fricatives are extremely weak sounds acoustically and hence are in danger of being lost from speech unless they are very carefully articulated. Moreover, several of them differ only slightly from each other in pitch and quality and hence are particularly difficult to discriminate. The two sounds [f] and [θ], for example, fit into both these categories; they are notably weak sounds and it is difficult to distinguish one from the other, *fin* sounding very much like *thin*. Careful and precise articulation is just as important for the fricatives as it was found to be for the plosives, perhaps even more so, for the reasons mentioned above.

THE CONSONANTS [f] AS IN [faɪn] *fine* AND [v] AS IN [vaɪn] *vine*

These two fricatives are known as labio-dentals, since they are formed with the lower lip held against the cutting edge of the upper front teeth. They depend for their distinctness almost entirely upon the activity of the lower lip. The sound of [f] is commonly spelled with *f* or *ff*, though occasionally one finds *gh* as in *rough* and *ph* as in *diphthong* [dɪfθɔŋ] and *phonograph* [fonəgræf]. [f] is the voiceless sound, and [v] the voiced.

No particular difficulties are normally encountered in the articulation of [f] and [v], aside from general indistinctness that may come from sluggish lip activity. Some confusion in voicing between [f] and [v] may occur among individuals whose speech exhibits the influence of a foreign or regional dialect. This confusion is most likely to occur in the final position and consists of unvoicing the [v], in which case *brave* will sound like [bref] and *have* will resemble [hæf]. Further confusion between [v] and [w] may also be traced to dialectal influences, the tendency being for the [v] to be pronounced like [w], making *vine* sound like 'wine' [waɪn].

In the practice material that follows, work for a clear, easy articulation of [f] and [v] and guard against any tendency to distort them or substitute other sounds for them. Compare the two sounds in the words paired below:

Comparing [f] *and* [v]:

INITIAL		MEDIAL		FINAL	
fine	vine	wafer	waver	life	live
fear	veer	rifle	rival	safe	save
feel	veal	deafen	Devon	proof	prove
face	vase	infest	invest	surf	serve
fast	vast	shuffle	shovel	leaf	leave
fault	vault	define	divine	shelf	shelve

Comparing [v] *and* [w]:

INITIAL		MEDIAL		FINAL	
wine	vine	weal	veal	weird	veered
west	vest	went	vent	Walt	vault
worse	verse	wary	very	wane	vane

Sentences with [f] *and* [v]:

1. Will found the drive to be very invigorating.

2. The victim lost a valuable watch when thieves entered the tavern.

3. Fred refused to view his defeat as final.

4. Stephen was forced to leave the valley where he had lived for five years.

5. Vivian carefully vacuumed the floor in front of the stove.

6. Very few people ever saw the cave.

7. 'Fee, fie, foe, fum,' roared the giant.

8. During his vacation Frank became quite proficient at volley ball.

9. Fair is foul and foul is fair:
    Hover through the fog and filthy air.

10. Forty flags with their silver stars,
    Forty flags with their crimson bars,
    Flapped in the morning wind.

11. The fair breeze blew, the white foam flew,
    The furrow followed free;
    We were the first that ever burst
    Into that silent sea.

12. A fly and a flea in a flue
    Were imprisoned, so what could they do?
      Said the fly, 'Let us flee!'
      'Let us fly!' said the flea,
    So they flew through a flaw in the flue.

13. Ay me! for aught that I ever could read,
    Could ever hear by tale or history,
    The course of true love never did run smooth.

14. The vaulted void of purple sky
    That everywhere extends,
    That stretches from the dazzled eye,
    In space that never ends.

15. A few vices are sufficient to darken many virtues.

16. There's no dew left on the daisies and clover,
    There's no rain left in heaven;
    I've said my 'seven times' over and over,
    Seven times one are seven.

THE CONSONANTS [θ] AS IN [θɪn] *thin* AND [ð] AS IN [ðɪs] *this*

Since the spelling of these two lingua-dentals does not distinguish them, we must learn from observation when *th* is to be voiced, as it is in *this* [ðɪs], and when it is unvoiced as in *thin* [θɪn]. Although on first thought one might say that the tip of the tongue was actually between the teeth during the production of these sounds, closer observation reveals that it is the outrush of air through the highly constricted space between the tongue tip and the sharp edges of the upper teeth (incisors) which causes the friction-like noises we recognize as [θ] and [ð].

Since English is one of the few languages containing these sounds, the individual with a foreign language background invariably has difficulty with them. Certain distortions and substitutions are also found among those speakers whose speech reflects certain regional dialectal influences. The most common fault in all these cases is the substitution of [t] for [θ], 'tin' for *thin,* and [d] for [ð], 'dis' for *this.* Occasionally in foreign dialect [s] or [z] will be heard in place of the lingua-dentals. The distinction between [t] and [d] and [θ] and [ð] is not difficult to explain, since these two fricatives are readily visible and can thus be observed as well as heard. They are also continuants, of course, while [t] and [d] are stops. While it may be simple to point out the difference, actually eradicating the substitution from one's speech after perhaps several years of habitual use may be quite another story. The technique of paired words can again be used to direct attention to the essential difference between the word pronounced with [t] or [d] and the accepted pronunciation with [θ] or [ð]. This initial ear training should be followed by sufficient practice to eradicate the old habit and establish the new one. The lists below can be used as a starting point, to which new examples can be added.

Minor problems often occur in the articulation of [θ] and

[ð] when they appear in difficult combinations with certain other front-of-the-tongue consonants, notably [s], [z], and [ʃ], such as occur in *baths* [bæðz], *widths* [wɪdθs]. In certain words, also, [θ] and [ð] are used almost interchangeably in the speech of many individuals. For example, is *with* pronounced [wɪθ] or [wɪð]? And would the pronunciation be the same in the phrase *with him* as it would be in the phrase *with them*? If not, what is the difference, and why? Do you use [θ] or [ð] in the following words?

oaths	wreaths	baths	cloths
laths	moths	youths	truths
thither	booths	widths	mouthy

PRACTICE MATERIAL FOR [θ] AND [ð]

Comparing [θ] *and* [t]:

INITIAL		MEDIAL		FINAL	
tin	thin	fateful	faithful	toot	tooth
tree	three	nutting	nothing	Pat	path
tank	thank	eater	ether	boat	both
tie	thigh	mits	myths	fort	fourth
team	theme	rootless	ruthless	fate	faith
taught	thought	pity	pithy	Bret	breath
true	through	latter	lather	sheet	sheath
tread	thread	rooty	Ruthie	brought	broth

Comparing [ð] *and* [d]:

INITIAL				MEDIAL	
doze	those	dare	there	loading	loathing
Diss	this	den	then	riding	writhing
dough	though	Dee	thee	ladder	lather
Dow	thou	dense	thence	breeding	breathing
day	they	Dan	than	fodder	father
dine	thine	die	thy	wordy	worthy

Phrases, Sentences, and Selections with [θ] *and* [ð]:

this and that	The Prince and the	these or those
around the town	Pauper	I thank you
through the street	this one or that one	then and there

1. The Bible states that out of the mouths of babes many truths shall come.

2. Next Thursday Theodore will have his seventh birthday.

3. I thought I saw Thelma buying some thread at the store.

4. Tom thought that he could find the path through the woods.

5. Martha had trouble getting the heavy thread through the thick tick.

6. The three brothers wanted to travel through the country.

7. All day they were so thirsty they thought they were going to die.

8. Ruth usually thinks things out thoroughly.

9. The player got three free throws at the basket.

10. The farmer gathered all of the thorns and thistles together.

11. The wind bloweth where it listeth, and thou hearest the sound thereof, but canst not tell whence it cometh or whither it goeth.

12. Bertha sews with thin thread,
    Martha sews with thick,
    For Bertha sews a thin silk scarf,
    But Martha sews a tick.
    So Bertha sews with thin thread,
    Though Martha uses thick.

13. For healthy warmth in all the weathers
    Some birds build nests with snug warm feathers;
    Feathers thick and feathers thin,
    With thick without, and thin within.

14. Breathes there a man with soul so dead
    Who never to himself hath said,
    'This is my own, my native land.'

15. Poet who sleepest by this wandering wave!
    When thou was born, what birth-gift hadst thou then?
    To thee what wealth was that the Immortals gave,
    The wealth thou gavest in thy turn to men?

16. Fathers who have hobbies rarely lose their minds. However, you can't say the same thing of their families.

> 17. Something old, something new,
>   Something borrowed, something blue.

18. We hold these truths to be self-evident; That all men are created equal; That they are endowed by their creator with inalienable rights; That among these are life, liberty and the pursuit of happiness.

> 19. And now abideth Faith, Hope and Charity, these three;
>   But the greatest of these is charity.

20. It is dishonorable to say one thing and think another; how much more dishonorable to write one thing and think another.

21. On the thirty-second day of the thirteenth month of the eighth day of the week,
>   On the twenty-fifth hour and the sixty-first minute, we'll find all things that we seek.

> 22. Thirty thousand thoughtful boys
>   Thought they'd make a thundering noise;
>   So, with thirty thousand thumbs,
>   They thumped on thirty thousand drums.

23. A family of fashion were gathered together,
    All of them deeply considering whether
    They ought to stay in on account of the weather.
    'Rain,' said the mother, 'would ruin my feather.'
    'Dust,' said the father, 'would dim my shoe leather.'
    'Sun,' said the brother, 'though out but an hour,
    Would probably wither my buttonhole flower.'
    And thus they concluded, agreeing together,
    There's danger to clothing in all sorts of weather.
    So they bought a big bandbox, together climbed in it,
    Shut down the lid, and they're there to this minute.

THE CONSONANTS [s] AS IN [sil] *seal* AND [z] AS IN [zil] *zeal*

Of all speech defects involving faulty articulation, improper formation of [s] and [z] is probably the most common. Not only is keen hearing essential to the proper production of [s], which has the highest frequency of all English speech sounds, but the complexity of the adjustment required for its formation is such as to make it a very difficult sound to articulate correctly. All of the speech organs must be adjusted with such co-ordination that even a slight deviation may be sufficient to change radically the quality of the resulting sound. These deviations may spring from structural irregularities in the mouth, especially various forms of malocclusions and dental misalignment, or they may arise merely from improper adjustments of the articulatory organs. Of course, what is said of [s] in this respect applies with equal force to its voiced analogue [z], except that [s] occurs much more frequently in speech than [z], and irregularities of formation are likely to show up more prominently in the resulting acoustic effect, in the case of [s].

Briefly stated, the hiss-like sound we call *s* is produced with the tip of the tongue retracted slightly from the position for [t], and with the sides of the tongue in tight contact with the upper teeth and gums approximately as far forward in the mouth as the canine teeth. A fine stream of air is then blown through the narrow groove formed between the tongue tip and the front of the hard palate, really the upper gum ridge.* This air stream is directed against the sharp cutting edges of the front teeth (incisors), which should be held fairly close together but not tightly closed. The resulting sound should be relatively high in pitch and its quality should be that of a clear hiss, but not a whistle.

From a mechanical point of view, the minimum essentials are that a thin stream of air should be directed against a sharp cutting edge. Whenever these essentials are present, we have the potentials of a good *s*; the thin stream of air

---

* In the speech of certain individuals the tongue position for [s] varies from that described here. These speakers keep the tip of the tongue back of the lower teeth and arch the middle front of the tongue upward toward the gum ridge to make the narrow groove described above. The sounds produced in these two positions are acoustically similar.

is formed in the groove over the tongue tip, or middle front of the tongue, depending upon which basic position is used, and the sharp cutting edges are provided by the incisors, as was mentioned. When some factor operates to interfere with this mechanism, a defective [s] or [z] is likely to result. Such deviations in the basic adjustment as (1) keeping the tongue too low in the mouth, (2) allowing too much space between the edges of the upper and lower incisors, (3) blanketing the sharp cutting edges of the incisors with the tongue or lower lip, or (4) directing the air stream out the side of the mouth where the cutting edge of the teeth is dull may very likely result in an unacceptable sound. Some of the more common problems in the production of [s] and [z] will be explained briefly in the paragraphs which follow.

Faults of [s] *and* [z]. 1. Perhaps the most common fault is that of allowing the tongue to remain too low in the front of the mouth during the formation of these sounds. Often the tongue tip approximates the lower edges of the upper incisors in a position similar to that for the lingua-dentals, resulting in a sound bearing a close resemblance to [θ] or [ð]. Sometimes the tongue tip actually protrudes between the teeth. This substitution is most commonly referred to as a lisp, resulting in such well-known deviations as 'lithp' for *lisp* and 'thithter' for *sister,* or approximations of these pronunciations. An excessively low tongue position, often combined with other deviations in the basic mechanism for [s], can result in other distortions of the sound. It may resemble [ʃ] in some cases or it may simply become dull and 'mushy' as a result of having too wide a space between the upper surface of the tongue and the gum ridge. While there are many structural conditions involving the tongue, teeth, and palate which can, and do, contribute to the malpositions of the tongue described above, in a surprising number of instances there is nothing more serious involved than bad speech habits induced by imitation or some other such factor. Often when such habits are found in the adult, it is difficult to discover where or why they may have originated.

2. A defective [s] is likely to result if the space is too wide between the edges of the upper and lower incisors. Instead of being directed against the sharp edges of the front teeth, the air is allowed to rush out between them if the opening is too wide, with a resulting low pitched, 'mushy' [s]. Dental irregularities or a malocclusion may make it impossible to approximate the incisors, in which case there may be an interdental protrusion of the tongue tip in an effort to obstruct the breath stream sufficiently to produce a sound resembling an *s*. In these cases the sound is almost always defective. On the other hand, the structure may be normal and poor speech habits alone may account for the deviation.

3. Another type of defect known as a lateral *s*, or a lateral lisp, is produced if any air is allowed to escape out the sides of the tongue over the canines or bicuspid teeth. Since these teeth are not sharp enough to provide a suitable cutting edge for the stream of air emitted, the resulting sound will be dull and 'fuzzy' and in extreme cases suggestive of a voiceless [l]. The presence of a lateral lisp is sometimes betrayed by a slight lifting of the upper lip on the side where the sound is emitted. This defect results from failure of the tongue to maintain tight contact with the upper teeth and gums on one or both sides. Irregularities of the teeth or structural deficiencies of the tongue may account for a lateral *s* in some cases, but, again, in many instances it appears to be merely a matter of speech habits.

4. Occasionally one finds the [s] defective simply because there is too much of it. The [s] is at best a rather prominent sound, and the frequency with which it occurs in average speech may very easily contribute to an unpleasant effect if in any way it is excessively prolonged or otherwise allowed to become too obvious in one's speech. A whistled effect

may result if the tongue is allowed to groove too deeply in the middle as it is brought up into position.

5. In areas where dialectal influences are present some confusion in voicing and unvoicing [s] and [z] may be heard. That is, [s] may be improperly voiced, resulting in such mispronunciations as [gæz] for 'gas' in a phrase such as 'gas meter' or [bezbɔl] for 'baseball.' Somewhat more common especially among speakers with certain foreign language backgrounds, is the unvoicing of final [z] in such words as 'his,' 'goes,' and 'bellows,' resulting in [hɪs], [gos], and [bɛləs].

Improving the Articulation of [s] *and* [z]. In the effort to attain a pleasant, clear-cut, yet not too prominent [s], the following suggestions should be followed carefully:

1. Care should be taken not to build up too much breath pressure in the production of this sound. No great amount of breath is required for a good [s], provided the articulatory adjustments are right.

2. The [s] should not be unduly prolonged. The sound is likely to be more pleasant if one passes over it quickly and easily, stressing instead the sound immediately following it. Care must be taken that in this process the [s] is not 'swallowed,' however.

3. The sides of the tongue should at all times maintain tight contact with the upper teeth and gum ridge as far front as the canine teeth.

4. The tip of the tongue should never be allowed to fall so low in the production of [s] or protrude in such a way that it approaches the interdental position or blankets the sharp, cutting edges of the upper and lower incisors.

5. The incisors should be so adjusted that their sharp edges intercept the breath stream as it is directed over the tip, or middle front, of the tongue. The edges should be fairly close together, with the upper teeth slightly in advance of the lower, leaving a thin space between them. The lips must be spread sufficiently to keep the edges of the teeth free.

In the improvement of [s] and [z], as in the correction of all speech deviations, the quality of the acoustic end-result is more important than the mechanics involved, provided, of course, that speech is produced without excessive effort or unpleasant visible components. Therefore, in the improvement of voice and speech, it is always advisable to begin with some serious ear training directed at enabling the individual to hear his own speech and voice and compare what he hears with some standard or concept of what is 'normal' or acceptable. When he becomes aware of what is wanted, he may be able, without further instruction, to produce the effect perfectly, often without being conscious of the particular mechanics involved. Therefore, it is always wise to begin by supplying the individual with the desired acoustic pattern, teach him to listen to it discriminatingly, and then attempt to imitate it. Often that is all that is needed.

In many other instances, however, the acoustic approach alone will prove inadequate and in those cases it will be found helpful to give direct attention to the positions and movements of the articulatory mechanism involved. One of the helpful devices in achieving this understanding is the technique of paired words, already used to some extent in this chapter. One can learn a great deal about the production of a new sound by comparing it with the positions and movements involved in a familiar sound which is produced correctly, and which it resembles in one or more important respects. We thus proceed from the known to the unknown, following an established educational principle.

In the improvement of s, therefore, it will often be found expedient to approach the problem of a good tongue position for [s] by studying the position for [t] and noting the similarity between the two, assuming, of course, that the individual keeps the tip of his tongue up, rather than assuming the lower tongue position described earlier in this section. In any case, this technique can be used to aid the individual in keeping his tongue away from the cutting edges of the front teeth.

Practice carefully the following pairs of words, observing that the tongue is in many respects in the same position for [s] as it is for [t]. Try to carry over the feel of the *t* position into the production of [s].

tea—sea	teal—seal	tell—sell	till—sill
told—sold	tame—same	tip—sip	taupe—soap
top—sop	taw—saw	tight—sight	tat—sat
too—Sue	tub—sub	turf—serf	toil—soil

Paired words can also be used for an opposite purpose—to demonstrate essential differences between sounds that may be confused. Distinguish carefully between the articulatory position for [θ] and that for [s] in the following pairs:

thin—sin	thaw—saw	neath—niece	bath—bass
thumb—sum	thank—sank	growth—gross	myth—miss
theme—seem	think—sink	lath—lass	truth—truce
thigh—sigh	thill—sill	worth—worse	forth—force
thong—song	thicken—sicken	Ruth—Roos	faith—face

Distinguish between [ð] and [z] in the following pairs. Note that the difference between these two sounds is similar to the difference noted above between [θ] and [s].

bathe—bays	scythe—size	teethe—tease	clothe—close
seethe—sieze	writhe—rise	breathe—breeze	lithe—lies

Distinguish carefully between [s] and [z] in the following pairs. Be sure you hear the voice element in the second member of each pair. If you have any tendency to unvoice final [z], making it sound like [s], give special emphasis to the final sound of those words where [z] should occur, prolonging it until you are sure you hear the 'buzzing' sound characteristic of [z].

Initial and Medial [s] *and* [z]:

seal—zeal	sounds—zounds	sip—zip	lacey—lazy
sink—zinc	cellar—Zeller	sag—zag	ceasing—seizing
sown—zone	Sue—zoo	scion—Zion	racer—razor

Final [s] *and* [z]:

hiss—his	niece—knees	fuss—fuzz	dice—dies
Joyce—joys	dose—doze	close—close	bus—buzz
price—prize	Boice—boys	lease—lees	Grace—graze
place—plays	loss—laws	ice—eyes	loose—lose

PRACTICE MATERIAL FOR [s] AND [z]

INITIAL		MEDIAL	FINAL
seem	swan	acid	this
sick	sleep	lesson	rice
sang	spin	missing	dates
save	skate	peaceful	grapes
send	smile	aside	box
soap	snow	resting	rugs
sun	stop	whisper	juice
soon	scrape	catsup	tease
south	splash	accent	once
sign	street	master	noise

spick and span	sink or swim	small and slender
sour and sweet	step by step	soft and smooth
his and hers	hustle and bustle	soft as satin

1. Six times six is thirty-six.
2. He that would thrive must ask his wife.
3. Some sailors came to see the starfish.
4. Nancy said, 'How much does a bus ticket cost?'
5. Susan went skating with Buster and slipped on the ice.
6. This is the place where the wild flowers first appear.
7. Alice goes to the store twice a day.
8. Seven birds sang in the sun.
9. Sister Susie is sewing shirts for sick soldiers.

10. A wise loser always tries to eliminate the cause of his failure.

11. Wealth is not his that has it, but his that enjoys it.

12. The wisest man is generally he who thinks himself the least so.

13 There is no vice so simple but assumes some mark of virtue on his outward parts.

14. Think all you speak, but speak not all you think. Thoughts are your own; your words are so no more.

15. Silence is sometimes the severest criticism.

16. My good blade carves the casques of men,
My tough lance thrusteth sure.

17. Was this the face that launch'd a thousand ships,
And burnt the topless towers of Ilium?

18. Listen: With faint dry sound, like steps of passing ghosts,
The leaves frost crisped, break from the trees and fall.

19. Swan swim over the sea;
Swim, swan, swim.
Swan swim back again;
Well swam, swan.

20. Swiftly, swiftly flew the ship,
Yet she sailed softly too:
Sweetly, sweetly blew the breeze—
On me alone it blew.

21. Words are like leaves; and where they most abound,
Much fruit of sense beneath is rarely found.

22. That hour it was when heaven's first gift of sleep
On weary hearts of men most sweetly steals.

23. The sequestered situation of this church seems always to have made it a favorite haunt of troubled spirits. However, to look upon its grass-grown yard, where the sunbeams seem to sleep so quietly, one would think that there at least the dead might rest in peace.

24. When to the sessions of sweet silent thought
I summon up remembrance of things past,
I sigh the lack of many a thing I sought,
And with old woes new wail my dear time's waste.

25. Folks say, a wizard to a northern king
    At Christmas-tide such wondrous things did show,
    That through one window men beheld the spring,
    And through another saw the summer glow.

26.   As I was going to St. Ives,
       I met a man with seven wives,
       Each wife had seven sacks,
       Each sack had seven cats,
       Every cat had seven kits:
    Kits, cats, sacks, and wives,
    Now tell me how many were going to St. Ives.

27. As, when the air is serene in the sultry solstice of summer,
    Suddenly gathers a storm, and the deadly sling of the hail-
       stones
    Beats down the farmer's corn in the field and shatters his
       windows,
    Hiding the sun, and strewing the ground with thatch from
       the house-roofs,
    Bellowing fly the herds, and seek to break their enclosure;
    So on the hearts of the people descended the words of the
       speaker.

                            LONGFELLOW, *Evangeline*

28.   Boats sail on the rivers,
          Ships sail on the seas;
       But clouds that sail across the skies
          Are prettier far than these.

29.   Swift and sure the swallow,
          Slow and sure the snail;
       Slow and sure may miss his way,
          Swift and sure may fail.

30. There's no dew left on the daisies and clover,
        There's no rain left in heaven;
     I've said my 'seven times' over and over—
        Seven times one are seven.

31. I sent my Soul through the Invisible,
        Some letter of that After-life to spell:
     And by and by my Soul returned to me,
        And answered 'I myself am Heav'n and Hell.'

Heav'n but the Vision of fulfilled Desire,
And Hell the Shadow from a Soul on fire
   Cast on the Darkness into which Ourselves,
So late emerg'd from, shall so soon expire.

FITZGERALD, The Rubaiyat of Omar Khayyam

32. In all societies it is advisable to associate if possible with the highest; not that the highest are always the best, but because, if disgusted there, we can at any time descend. But if we begin with the lowest, to ascend is impossible.

COLTON

33. The sun is set; the swallows are asleep;
   The bats are flitting fast in the gray air;
   The slow soft toads out of damp corners creep;
   And evening's breath, wandering here and there
   Over the quivering surface of the stream,
   Wakes not one ripple from its silent dream.

SHELLEY

34. He who sedulously attends, pointedly asks, calmly speaks, coolly answers, and ceases when he has no more to say, is in possession of some of the best requisites of man.

LAVATER

35. So through the Plymouth woods John Alden went on his
    errand;
   Came to an open space, and saw the disk of the ocean,
   Sailless, sombre, and cold with the comfortless breath of the
    east-wind.

THE CONSONANTS [ʃ] AS IN [ʃɪp] *ship* AND [ʒ] AS IN [æʒɚ] *azure*

There is no consistent symbol in conventional spelling to represent either of these two lingua-palatal fricatives, each one being spelled in a number of different ways. Although the most common spelling of [ʃ] is probably with *sh*, it is a distinctly different sound from either [s] or [h], and is also spelled with *s* as in *sure*, with *ss* as in *mission*, and even with *c* as in *ocean*. [ʒ] may be spelled with *z, s,* or *g,* as in *azure, usual,* and *rouge.*

These sounds are formed with the point or middle front

of the tongue somewhat retracted and lowered from its position for [s] and with the middle of the tongue considerably more raised toward the hard palate and less grooved. Also in contrast to [s], there is a noticeable lip rounding in the production of [ʃ]. The wider space over the tongue, plus the lip rounding, accounts for the lower pitch characteristic of [ʃ] when compared with [s]. The manner of formation is, of course, similar for both [ʃ] and [ʒ], except that the latter is voiced.

But few difficulties are ordinarily encountered in the production or use of either of these sounds. An infrequent defect is the substitution of [s] for [ʃ], making *ship* sound like 'sip.' A more common defect of [ʃ] occurs when the middle front of the tongue is allowed to rise too high toward the hard palate, in which case it becomes much higher in pitch and takes on a quality suggesting the sound of the German *ch* as in *ich*. This defect may be accompanied by inadequate lip rounding in the formation of [ʃ].

In almost every instance of a defect of [ʃ], the quality of the sound can be improved if the individual remembers to round his lips adequately when pronouncing it. If the sound suffers because its pitch is too high and it resembles a lisp, an improvement in its quality can be made by keeping the middle front of the tongue lower in the mouth, thus allowing a more open passageway for the escaping air.

Both the lip rounding and the more open passageway can be facilitated if the [ʃ] is practiced in combination with the low-middle and back vowels, especially those involving some lip rounding, such as [ɔ], [o], and [u]. Practice on such combinations, therefore, as [ʃɔ], [ʃo], and [ʃu] will prove helpful, as well as with such open vowels as found in words like *shop, hush, shout,* and *shore.*

Both [ʃ] and [ʒ] also figure in a few groups of words involving certain problems in pronunciation. In some words, for example, usage varies between [ʃ] and [ʒ]. The word *luxurious* belongs to this group. The variation is between [ʃ] and [s] in such words as *association*. In another group of words borrowed from the French, the original [ʒ] is often pronounced as [dʒ] in popular usage. *Garage* is an example of this class.

Study the pronunciation of the following words:

rouge	massage	Asia	issue	peninsula
mirage	corsage	erasure	sumac	emaciated
regime	gendarme	nausea	chassis	insular
prestige	camouflage	luxury	enunciate	appreciation

To correct the [s] substitution for [ʃ], the technique of paired words can again be used to illustrate the essential differences between these two sounds, both as to acoustic quality and manner of production, especially the factor of lip rounding.

seat–sheet	sown–shown	Sue–shoe	sip–ship
sake–shake	Sam–sham	so–show	Sal–shall
sun–shun	save–shave	saw–Shaw	sign–shine

Practice Material for [ʃ] and [ʒ]

INITIAL		MEDIAL		FINAL	
shade	shout	wishing	notion	hush	selfish
short	shop	ocean	insure	wash	wish
shark	shut	bushel	bashful	bush	crash
shook	should	casual	leisure	rush	leash
shore	shawl	evasion	collision	fresh	mash
shoot	sheep	division	seizure	marsh	dish

1. She sells seashells at the seashore.
2. We usually buy some dishes in this shop.
3. The sheep were rushing about in every direction.
4. She climbed aboard as the fishing boat left the shore.
5. What is usually called chamois skin is actually a specially processed sheepskin.
6. Shirley put the dishes back on the shelf.

7. She believed that a little rouge judiciously used could enhance the facial expression.

8. His regime was marked by a sharp increase in racial tension.

9. Now air is hushed, save where the weak-eyed bat
   With short shrill shriek flits by on leathern wing.

10. There is no such thing as real pleasure in life. The justest definition that was ever given was 'A tranquil acquiescence under an agreeable delusion.'

11. There is in a man a conscience which outlives the sensations, resolutions, and emotions of the hour, and rises above them all.

12. When I go fishing
    I'm always wishing
    Some fishes I will get;
    But while I'm fishing,
    The fish are wishing
    I won't; just harder yet.

    And all those wishes
    Of the fishes,
    Every one come true;
    So all my wishes
    To get the fishes
    Never, never do.

    UNKNOWN

13. Rich the treasure,
    Sweet the pleasure,
    Sweet is pleasure after pain.

14. No man is happy without a delusion of some kind. Delusions are as necessary to our pleasures as realities.

15. The keen spirit
    Seizes the prompt occasion—makes the thought
    Start into instant action, and at once
    Plans and performs, resolves and executes.

16. When providence, for secret ends
    Corroding cares, of sharp affliction, sends;
    We must conclude it best it should be so,
    And not desponding or impatient grow.

17.   Oh, philosophers may sing
      Of the troubles of a King,
   But of pleasures there are many and of worries there are
      none;
   And the culminating pleasure
   That we treasure beyond measure
   Is the gratifying feeling that our duty has been done!

W. S. GILBERT, *The Gondoliers*

18. Imagination is that faculty which arouses the passions by the impression of exterior objects; it is influenced by these objects; its fear or courage flies from imagination to imagination.

THE CONSONANT [h] AS IN [hæt] *hat*

The consonant [h], also known as a glottal fricative or glottal aspirate, can scarcely be considered a separate sound entity at all, but rather it is merely a method of beginning vowel sounds and certain of the glides. That is to say, when a syllable or word is to begin with [h], the articulators are set in position for the sound which is to follow the [h] and breath is then blown through the partially closed vocal folds before the voicing for the following sound begins. For this reason the *h* takes on the quality of whatever sound follows it, so that in reality there are as many different *h*'s as there are speech sounds that may be used after it.

To disclose the true nature of [h] as a sound, pronounce very carefully and slowly the vowel [i], holding it for a moment. Almost immediately pronounce [hi]. In comparing the two performances, observe that there is no noticeable change in the position of the tongue, jaw, or lips; the only difference is that [hi] begins with breath, while [i] begins with voice. The variable nature of [h] as a speech sound is seen when the syllable [hi] is compared with [hɑ] or with [hu]. If these syllables are whispered, the distinctly different quality of the [h] in each instance can easily be heard.

Only in a few special cases does this sound present any speech problem. Those whose speech reflects a foreign language background may omit the [h], *hope* being pronounced as [op] and *hall* as [ɔl] by these individuals. This, of course, is a noticeable deviation from standard pronunciation and should be avoided. Where [h] begins an unstressed syllable within a word or an unstressed word within a phrase, it is often omitted in informal, natural speech. Thus, the *h* is customarily omitted from such words as *forehead, annihilate,* and *vehicle* and it may properly be dropped out in such statements as 'I saw her there' [aɪ sɔ ɚ ðɛr] and 'He said he saw him' [hi sɛd i sɔ ɪm] when the words containing the *h* are unstressed, and when there is no problem of intelligibility involved.

The initial *h* is universally disregarded in such words as *heir, hour,* and *honest,* but there is less uniformity in the pronunciation of another group of words spelled with *h,* of which *humble, herb,* and *homage* are examples. As was stated, [h] is found in English speech not only preceding vowels but also as an approach to two of the glides, [w] and [j], as found in the words *where* [hwɛr] and *hue* [hju]. Usage varies considerably over the country with respect to the sounding of [h] in such words as these. In the speech of certain individuals it is omitted, and *whether* is pronounced like 'weather' and *hue* is indistinguishable from 'you,' resulting in a number of homophones (words that sound alike but have different meanings). With the possible exception of the Eastern region, where it is more common than in other sections of the country and where opinion is divided, this practice of omitting the [h] approach to the [w] and [j] glides, as in the examples shown, is not generally accepted as the best usage.*

The individual wishing to improve his speech, therefore, would be well advised to make a clear distinction in pronunciation between [w] and [hw] † (usually spelled *wh*), and

---

* Wise, Claude M., *Applied Phonetics,* pp. 200-201, Prentice-Hall, Inc., Englewood Cliffs, N. J., 1957.

† This sound is also described by some phoneticians as a voiceless [w], in which case it is represented by the symbol [ʍ].

likewise between [j] and [hj], in the case of those words in which prevailing good usage in his section of the country recognizes an *h* approach. The individual who is prone to have *wh* trouble may help himself by remembering that the most usual spelling, which is with *wh,* is actually reversed in pronunciation, becoming [hw]. In other words, the [h] is pronounced *before* the [w], not after, as it is spelled. It may be worth noticing in passing that the various forms of *who* and *whole,* although spelled with *wh,* are pronounced simply with [h].

Compare the pronunciation of the words in the following pairs. 'Get set' for the second member of each pair by expelling some unvocalized breath while the articulatory mechanism is in position for the [w], which produces the [h] effect. Follow this with the voiced [w]. Hold your hand close to your mouth; can you feel the emitted breath when you pronounce *where, whether,* etc.?

wear—where	wail—whale	Wac—whack
weather—whether	wine—whine	wig—Whig
wet—whet	way—whey	Wight—white
wile—while	weal—wheel	were—whir
witch—which	watt—what	wit—whit
wen—when	world—whirled	wither—whither

Investigate the recommended pronunciation of the following words and compare it with your own:

huge	human	humor	humble
whoop	heir	herb	why (interjection)
homage	hue	humid	forehead

PRACTICE MATERIAL FOR [h], [hw], AND [hj]

1. The horn of the hunter was heard on the hill.
2. Many a wit is not a whit wittier than Whittier.
3. We all enjoy a little humor, human nature being what it is.

4. When, whence, where, and why are adverbs, whereas which, what, and who are pronouns.

5. Humphrey had the humility to wear his new honors with discretion.

6. They played whist whenever they went anywhere.

7. White hawthorne was blooming everywhere along the high-way.

8. Hugh painted the wheel white with a blue hub.

> 9. Home is the sailor, home from the sea,
> And the hunter home from the hill.

> 10. To the gull's way and the whale's way
> Where the wind's like a whetted knife.

11. The wind bloweth where it listeth, and thou hearest the sound thereof, but canst not tell whence it cometh, and whither it goeth.

12. It is good to be out on the road, and going one knows not where,
Going through meadow and village, one knows not whither nor why.

> 13. Wherefore rejoice? What conquest brings he home?
> What tributaries follow him to Rome,
> To grace in captive bonds his chariot wheels?

14. We are rich only through what we give, and poor only through what we refuse.

> 15. O what a tangled web we weave,
> When first we practice to deceive!

16. Men now are precisely what they were when they thrust Jeremiah into a hole and took off the head of John the Baptist.

> 17. Home is the place where, when you have to go there,
> They have to take you in.

> 18. Into this Universe, and *Why* not knowing
> Nor *Whence*, like Water willy-nilly flowing;
> And out of it, as wind along the waste,
> I know not whither, willy-nilly blowing.

What, without asking, hither hurried whence?
And, without asking, whither hurried hence?
    Oh, many a cup of this forbidden wine
Must drown the memory of that insolence!
                    FITZGERALD, *The Rubaiyat of Omar Khayyam*

19. See the mermaid on the whale,
    'Whoa!' she cries, 'Don't whisk your tail!'
    'Whoa!' she cries, 'It makes me slip.
    Must I whack it with my whip?'
    Said the whale with mournful whine,
    'Your tail whisks as well as mine;
    Tails were made to whisk and flop,
    Whacking will not make them stop.'

                                        UNKNOWN

20. High on the shore sat the great god Pan,
    While turbidly flowed the river;
    And hacked and hewed as a great god can,
    With his hard bleak steel at the patient reed,
    Till there was not a sign of the leaf indeed
    To prove it fresh from the river.

                                        E. B. BROWNING

THE GLIDES

There are four glide sounds in English, [l], [r], [j], and [w].
The glides are transition sounds resulting from the movement of the articulatory mechanism from one vowel, or
vowel-like, position to another during continuous voicing.
The first three depend principally upon movement of the
tongue, while the fourth is also materially dependent upon
activity of the lips. From the point of view of sonority and
resonance, the glides have much in common with the vowels
and diphthongs.

THE CONSONANT [l] AS IN [lip] *leap*

The sound [l] is emitted laterally around the sides of the
tongue, the point remaining in contact with the upper gum
ridge in front momentarily or for a longer time, depending

upon the position which [l] occupies in relation to the other sounds in the word or syllable. As a matter of fact, this sound is an extremely variable one, there being virtually as many varieties as there are sounds which may precede or follow it.

The shape and position of the body of the tongue as well as the shape of the lips determine the particular resonance or quality which the [l] will have. When [l] precedes a vowel, particularly a high front vowel, as in the word *leap,* the point of elevation of the tongue is likely to be farther forward in the mouth and the lip opening somewhat wider than when [l] is used in the final position as in *haul,* or when it precedes a consonant as in *help,* or when it is used syllabically as in *little* [lɪtl̩]. In the former instance the characteristic resonance of the [l] resembles that of the front vowels and it is called a 'clear' or 'light' *l.* In the latter case the resonance is more like that of the back vowels and the sound is referred to as a 'dark' *l.*

It is in connection with this characteristic of the *l* to move backwards in the mouth, as it were, under the influence of certain conditions that we find the chief problems involved in its pronunciation. There is a strong tendency noticeable in the speech of many people to allow the [l] to become too dark generally. It is formed so far back in the mouth and with so little movement of the front of the tongue that it strongly resembles the back vowel [u], or in some cases [ɔ] or the neutral vowel [ə]. Thus *help* tends to become [hɛəp], *hill* becomes [hɪə] or [hɪɔ], and *little* sounds like [lɪtu] in the speech of these individuals. In such cases the [l] might be said to be 'swallowed.'

The so-called syllabic *l* is found in such words as *bottle* [batl̩] and *saddle* [sædl̩], in which the [l̩] forms a syllable by itself without the aid of another vowel sound. Used in this way, the [l̩] takes on many of the qualities of a true vowel and is so classified by some phoneticians. In such words the tongue moves directly from the preceding consonant to the [ḷ] position without any vowel intervening. In the case of the preceding [t] and [d] illustrated above, they are exploded around the sides of the tongue and into the [ḷ] instead of over the tip of the tongue as in the usual manner. The reader is referred at this point to the earlier discussion of [t] and [d], where it was pointed out that where syllabic *l* occurs, there is danger of the glottal stop [ʔ] becoming substituted for the preceding [t] or [d], giving us such sub-standard pronunciations as [bɑʔl̩] for *bottle* and [lɪʔl̩] for *little*. This fault is particularly prevalent in New York City.

The best approach to the improvement of this sound will often be to capitalize on the similarity between [d] and [l] with respect to the position of the tip of the tongue. Compare the paired words below and observe the position of the tongue tip as you pronounce the first word beginning with [d]. Try to carry over this feeling as you begin the [l] in the second word. Before the [l] is released, it should feel very much like the [d], the tongue being in a similar position, the tip resting against the upper gum ridge. As the [l] is pronounced, the sides are released first and then the tip is dropped as the tongue passes from [l] into position for the following sound.

deep—leap	dome—loam	dip—lip
dead—lead	dove—love	dark—lark
dine—line	dawn—lawn	dame—lame
dad—lad	doom—loom	dear—leer

In pronouncing [l], the two important points to observe are that (1) the tongue tip rests against the upper gum ridge and (2) the release first comes around the sides of the tongue. These characteristics can be demonstrated readily if the transition between [d] and [l] is observed in the combination [dl̩], as in the final syllable of *saddle,* being sure to produce a syllabic *l* as described previously. Pronounce the [dl̩] syllable slowly and carefully, observing where the release comes as you pass from *d* to *l*. Hold the [l] portion long enough to study its formation. You will note that the tongue tip is still against the upper gum ridge and the tongue as a whole is in position for the start of the glide [l], as found in such words as *leap* and *lad*.

Good articulation demands a clearly formed [l] produced by lively action of the tongue centering not too far back in the mouth. Begin with initial [l] and medial [l] followed by a vowel, preferably a high front vowel, as in *lip* and *hilly*. Proceed from there to the more difficult pre-consonantal, final, and syllabic positions, as in *milk, fail,* and *rattle.* At the beginning it will be found helpful to practice the *l* in various nonsense syllables followed by the several vowels, as [li, le, lɑ, lo, lu, etc.]. Other helpful exercises will be found in the previous chapter under 'Exercises for the Tongue.'

PRACTICE MATERIAL FOR [l]

INITIAL		MEDIAL			FINAL	
lady	late	alone	cliff	help	heel	little
leave	left	fellow	blame	milk	hill	camel
let	lunch	melody	play	colt	sale	saddle
lie	lard	Ellen	sleep	heels	pal	uncle
lamp	loud	silly	flock	field	ball	giggle
law	leap	eleven	glass	health	pole	whistle
loop	lip	alive	split	wolf	full	puzzle
load	lead	belong	slope	lily	file	table

1. The lithe athlete went leaping nimbly over the low hurdles.
2. Beautiful yellow flowers grew all along the lane.
3. Not a single fellow lifted his little finger to offer help.
4. Nellie fell into the lake and yelled for help.
5. Learning to listen is an important preliminary to clearer articulation.
6. The pilot landed the plane safely.
7. Last week little blue violets were growing all over that hill.
8. The lady laughed at the little children playing ball.
9. A meadow lark flew up onto a limb of that tall tree.

10. Central High School's star basketball player was limping as he left the floor.

11. Willie was a piper's son,
    He learned to play when he was young;
    But the only tune that he could play,
    Was 'Over the Hills and Far Away.'

12. The fields fall southward, abrupt and broken,
    To the low last edge of the long lone land.

13. The curfew tolls the knell of parting day,
    The lowing herd winds slowly o'er the lea;
    The plowman homeward plods his weary way,
    And leaves the world to darkness and to me.

14. Don't you love to lie and listen
      Listen to the rain,
    With its little patter, patter,
    And its tiny clatter, clatter,
    And its silvery spatter, spatter,
    On the roof and on the pane?

15. The student has his Rome, his Florence, his whole glowing Italy, within the four walls of his library. He has in his books the ruins of an antique world and the glories of a modern one.

16. Liberty is to the collective body, what health is to every individual body. Without health no pleasure can be tasted by man; without liberty, no happiness can be enjoyed by society.

17. It was night, and the rain fell: and, falling, it was rain, but, having fallen, it was blood. And I stood in the morass among the tall lilies, and the rain fell upon my head—and the lilies sighed one unto the other in the solemnity of their desolation.

EDGAR ALLAN POE, 'Silence—A Fable'

18. In the dooryard fronting an old farm-house near the white-wash'd palings,
    Stands the lilac-bush tall-growing with heart-shaped leaves of rich green,
    With many a pointed blossom rising delicate, with the perfume strong I love,
    With every leaf a miracle—and from this bush in the door-yard,

With delicate-color'd blossoms and heart-shaped leaves of
  rich green,
A spring with its flower I break.

WALT WHITMAN, 'When Lilacs Last in the
Dooryard Bloom'd'

19. All through the windless night the clipper rolled
    In a great swell with oily gradual heaves
    Which rolled her down until her time-bells tolled,
    Clang, and the weltering water moaned like beeves.
    The thundering rattle of slatting shook the sheaves,
    Startles of water made the swing ports gush,
    The sea was moaning and sighing and saying 'Hush!'

JOHN MASEFIELD, 'Dauber'

20. When the night wind howls in the chimney cowls, and the
    bat in the moonlight flies,
    And inky clouds, like funeral shrouds, sail over the midnight
    skies—
    When the footpads quail at the night-bird's wail, and black
    dogs bay the moon,
    Then is the spectre's holiday—then is the ghosts' high noon!

W. S. GILBERT, *Ruddigore*

THE CONSONANT [r] AS IN [rʌn] *run*

The lingua-palatal glide consonant [r] is begun from a
typical articulatory position that can be described as follows:
The sides of the tongue are in contact with the inner borders
of the teeth as far forward as the first or second bicuspid.
The tip is elevated toward, but does not touch, the hard
palate slightly back of the upper gum ridge. From this starting position, which is approximately that for the vowel [ɝ]
as in *her*, the tongue moves, or glides, to the position required for the sound that follows. This movement usually
involves a dropping of the tongue tip. When [r] follows a
vowel, the process is reversed and also considerably modified.

Since [r] is largely an invisible sound and since the tongue
does not make actual contact with the palate, the position

and shape of the tongue must be judged largely through the kinesthetic sense. This fact explains, for the most part, why it is difficult to determine definitely just where the tongue actually is and what it does; and it also partially explains why there is considerable variation from individual to individual in the way [r] is produced. This variation involves chiefly the degree of curling backward (retroflexion) of the tongue tip and the degree and place of elevation of the rest of the tongue. It should be noted in passing that [r] is primarily a tongue sound; it should be produced with a minimum of dependence on lip movement.

It should be made clear that the sound thus far described is the pre-vocalic [r] (followed by a vowel) as found in the words *red,* where it is initial, and *around,* where it is medial. When the [r] follows a vowel or is in the final position, as in *cart* or *fear,* it is pronounced somewhat differently and varies considerably in the manner of its production, not only among individuals, but from one section of the country to another. Through the Middle West and West, where [r] is generally pronounced in all positions, the post-vocalic variety is typically weaker than the pre-vocalic [r], receiving less stress and being characterized by less retroflexion of the tongue. Throughout sections of the East and South post-vocalic [r] disappears altogether or is replaced by the neutral vowel [ə]. Thus, *cart* becomes [kɑːt] and *fear* is pronounced [fɪə] in these areas.

In regard to this problem of handling the post-vocalic *r,* the individual would be well advised to follow the accepted practice of the best speakers of the particular section of the country in which he happens to live. This is one case in which the problem of speaking clearly can be kept more or less distinct from the problem of speaking 'correctly.' In any event, it should be remembered that *r* before a vowel is always pronounced.

The principal problems in the production and use of [r] can be summarized briefly as follows:

1. A *w* or *w*-like substitution for *r* is not uncommon among children and also among others where excessive lip action is present in the formation of [r], often as a compensation for inadequate tongue activity.

2. A 'dark' vowel-like quality, sometimes referred to as a 'back *r*,' may result if the front of the tongue is kept too low and too far forward in the mouth and the principal humping of the tongue is too far back.

3. The *r* is ordinarily not trilled in American speech. A trilled *r* suggests a foreign language background.

4. Both [l] and [r] may be confused and interchanged by individuals with an Oriental language background.

5. The [r] can become unpleasantly conspicuous if it is unduly stressed or prolonged in one's speech, or if it is produced with the tongue in an excessively retroflexed position. This is sometimes referred to as the 'burred *r*' and becomes particularly noticeable if it occurs in the post-vocalic position.

In the improvement of [r], the important points to remember are that a definite and vigorous movement is required and that it is the tongue that is chiefly involved. Sluggishness of tongue action has a devastating effect upon the [r], just as it has upon the [l], and where compensating lip activity has been developed to make up for deficient tongue action, the [r] will take on a definite *w*-quality. For those individuals in whom excessive lip activity has tended to replace adequate tongue functioning, the pairing of words beginning with [w] and [r] will tend to make the distinction between these two sounds more obvious. Note that [w] is primarily a lip sound; in pronouncing [r], although there may be some lip activity still present, it is the tongue that is principally involved.

wing—ring	won—run	woo—rue	weep—reap
wipe—ripe	way—ray	wake—rake	wed—red
wag—rag	wail—rail	woe—roe	wow—row

The tongue position for [r] may be facilitated by comparing it with the position for [d]. When the beginning of the two syllables [de] and [re] is compared, for example, it will be found that in the production of [r] the tip of the tongue is drawn back and elevated slightly from the gum ridge where it rests for [d]. With a point of departure thus established, the position from which the glide [r] is begun will be easier to determine. Paired words such as the following can be used to exploit this comparison still further:

doe—roe	Dan—ran	dope—rope	dip—rip
dub—rub	doom—room	deem—ream	day—ray
dice—rice	dead—red	dent—rent	dim—rim

PRACTICE MATERIAL FOR [r]

INITIAL		MEDIAL		POST-VOCALIC AND FINAL	
rock	Richard	arrive	story	farm	fire
reel	ripple	tomorrow	marry	heart	store
rap	rabbit	arrow	parachute	harp	car
room	robin	very	borrow	fork	here
rope	rowboat	parade	hearing	yarn	hour
rough	wretched	carrot	terrible	weird	moor
rip	review	berate	glory	garb	air
rice	reduce	fearing	nourish	Carl	care

BLENDS WITH [r]

rap—trap—strap	rag—brag—crag
ride—tried—stride	rink—drink—shrink
roll—troll—stroll	rank—Frank—shrank
ripe—tripe—stripe	rill—grill—frill—shrill
rest—pressed—crest	rim—prim—brim—trim

ray—pray—bray—tray	rue—crew—true—through
rye—pry—fry—try	ray—dray—gray—fray
rip—trip—drip—strip	roe—crow—grow—fro
rank—drank—prank—crank	roan—drone—groan—throne

rough and ready	round and round	wrack and ruin
criss-cross	round robin	right or wrong

1. Around the rough and rugged rock the ragged rascal ran.

2. Henry Clay once said, 'I would rather be right than be President.'

3. Truth crushed to earth will rise again.

4. Ruth wore a brown dress to the races.

5. Everywhere in the country one saw the bright broom blossoms.

6. He tried to drive the car through the narrow door.

7. The cart creaked and groaned as he drove along the crooked road.

8. The attractive winner wore a cotton dress with prominent red stripes.

9. Harry ran down to the river in the rain.

10. A large green frog suddenly leaped from his rock into the water.

11. 'Tis strange but true; for truth is always strange—stranger than fiction.

12. In September many people return from the summer resorts for a greatly needed rest.

13. By the rude bridge that arched the flood,
    Their flag to April's breeze unfurled,
Here once the embattled farmers stood,
    And fired the shot heard round the world.

14. When a merry maiden marries,
Sorrow goes and pleasure tarries;
Every sound becomes a song.
All is right and nothing wrong!

15. Water, water, everywhere,
And all the boards did shrink;
Water, water, everywhere
Nor any drop to drink.

16. I heard the trailing garments of the Night
    Sweep through her marble halls!
 I saw her sable skirts all fringed with light
    From the celestial walls!

17. Row, vassals, row, for the pride of the Highlands!
    Stretch to your oars, for the evergreen Pine!
 O that the rosebud that graces yon islands
    Were wreathed in a garland around him to twine!

18. Ambition has but one reward for all;
    A little power, a little transient fame,
    A grave to rest in, and a fading name!

19. Drip, drip, the rain comes falling,
    Rain in the woods, rain on the sea;
 Even the little waves, beaten, come crawling
    As if to find shelter here with me.

20. Our purses shall be proud, our garments poor.
    For 'tis the mind that makes the body rich;
 And as the sun breaks through the darkest clouds,
    So honor peereth in the meanest habit.

21. A good reader is nearly as rare as a good writer. People
bring their prejudices, whether friendly or adverse.

22. The rain is raining all around,
    It falls on field and tree;
    It rains on the umbrellas here
    And on the ships at sea.

23. Sherwood in the twilight, is Robin Hood awake?
 Gray and ghostly shadows are gliding through the brake,
 Shadows of a dappled deer, dreaming of the morn,
 Dreaming of a shadowy man that winds a shadowy horn.
 Oberon, Oberon, rake away the gold,
 Rake away the red leaves, roll away the mold,
 Rake away the gold leaves, roll away the red,
 And wake Will Scarlett from his leafy forest bed.
                    ALFRED NOYES, 'A Song of Sherwood'

24. In a coign of the cliff between lowland and highland,
    At the sea-down's edge between windward and lee,
Walled round with rocks as an inland island,
    The ghost of a garden fronts the sea.
A girdle of brushwood and thorn discloses
    The steep square slope of the blossomless bed
Where the weeds that grew green from the graves of its roses
    Now lie dead.

A. SWINBURNE, 'The Forsaken Garden'

THE CONSONANT [j] AS IN [jɛs] *yes*

This lingua-palatal glide is most commonly spelled with *y* as in *yesterday,* although we also find the sound spelled differently in such words as *ewe, Europe, volume,* and *opinion.* To form the glide [j] the tongue begins from a position approximately that for the vowel [i], then shifts rapidly to the position for the vowel that follows. The sound of [j] is the result of this relatively rapid shift during continuous voicing. To illustrate, pronounce the vowel [i], holding it for a moment; without interrupting the flow of tone, shift abruptly into the vowel [u]. The result should resemble closely the word *you* [ju]. Note that [j] is primarily a tongue sound, although the lips may also be involved, as they were in the example just cited.

Since [j] presents no serious problems for the majority of individuals, nothing further will be said about it and no practice material for it will be included. The *h*-approach to [j], as in the word *human* [hjumən] was discussed in a previous section under the consonant [h].

THE CONSONANT [w] AS IN [we] *way*

The bilabial glide [w] is the only one of the glides dependent to any great extent upon activity of the lips. In its formation the lips open rapidly from their shape and position for the vowel [u], which is the position from which [w] begins, to the shape which they assume for the vowel that follows.

Of course, the tongue also changes position during this transition, but the sudden widening of the lip orifice is very important. Reversing the demonstration suggested for [j] in the foregoing section, pronounce the vowel [u] and then quickly shift to the vowel [i] during continuous voicing. The result should be the word *we* [wi].

Although individuals with a foreign language background may interchange [w] and [v], the only real problem confronting a native speaker of English is a possible muffling of the [w] through lack of precise and vigorous lip action. Much of what was said earlier in this chapter regarding the importance of adequate lip activity in the articulation of *p, b,* and *m* applies with equal force to *w,* perhaps more so, since a somewhat more complicated lip activity is involved. Exercises and selections containing numerous *w*'s, therefore, make excellent drill material for developing clearness of articulation generally, especially as it relates to activity of the lips. Since lip movements are clearly visible, it may prove helpful to practice some of the following materials with the aid of a small hand mirror. The reader is also referred at this point to the exercises for the lips included in the previous chapter, several of which involve the glide [w].

Practice Material for [w]

1. Walter went away for a while with William.
2. We went walking in the winter wonderland.
3. Wilda stood watching as Warren washed the window.
4. The wagon wobbled along on crooked wheels.
5. The men lay quietly in their tent listening to the wind wailing in the willows.
6. The winning play was credited to some quick work by the wily quarterback.
7. 'O, wild West Wind, thou breath of Autumn's being!'
8. With what wistful look did he eye every trembling ray of light streaming across the waste fields from some distant window.
9. Great souls have wills; feeble ones have only wishes.
10. All bow to virtue, and then walk away.

11. No man is born into the world whose work
Is not born with him; there is always work,
And tools to work withal, for those who will.

12. The western wind was wild and wet with foam,
And all alone went she.

13. We think our fathers fools, so wise we grow;
Our wiser sons, no doubt, will think us so.

14. We judge ourselves by what we feel capable of doing, while others judge us by what we have already done.

15. 'Tis well to be merry and wise,
'Tis well to be honest and true;
'Tis well to be off with the old love
Before you are on with the new.

16. The west winds blow, and, singing low,
I hear the glad streams run;
The windows of my soul I throw
Wide open to the sun.

The woods shall wear their robes of praise,
The south-wind softly sigh,
And sweet, calm days in golden haze
Melt down the amber sky.

J. G. WHITTIER, 'My Psalm'

17. With what wistful look did he eye every trembling ray of light streaming across the waste fields from some distant window.

18. It's a warm wind, the west wind, full of birds' cries;
I never hear the west wind but tears are in my eyes.
For it comes from the west lands, the old brown hills,
And April's in the west wind, and daffodils.

JOHN MASEFIELD, 'The West Wind'

19. Whichever way the wind doth blow,
Some heart is glad to have it so.
Then blow it east or blow it west,
The wind that blows, that wind is best.

IX

The Pronunciation of Vowels and Diphthongs

As was explained in an earlier chapter, vowels are resonance tones that owe their characteristic quality to the shape and size of the resonance cavities of the mouth, and the shape and size of the openings into and out of them. The articulatory organs chiefly responsible for the adjustments required in the formation of each vowel sound are the lips, jaw, tongue, velum, and the walls of the pharynx. Of these organs the tongue is probably the most important single one because of its extreme mobility and also because of the strategic position which it occupies, forming as it does not only the complete floor of the mouth cavity but the anterior wall of the lower pharynx as well. Any change in the shape or position of the tongue cannot fail to effect some consequent change in these resonance chambers.*

THE CLASSIFICATION OF VOWELS

In the previous chapter it was seen that a meaningful classification of consonants could be built upon the place and manner of their formation in the mouth. A similar treatment is feasible for the vowels, and some light may be thrown upon their identifying characteristics if a superficial examination is made of the processes involved in vowel formation.

Lip Rounding. The importance of the lips in the formation of vowel tones should by no means be overlooked. With-

---

* As a preliminary to his study of vowel pronunciation in this chapter, the reader is advised to review the section on *oral resonance* in Chapter IV.

out appropriate activity of these organs, proper sounding of certain of the back vowels especially becomes impossible. With the aid of a mirror, study the shape and position of the lips during the pronunciation of the back vowels [u, ʊ, o, ɔ, and ɒ]. If these vowels are properly formed, it will be seen that the lips are markedly protruded and rounded for [u] and [o] especially, somewhat less so for the others. Because of this characteristic, the back vowels, with the exception of the low back vowel [ɑ], are commonly referred to as 'rounded.' While the lips play a less prominent part in the formation of these sounds when they occur in connected speech, some degree of rounding is still necessary if the true quality of these vowels is to be maintained.

Still using the mirror, contrast the lip positions just described with the positions which characterize the front vowels [i, ɪ, e, ɛ, and æ]. In forming these sounds the lips are spread to a greater or less degree and somewhat retracted at the corners. The lips could be described as neutral for [a] and [ɑ] and the so-called central vowels. The importance which the lips play in the formation of the glide [w] has already been discussed. Some lip activity is also involved in the production of the diphthongs [ɑʊ] and [ju]. For these reasons speech habits involving lip laziness produce disastrous results in terms of vowel quality and hence general voice quality as well as seriously impairing clearness of articulation.

The Shape and Position of the Tongue. The tongue is even more important than the lips in achieving the distinctive quality that should characterize each vowel sound. In the discussion of oral resonance in Chapter IV, it was explained that as the tongue is lowered through progressive steps from a position in which it is 'bunched up' high in the front of the mouth to a position in which it lies more or less flat, the so-called front vowels [i, ɪ, e, ɛ, æ, and a] are sounded. As the back of the tongue is then raised through similar steps toward the back of the mouth until the point of greatest tension or 'bunching' is high in the back, with certain accompanying changes in lip position, the so-called back vowels are produced. These are in order from lowest to highest [ɑ, ɒ, ɔ, o, ʊ, and u]. Activity of the tongue in the middle of the mouth gives us the central vowels [ʌ, ə, ɚ, ɜ, and ɝ]. The tip of the tongue remains back of the lower teeth for all of the vowel sounds.

Two points of reference are thus provided by the activity of the tongue described above: (1) whether the bunching or greatest tension of the tongue takes place near the front, the back, or the central portion, on the basis of which, vowels are classified as front, back, or central; and (2) the degree of elevation of the 'bunched' portion of the tongue, according to which vowels can be classified as high, mid, or low. In relation to these points of reference, therefore, [i] would be classified as a high, front vowel, along with [ɪ]; [e] and [ɛ] would be mid, front and [æ] and [a] would be low, front. [u] and [ʊ] would be high, back, and rounded; [o] would be mid, back, and rounded, and [ɔ] and [ɒ] would be low, back, and rounded. [ɑ] would be called a low, back vowel, and those referred to in the previous paragraph as central vowels would be classified as mid, central.

In addition to the progressive lowering of the tongue in the formation of the front vowels beginning with [i], the jaw is also lowered a little further for each succeeding vowel. Likewise the jaw is raised slightly for each vowel in the back series progressing upward from [ɑ]. The change in the shape and position of the lips has already been referred to.

Length and Tenseness as Vowel Characteristics. There are also other factors which contribute to produce changes in vowel quality and quantity. Among them are (1) the length of the vowel and (2) the tenseness or laxness of the articulatory mechanism. As to length, such vowels as [i], [ɑ], and [ɔ] are as a rule relatively longer than such so-called short vowels as [ɪ], [ɛ], and [ʌ]. Regarding the second of these factors, it is generally agreed that at least a part of the difference in quality between the two vowels [i] and [ɪ], for example, can be traced to the relative tenseness of the mechanism during the sounding of [i], while for [ɪ] the musculature is more lax. A similar explanation accounts in part for the difference between [e] and [ɛ], and [u] and [ʊ], the former in each case being more tense than the latter.

The Vowel Diagram. We see from the preceding discussion that there are in reality seventeen vowels common to American speech instead of the traditional *a, e, i, o,* and *u.* If we should attempt to represent these seventeen sounds diagrammatically with respect to the approximate position in the mouth at which the bunching, or chief point of tension, of the tongue occurs, we should have some such arrangement as the following:

	Front of the mouth	*Central*	*Back of the mouth*
High	i—he ɪ—will		u—who ʊ—would
Mid	e—pay ɛ—them	ɝ, ɜ—bird ɚ—ever ə—upon ʌ—cut	o—go ɔ—call
Low	æ—back a—last		ɒ—on ɑ—father

Fig. 18. Classification of the vowels upon the basis of (1) elevation of the tongue and (2) location of the point of greatest tension. For a more complete orientation, superimpose this diagram upon the tongue and oral cavity as shown in Figure 1 in Chapter II, or compare it with the tongue positions shown in Figures 15 and 16 in Chapter IV.

Of course, it must be understood that a diagram of this sort is purely schematic and as such conveys but little exact information; it must not be taken to represent actual tongue placement. It does serve, however, to give some notion of the relative positions of the tongue as well as its direction of movement and change in the production of the various sounds.

Upon the care and precision with which the vowel sounds are formed the quality of the voice will ultimately depend, since quality is a characteristic of tone, and tone, as far as the voice is concerned, means a vowel. In order that each vowel may be given its true quality the speaker should have clearly in mind the essentials of its proper formation. In the following pages each vowel will be discussed and its production described briefly. Attention will also be called to any unacceptable forms which may be common enough to warrant mentioning.

THE VOWEL [i] AS IN [it] *eat*

This vowel, the long *e* of conventional spelling, is, as we have seen, the highest of the front vowels, being formed with the front of the tongue humped up high in the mouth toward the hard palate. The teeth are fairly close together and the lips are drawn back in the smile position. The vowel is relatively long and the mechanism is relatively tense during its production. The characteristic quality of this vowel is one of crispness and brilliance, the impression being that it is formed just back of the front teeth.

The vowel [i] is a common sound in speech, being spelled, as we have already seen, in a number of different ways. It is also a common sound in other languages, but it is inclined to be pronounced somewhat more abruptly in most foreign languages than in English, where it is characteristically prolonged. Therefore, the [i] may not sound entirely normal in the speech of an individual with a foreign language background, having a short, clipped quality faintly suggestive of a sound somewhere between our [i] and [ɪ]. It normally presents no difficulty to a native speaker of English.

THE VOWEL [ɪ] AS IN [hɪt] *hit*

With the tongue slightly lowered from the [i] position and with the teeth opened a little wider, the vowel [ɪ] is produced. It is also normally a somewhat shorter sound than the vowel [i] and the musculature of the speech mechanism is in a more lax condition. This sound is the short *i* found in such words as *him, sit,* and *pity.* While this is a very difficult sound for individuals with a foreign language background to master because of their tendency to confuse it with [i], it ordinarily presents no problems for one who speaks English as his native language.

Since the vowel [ɪ] is missing from many of the other languages of the world, the foreigner will substitute for it the sound from his own language which it most closely resembles. This is usually the foreign variety of [i] mentioned above. In foreign dialect, therefore, the word *sit* sounds to us like 'seat,' and *hit* resembles 'heat.' To correct this fault, the tongue must be lowered slightly in the front of the mouth and made a bit more lax.

Pairing words with [i] and [ɪ] will serve to call attention to the difference between these two vowels, since it is obvious that the two words in each pair are different words. If the second member of each pair is pronounced to sound just like the first, then it is clear something is wrong. With a familiar point of departure thus established in the first word, it will be easier to make the necessary change in the second. Pairs like the following will be found valuable:

heat—hit	seep—sip	deem—dim	keel—kill
wheat—whit	leak—lick	seek—sick	team—Tim
seen—sin	leap—lip	sheep—ship	seat—sit
feast—fist	keen—kin	beetle—little	lead—lid

PRACTICE MATERIAL FOR [i] AND [ɪ]

INITIAL		MEDIAL			
eat	it	meal	mill	greet	grit
each	itch	weak	wick	beet	bit
eel	ill	steeple	stipple	deed	did
ease	is	bean	bin	reed	rid
e'en	in	seal	sill	deep	dip
east	idiom	least	list	scream	scrim

1. Tim's teacher took him to see the big city.
2. The little kitten quickly ran up the tree.
3. In the dim light the last of the wheat was put into the bin.
4. If you wish a thing done quickly, ask a busy man to do it.
5. His business was good but not as big as he wished it to be.
6. Edith was singing as she came down the hill.
7. Jim listened to the wind singing in the trees.
8. His sister was busy knitting things for Christmas.
9. Neal made a quick trip to the city to see his children.
10. Dick wanted to build a bridge over the stream, but Lee didn't agree.

11.   A little house well filled,
       A little field well tilled,
       A little wife well willed,
       Are great riches.

12. It is a most peculiar thing that when a maid's sixteen,
    She wants to pass for thirty and be dangerous and keen.
But when a woman's thirty, she muffles down her wit,
    And acts sixteen, and really thinks she gets away with it!

13. The Moving Finger writes; and, having writ,
    Moves on; nor all your Piety nor wit
       Shall lure it back to cancel half a line,
    Nor all your tears wash out a word of it.

14. And long will be the way,
       And high will be the hill,
       And dark will be the day,
       Before my feet are still.

15. So, naturalists observe, a flea
Has smaller fleas that on him prey;
And these have smaller still to bite 'em;
And so proceed ad infinitum.

16. A primrose by a river's brim
A yellow primrose was to him,
And it was nothing more.

17. All earth's full rivers can not fill
The sea, that drinking thirsteth still.

18. The history of the past is a mere puppet show. A little man comes out and blows a little trumpet, and goes in again. You look for something new, and lo! another little man comes out and blows another little trumpet, and goes in again. And it is all over.

H. W. LONGFELLOW

19. The appearance of Rip, with his long grizzled beard, his rusty fowling-piece, his uncouth dress, and an army of women and children at his heels, soon attracted the attention of the tavern politicians. They crowded round him, eyeing him from head to foot with great curiosity.

WASHINGTON IRVING

20. Only reapers, reaping early
In among the bearded barley,
Hear a song that echoes cheerly
From the river winding clearly,
    Down to Tower'd Camelot;
And by the moon the reaper weary,
Piling sheaves in upland airy,
Listening, whispers, ' 'Tis the fairy
    Lady of Shalott.'

TENNYSON, 'The Lady of Shalott'

THE VOWEL [e] AS IN [sem] *same*

Although this sound, which is the long *a* of words like *mate, able,* and *say,* is represented here as a vowel, in the actual speech of a majority of speakers it becomes a diphthong when it occurs in a syllable which is accented or stressed. That is, there are in reality two sounds blended together instead of just the one, even though both may be represented in spelling by the one letter as in the examples given above. The two sound elements, which can easily be heard and identified if the diphthong is prolonged, are [e] and [ɪ], the first one stressed, the second but lightly touched; they are often represented phonetically as [eɪ]. To demonstrate, pronounce the word, *say,* slowly and you will distinctly hear that it ends in a sound strongly resembling [ɪ]. You will also note that your tongue has moved slightly during the sounding of this vowel. For this reason *say* is often written phonetically as [seɪ] and *mate* as [meɪt]. However, for the sake of simplicity the one symbol [e] is frequently used to represent this sound.

Since [e] is actually a pure vowel in most other languages instead of a diphthong, the foreigner will likely use this sound with which he is familiar when he speaks English. As a result, *gate* will sound to us somewhat like 'get' and *rain* will remind us of 'wren.' Such an individual needs to prolong the [e] more than he is accustomed to doing, allowing his tongue to rise slightly near the end of the sound toward the [ɪ] position.

There is some danger of [e] taking on a flat and nasal quality in certain types of American speech, especially when it is found in words containing adjacent nasal consonants, as in *same, name,* and *main.* To avoid this unpleasant quality, care must be exercised to insure that the sound is emitted properly through the mouth. The jaw should not be too rigid nor the tongue too tense, and the throat must be properly opened and relaxed.

Listen to the [e] carefully as you pronounce the following words; work for an 'open' pleasant sound:

frame	aim	tame	vain	nation
manger	angel	maintain	claim	maiden
rain	maim	fame	nature	make

PRACTICE MATERIAL FOR [e]

INITIAL		MEDIAL		FINAL	
able	acorn	vacate	grade	bray	clay
eight	apex	grape	game	say	away
age	apron	cable	cane	play	stay
acre	Avery	waiting	waver	sway	spray
alien	April	station	vapor	weigh	dray
ancient	amiable	name	main	may	neigh

Comparing [e] *and* [ɛ]:

laid—led	rake—wreck	Bain—Ben
wade—wed	age—edge	fail—fell
freight—fret	tail—tell	wage—wedge
shale—shell	gate—get	late—let
bacon—beckon	rain—wren	mate—met

1. Am I to blame if Mabel came too late?
2. The maiden claimed to be related to the late steel magnate.
3. Day after day the rain came down upon the plain.
4. Jane maintained that she should make a cake.
5. The location of the firm was changed, but the name remained the same.
6. Nell can explain this strange mistake.
7. Fred's birthday came on the same day as Hazel's.
8. Ned made a bookcase for James.
9. The sole basis of the candidate's claim to fame lay in the prestige of his family name.
10. With the aid of his cane, the old man made his way along the wet lane.

11. Out upon the wharfs they came,
    Knight and burgher, lord and dame,
    And round the prow they read her name,
    The Lady of Shalott

12. The ceaseless rain is falling fast,
    And yonder gilded vane,
    Immovable for three days past,
    Points to the misty main.

13. For what avail the plough or sail,
    Or land or life, if freedom fail?

14. Diplomacy is to do and say
    The nastiest things in the nicest way.

15. If the nose of Cleopatra had been shorter, the whole face
of the earth would have been changed.

16. A man who would woo a fair maid,
    Should 'prentice himself to the trade;
        And study all day,
        In methodical way,
    How to flatter, cajole, and persuade.
    He should 'prentice himself at fourteen,
    And practice from morning to e'en;
        And when he's of age,
        If he will, I'll engage,
    He may capture the heart of a queen!
                    W. S. GILBERT, *The Yeoman of the Guard*

17. So fades a Summer cloud away;
    So sinks the gale when storms are o'er;
    So gently shuts the eye of day;
    So dies a wave along the shore.

18. For he who fights and runs away
    May live to fight another day;
    But he who is in battle slain
    Can never rise and fight again.

THE VOWEL [ɛ] AS IN [gɛt] *get*

This vowel, often designated as the short *e*, is found in
such words as *bed, head, said, many,* and *friend.* As can be
seen from these examples, it is spelled in a variety of ways.
In the speech of a large number of individuals, [ɛ] is a relatively unstable vowel; there is a pronounced tendency to
substitute a number of other sounds for it when it occurs in
certain combinations. Representative substitutions are illustrated in the examples which follow.

1. Take care to pronounce [ɛ], not [ɪ], in such words as the following:

men	pen	get	many	emery	emphasis
when	ten	let	forget	empty	yes
them	penny	Jenny	chest	instead	yet
sent	mend	steady	any	end	engine

Practice on such pairs as the following will help to make clear the difference between [ɛ] and [ɪ]:

Min—men	tin—ten	Sid—said	pin—pen
kin—ken	hid—head	since—sense	in—N
lint—lent	tinder—tender	bin—Ben	him—hem

2. Do not allow the [ɛ] to become diphthongized to [eɪ] in the following words and similar ones:

| egg | measure | hair | keg | pleasure |
| leg | treasure | there | beg | care |

3. When [ɛ] is unduly prolonged, there is some danger of its becoming diphthongized to [ɛə], resulting in such pronunciations as [hɛəd] for *head* and [drɛəs] for *dress*. In the following words and similar ones pronounce a 'clean, crisp' [ɛ]; be careful not to drawl it out to [ɛə]:

head	bed	met	said	wet	kept
dress	next	pet	step	men	best
left	lend	gem	belt	desk	tell

4. The vowel is [ɛ], not [ɝ], in the following words:

| very | bury | where | America | merry |
| cherry | terrible | ferry | everywhere | there |

Study the pronunciation of the following words:

| thresh | kettle | chest | against | well |
| chair | care | bear | wrench | edge |

Practice Material for [ɛ]

1. Ten men were sent to tear down the old ferry.
2. The little red hen pecked at the empty keg.
3. They treasured the old cherry chest which was sent from America.
4. Sell the cherries to Jenny for a penny a measure.
5. Emory was very merry as he went to get the eggs.
6. Ellen takes pleasure in caring for her beautiful hair.
7. He had too much sense to sell the very, very old kettle.
8. They buried the old treasure chest near the spot where the empty hull rested.
9. Jenny's terrible experience, instead of shocking them, merely served to emphasize their desire to forget the entire affair.
10. She kept the yellow pencil in the desk.

11. Said a very small wren
     To a very large hen,
     'Pray why do you make such a clatter?
     I never could guess
     Why an egg more or less
     Should be thought so important a matter.'

12. Oft to his frozen lair
     Tracked I the grizzly bear,
     While from my path the hare
     Fled like a shadow.

13. Early to bed and early to rise,
     Makes a man healthy, wealthy, and wise.

14. Never ask of money spent
     Where the spender thinks it went.
     Nobody was ever meant
     To remember or invent
     What he did with every cent.

ROBERT FROST

15. The Reverend Henry Ward Beecher
     Called a hen a most elegant creature.
     The hen, pleased with that,
     Laid an egg in his hat,
     And thus did the hen reward Beecher.

O. W. HOLMES

16. If I ever reach heaven I expect to find three wonders there: first, to meet some I had not thought to see there; second, to miss some I had expected to see there; and third, the greatest wonder of all, to find myself there.

JOHN NEWTON

17. One evening as I wandered forth
Along the banks of Ayr,
I spied a man, whose aged step
Seemed weary, worn with care,
His face was furrowed o'er with years
And hoary was his hair.

BURNS, 'Man Was Made to Mourn'

18. Shall I, wasting in despair,
Die because a woman's fair?
Or make pale my cheeks with care,
'Cause another's rosy are?
Be she fairer than the day,
Or the flowery meads in May,
If she be not so to me,
What care I how fair she be?

WITHER, 'Shall I Wasting in Despair'

THE VOWEL [æ] AS IN [sæt] *sat*

This is the so-called short *a* of such words as *had, sand,* and *sack,* a very common vowel in American speech. It is formed with the tongue somewhat lower in the mouth than for [ɛ] and with a correspondingly wider jaw opening. If the tongue is allowed to become too tense in the production of [æ], the result is a disagreeable, flat, nasal quality. As in the case of [e], this is especially noticeable when [æ] is preceded or followed by a nasal consonant, in which case assimilation nasality plays an important part.

Practice the following words carefully, eliminating all traces of flatness and nasality from the pronunciation:

man	manner	rang	hand	plank	jam
mangle	mantle	bank	damp	angle	map
fancy	hang	camp	Manx	pan	ham

When other vowels become substituted for [æ], we have such mispronunciations as *gether* [gɛðɚ] for *gather* [gæðɚ], *ruther* [rʌðɚ] or *rether* [rɛðɚ] for *rather* [ræðɚ],* and *kin* [kɪn] for *can* [kæn]. Study the pronunciation of the following words:

rather	narrow	radish	happy	carry
barrel	catch	marry	Harold	Harry
arrow	Clara	claret	Paris	tarry
bade	barren	wheelbarrow	parrot	parish

Since the vowel [æ] does not occur in a number of foreign languages, the individual whose speech exhibits foreign influences will tend to substitute [ɑ] for it. Paired words containing [ɑ] and [æ] will help to illustrate the difference between these two sounds: †

cot—cat	hot—hat	odd—add	bog—bag
knock—knack	cop—cap	sock—sack	flog—flag
top—tap	volley—valley	don—Dan	sod—sad
pod—pad	shock—shack	con—can	calm—cam

In the regional dialect of certain sections of this country, particularly in New York City, [æ] is sometimes pronounced as [ɛ], or more likely [ɛə], resulting in such sub-standard pronunciations as [hɛənd] for *hand* and [glɛəd] for *glad*. Study carefully the words that should be pronounced with [æ] in the list that follows; compare these with the preceding member of each pair containing [ɛ]. Remember that [æ] requires a lower tongue position than does [ɛ]; be careful that the tongue does not become tense, and that it does not change position while the vowel is being pronounced.

---

* While the most common pronunciation of this word is with [æ] throughout the United States, pronunciations with [ɑ] and [a] are sometimes heard and are quite acceptable.

† The efficacy of this exercise is based upon the assumption that these and similar words spelled with the so-called 'short *o*' are pronounced with [ɑ]. It loses much of its point when, as is sometimes the case, the individual pronounces these words with [ɒ], a quite acceptable pronunciation.

ketch—catch	wreck—rack	head—had	send—sand
met—mat	set—sat	ken—can	pen—pan
shell—shall	gem—jam	wren—ran	slept—slapped
beg—bag	bend—band	hem—ham	neck—knack

In other sections of the country where [æ] may become unduly prolonged with a drawling effect, the vowel may again change into a diphthong, this time with the neutral vowel [ə] as the second element and [æ] as the first. This results in such pronunciations as [hæəd] for *had,* [hæənd] for *hand,* and [kæəp] for *cap.* This tendency should be avoided. [æ] is usually classified as a short vowel; it should be kept so.

PRACTICE MATERIAL FOR [æ]

1. Nancy, thank the man for the candy.
2. The bell on the bank door rang out with a great clang.
3. He sat with his hat in his hand holding the lamp in his lap.
4. Hand in hand, the man and the little boy ran rapidly over the damp sand.
5. Angus squatted near the campfire, pan in hand.
6. Nan's manner was grim as she reached to hang up the damp rag.
7. Francis stood on the plank to rescue his Manx cat from the overhanging bank.
8. Albert and Frank had inherited the land from their grandfather.
9. Andy sang every evening in camp.
10. The man at the fruit stand sold Dan a basket of red apples.

11. Sometimes a troop of damsels glad,
    An abbot on an ambling pad,
    Sometimes a curly shepherd-lad,
    Or long-hair'd page in crimson clad,
       Goes by to tower'd Camelot.

12. When of old Hildebrand
    I asked his daughter's hand,
    Mute did the minstrels stand
       To hear my story.

13. Rats!
They fought the dogs and killed the cats
    And bit the babies in the cradles,
And ate the cheeses out of the vats,
    And licked the soup from the cooks' own ladles,
Split open the kegs of salted sprats,
Made nests inside men's Sunday hats,
And even spoiled the Women's chats
    By drowning their speaking
    With shrieking and squeaking
In fifty different sharps and flats.

ROBERT BROWNING

14. Flower in the crannied wall,
    I pluck you out of the crannies,
    I hold you here, root and all, in my hand,
    Little flower—but *if* I could understand
    What you are, root and all, and all in all,
    I should know what God and man is.

TENNYSON

15. I recollect a nurse called Ann,
    Who carried me about the grass,
    And one fine day a fine young man
        Came up, and kissed the pretty lass:
    She did not make the least objection!
        Thinks I, 'Aha!
        When I can talk, I'll tell Mamma.'
    —And that's my earliest recollection.

FREDERICK LOCKER LAMPSON

16. And hand in hand, on the edge of the sand,
    They danced by the light of the moon,
        The moon,
        The moon,
    They danced by the light of the moon.

EDWARD LEAR

THE VOWEL [a] AS IN [ask] *ask*

The intermediate vowel [a] lies somewhere between [æ]
and [ɑ]. In its production the tongue is somewhat lower in

the mouth than it is for [æ], and the place of greatest tension is farther back. The use of this so-called 'compromise' vowel is very limited throughout the United States, being confined largely to certain areas along the Eastern seaboard. When it is found outside of these rather limited areas, in the majority of instances it is an acquired, or cultivated, sound. Many people do not use this vowel at all, pronouncing either [æ] or [ɑ] in its place. Of these two choices, [æ] is by far the more common in America.

The words for which this sound may be used comprise a small group sometimes referred to as the *ask* words, because *ask* happens to be one of the most typical. Other examples include *laugh, past, aunt,* and *dance.* There are only about 150 of them in all; they can be recognized as those words which the Englishman, and the American in certain areas of this country, pronounce with [ɑ], but which the majority of Americans pronounce with [æ].

It is difficult and perhaps unwise to attempt to offer dogmatic recommendations regarding the use of this sound. If one does not already have it in his speech, the value of acquiring it is probably not worth the time and effort involved. Even if one does succeed in incorporating it into his speech, it is doubtful whether he will ever be able to use it without a certain degree of self-consciousness.

In any case, two important points should be kept in mind in the pronunciation of the *ask* words. In the first place, whether one uses [æ], [a], or [ɑ], he should use the one sound consistently for all of the words belonging to this group. One should not, for example, say [ɑsk] and [ɑnt] for *ask* and *aunt,* using the 'broad' *a,* while in the next breath he pronounces *path* and *example* as [pæθ] and [ɛgzæmpl]. Furthermore, if the speaker habitually uses [æ] in all of the *ask* words, care should be taken to avoid undue flatness and nasalization in their pronunciation. In fact, all of the cautions mentioned in the previous section in connection with the use of [æ] likewise should be carefully observed in the case of these words.

On the other hand, if one does have this intermediate sound in his speech, he should exercise care to make sure that he does not use it for words which normally take the vowel [æ]. That is, he should be careful not to say [hand] for *hand* [hænd], [man] for *man* [mæn], or [hat] for *hat* [hæt]. Such pronunciations will impart to his speech an air of artificiality and affectation.

Practice the following words, sentences, and selections carefully, employing a vowel that is consistent for all of the *ask* words and one in which there is no trace of flatness or nasality:

PRACTICE MATERIAL FOR [a]

after	bath	mast	example
laugh	path	pass	advantage
half	ask	task	aunt
craft	cast	disaster	answer
staff	fast	class	dance
draft	glass	grass	grant

1. He laughs best who laughs last.

2. This is an example of a basket fashioned by a master craftsman.

3. We took advantage of the chance to see the samples of old glass, pewter, and brass.

4. The breeze rippled the grass and set the tulips dancing in its path.

5. Knowledge advances by slow steps with a staff, and not by an easy path.

6. Chance often gives us that which we should not have presumed to ask for; or have attempted to grasp.

7. Man thinks, and at once becomes the master of the class that does not think.

8. Dance, laugh, and be merry, but do not tread the primrose path.

9. And when Yourself with silver Foot shall pass
   Among the Guests Star-scattered on the Grass,
   And in your joyous errand reach the Spot
   Where I made One—turn down an empty Glass!

10. Then launched they to the blast,
    Bent like a reed each mast,
    Yet we were gaining fast,
       When the wind failed us.

11. A thousand dancing flowers
    Amid the dewy grass
    Glance at you with laughter
    And greet you as you pass.

12. And ever, when a louder blast
    Shook beam and rafter as it passed,
    The merrier up its roaring draught
    The great throat of the chimney laughed.

13. Fair stood the wind for France
    When we our sails advance,
    Nor now to prove our chance
       Longer will tarry.

14. And down the river's dim expanse
    Like some bold seer in a trance,
    Seeing all his own mischance—
    With a glassy countenance
    Did she look to Camelot.

THE VOWEL [ɑ] AS IN [fɑðɚ] *father*

This is the lowest of the back vowels and most open of any, made with the tongue relaxed and more or less flat in the mouth, the jaw dropped as far as for any speech sound, and the lips in a neutral, relaxed position. No serious problems are involved in its production, though care should be taken to give full value and prominence to the resonance in the front of the mouth, a condition referred to in Part 1 as 'forward placement.' If subjectively the [ɑ] appears to be concentrated too far back in the mouth and throat, it will take on a quality suggestive of [ɒ] or [ɔ]. An open, relaxed throat with careful management of the resonance in the front of the mouth will produce a sound of true fidelity, possessing a rich, vibrant quality.

The most widespread occurrence of this vowel in America is in the word *father,* or perhaps in the exclamation *ah!* It is also rather uniformly used in words spelled with *a* followed by *r,* such as *cart,* with the exception of the substitution mentioned below. The majority of Americans use [ɑ] in words spelled with so-called short *o,* such as *cot, rod,* and *not,* although [ɒ], to be discussed in the following section, is also heard in these words.

In New England and certain other parts of the East, the vowel [a] is often substituted for [ɑ] in words like *car* and *cart,* where the *a* is followed by final *r* or *r* plus a consonant. These words are pronounced as [kaː] and [kaːt] in these areas, and, of course, without the [r]. This change of vowel is a part of the accepted speech pattern in these areas of the East.

Not as common and not considered acceptable is a substitution of the vowels [ɒ] or [ɔ] for [ɑ] in the group of words referred to in the preceding paragraph, especially characteristic of substandard New York City speech. In such speech *car* sounds like 'caw,' and *cart* resembles 'caught,' although [r] is sometimes heard in these and similar words. Practice on the following list of paired words should illustrate the essential difference between the two vowels, [ɑ] and [ɔ]. If the second member of each pair resembles the first to the point where there is any danger of confusing the two, it is obvious that the [ɑ] is faulty, provided, of course, that the [ɔ] is reasonably close to standard.

form—farm	caught—cart	laud—lard	for—far
raw—rah	ought—art	or—are	caw—car
awe—ah	Shaw—shah	law—lah	yaw—yah
paw—pa	dawn—don	yawn—yon	cord—card

PRACTICE MATERIAL FOR [ɑ]

1. Arthur's father and grandfather before him had lived on the old farm.

2. In spite of the dark clouds, the farmer calmly hitched his oxen to the cart and started for the field.

3. Before dark father always drove his car into the garage.

4. Palm trees grew in a small plot near the center of the park.

5. The guard was charged with the responsibility of watching the car.

6. The drama students argued with the author about the plot of the story.

7. The olives are larger in this jar.

8. Bob calmly told his father that he wanted to join the army.

9.
> All that I know
> Of a certain star
> Is, it can throw
> (Like the angled spar)
> Now a dart of red,
> Now a dart of blue;
> Till my friends have said
> They would fain see, too,
> My star that dartles the red and the blue!

ROBERT BROWNING

10. Awake, Sir King, the gates unspar!
Rise up and ride both fast and far!
The sea flows over both and bar.

11. It is the lark that sings so out of tune,
Straining harsh discords and unpleasing sharps.

THE VOWEL [ɒ] AS IN [sɒft] *soft*

In the pronunciation of this low, back vowel the tongue is raised at the back slightly from the position for [ɑ], and there is just the beginning of the lip rounding which characterizes the back vowels generally. The vowel [ɒ] is an intermediate sound midway between [ɑ] and [ɔ], with both of which sounds it shares some affinity acoustically. It is typically a shorter sound than either [ɑ] or [ɔ], however, both of which are considered long vowels.

The sound [ɒ] is found sporadically and often accidentally in the speech of many individuals, but few speakers in America are at all consistent in its use. As a matter of fact, many individuals are not conscious of it as a separate sound. Among the words in which [ɒ] may occur are the so-called short *o* words, of which *lock, stop, odd,* and *not* are examples. It is likely that the most typical and widespread use of this vowel is in the Englishman's pronunciation of *not* [nɒt], although this and similar short *o* words are commonly pronounced with [ɒ] by certain individuals in this country, especially among those who speak Eastern American. This sound may also be heard in other groups of words, of which *want, water, Morris, swallow,* and *soft* are examples.

An examination of the words cited above, as well as those in the list which follows, discloses that acceptable usage varies all the way from [ɑ] to [ɔ] in their pronunciation, and not only among different speakers but also in the speech of a single individual. A person may very well pronounce *swallow* habitually as [swɑlo], but use the vowel [ɔ] in *soft* [sɔft]. Even among similar words there may be considerable variation; an individual may say [ɑd] for *odd,* but pronounce *fog* as [fɔg]. Let us try an even more striking example—pronounce the sentence 'In the fog the dog barked at the frog on the log in the bog.' Do you pronounce all five *og* words in this sentence with exactly the same vowel quality? Or, for example, does *log* sound a little like [lɔg], and *bog* like [bɑg]? Try it on several of your friends and you may notice even more variation. If you extend your observation sufficiently, you will conclude that only a few individuals employ the intermediate vowel [ɒ] with any degree of consistency for these and similar words; variation rather than uniformity appears to be the norm in these instances.

A rather simple explanation may be adequate at this point

to account for the lack of widespread use of the intermediate vowel [ɒ]—for many people it simply does not exist as a separate speech sound, or more properly, separate phoneme.* For these individuals there is no real, identifiable vowel between [ɑ] and [ɔ]; in-between sounds are merely variations of one or the other of these vowels, and as such have failed to become stabilized in use, but rather have remained haphazard and accidental. Thus, individuals may, and often do, actually use this vowel in certain words without being aware of it. For example, do you pronounce the first syllable of *orange* as if it were *are,* or does it sound like *or?* Or is it somewhere in between? If it is the latter, it is likely that you are using the intermediate vowel [ɒ].

Recommendations regarding the use of [ɒ] are difficult to formulate, and perhaps are unnecessary. Some authorities have expressed the view that there is an observable trend toward increased use of [ɒ] as a 'compromise' vowel for those words for which usage is so variable between [ɑ] and [ɔ]. According to this point of view, if an individual uses [ɒ] for such words as *soft, forest,* and *fog,* he is close enough to both extremes of pronunciation of these words to avoid the element of conspicuousness in his speech. In other words, he fits in fairly well with both the [ɑ]-speakers and the [ɔ]-speakers. Others have failed to see such a trend developing.

Whether the deliberate cultivation of the use of [ɒ] is worth the time and effort that would be involved must be determined in individual instances by such factors as prevailing practices and preferences in the area where the individual lives and the particular conditions which affect his own use of speech. In the end, one cannot say which is 'right' and which is 'wrong'; it is a matter of individual preference and expediency.

* For a more complete discussion of the 'phoneme principle' as it applies to problems of pronunciation, consult one of the works on phonetics listed in the Bibliography at the end of this book, such as Thomas, *An Introduction to the Phonetics of American English* or Kenyon, *American Pronunciation.*

Following is a list of words in which this intermediate sound is often heard. As has been pointed out, considerable variation is common in their pronunciation, however. For certain of these words, such as *odd, hot,* and *cot,* for example, many speakers will use [ɑ] or at least a vowel that approaches very closely to it. For other words such as *wash, loss,* and *wrong,* the vowel may approximate [ɔ]. Compare your own pronunciation of these words with the preferred usage in your community. What does the dictionary recommend?

not	want	Morris	cost	log
cot	water	soft	gloss	cough
hot	sorry	coffee	watch	dog
odd	long	offer	wallet	off
stock	song	often	cloth	on
lot	quarrel	office	wash	forest

1. Tom had wanted to watch the stock car races but he had to return to his job in the parking lot.

2. Dorothy's boxer won first prize in the dog show.

3. The officer was sorry that his men had to cross the desert on such a hot day.

4. The boss often left his office to get a cup of coffee.

5. When the foreigner became quarrelsome over what he had said, Warren tried to toss it off as a joke.

6. Doris was warned to use care in washing the soft cloth.

7. Morris got used to the long haul required to bring the logs from the forest to the sawmill.

8. Donald was sipping his orange juice on the terrace as he listened to the song of the mockingbird.

THE VOWEL [ɔ] AS IN [sɔ] *saw*

The tongue is bunched somewhat higher at the back for this low, back, rounded vowel than for the preceding one, and the lips are more rounded. More of the resonance appears subjectively to be concentrated in the back of the mouth and throat. The use of this vowel is typical in such words as *awful, talk, wall, quart,* and *war.* In Southern British speech and among certain Eastern American speakers [ɔ] is produced somewhat higher in the back of the mouth with a quality closer to [o] than is characteristic of the country as a whole. On the other hand, a quality closer to [ɑ] can be heard in other sections of the country. Thus, there is considerable variability in the pronunciation of [ɔ]. No serious problems are ordinarily encountered in the production and use of this vowel, other than its involvement in the [ɑ]-[ɒ]-[ɔ] situation discussed in the previous section.

PRACTICE MATERIAL FOR [ɑ, ɒ, and ɔ]

Comparing [ɑ, ɔ, and o]:

cot—caught—coat	lah—law—low
not—naught—note	sod—sawed—sowed
hocks—hawks—hoax	tot—taught—tote
are—or—oar	ah—awe—oh
chock—chalk—choke	Lon—lawn—loan
pa—paw—Poe	rah—raw—roe

1. Morris caught cold when he slept outside on the cot.
2. From his office John could watch the foreign cars parade by.
3. Norman took the wrong road where it forked, which was the cause of all his trouble.
4. The author posed with his daughter at the door of the transcontinental plane.
5. Dorothy was forced to park her car in an awkward position.
6. Oranges cost much more when bought in small quantities.
7. Don wanted to borrow the sorrel horse from his brother Lawrence.
8. Paul's audience responded warmly to his last song.
9. As Tom turned a corner he caught a glimpse of the outlaw.
10. Doris found Charles out in the yard mowing the lawn.
11. Robert wanted a job hauling logs out of the forest.
12. In the fog the dog barked at the frog on the log in the bog.

> 13. As a rule man is a fool,
> When it's hot he wants it cool,
> When it's cool he wants it hot,
> Always wanting what is not.

14. To sit in solemn silence in a dull, dark dock
    In a pestilential prison, with a life-long lock,
    Awaiting the sensation of a short, sharp shock,
    From a cheap and chippy chopper on a big black block!

15. The leaves are falling, falling,
        Silently and slow;
    Caw! Caw! the rooks are calling,
        It is a sound of woe,
        A sound of woe!
        LONGFELLOW, 'Midnight Mass for the Dying Year'

16. The desire of the moth for the star,
        Of the night for the morrow,
    The devotion to something afar
        From the sphere of our sorrow.

17. They proceeded into the wood, making as broad and obvious a trail as possible. They soon reached a water-course, which they crossed, and continued onward, until they came to an extensive and naked rock. At this point, where their footsteps might be expected to be no longer visible, they retraced their route to the brook, walking backwards, with the utmost care.

JAMES FENIMORE COOPER, *The Last of the Mohicans*

18. I know not whether Laws be right,
        Or whether Laws be wrong;
    All that we know who lie in gaol
        Is that the wall is strong;
    And that each day is like a year,
        A year whose days are long.
        OSCAR WILDE, 'The Ballad of Reading Gaol'

19. The number of things that a small dog does naturally is strangely small. Enjoying better spirits and not crushed under material cares, he is far more theatrical than average man. His whole life, if he be a dog of any pretension to gallantry, is spent in a vain show, and in the hot pursuit of admiration. Take out your puppy for a walk, and you will find the soft little ball of fur clumsy, stupid, bewildered, but natural. Let but a few months pass, and when you repeat the process you will find nature buried in convention. He will do nothing plainly; but the sim-

plest procedures of our material life will all be bent into the forms of an elaborate and mysterious etiquette.

R. L. STEVENSON, 'The Character of Dogs'

20. Day by day autumn draws on. This is the season when earth pauses for an interlude to marshall its strength for the glory time ahead. There is a soft bluish haze on mountain brows and over the upland mowings. In the perennial border beneath the south windows of the farm kitchen the last blossoming of the delphiniums are small tender spikes of blue; exclamation points to punctuate the garden's last sentence.

Wide-leaved chicory holds aloft its stems with their pale, almost transparent deep-bell flowers. Along the roadside by the weathered stone walls, in the fence corners and around the stone piles in upper fields patches of asters make patterns of soft blue against the browning weeds and grasses.

Quiet mill ponds and sandy-bottomed northern lakes are smooth blue mirrors on windless days. Flocks of bluebirds gather in the old orchard behind the barn, organizing for the hegira southward. Blue jays flash across the field screaming that autumn is near.

The New York Times

21. On the verge of the forest we paused to inquire our way at a log house, owned by a white settler or squatter, a tall rawboned old fellow, with red hair, a lank lantern visage, and an inveterate habit of winking with one eye, as if everything he said was of knowing import. He was in a towering passion. One of his horses was missing; he was sure it had been stolen in the night by a straggling party of Osages encamped in a neighboring swamp; but he would have satisfaction! He would make an example of the villains. He had accordingly caught down his rifle from the wall, that invariable enforcer of right or wrong upon the frontiers, and, having saddled his steed, was about to sally forth on a foray into the swamp; while a brother squatter, with rifle in hand, stood ready to accompany him.

WASHINGTON IRVING, *A Tour of the Prairies*

THE VOWEL [o] AS IN [kot] *coat*

All that was said in an earlier section regarding the diphthongal quality of the vowel [e] when stressed applies with equal force to this mid, back, rounded vowel [o]. In this case the first element is [o], the second is [ʊ]; the two sounds blend together to form the 'long o' of such words as *go, tone,* and *coat.* For the sake of simplicity, as in the case of [e], the single symbol [o] has been used in this book to represent this sound, whether it is stressed or unstressed.

In most foreign languages [o] is actually a simple vowel instead of a diphthong, as it usually is in English. Consequently the foreigner's pronunciation, with his 'version' of the vowel [o], may suggest the vowel [ɔ] to us, who are accustomed to hearing the diphthong [oʊ]. Thus, the foreigner's pronunciation of *coat* and *low* may sound to us somewhat like 'caught' and 'law.' Prolongation of the sound with a slightly higher tongue position and a definite rise of the tongue toward the end producing a pronounced [ʊ]-element should take care of this problem. Practice on such pairs as the following should also be helpful in demonstrating the difference between [ɔ] and [o] and can be used to call attention to the diphthongal quality of [oʊ], as well as its pronounced lip-rounding:

caught—coat	law—low	saw—sow	ball—bowl
lawn—loan	laud—load	bought—boat	shawl—shoal
stalk—stoke	pause—pose	walk—woke	hall—hole

Without this lip rounding, it becomes difficult, if not impossible, to produce an [o] of good quality, particularly when the sound is stressed or held for any length of time. In practicing the selections with [o] which follow, give special attention to adequate lip rounding, as well as to the diphthongal quality of this sound.

PRACTICE MATERIAL FOR [o]

1. Won't you go home?
2. Joe has sold the old boat.
3. The roses still grow over the gate post.

4. Our goal is to get the most votes by tomorrow.
5. The tones of the choir floated through the open windows into the grove.
6. Joe bought the old boat from Mr. Hogan.
7. Mr. Jones caught his coat in the door.
8. Olsen brought only an old pair of overalls from home.
9. Call Mr. Lowe and order a load of coal.
10. The law provided for low interest on the loan.

11. He who knows and knows that he knows,
   He is wise; follow him.

12. Alone, alone, all, all alone,
   Alone on a wide, wide sea.

13. Over the rolling waters go,
   Come from the dying moon and blow,
   Blow him again to me.

14. I was a Viking old!
   My deeds though manifold,
   No Skald in song has told,
   No Saga taught thee!

15. And up and down the people go,
   Gazing where the lilies blow
   Round an island there below,
   The island of Shalott.

   .   .   .

   Down she came and found a boat
   Beneath a willow left afloat,
   And round about the prow she wrote
   The Lady of Shalott.
                    TENNYSON, 'The Lady of Shalott'

16. There is a bird who by his coat,
   And by the hoarseness of his note,
   Might be supposed a crow.

17. Oh, this is the joy of the rose:
   That it blows,
   And goes.

18. The greatest poem ever known
   Is one all poets have outgrown:
   The poetry, innate, untold,
   Of being only four years old.

19. Of all the horrid, hideous notes of woe,
   Sadder than owl-songs or the midnight blast;
   Is that portentous phrase, 'I told you so.'

THE VOWEL [ʊ] AS IN [pʊt] *put*

[ʊ] is a high, back, lax vowel, sometimes referred to as the short *oo,* found in such words as *wood, could,* and *pull.* The tongue is elevated moderately in the back from the position required for [o] and the jaw is raised slightly. The lips are rounded, but not as much as for [o] or [u].

Since this vowel is missing in most foreign languages, the foreigner is likely to have trouble with it, usually substituting [u] for it and pronouncing *foot* as [fut] and *would* as [wud]. An individual having this difficulty can be helped if he is reminded that the back of the tongue is slightly lower for [ʊ] than for [u], the lips are not so rounded, the whole articulatory mechanism is less tense, and the sound is a shorter one than [u]. With this, as with other problems of pronunciation, however, the direct acoustic approach is probably the best, involving intensive ear training. The following paired words can be used to illustrate the difference in quality between [ʊ] and [u]:

wooed—wood	shoed—should	Luke—look	pool—pull
stewed—stood	fool—full	who'd—hood	food—foot
cool—cook	boot—book	noon—nook	tool—took

Those who speak English as their native language should have no difficulty with this vowel. A few minor variations in its use occur locally here and there over the country, but they could hardly be called serious. One of these involves a substitution of [or] for [ʊr] in *sure, poor,* and a few similar words, resulting in such substandard pronunciations as [ʃor] and [por]. Some individuals are guilty of allowing this vowel to shift toward the middle of the mouth with an accompanying unrounding of the lips. Such a practice results in a sound suggesting the vowel [ʌ], making *book* sound like [bʌk] and *look* like [lʌk].

Practice material for [ʊ] will be included with that for [u] at the end of the following section.

THE VOWEL [u] AS IN [hu] *who*

This is the highest of the back vowels, made with the lips protruded and rounded and the back of the tongue high in the mouth. One of the serious faults associated with the pronunciation of this sound is the failure to round the lips sufficiently to produce a good quality of tone. Resonance appears to be concentrated in the back of the mouth and throat, and the tone must be carefully molded by the lips. During the production of [u] the articulators are in a relatively tense condition in comparison with [ʊ], which is a more lax vowel.

The vowel [u] is represented in conventional spelling in a number of different ways, one of the most common being with *oo*. Not all of the words spelled with *oo* are pronounced with [u], however. The following regularly take the lower vowel [ʊ]: *book, cook, foot, good, hook, look, shook, stood,* and *took.* Pronunciation with [u] is fairly uniform in these words: *behoove, bloom, boot, booth, choose, doom, fool, gloom, groove, loop, loose, moon, proof, shoot,* and *tooth.* There is little agreement as to the vowel to be used in the following list of words, both [ʊ] and [u] being heard in the speech of different individuals and throughout different sections of the country. Study carefully the pronunciation of each of these words. Perhaps the safest guide is to follow the practice of the best speakers in whatever section of the country one happens to live. What does the dictionary recommend?

broom	hoof	soon	whooping cough
coop	hoop	soot	rooster
groom	roof	spoon	rook
Cooper	root	room	bedroom

Watch carefully the pronunciation of [ʊ] and [u] in the words and selections which follow Make a special study of any words about which there is any doubt; that is, consult the dictionary, listen to their pronunciation in the speech of others, and so forth.

PRACTICE MATERIAL FOR [ʊ] AND [u]

WORDS WITH [ʊ]		WORDS WITH [u]	
nook	butcher	moon	fool
put	sugar	gloom	pool
wolf	woman	chew	group
wood	wool	mood	flew
should	could	stoop	wound
bush	bullet	do	food
your	tourist	boot	spook
pudding	push	who	school
forsook	sure	move	shoe
poor	jury	grew	shoot

Sentences with [ʊ]:

1. She took the book from the shelf and put it on the table.
2. Are you sure that the woman stood on just one foot?
3. The cook took a good look at the poor tramp on the door step.
4. He could go if he would.
5. The crooked sapling which stood near the edge of the brook shook violently as the wind threatened to push it over.

Sentences with [u]:

1. The moonlight streamed into the room.
2. The small group of men were soon seen to be moving silently through the gloom.

3. The fool took off his shoe and threw it across the room.
4. The pool of clear, cool water sparkled in the sun at noon.
5. Bruce swept out the schoolroom with the new broom.

Sentences and selections with [ʊ] *and/or* [u]:

1. Mrs. Cooper's little girl came down with the whooping cough soon after she started to school.
2. The rooster stood on the roof of the chicken coop.
3. The groom could hear hoof beats on the track outside his room.
4. The natives were looking for roots to use for medicines and food.
5. Ruth asked the doctor how soon her baby could take solid food with a spoon.

6. She left the web, she left the loom,
   She made three paces through the room,
   She saw the water-lily bloom,
   She saw the helmet and the plume.

7. The harbour-bay was clear as glass,
   So smoothly it was strewn!
   And on the bay the moonlight lay,
   And the shadow of the moon.

8. The moon looks
   On many brooks,
   The brook can see no moon but this.

9. We may live without friends; we may live without books;
   But civilized man cannot live without cooks.

10. The cook was a good cook, as cooks go, and as cooks go she went!

11. And this our life exempt from public haunt
    Finds tongues in trees, books in the running brooks,
    Sermons in stones and good in everything.
    I would not change it.

12. The moon above the eastern wood
    Shone at its full; the hill-range stood
    Transfigured in the silver flood.

13. And sometimes thr' the mirror blue
The knights come riding two and two:
She hath no loyal knight and true
The Lady of Shalott.

14. In May, when sea-winds pierced our solitudes,
I found the fresh Rhodora in the woods,
Spreading its leafless blooms in a damp nook,
To please the desert and the sluggish brook.
The purple petals, fallen in the pool,
Make the black water with their beauty gay;
Here might the red-bird come his plumes to cool,
And court the flower that cheapens his array.

R. W. EMERSON

15. The time I've lost in wooing,
In watching and pursuing
The light that lies
In woman's eyes,
Has been my heart's undoing.
Though Wisdom oft has sought me,
I scorn'd the lore she brought me,
My only books
Were woman's looks,
And folly's all they've taught me.

THOMAS MOORE

THE VOWEL [ʌ] AS IN [ʃʌt] *shut*

This vowel, the 'short *u*' of such words as *up, come,* and *double,* is variously referred to as a mid, central vowel or mid, back vowel. In any case, it is a short vowel and is further described as lax and unrounded. In the speech of the majority of individuals it is formed in the mid, back-central portion of the mouth, above and somewhat forward of [ɑ]. The jaw is quite open and the lips are in a neutral position.

Certain dialectal problems, of both the foreign and 'domestic' variety, are involved in the use of this vowel, the most common doubtless being the substitution of [ɑ] or a sound closely resembling it. This substitution produces such

non-standard pronunciations as [maðɚ] for *mother,* [lɑv] for
love, and [rɑbɚ] for *rubber.* Paired words such as the following can be used to teach the difference between [ʌ] and [ɑ];
it will be helpful to keep in mind that the vowel in the
second member of each pair is always a shorter sound than
the vowel in the first, assuming, of course, that the individual uses [ɑ] as the vowel in the first member.

psalm—some	calm—come	cop—cup	cob—cub
hot—hut	cot—cut	chock—chuck	lock—luck
shot—shut	fond—fund	stock—stuck	wan—one
robber—rubber	Don—done	shock—shuck	crocks—crux

Examples of miscellaneous minor substitutions heard here
and there over the country include [brɛʃ] for *brush,* [kɪvɚ]
for *cover,* [dʒɪst] for *just,* [ɔnhæpɪ] for *unhappy,* [gums] for
gums and [mɜˑʃ] for *mush.*

It should also be pointed out in passing that [ʌ] is always
a stressed vowel. That is, the stressed vowel [ʌ] in *supper*
[sʌpɚ], for example, is a different vowel from the one in the
first syllable of support [səport], an unstressed vowel. This
latter will be discussed in the following section.

Study the following words; how many different pronunciations have you heard for some of them?

comfort	become	color	something
above	upper	subway	rough
judge	hush	plover	shut
touch	just	cover	covert

PRACTICE MATERIAL FOR [ʌ]

1. The Bible tells us to love one another.
2. Unless he has unusual luck, the robber will be unable to
break that lock.
3. Mr. Hull's brother lived in luxury in the suburbs.
4. On a hunch Cousin Douglas began looking for honey.
5. When Russell tried to come through the garden, his rubbers
stuck in the mud.

6. Duncan's mother took him to Judge Avenue to see his uncle.

7. Cut up the onions and put them in this cup.

8. Something must be done to get some more money for the club.

9. Doves, gulls, plovers, and thrushes are all birds of one kind or another.

10. Chuck wondered why the ducks wandered around in the muck.

11. And doubly dying shall go down
    To the vile dust from whence he sprung,
    Unwept, unhonored and unsung.

12. When I read Shakespeare, I am struck with wonder
    That such trivial people should muse and thunder
    In such lovely language.

13. Life's race well run,
    Life's work well done,
    Life's victory won,
    Now cometh rest.

14. For some we loved, the loveliest and the best
    That from his Vintage rolling Time has prest,
    Have drunk their Cup a Round or two before,
    And one by one crept silently to rest.

15. O young Lochinvar is come out of the West,—
    Through all the wide Border his steed was the best!
    And, save his good broadsword, he weapon had none,—
    He rode all unarmed, and he rode all alone.
    So faithful in love, and so dauntless in war,
    There never was knight like the young Lochinvar.

                                                    SCOTT

16. It is done!
    Clang of bell and roar of gun!
    Send the tidings up and down.

17. In came the moon and covered me with wonder,
    Touched me and was near me, and made me very still.
    In came a rush of song, raining as from thunder,
    Pouring importunate on my window-sill.

18. But the Raven, sitting lonely on the placid bust, spoke only
That one word, as if his soul in that one word he did out-
pour.
Nothing further then he uttered—not a feather then he flut-
tered—
Till I scarcely more than muttered 'Other friends have flown
before—
On the morrow he will leave me, as my hopes have flown be-
fore.'
Then the bird said, 'Nevermore.'

EDGAR ALLAN POE, 'The Raven'

19. There was a rustling that seemed like a bustling
Of merry crowds justling at pitching and hustling.

THE VOWEL [ə] AS IN [əbʌv] *above*

The vowel [ə] * is often identified as the unstressed, weakened form of [ʌ], described above. Without doubt, the two
have much in common. Since [ə] is always unstressed, however, it is a difficult sound to identify and to describe. As
found in the natural melody patterns of speech, it is passed
over so lightly and so rapidly that one is often not sure just
what sound he has heard or has used. It can best be described
as the first sound of *about* and the last sound of *sofa,* as well
as the final sound of *ever* as pronounced by people who 'drop
their *r*'s.' As a matter of fact, however, almost any vowel
when it is unstressed sufficiently tends to become this neutral
vowel, sometimes also referred to as the 'vowel murmur' or
schwa. A few words in which this sound occurs will illustrate
this point.

*a*round	postm*a*n	judgm*e*nt	pr*o*pose
por*ou*s	dist*a*nce	spec*i*men	s*u*pport
bo*a*	qui*e*t	Apr*i*l	th*e* man

Observe that the sound is spelled in a variety of ways and
also that there is no method of determining from the spelling how the syllable is to be pronounced unless one happens

* The nature and use of this vowel can best be understood in connection with the discussion of stress in Chapter X.

to know which syllables are unstressed. As will be explained in more detail in Chapter X, unstressing works profound changes within syllables and words, the [æ] of *man* changing to [ə] in *postman* [postmən], as an example.

Words as well as syllables are pronounced with this neutral vowel when they become unstressed in the phrase or sentence. Thus, *to* is no longer [tu] in the expression *he wanted to go*. Here it becomes [tə] in informal speech because it is unstressed. A like change takes place in the vowel sounds of such words as *but, an, of, was,* and *can* when they are similarly unstressed. For example, *was* has an original stressed form of [wɑz] or [wɒz], which might be heard in such an expression as *I was, too!* However, used in the sentence *I was ill last week,* the same word is now unstressed and becomes [wəz]. Such words, pronounced in two different ways according to the degree of prominence given them in speaking, are said to have both a stressed and an unstressed form.

It should be noted that this vowel, properly used, has a perfectly legitimate and necessary place in spoken English, which is characterized by patterns of alternating light and heavy stress. This variation in stress is to a great extent reflected in an actual change in the quality of the vowel that forms the syllable. Observe in the following list of words how the vowel in the stressed syllable in the first column changes to [ə] when it becomes unstressed in the examples given in the second column.

STRESSED	UNSTRESSED
compose [kəm'poz]	composition [ˌkɑmpə'zɪʃən]
man [mæn]	gentleman ['dʒentḷmən]
contract ['kɑn,trækt]	contract [kən'trækt]
papa ['pɑpə]	papa [pə'pɑ]
momentum [mo'mentəm]	moment ['momənt]
install [ɪn'stɔl]	installation [ˌɪnstə'leʃən]
able ['ebḷ]	ability [ə'bɪlətɪ]

Study the use of [ə] in the following practice material. Note especially those syllables in which there might be a choice between [ə] and the vowel that would normally occur in the same syllable if it were given slightly more stress. For example, do you pronounce *selection* as [səlɛkʃən] or do you say [sɪlɛkʃən]? Do you say [falo] or [falə] for *follow?* In each example in the passages following, which is easier to articulate in the unstressed words and syllables, [ə] or a slightly stronger, more stressed form of the original vowel? Which appeals to you as constituting the better usage? Refer to the section on stress in Chapter X for further discussion of these points.

PRACTICE MATERIAL FOR [ə]

debate	parent	about	salute
divide	aroma	taken	confide
parade	forum	reform	coma
umbrella	university	unit	potato

1. He tried to arouse the nightwatchman when he saw that the place was on fire.

2. It is difficult to account for the lack of interest in the election.

3. Do you believe in the universal brotherhood of man?

4. He was a typical man-about-town.

5. A mischievous boy aroused the teacher to violent action.

6. Barbara took the dress back to exchange it for another.

7. The scientist was rewarded for his contributions to the benefit of mankind.

8. The university professor decided to travel abroad during his vacation.

9. Sing a song of sixpence
   A pocket full of rye,
   Four and twenty blackbirds,
   Baked in a pie.
   When the pie was opened,
   The birds began to sing,
   Wasn't that a dainty dish
   To set before the King?

10. Composition is, for the most part, an effort of slow diligence and steady perseverance, to which the mind is dragged by necessity or resolution.

11. Tomorrow, and tomorrow, and tomorrow,
Creeps in this petty pace from day to day
To the last syllable of recorded time.

12. Men are so inclined to content themselves with what is commonest; the spirit and the senses so easily grow dead to the impressions of the beautiful and perfect, that everyone should study, by all methods, to nourish in his mind the faculty of feeling these things.

13. There are worse ills to face
Than foemen in the fray;
And many a man has fought because—
He feared to run away.

14. Better to see your cheeks grown hollow,
Better to see your temple worn,
Than to forget to follow, follow,
After the sound of a silver horn.

Better to bind your brow with yellow
And follow, follow until you die,
Than to sleep with your head on a golden pillow,
Nor lift it up when the hunt goes by.

Better to see your cheeks grown sallow
And your hair grown gray so soon, so soon,
Than to forget to hallo, hallo,
After the milk-white hounds of the moon.

ELINOR WYLIE, 'Madman's Song'

15. Afoot and light-hearted I take to the open road,
Healthy, free, the world before me,
The long brown path before me leading wherever I choose.

Henceforth I ask not good-fortune, I myself am good-fortune,
Henceforth I whimper no more, postpone no more, need nothing,
Done with indoor complaints, libraries, querulous criticisms,
Strong and content, I travel the open road.

WALT WHITMAN, 'Song of the Open Road'

16. It is a very good world to live in,
    To lend, or to spend, or to give in;
    But to beg or to borrow, or to get a man's own,
    It is the very worst world that ever was known.

THE VOWELS [ɝ] AND [ɜ] AS IN *heard* [hɝd] OR [hɜd]

These symbols [ɝ] and [ɜ] represent two different pronunciations, and hence two different vowels, for such words
as *bird, word,* and *turn.* Both of these are mid vowels, the
[ɝ] of General American speech being formed by slightly
retracting the tongue and elevating the middle portion of it
upward toward the hard palate. The tongue position is extremely variable in the production of [ɝ], however, many
speakers raising the front of the tongue and curling it more
or less backward and upward toward the palate. This produces the 'retroflex' variety of [ɝ], though the degree of retroflexion, or curling backward, of the tongue varies considerably in different speakers.

The vowel [ɜ] is the sound used in this same group of
words by individuals who 'drop their *r*'s.' This pronunciation is commonly heard in certain sections of the East and
South. In producing [ɜ] the front of the tongue is held lower
and further forward than for [ɝ]. There is no retroflexion.
It is a sound somewhat higher and in advance of the vowel
[ʌ]. It does not occur at all in the speech of a great many
people.

Several dialectal problems should be noted in connection
with the production of these vowels. Since these are unfamil-
iar sounds to most foreigners, they will attempt a spelling-
pronunciation in most cases. That is, they will attempt to
pronounce *word* as [word], *her* as [hɛr], and *heard* as something like [hɪrd]. Probably the most common regional dialectal mispronunciation is the substitution of a diphthong, [ɜɪ],
for [ɜ], often popularly written as 'boid' for *bird* and 'hoid'
for *heard.* The actual substitution is more nearly [ɜɪ], how-

ever, *bird* being pronounced as [bɜɪd] and *heard* as [hɜɪd]. Practicing paired words with [ɔɪ] and [ɝ] or [ɜ] can still be helpful in demonstrating the true quality of the vowel in contrast with the substandard diphthong:

Boyd—bird	Coit—curt	loin—learn	Hoyt—hurt
boil—burl	coil—curl	voice—verse	oil—Earl
foist—first	doit—dirt	hoist—Hearst	avoid—averred

In the production of [ɝ], care must be taken to avoid excessive retroflexion of the tongue, else a sound which many people find unpleasant may result. Neither should [ɝ] be prolonged unnecessarily, although both this vowel and [ɜ] are always found in a stressed position. The previously discussed schwa vowel [ə] will replace [ɜ] in an unstressed position, and in a similar situation the stressed [ɝ] will become the unstressed [ɚ], to be discussed in the following section. Thus, *murmur* would be pronounced [mɝmɚ] in General American speech, and [mɜmə] in the Eastern and Southern regions.

PRACTICE MATERIAL FOR [ɝ] AND [ɜ]

INITIAL	MEDIAL		FINAL
early	turn	myrtle	were
ermine	pearl	word	fur
urn	journey	pert	purr
earth	colonel	burn	her
urban	stirring	bird	sir
err	preferring	term	blur
earn	murky	perfect	infer
urge	purple	third	stir
irksome	burden	worthy	incur
erg	kernel	virtue	deter

1. A worthy thought—the early bird catches the worm, so we have heard.

2. The pert little girl with the long curls is Shirley.

3. Bert flew around the world in thirty days.

4. The third word in the second verse is an adverb.

5. The perverse animal reversed his first position and then turned again.

6. In astronomy Earl learned all about the earth and its place in the universe.

7. Verna was sure she had never heard such an earnest sermon.

8. Herbert would always try to shirk when the work became irksome.

9. Judge Curtis adjourned the murder trial until Thursday.

10. They were determined to prevent Herman from serving a third term as treasurer.

> 11. Learn to live, and live to learn,
> Ignorance like a fire doth burn,
> Little tasks make large return.

> 12. This truth within thy mind rehearse,
> That in a boundless universe
> Is boundless better, boundless worse.

> 13. To dig and delve in nice clean dirt
> Can do a mortal little hurt.

14. Everything is worth what its purchaser will pay for it.

> 15. Below they lie, their sails unfurled,
> The ships that go around the world.

16. A peasant girl, a shepherdess, dreaming on the hills of France, feels her simple heart burn with the story of her country's wrongs. Its army beaten, shattered and dispersed; its fields laid waste; its homes pillaged and burned; its people outraged and murdered; its prince fleeing for life before a triumphant and remorseless foe.

JOHN M. THURSTON

> 17. There the river eddy whirls
> And there the surly village churls
> And the red cloaks of market girls,
> Pass onward from Shalott.

18. If we crave advancement in this world's work, we must set out to earn it. He only is worthy to rule who has learned first to serve.

19. The world is content with words; few think of searching into the nature of things.

20. Man must work. That is certain as the sun. But he may work grudgingly or he may work gratefully. He may work as a man, or he may work as a machine. There is no work so rude, that he may not exalt it; no work so impassive, that he may not breathe a soul into it; no work so dull that he may not enliven it.

HENRY GILES

21. Then to the lip of this poor earthern Urn
   I lean'd, the secret Well of Life to learn:
     And Lip to Lip it murmured—'While you live,
Drink!—for, once dead, you never shall return.'

THE VOWEL [ɚ] AS IN [ɛvɚ] *ever*

As mentioned previously, when [ɝ] becomes unstressed in a word or syllable, it takes the form of [ɚ]. Both are mid vowels and have somewhat similar tongue positions, but [ɚ] is a much shorter, weaker sound than [ɝ]. It is always un- stressed. The word *perverse,* as pronounced in General American, contains both vowels—[pɚvɝs], as do also such words as *worker* [wɝkɚ], *further* [fɝðɚ], and *murmur* [mɝmɚ]. The relationship of [ɚ] to [ə] is very similar to that of [ɝ] to [ɜ], so far at least as usage is concerned. That is, in those words and syllables for which an individual would use [ɜ] in the stressed position, he would use [ə] in the un- stressed syllables. Thus, *perverse* in the speech of such an individual would be pronounced [pəvɜs], *worker* would be [wɜkə], et cetera.

In General American [ɚ] forms the final syllable of a large group of words spelled variously with *-ar, similar* [sɪmələɚ]; *-er, father* [fɑðɚ]; *-or, tailor* [telɚ]; *-ur, murmur* [mɝmɚ]; and *-ure pleasure* [plɛʒɚ]. In natural, unaffected speech these endings are all pronounced alike, with [ɚ], no effort being made to distinguish them.

Special care should be taken at all times to keep this sound strictly in the category of an unstressed vowel. It should not be prolonged, nor should any degree of prominence be given to it in any way. Excessive retroflexion of the tongue should be avoided.

If you speak General American, in which dialect [ɝ] and [ɚ] are commonly used, compare these two vowels in the paired words which follow. Note how the lighter, shorter [ɚ] in the second word of each pair differs from the more prominent, stressed [ɝ] of the first word. Note also that [ɚ] has less of the *r*-coloring quality than the stressed [ɝ]:

av*er*—ev*er*	p*er*spiration—p*er*spire	p*er*t—p*er*tain
det*er*—bett*er*	p*ur*pose—p*ur*port	ref*er*—reef*er*
b*ir*d—cupbo*ar*d	w*or*d—backw*ar*d	h*er*—h*er*self
st*ir*—mist*er*	w*or*k—bulw*ar*k	*ir*k—New*ar*k

PRACTICE MATERIAL FOR [ɚ]

MEDIAL	FINAL	
s*ur*prise	debtor	altar
rec*or*d (noun)	tapir	glamour
lant*er*n	picture	martyr
p*er*verse	actor	calendar
wand*er*ed	bachelor	treasure
must*ar*d	never	humor
South*er*n	color	pillar
bett*er*ment	augur	paper
c*ur*tail	harbor	measure
p*er*ceive	offer	liar

1. Since winter was getting nearer, Arthur could no longer hope for any betterment in the weather.

2. After the batter struck out, the pitcher and catcher conferred together earnestly for a moment.

3. The brothers searched through the orchard for their sister's lost rubbers.

4. Albert persuaded the actor to undertake the energetic assignment.

5. Mr. and Mrs. Lester were among the wealthier passengers.

6. Fishermen in the harbor were working overtime while the good weather lasted.

7. The inventor was working to perfect a method of measuring very low pressures.

8. Robert offered to drive Esther over to see her mother that afternoon.

9. Never here, forever there,
   Where all parting, pain, and care,
   And death, and time shall disappear,—
   Forever there, but never here!
   The horologue of Eternity
   Sayeth this incessantly,—
     'Forever—never!
     Never—forever!'
   H. W. LONGFELLOW, 'The Old Clock on the Stairs'

10. Willows whiten, aspens quiver,
    Little breezes dusk and shiver
    Through the wave that runs forever
    By the island in the river
      Flowing down to Camelot.

    Four gray walls and four gray towers,
    Overlook a space of flowers,
    And the silent isle embowers
      The Lady of Shalott.
              . . . . .
    All in the blue unclouded weather
    Thick-jewell'd shone the saddle-leather.
    The helmet and the helmet-feather
    Burned like one burning flame together,
      As he rode down to Camelot.
                    TENNYSON, 'The Lady of Shalott'

11. Jefferson once said, 'I have never been able to conceive how any rational being could propose happiness to himself from the exercise of power over others.'

12. Emerson told us, 'We are reformers in spring and summer; in autumn and winter we stand by the old; reformers in the morning, conservers at night.' Emerson was a speaker as well as

a writer. Of speech, he said, 'Speech is power; speech is to persuade, to convert, to compel.'

13. Lord Chesterfield offered this advice: 'Never hold any one by the button, or by the hand, in order to be heard out; for if people are unwilling to hear you, you had better hold your tongue than them.'

14. The best teacher is the one who suggests rather than dogmatizes, and inspires his listener with the wish to teach himself.

THE PRONUNCIATION OF DIPHTHONGS

In addition to the diphthongs [oʊ] and [eɪ], which were discussed in connection with the vowels [o] and [e], there are four other diphthongs in American speech, [aɪ] as in *ride,* [aʊ] as in *how,* [ɔɪ] as in *voice,* and [ju] as in *few.* Diphthongs are continuous glide sounds in which the articulatory mechanism moves from the position for one vowel sound to that for another. The two positions are indicated by the two symbols employed to designate each diphthong. Thus, in [ɔɪ], for example, as pronounced in *voice* [vɔɪs], the mouth is set for the vowel [ɔ], but before there has been time to produce a clearly defined vowel, the mechanism has moved to a position approximately that for the vowel [ɪ]. It is not difficult to hear these two vowel elements in [ɔɪ], especially when it is pronounced slowly, but it is somewhat more difficult to identify the two vowels which become fused together when [aɪ] is formed. In this case we are further confused by the spelling of this diphthong, which is often with the single alphabet symbol *i,* as in *nice* [naɪs].

THE DIPHTHONG [aɪ] AS IN [raɪd] *ride*

This speech sound, the so-called long *i* of such words as *ride* [raɪd] and *sight* [saɪt] is, of course, a combination of the two vowels, [a] and [ɪ], or close approximations of them, closely joined through continuous voicing. In certain sections of the country the first element is more likely to be [ɑ] than [a], though the untrained ear would likely detect but little difference between the two forms. Both are quite acceptable throughout the country. If the first element shifts too far toward [ɒ], however, a substandard pronunciation is likely to result.

In pronouncing this diphthong, one should not allow either of its two elements to become disproportionately stressed or prolonged at the expense of the other. Normally in this sound the first element is stressed more than the second, but if the [a] is held too long and if the tongue fails to rise properly in front toward the [ɪ] position at the end of the diphthong, the result will be such pronunciations as [nas] for *nice* and [fan] for *fine*. This variation is especially likely to be heard in certain sections of the South. On the other hand, unusual emphasis upon the second element of the diphthong gives us a pronunciation for these words suggesting [na-is] for *nice* and [fa-in] for *fine*. Both of these extremes should be avoided.

With respect to the final syllable in certain groups of words, usage varies between preference for [aɪ] and for [ɪ], not only between Britain and the United States, but among different sections of this country as well in some instances. Study the pronunciation of the following words, especially with reference to the vowel or diphthong to be used in the final syllable. What do you hear most often in your section of the country? Is it [dʒuvənaɪl] or [dʒuvənɪl], for *juvenile*, for example? What does the dictionary recommend? Should [ə] be used for some of them?

favorite	genuine	cowardice	quinine
juvenile	reptile	agile	docile
hostile	textile	vitamin	servile

Practice Material for [aɪ]

1. Mr. Frye brightly greeted the sightseers with a cheerful 'Hi!'
2. Clyde twice tried to climb up the fire escape.

3. The guide tried to lead them down the mountainside at night.

4. Irene was delighted by the sight of the bright fire.

5. The child was frightened by the sight of the tribesmen fighting.

6. The light was so bright that it blinded his eyes.

7. Inez tried to hide behind the sofa so the others couldn't find her.

8. Write to me when you can find the time.

9. A violet by a mossy stone
Half hidden from the eye;
Fair as a star, when only one
Is shining in the sky.

10. Love looks not with the eyes, but with the mind,
And therefore is winged cupid painted blind.

11. The apple grows so bright and high,
And ends its day in apple pie.

12. Music that gentler on the spirit lies
Than tired eyelids upon tired eyes.

13. The night has a thousand eyes,
And the day but one;
Yet the light of the bright world dies,
With the dying sun.

14. She walks in beauty, like the night
Of cloudless climes and starry skies;
And all that's best of dark and bright
Meet in her aspect and her eyes.

15. Why, I, in this weak piping time of peace
Have no delight to pass away the time,
Unless to spy my shadow in the sun.

16. The sun was shining on the sea,
Shining with all his might;
He did his very best to make
The billows smooth and bright—
And this was odd, because it was
The middle of the night!

LEWIS CARROLL

17. Into the street the Piper stept,
Smiling first a little smile,
As if he knew what magic slept
In his quiet pipe the while.

18. Lying, robed in snowy white
That loosely flew to left and right—
The leaves upon her falling light—
Thro' the noises of the night
She floated down to Camelot.

THE DIPHTHONG [ɑʊ] AS IN [hɑʊs] *house*

Probably the most common spellings of this diphthong are with *ou* as in *house* [hɑʊs] and *ow* as in *down* [dɑʊn]. The vowel [a] becomes the first element of this diphthong in the speech of many individulas, who pronounce *house* as [haʊs] and *down* as [daʊn]. Both forms are quite acceptable. However, if the tongue is allowed to rise still farther in front as this diphthong is begun, the first element will approximate the sound of [æ] and such pronunciations as [hæʊs] and [dæʊn] will result. Very often there is more or less nasalization of the [æ]. While the form [æʊ] is common in certain localities, it is not considered as standard throughout the country as a whole. The speaker would do well to avoid it in those sections of the country where it is looked upon as a fault.

If you are inclined to pronounce [ɑʊ] as [æʊ], practice the following paired words, listening carefully for the vowel you use at the beginning of the diphthong in the second member of each pair. Keep it from sounding like the [æ] in the first word of each pair. Put the diphthong in 'slow motion'; hold the beginning of it long enough to hear it clearly and determine just what sound you are using.

| pat—pout | Dan—down | clad—cloud | hand—hound |
| cant—count | Al—owl | lad—loud | tan—town |

Now experiment with the following pairs. Here the first member contains the vowel [ɑ] (for most individuals) and the object is to begin the diphthong in the second word in each pair with a sound as close to [ɑ] as possible. This will give you the diphthong [ɑʊ] or at least [aʊ]; in any case, if it works successfully, you will keep away from [æʊ].

pond—pound	pot—pout	Scott—scout	spot—spout
Don—down	ha—how	dot—doubt	prod—proud
par—power	are—hour	trot—trout	shot—shout

Practice the following exercises, paying careful attention to adequate mouth opening at the beginning of this diphthong and some degree of lip rounding at the end.

PRACTICE MATERIAL FOR [ɑʊ]

allow	cow	mound	plow
flour	house	bough	mouth
sauerkraut	sound	announce	mountain
down and out	round about	down town	how now

1. There is no doubt about it.

2. He has now got to be quite a man about town.

3. Low flying clouds made the trip down the mountain very hazardous.

4. He opened his mouth and shouted loudly for help.

5. A low hanging bough allowed him to lift himself off the ground.

6. They found the brown house out on the edge of town.

7. When he bought the cows, he had not counted on such a long drought.

8. Somehow he got the ground plowed around the house.

9. Till like one in slumber bound,
Borne to ocean, I float down, around,
Into a sea profound of everlasting sound.

10. Oh, London is a man's town, there's power in the air;
And Paris is a woman's town, with flowers in her hair.

11. Look out how you use proud words.
     When you let proud words go, it is not easy to call them back.
     They wear long boots, hard boots. . . .
     Look out how you use proud words.

> 12. Around, around flew each sweet sound,
>   Then darted to the sun;
>   Slowly the sounds came back again,
>   Now mixed, now one by one.

> 13. There for my lady's bower
>   Built I the lofty tower,
>   Which to this very hour,
>   Stands looking seaward.

14. The owl looked down with his great round eyes
     At the lowering clouds and the darkening skies,
       'A good night for scouting,' says he,
     'With never a sound I'll go prowling around.
     A mouse or two may be found on the ground
       Or a fat little bird in a tree.'
     So down he flew from the old church tower,
     The mouse and the birdie crouch and cower,
     Back he flies in half an hour,
       'A very good supper,' says he.

UNKNOWN

THE DIPHTHONG [ɔɪ] AS IN [bɔɪ] *boy*

This sound, spelled typically with *oy* as in *boy* and with *oi* as in *noise*, presents no serious problems for the majority of American speakers. Two substandard dialectal variations are worth mentioning, however. Occasionally one hears, often in remote areas, a substitution of [aɪ] for [ɔɪ] in certain words, of which *boil* and *join* are examples. These words become [baɪl] and [dʒaɪn]. Other examples would include *joint* [dʒaɪnt], *oil* [aɪl], *joist* [dʒaɪst], and *hoist* [haɪst].

In substandard New York City dialect and in certain areas of the South a common substitution is the non-standard diphthong [ɜɪ] for [ɔɪ], resulting in [vɜɪs] for *voice* and [ɜɪl] for *oil.* Comparing this substitution with a similar one for the vowels [ɝ] and [ɜ] discussed in an earlier section reveals that in these dialectal areas the words *oil* and *earl*, *voice* and *verse* would resemble each other, both members of each pair being pronounced with [ɜɪ]. Thus, [vɜɪs] might be either *voice* or *verse*. The correction of this fault involves beginning the diphthong [ɔɪ] with the tongue lower in the mouth and with the bunching of the tongue located farther back. A moderate degree of lip rounding will also help to achieve the quality of [ɔ] as the starting point for this diphthong.

An exercise involving paired words, similar to that suggested for [ɝ] and [ɜ] in a previous section, will be found helpful in demonstrating the difference between the vowel [ɝ] or [ɜ] and the diphthong [ɔɪ]. This time the pairs will be reversed.

bird—Boyd	curt—Coit	learn—loin	hurt—Hoyt
burl—boil	curl—coil	verse—voice	Earl—oil
first—foist	dirt—doit	Hearst—hoist	averred—avoid

Practice Material for [ɔɪ]

1. The boy made but little noise as he quietly played with the coil of rope.
2. Mr. Doyle was appointed to the joint committee on finance.
3. Noise is generally annoying and is to be avoided.
4. Hoyt made an appointment to meet him later down town.
5. The boys were given some coins to buy toys.
6. Raw oysters are considered to be very choice.
7. Lloyd joined in the singing with his strong bass voice.
8. Floyd enjoyed working in Detroit.

9. When you appoint a leader, avoid making choice of the man who is in any measure devoid of those essential qualities that inspire and enjoin wholehearted loyalty.

10. Then read from the treasured volume
   The poem of thy choice,
   And lend to the rime of the poet
   The beauty of thy voice.

11. Has any old fellow got mixed with the boys?
    If there has, take him out, without making a noise.

12. Let not ambition mock their useful toil,
    Their homely joys, and destiny obscure;
    Nor grandeur hear with a disdainful smile,
    The short and simple annals of the poor.

13. Your own proud land's heroic soil
    Shall be your fitter grave:
    She claims from war his richest spoil—
    The ashes of her brave.

14. The saddest noise, the sweetest noise,
    The maddest noise that grows,—
    The birds, they make it in the spring,
    At night's delicious close.

THE DIPHTHONG [ju] AS IN [kjut] *cute*

There are several varieties of this sound, but the most common phonetic representation of it is with the symbols [ju]. It will be seen that the first element of this diphthong is the glide [j], which was discussed in some detail near the end of the previous chapter dealing with consonants. For a better understanding of this present diphthong, a review of this earlier discussion is recommended.

[ju] is often referred to in spelling as the long *u*, although not all words containing this sound are spelled with *u*. It regularly occurs in words like *cute* [kjut], *pupil* [pjupl], and *unit* [junɪt]. [ju], or a sound closely resembling it, is also heard in the speech of many individuals following such consonants as [t, d, θ, n, and s]. Examples of words falling under this classification include *new, suit, Tuesday, due, tune,* and *enthusiasm.* That is, *new* may be heard as [nju] or [nu], *suit* as [sjut] or [sut], and so forth. Usage is so sharply divided between [ju] and [u] in these and similar words over various sections of the country, and within any given section, that no

dogmatic recommendation regarding the use of one or the other of these sounds in such words would be advisable. One hears individuals of education and prominence using either form. Again, the trend of usage among respected individuals in any given locality would probably be one's best guide regarding this problem.

Study the pronunciation of the words which should, or may, take the diphthong [ju] in the exercises that follow. Compare your own pronunciation with what you hear most often in your own locality and over the radio and on television. Arrive at some decision as to what seems best for you.*

PRACTICE MATERIAL FOR [ju] AND/OR [u]

1. The youthful student carefully studied the solution in the test tube.

2. It is only human nature to be intrigued by what is new.

3. Hubert, as usual, commented on the beautiful view.

4. Hugh bought himself a new suit at one of the few shops down on the avenue.

5. Union members accused the officers of raising the dues.

6. A huge class graduated from the new school.

7. The band played a lively tune as the uniformed men passed in review.

8. The young campers assumed that the humid weather would not continue beyond Tuesday.

9. Waste not your Hour, nor in the vain pursuit
   Of This and That endeavor and dispute;
   Better be jocund with the fruitful Grape
   Than sadden after none, or bitter, Fruit.

10. Whither, midst falling dew,
   While glow the heavens with the last steps of day,
   Far, through their rosy depths, dost thou pursue
   Thy solitary way?

* Consult a good dictionary. Further help may be had from the discussion of [ju] in one of the phonetic texts listed in the Bibliography, such as Kenyon, *American Pronunciation* or Thomas, *Introduction to the Phonetics of American English.*

11.   Hie hence, be gone, away!
   It is the lark that sings so out of tune,
   Straining harsh discords and unpleasing sharps.

12. All sights were mellowed, and all sounds subdued,
    The hills seemed farther, and the streams sang low;
   As in a dream the distant woodman hewed
    His winter log with many a muffled blow.

   13. Expression is the dress of thought, and still
       Appears more decent, as more suitable.

   14. Regard not then if wit be old or new,
       But blame the false, and value still the true.

    15. Transparent forms, too fine for mortal sight,
        Their fluid bodies half dissolved in light.
        Loose to the wind their airy garments flew,
        Thin glittering textures of the filmy dew.

     16. I am not fond of uttering platitudes
         In stained-glass attitudes.

X

Some Problems of Connected Speech

THE concept of spoken language as a moving, dynamic process has been referred to several times thus far in this book. However, when it becomes necessary to examine individual speech sounds as separate units, as we have done in the preceding two chapters, we tend to forget that the functional unit of speech is not the individual speech sound or phoneme, but rather the word, the phrase, or longer thought-unit. That is, we do not speak in terms of separate, discrete speech sounds, as [k] plus [æ] plus [t] equals [kæt], but rather in terms of what have been called thought-groups, which may be words, phrases, or even larger entities. For example, we say, 'How are you?' as [hɑʊɑrju] with all the sounds blended together through continuous movement, just as if it were all one word. Even in a longer example, such as the sentence, 'How would you like to go with me?' spoken in a normal manner, the ear can scarcely detect any interruption in the steady flow of sound from the beginning to the end of the thought-group. The individual sounds, and even the words, are molded and blended together.

In this dynamic process of continuous speech are to be found some of the most troublesome, and at the same time most interesting, problems of articulation, including some related specifically to pronunciation. Certain things happen to sounds when they become a part of a dynamic process such as this. Some of these 'things' will be discussed in more detail in later sections of this chapter. As one feature of this process, researchers have recently become especially interested in the importance to the communicative process of the transition sounds which result from movements of the articulatory mechanism from the approximate position for one speech sound into that for another. There is evidence to indicate that speech intelligibility is as much, or more, dependent on these transition phenomena, as on the actual speech sounds themselves. Experiments indicate that when these transition sounds are eliminated from speech and only the individual discrete sound units themselves are presented, speech becomes virtually unintelligible. We must conclude from these results, as well as from general experience, that it is the whole process of speech that is involved in intelligibility, not just the articulation or pronunciation of isolated sounds. It is the purpose of this chapter to examine some of the implications arising from this point of view.

STRESS

The patterns of spoken language are usually very complex and often obscure. For this reason they cannot be studied and demonstrated as readily and objectively as the rhythms of poetry can be, for example, but the elements of the two are essentially the same, consisting as they do of various combinations of alternating light and heavy stress. In English especially these variations tend to be extreme, and the alternations are inclined to be regular and repeated frequently, in contrast with certain other languages such as Turkish and Hawaiian, which are marked by a relatively even stress on all syllables. As an illustration, if we should say, 'I wént to tówn and bóught some shóes,' we would have a perfect example of alternating light and heavy stress, as easily scannable as a line of iambic verse. Most prose rhythms, of course, are hardly as obvious as we find in this rather extreme example.

The basis of speech melody is stress—the process of giving prominence to a syllable or a word. Stress involves (1) changes in pitch, (2) changes in force, and (3) changes in the length or duration of the sound being emphasized. Since pitch variation is a problem of voice, and has already been dealt with at some length in an earlier portion of this book, we are primarily concerned at this point with the last two of these factors.

Relationship of Stress to the Quantity and Quality of Speech Sounds. As we have stated, duration and force, or loudness, are two important elements of stress. These two go to make up what might be termed quantity—the actual amount of the speech sound that is heard. Stress functions in two different ways—(1) It may be applied to syllables or words within a thought-group, in which case it becomes a part of the expressional pattern of speech related to the meaning and intention of the speaker, a process that is known as emphasis, discussed in more detail in a previous chapter. (2) Stress may also be applied to certain syllables in polysyllabic words, in which case, as we have seen, it becomes one of the important elements in pronunciation and is known as accent. The difference between the two pronunciations of *papa*, [pəpɑ] and [pɑpə], is basically a difference of accent. The fact that the vowel sound likewise changes under the influence of a change of stress is an important point and should be kept carefully in mind for a later reference. Such a common word as *tapioca* [tæpɪokə] becomes virtually unrecognizable as a result of a change of stress (accent) to [təˈpaɪəkə].

A similar transformation takes place in certain words when they become unstressed within a phrase or sentence. Thus, *am, at, but, was,* and *a* are pronounced [æm], [æt], [bʌt], [wɑz] or [wɒz], and [e] when they stand alone or are stressed; but in the sentence, 'I'm at hóme nów, but I was óut a móment agó,' these same words become [m], [ət], [bət], [wəz], and [ə]. Note the difference between the pronunciation of *or* and *and* in the sentence, 'I didn't say *or;* I said *and,*' and the sound which these same words have in such phrases as *boy or girl* [bɔɪ ɚ gɝl], *bread and butter* [brɛd n̩ bʌtɚ]. Of course, the spelling of the word does not always change with the change of sound. The last syllable of *postman* [postmən] is spelled exactly like the word *man* [mæn], but it is obvious that they are pronounced quite differently. This similarity of spelling for sounds that are in reality different is confusing and it often blinds us to the importance of the transformation that has taken place as a result of a shift of stress or accent.

In general, four things may happen to a speech sound as a result of unstressing: (1) In some instances a vowel may change into a sound resembling very closely the vowel [ɪ] in a slightly weaker form, as in *always* [ɔlwɪz] and *Sunday* [sʌndɪ]. (2) If the word or syllable when stressed contains the vowel [ɝ], the sound will become [ɚ] when unstressed, as in the sentence, *I saw her come* [aɪ sɔ hɚ kʌm]. A similar change may also occur when the syllable contains the consonant [r] with a vowel, as we find in *come for me* [kʌm fɚ mi]. (3) Much more commonly, however, as was pointed out in Chapter IX, the unstressed vowel takes the form of the obscure vowel [ə], as it has in so many of the examples used as illustrations in this chapter. (4) Finally, individual sounds may be lost altogether, as *and* becomes simply [n̩] when unstressed sufficiently.

In a certain group of words, of which the following are representative, usage varies between [ɪ] and [ə] in the unstressed syllable, many speakers preferring to use [ɪ] as representing more careful pronunciation. Study the list carefully; which words do you think require an unstressed form of [ɪ] in the unstressed syllable and for which do you feel that [ə] would be quite acceptable in good conversational speech?

village	pity	bur*ie*d	spin*a*ch	r*e*volt
with*ou*t	b*e*lieve	*e*vent	Engl*i*sh	im*a*ge
Mex*i*co	*e*nough	d*e*note	alw*a*ys	needl*e*ss

In another group of words in which the unstressed syllable is spelled with *o* or *ow,* usage again varies between a choice of an unstressed [o] and a choice of [ə] in the unstressed syllable. When the syllable is final, as it is in *piano* and *mellow,* the use of [ə], while common enough in certain localities, is not generally acceptable throughout the country. In certain other instances when the syllable containing the *o* is not final, as in *desolation,* both [o] and [ə] are commonly heard. In some examples [o] is more common, in others the reverse is true. Study the following words. Decide what sound should be used in pronouncing the unstressed syllables indicated by italics.

p*o*tato	holl*ow*	mell*ow*	yell*ow*	foll*ow*
sopran*o*	borr*ow*	tomorr*ow*	pian*o*	l*o*cation
thor*ough*	den*o*tation	r*o*tation	p*o*lite	p*o*lice

In connection with this general problem of stress and vowel quality, it should be noted that there are *degrees* of unstressing, each step being marked by some change in the character of the sound or sounds involved. Illustrating with *and* again, we find that the stressed form is [ænd]. The first stage of unstressing would give us [ənd], the next would be [ən] or [ṇd], and finally complete unstressing would result in merely [ṇ], as we have already seen. Not uncommonly an entire syllable may be lost, as it is when *probably* is pronounced [prɑblı]. Thus, as a sound becomes progressively weakened by unstressing, less and less time and care are given to it and it assumes a form more and more remote from that which it had originally until it may take the form of the obscure vowel [ə], if it is a vowel, or it may disappear altogether.

Up to a certain point this is a perfectly natural and desirable process; as has been pointed out, a marked variation in stress is a dominant characteristic of English speech closely bound up with the history of the language. No one can speak English acceptably without observing its natural patterns of stress and accent. However, the individual interested in achieving easy intelligibility and an acceptable standard of pronunciation in his speech will see that this tendency of unstressed words and syllables to become blurred and obscured in pronunciation constitutes a serious problem in articulation. The problem is not whether these words and syllables should be given sufficient attention to restore their full value; in that case the distinctive pattern of English would be destroyed. Rather, the problem is, how far should this process of unstressing be allowed to go in the natural flow of speech within the phrase or sentence? To what extent should sounds be allowed to change from their original form under the influence of unstressing?

The reason for concern over the unstressed sounds is simply this: In the speech of an individual whose articulation is faulty to the point at which intelligibility suffers and an impression of slovenliness is created, it is the unstressed syllables and words that suffer most. He may 'hit the high spots' in his speech, but the high spots will be the stressed syllables. Many of the low spots may be omitted entirely or may be so changed from their original form as to be unrecognizable and to make the entire word or phrase difficult to understand.

A few examples will serve to make this point more clear. The sentence *I should like to see you come* might be spoken very carefully as [aɪ ʃʊd laɪk tʊ si jʊ kʌm]. Or in informal speech we might hear [aɪ ʃəd laɪk tə si jə kʌm]. While considerable unstressing has now taken place in the syllables which are less important to the meaning and natural rhythm of the sentence, most individuals would probably find this pronunciation quite acceptable. When, however, as often happens within a phrase, *interested* becomes [ɪnɚstəd], *tendency* sounds like [tɛnəsɪ], and *let me give them a pretty poem* turns into [lɛmɪ gɪvm̩ ə pɚtɪ pom], we have a type of speech that does not measure up to a standard which most people are willing to accept. Likewise we hear all too frequently such pronunciations as [gʌvmənt] for *government*, [kɑntɚdɪk] for *contradict*, [fɪgɚ] for *figure*, [hʌndɚd] or even [hʌnɚd] for *hundred*, [ʃudə] for *should have*, and [dəno] for *don't know*. It is clear from these examples that it is the unstressed syllables that suffer the greatest change under the influence of poor articulation.

What is the answer? Somewhere between the extreme of too-careful, over-precise, pedantic speech, on the one hand, and careless, slovenly, relatively unintelligible speech, on the other, there is a type of pronunciation that is both easy, natural, and informal and reasonably clear, easily intelligible, and generally acceptable to those who hear it. Each individual must find this type of speech for himself; it is difficult to set up fixed, arbitrary standards for all occasions and all circumstances and all individuals.

Some of the problems which have just been discussed are illustrated in the following words and practice material. For many of the words weakened forms are commonly heard, some of which have a more doubtful standing than others. For each word and each phrase decide upon a pronunciation that you consider to be entirely acceptable for good, informal speech. In the case of the words listed, construct and pronounce aloud short sentences in which the words are used, testing out the pronunciation that you have chosen for each of the words in question. Give special attention to the way in which, in your opinion, the unstressed syllables and words should be handled. Avoid both slovenliness, on the one hand, and labored, over-precise articulation, on the other.

February	pretty	hundred	tomorrow
library	laboratory	secretary	poetry
similar	mutual	generally	village
figure	usually	terrible	all right
circulation	finally	particular	gradually
government	regulation	philosophy	hello
manufacture	probably	comfortable	introduction
recognition	orange	syrup	tendency
president	actually	individual	argument
visitor	telephone	company	idea
quantity	naturally	everybody	candidate
sophomore	captain	hesitation	gentlemen

1. Afoot and light-hearted, I take to the open road,
   Healthy, free, the world before me,
   The long brown path before me, leading wherever I choose.

   Henceforth I ask not good-fortune—I myself am good-fortune;
   Henceforth I whimper no more, postpone no more, need noth-
        ing,
   Strong and content, I travel the open road.
                          WALT WHITMAN, 'Song of the Open Road'

2. I met a traveller from Arkansas
   Who boasted of his state as beautiful
   For diamonds and apples. 'Diamonds
   And apples in commercial quantities?'
   I asked him, on my guard. 'Oh, yes,' he answered,
   Off his. The time was evening in the Pullman.
   'I see the porter's made your bed,' I told him.

   I met a Californian who would
   Talk California—a state so blessed,
   He said, in climate, none had ever died there
   A natural death, and Vigilance Committees
   Had had to organize to stock the graveyards
   And vindicate the state's humanity.
   'Just the way Steffanson runs on,' I murmured,
   'About the British Arctic. That's what comes
   Of being in the market with a climate.'
                          ROBERT FROST, 'New Hampshire'

3. Arthur, the Shirker

Once there was a young rat named Arthur, who could never make up his mind. Whenever the other rats asked him if he would like to go out with them, he would answer, 'I don't know.' And when they said, 'Would you like to stop at home?' he wouldn't say yes or no either. He would always shirk at making a choice.

One day his aunt said to him, 'Now, look here. No one will ever care for you if you carry on like this; you have no more mind than a blade of grass!' The young rat coughed and looked wise as usual, but said nothing.

'Don't you think so?' asked his aunt, stamping with her foot, for she couldn't bear to see the young rat so cold-blooded. 'I don't know' was all the young rat ever answered. And then he would walk off and think for an hour whether he should stay in his hole in the ground or go out and walk.

One night the rats heard a great noise in the loft. It was a dreary old loft. The roof let in the rain; the beams and rafters were all rotten, so that the place was rather unsafe. At last, one of the joists gave way and the beams fell with one end on the floor. The walls shook and the rats' hair stood on end with fear and horror.

At once the chief sent out scouts to look for a new home. When they had found one, he ordered all the rats to stand in line and to prepare to move to their new abode. Just then he caught sight of young Arthur, the shirker. He was not in the line and he was not exactly out of it either; he was just by it.

'Aren't you coming?' asked the chief.

'I don't know,' said Arthur calmly.

'Surely you don't think this place is safe,' exclaimed the chief in surprise.

'I'm not certain,' said Arthur, undaunted. 'The roof may not come down just yet. I think I'll go tomorrow. And then again, I don't know; it's so nice and snug here. Maybe I should go back to my hole and think it over.' And the long line of rats marched out to their new home and left him there alone.

That night there was a big crash. In the foggy morning some men rode up to look at the old barn that had fallen down. One

of them moved a board and saw a young rat, quite dead, half in
and half out of his hole. Thus the shirker got his due.

Adapted from 'The Young Rat'

Stressing and Diphthongization. Looking for a moment at
the other side of the picture, we find that excessive stressing
accompanied by undue prolongation of vowel sounds leads
to a drawling type of utterance in which a number of non-
standard diphthongs are likely to appear. Sounds that should
normally be pure vowels become diphthongized in such
speech because the articulatory organs change their position
during the prolonged period that the sound is held, or as a
result of the peculiar pattern of stress applied to the syllable.
Illustrating this tendency, the vowel [æ] often becomes the
diphthong [æə], giving us such pronunciations as [kæəmp]
for *camp,* [læənd] for *land,* and [bæəd] for *bad.* Other vowels
become affected in a similar manner and we hear [wɛəl] for
well, [fuəl] or even [fuwəl] for *fool,* [hɪət] for *hit,* [meɪʒɚ] for
measure, and many others. None of these forms is to be recommended. Pure vowels should be kept pure, and should
not be prolonged to the point at which diphthongization is
likely to take place.

Restressing. Many short words, especially articles, prepositions, and conjunctions, are found so frequently in unstressed positions and occur so infrequently in stressed positions that their stressed form has been all but lost. The only
form which we remember readily is the unstressed one. Then
when we do have occasion to stress one of these words, we
simply substitute the stressed form of whatever weakened
vowel has been used. When this vowel is [ə], as it often is,
the sound changes to [ʌ] when the words become *restressed.*
For example, we so frequently use the preposition *from* in
its weak form, [frəm], as in the phrase *from time to time,*
that when we do want to stress it, we call it [frʌm], forgetting
that its original stressed form is [frɑm] or [frɒm]. Of course,
other vowels may be involved as well. *For* is so often un-

stressed to [fɚ] that it is often pronounced [fɝ] when stressed, instead of the proper [fɔr] (General American).

Exactly the same thing has happened to many of the words in the following list. In the case of some of them other factors may have been operative also in producing the form listed in the restressed column. In every instance restressing has probably played some part.

STRESSED FORM	UNSTRESSED FORM	RESTRESSED FORM
was [wɑz]	[wəz]	[wʌz]
of [ɑv]	[əv]	[ʌv]
what [hwɑt]	[hwət]	[hwʌt]
for [fɔr]	[fɚ]	[fɝ]
you [ju]	[jə]	[jʌ]
or [ɔr]	[ɚ]	[ɝ]
pretty [prɪtɪ]	[pɚtɪ]	[pɝtɪ]
because [bɪkɔz]	[bɪkəz]	[bɪkʌz]
can [kæn]	[kən] or [kn̩]	[kɪn]
nor [nɔr]	[nɚ]	[nɝ]
where [hwɛr]	[hwɚ]	[hwɝ]
from [frɑm]	[frəm]	[frʌm]

Of course, the unstressed form is quite all right to use when the word is really unstressed. However, not all of the restressed forms have become acceptable substitutes for the original stressed pronunciation,* although some of them, such as [frʌm], [ʌv], and [wʌz], are coming into rather widespread use. On the other hand, one could hardly consider such pronunciations as [fɝ], [bɪkʌz], and [kɪn] to be representative of the best usage. In the following sentences practice what you consider to be the most acceptable, and at the same time the most natural, pronunciation of the *italicized* words which should be spoken with rather definite emphasis:

* Kenyon, John S., *American Pronunciation,* p. 113, George Wahr, Publisher, Ann Arbor, Michigan, 10th Ed., 1951.

1. *Just what* do you want to know?
2. I *was* going out, but I have changed my mind.
3. We have government *of* the people, *by* the people, and *for* the people.
4. Webster said, 'Liberty *and* Union, now and *for*ever.'
5. He was walking *from* the depot.
6. *Can* you do it, *or* are you a bit doubtful?
7. *Where* do *you* think it is?
8. I was *pretty* angry *because* I couldn't go.

INCOMPATIBILITY OF SPEECH SOUNDS

Serious problems in diction arise out of certain combinations of sounds which require articulatory transitions that are particularly difficult. The sounds by themselves are not especially difficult to make; it is only when they occur together that trouble arises. Such consonants as [θ], [s], [ʃ], [f], [t], and their voiced analogues can be called incompatibles because they present real problems in articulation when they occur in such combinations as we find, for example, in *fifths, lists, statistics, warmth,* and the old tongue-twisters, 'she sells sea shells,' and 'Theophilus Thistle.' The problem is often solved in common practice simply (1) by omitting one or more of the offending sounds, (2) by substituting other less difficult but acoustically similar sounds, or (3) by inserting incidental, superfluous sounds to ease the transition. In this way, *fifth* often becomes [fɪft] or [fɪf] in pronunciation, *lists* becomes simply [lɪs], and *warmth* is often pronounced [wɔrmpθ].

In connection with this last example, it might be well to point out that a minor difficulty in articulation arises whenever a nasal is followed by a fricative within a word. The usual solution to this problem is to allow a stop consonant to appear between the nasal and the following fricative, the incidental consonant sound corresponding in place and manner of articulation to the preceding nasal. This gives us [wʌnts] for *once,* [kʌmpfɚt] for *comfort,* and [sɪŋgz] for *sings.* *

Again, the only advice that can safely be given is to exercise as much care in speaking as is consistent with ease and naturalness. The practices just described often cannot be avoided in informal speech, nor is this always necessary, provided the changes which occur in one's pronunciation are not too prominent and also provided the word does not suffer serious loss of intelligibility.

Practice the following words and selections with the foregoing principles in mind. Articulate each word and phrase as clearly as you can without causing your speech to sound labored or artificial.

fifths	thousands	oaths	lengths
eighths	widths	depths	hundredths
sixths	cloths	twelfths	months
strength	grasped	camphor	asks
frisked	answer	dance	fists
flings	diphtheria	statistics	something

1. Shave a cedar shingle thin.
2. He asks that thousands be held to answer with oaths.
3. Hundreds wandered up and down the length and breadth of the land for months.
4. Three-thousandths of an inch is the width of the line.
5. This is the zither he asks for.
6. Three-sixths equals six-twelfths.
7. In the production of plosives the breath stream is stopped.
8. It is estimated that three-fifths of the earth's surface is covered by the seas.

* It should be understood that the [g] of such combinations as this latter one is a very weak sound and must not be confused with the much more prominent [g] appearing under like circumstances in the speech of an individual with a foreign-language background. It is common practice to disregard all three of these incidental transition sounds except in close phonetic transcriptions in which minor changes and modifications of speech sounds are recorded. However, they can still be heard in the everyday speech of the average individual.

9. Three months ago the thief was seen in the thick of the thicket.

10. She stood at the door of Mrs. Smith's fish-sauce shop welcoming him.

11. I sometimes think that never blows so red
    The Rose as where some buried Caesar bled;
        That every Hyacinth the Garden wears
    Dropt in her Lap from some once lovely Head.

    Yet ah, that Spring should vanish with the Rose!
    That Youth's sweet-scented manuscript should close!
        The Nightingale that in the branches sang,
    Ah whence, and whither flown again, who knows!
                    FITZGERALD, *The Rubaiyat of Omar Khayyam*

12. Now air is hushed, save where the weak-eyed bat
    With short shrill shriek flits by on leathern wing,
        Or where the beetle winds
        His small but sullen horn.
                    WILLIAM COLLINS, 'Ode to Evening'

ASSIMILATION

Earlier in this chapter the continuous, dynamic nature of connected speech was pointed out. There it was seen that not only are separate sounds blended together to form words, but words themselves are fused together to form larger units of expression—phrases and thought-groups, with a more or less continuous flow of sound throughout the unit.

Herein lies an important problem in articulation, for each sound within a phrase is to a certain extent influenced in the manner of its production by the sound that precedes it and the one that follows it. That is to say, with the exception of the initial and final sounds of phrases, the articulatory mechanism is always coming into the position for a sound from some other sound, and it no sooner assumes a position than it begins to move out again in preparation for the sound that is to follow. Each sound is formed 'on the run,' as it were, as a result of movement almost as much as the result

of position. The effect of this process is to work some alteration in the quality of each sound, depending upon the nature
of the change which the mechanism must make from the
sound that precedes it and to the one that follows. Some of
these transitions are easy, others are difficult to negotiate;
some leave but little trace in the altered quality of adjacent
sounds, others work such a profound change that a sound
may be metamorphosed into a totally different one. This
general process is known as assimilation.

As a simple illustration, the two varieties of [k] in *keen*
[kin] and in *cool* [kul] are in reality quite different sounds,
as can readily be heard if the [k] is sounded in isolation in
each case. In *keen* the tongue is getting ready for a front
vowel and as a consequence the contact for this [k] is made
forward on the hard palate, while the back vowel which follows the [k] in *cool* brings the tongue much farther back in
the mouth for the initial sound. The *n* of *bank* and *ink* is
pronounced [ŋ] because anticipation of the [k] draws the
tongue backward away from the [n] position and into that
for [ŋ], which is similar to that for [k]. The same influence
can be seen operating in other words which normally have
an *n* before a [k], even though the two sounds may be in
different syllables. Examples of this are *income* and *Bancroft,*
often pronounced [ɪŋkʌm] and [bæŋkrɔft]. Another interesting example can be heard in the pronunciation [græmpɑ] for
grandpa. In this case the [d] is first lost, partly because of
unstressing, and the word becomes [grænpɑ]. However, because the [m] is formed with the lips in the same position as
for the [p], the [n] changes to [m] and we have [græmpɑ],
which naturally is the most easily pronounced of all three of
these forms.

An example of the opposite condition in which a sound
influences the one that follows it rather than the preceding
one is found in the behavior of *s* when it forms the plural
of words which end in a voiceless sound in contrast to its

quality when it follows a voiced sound. Thus, in *bids s* is pronounced as [z], but in *bits* it becomes [s] because the sound that precedes it, [t], is also unvoiced. For the same reason *d* becomes [t] following a voiceless consonant in words like *looked* [lʊkt], *wished* [wɪʃt], and *whipped* [hwɪpt]. When *t* becomes [d] in *notice,* and the word is pronounced as [nodəs], a form sometimes heard, the *t* is influenced by the fact that a voiced sound, a vowel in this case, both precedes and follows it and it likewise becomes a voiced sound, [d]. The explanation is, of course, that it is easier to keep the voice going all the way through the word, once it is started, than it is for voicing to stop after [o] and then start again for [ə]. A similar circumstance gives us such pronunciations as [sædɚdɪ] for *Saturday,* [lɪdl̩] for *little,* and [guzbɛrɪ] for gooseberry.

An example of a third type of assimilation in which certain sounds combine to form an entirely new one is seen in the present-day pronunciation of *issue* [ɪʃu], which has come down to us from an earlier pronunciation of [ɪsju], a form that is still heard occasionally. In this case the [s] and the [j] have combined to form [ʃ]. The same change is seen in the pronunciation of the word *ocean* [oʃən]. A like explanation also underlies the often heard [mɪʃu] for the phrase *miss you.* Such pronunciations as [neʃən] for *nation,* [soldʒɚ] for *soldier,* and [fitʃɚ] for *feature* have become so common as a result of assimilative influences and have been standard for so long that in many instances we have forgotten that they ever were pronounced in any other way. It will be observed, however, that some of the examples cited, such as [nodəs] and [lɪdl̩], have not as yet attained to this level of universal acceptability.

Assimilation Within the Phrase. Not only does assimilation affect sounds within word units, but it operates in a similar manner for sounds in closely related words within a phrase or sentence. In this way, the phrase, *meet you,* usually becomes [mitʃu] in informal speaking, in reality pronounced as one word. A like change occurs in the examples *this show* [ðɪʃo], *horseshoe* [hɔrʃu], *won't you* [wontʃu], and many similar pronunciations which are often heard.

There is no question that assimilation constitutes a powerful influence in determining the development of spoken language and that it accounts for many of our present-day forms of pronunciation. The tendency to assimilation is present in our speech every time we open our mouths to utter a word. Whether it is a good or a bad influence depends in part upon how completely we surrender to it and allow it to dominate our articulation. To illustrate this point, we easily pass from the examples already cited, which are acceptable to most people, to such not uncommon pronunciations as [sʌmpm̩] for *something,* [kʌp m̩ sɔsɚ] for *cup and saucer,* and [sædɚdɪ] for *Saturday.* Proceeding another step in the direction of total surrender to the influences of assimilation aided by those arising from unstressing, we find such mutilated forms as [gadə] for *got to,* [gʌnə] for *going to,* and [dʒəgo] for *did you go.* Many similar examples could be cited.

Assimilation and Speech Standards. We may well ask, 'Just how far should we allow the influences illustrated in the foregoing to appear in our speech?' We must yield to a degree; no one would think of insisting upon the original spelling-pronunciations of *handkerchief, cupboard,* and *raspberry,* yet assimilative influences are chiefly responsible for the accepted forms of these words today. Most individuals believe that *nature* [netʃɚ] is preferable to the over-precise [netjʊr], and in like manner such pronunciations as *education* [ɛdʒukeʃən] for the more formal [ɛdjukeʃən], *fortune* [fɔrtʃən] instead of [fɔrtjun], and *literature* [lɪtərətʃɚ] for [lɪtərətjʊr] have gained, or are gaining, acceptance. But again we ask, 'How far should we go?' If these examples are passable for informal speech, then what of [pʌŋkən] for *pumpkin,* [græmɑ] for *grandma,* [sɛbm̩] for *seven,* and [dʒævə gutaɪm] for *did you have a good time?*

If we adhere too closely, however, to what might be called strict 'academic' standards, we run the risk of appearing stilted and artificial in our speech. In the other direction, too complete surrender to the natural tendency of allowing speech to become as easy and unrestrained as possible is liable to result in mutilated, all but unintelligible diction, as we have already seen in some of the examples cited.

It is obvious that we can expect but little help toward the solution of our problem from conventional spelling. If we were to follow spelling as a guide to pronunciation, we should soon become hopelessly confused.

A good dictionary, of course, is of great value in disclosing generally established forms of individual words, but it also has its limitations. In the first place, the dictionary attempts to reflect the general usage of the country as a whole. Yet in actual practice no such uniformity of usage is to be found. Instead, there are distinct variations of pronunciations heard in certain sections of the country that are quite acceptable in those areas. Some of the more common of these have been referred to in previous chapters. As yet no universally agreeable solution to the problem of determining what is 'correct' for the entire country has been found.

Moreover, dictionaries must of necessity present words merely as isolated units complete in themselves. There is no way of indicating what changes take place in the sound structure of these words as a result of stressing and unstressing or of indicating the influence of one sound upon another when the words become a part of connected speech. We have already seen what profound changes these factors may make in pronunciation. Knowing merely one way to pronounce a word and that only when it stands alone is frequently not enough, important as that may be.

Where then can we turn for guidance and help in the solution of our diction problems? The desire to be correct in our speech plus the wish to avoid the stigma of carelessness and unintelligibility function as restraining influences to keep our diction from deteriorating too seriously. On the other hand, there is little danger of the average individual becoming too careful and too precise in his speech. The seductive tendency to allow speech to become as effortless as possible, combined with the powerful influence of common usage, is more than sufficient in the majority of instances to prevent such a development. With speech, as with many other things, the path of least resistance does not lead upward.

In setting up our standards, we should be guided to a great extent by our observation of the actual speech habits of those around us whose speech we admire and who are generally regarded as speaking well. After all, the usage of those who are looked upon as leaders, as knowing what is 'right,' will in the end determine what is acceptable and correct. The best speech, after all, is that which does not call attention to itself either because it is too bad or because it is too 'good.' The best speech is natural, clear, and easily understandable, without suggesting the artificial and the pedantic. This, it will be recognized, is hardly an absolute standard nor is it anything that can be found merely by looking in a book. In the end, one must be guided by his sense of discrimination, by his judgment, and his good taste.

WORDS FREQUENTLY CONFUSED IN PRONUNCIATION

The following list contains a number of troublesome words as far as pronunciation is concerned. In some instances common usage is sharply divided and in other cases common usage is inclined to differ from recommended 'academic' pronunciation. Study the list carefully and discover in each case the pronunciation that is most generally acceptable as constituting good usage.

acclimate	condolence	gamut	orchestra
address	contractor	genuine	penalize
admirable	controversial	gesture	pianist
adult	coupé	gratis	posterior
advertisement	coupon	grievous	precedence
alias	creek	grimace	preferable
allies	data	harass	prestige
Alma Mater	debut	height	projectile
amateur	decadent	hilarious	pumpkin
amenable	decorous	hover	ration
apparatus	defect	illustrative	research
asked	deluge	incognito	respite
association	diphthong	infantile	romance
attacked	discretion	inquiry	saline
banquet	divan	integral	senile
barbarous	drama	inveigle	solace
blatant	dramatist	irreparable	status
bouquet	economic	isolate	theater
bravado	either	issue	toward
breeches	envelope	juvenile	tremor
carry	err	lamentable	vaudeville
chasm	exquisite	larynx	vehement
chassis	extraordinary	longevity	vice versa
chastisement	forehead	luxury	virile
clique	formidable	manor	viscount
column	frequented	medieval	vivacity
combatant	gala	mischievous	wandered
comely	gallant	often	zoology

1. Dr. Curry represents a small boy's rendition of the final stanza of Longfellow's 'The Psalm of Life' as follows:

Liza grape men allry mindus
Weaken maka Liza Blime

Andy Parting Lee B. Hindus
Footbrin Johnny sands a time.*

How many of the sound changes in this example can you explain on the basis of unstressing and assimilation? Compare this version with the original and note what sounds have been lost, substituted, or added. Read it the way you think it should be read. Compare your reading with the 'small boy's.'

2. Consider the acceptability of the pronunciations suggested in the following list—pronunciations that are often heard in certain types of speech. Can you explain them in terms of unstressing and assimilation? Use each phrase in an improvised sentence and speak the sentence in a way you would consider entirely acceptable in informal speech.

  a. [dʒə gou] for 'did you go?'
  b. [dʒit] for 'did you eat?'
  c. [harjə] for 'how are you?'
  d. [ɔdə] for 'ought to.'
  e. [dʒævə] for 'did you have a.'
  f. [mʌstə] for 'must have.'
  g. [sɪdaun] for 'sit down.'
  h. [gəbaɪ] for 'good-bye.'
  i. [gʌnə] for 'going to.'
  j. [swataɪ] for 'that is what I.'
  k. [lɛmɪ] for 'let me.'
  l. [pɝt nɪr] for 'pretty nearly.'

PRACTICE MATERIAL FOR GENERAL DICTION

1. When the hounds of spring are on winter's traces,
   The mother of months in meadow or plain
  Fills the shadows and windy places
   With lisp of leaves and ripple of rain.

* Curry, S. S., *Mind and Voice*, p. 429, Expression Company, Boston, 1910.

2. Why is it that the poets tell
So little of the sense of smell?
These are the odors I love well:

The smell of coffee freshly ground;
Or rich plum pudding, holly crowned;
Or onions fried and deeply browned.

The fragrance of a fumy pipe;
The smell of apples, newly ripe;
And printers' ink on leaden type.

Woods by moonlight in September
Breathe most sweet; and I remember
Many a smoky camp-fire ember.

Camphor, turpentine, and tea
The balsam of a Christmas tree,
These are whiffs of gramarye . . .
A ship smells best of all to me.

CHRISTOPHER MORLEY, 'Smells'

3. With malice toward none; with charity for all; with firmness in the right, as God gives us to see the right, let us strive on
to finish the work we are in; to bind up the nation's wounds; to
care for him who shall have borne the battle, and for his widow,
and his orphan—to do all which may achieve and cherish a just
and lasting peace among ourselves, and with all nations.

LINCOLN

4. Oh! a private buffoon is a light-hearted loon,
    If you listen to popular rumour;
From morning to night he's so joyous and bright,
    And he bubbles with wit and good humour!
He's so quaint and so terse, both in prose and in verse;
    Yet though people forgive his transgression,
There are one or two rules that all Family Fools
    Must observe if they love their profession.
       There are one or two rules,
         Half-a-dozen, maybe,
       That all family fools,
         Of whatever degree,
Must observe if they love their profession.

Though your head it may rack with a bilious attack,
  And your senses with toothache you're losing,
Don't be mopy and flat—they don't fine you for that,
  If you're properly quaint and amusing!
Though your wife ran away with a soldier that day,
  And took with her your trifle of money;
Bless your heart, they don't mind—they're exceedingly kind—
  They don't blame you—as long as you're funny!
           It's a comfort to feel
             If your partner should flit,
           Though *you* suffer a deal,
             They don't mind it a bit—
They don't blame you—so long as you're funny!
             W. S. GILBERT, *The Yeomen of the Guard*

    5. Out of the night that covers me,
       Black as the pit from pole to pole,
    I thank whatever gods may be
       For my unconquerable soul.

    In the fell clutch of circumstance
       I have not winced nor cried aloud.
    Under the bludgeonings of chance
       My head is bloody, but unbowed.

    Beyond this place of wrath and tears
       Looms but the horror of the shade,
    And yet the menace of the years
       Finds and shall find me unafraid.

    It matters not how strait the gate,
       How charged with punishments the scroll,
    I am the master of my fate;
       I am the captain of my soul.
             WILLIAM E. HENLEY

6. Rip Van Winkle, however, was one of those happy mortals, of foolish, well-oiled dispositions, who take the world easy, eat white bread or brown, whichever can be got with least thought or trouble, and would rather starve on a penny than work for a pound. If left to himself, he would have whistled life away in perfect contentment; but his wife kept continually dinning in his ears about his idleness, his carelessness, and the ruin he was

bringing on his family. Morning, noon, and night, her tongue was incessantly going, and everything he said or did was sure to produce a torrent of household eloquence. Rip had but one way of replying to all lectures of the kind, and that, by frequent use, had grown into habit. He shrugged his shoulders, shook his head, cast up his eyes, but said nothing. This, however, always provoked a fresh volley from his wife; so that he was fain to draw off his forces, and take to the outside of the house—the only side which, in truth, belongs to a hen-pecked husband.

WASHINGTON IRVING, *Rip Van Winkle*

7. 'You are old, Father William,' the young man said,
    'And your hair has become very white;
And yet you incessantly stand on your head—
    Do you think, at your age, it is right?'

'In my youth,' Father William replied to his son,
    'I feared it might injure the brain;
But, now that I'm perfectly sure I have none,
    Why, I do it again and again.'

'You are old,' said the youth, 'as I mentioned before,
    And have grown most uncommonly fat;
Yet you turned a back-somersault in at the door—
    Pray, what is the reason of that?'

'In my youth,' said the sage, as he shook his gray locks,
    'I kept all my limbs very supple
By the use of this ointment—one shilling the box—
    Allow me to sell you a couple?'

'You are old,' said the youth, 'and your jaws are too weak
    For anything tougher than suet;
Yet you finished the goose, with the bones and the beak—
    Pray, how did you manage to do it–'

'In my youth,' said his father, 'I took to the law,
    And argued each case with my wife;
And the muscular strength which it gave to my jaw,
    Has lasted the rest of my life.'

'You are old,' said the youth, 'one would hardly suppose
    That your eye was as steady as ever;
Yet you balanced an eel on the end of your nose—
    What made you so awfully clever?'

'I have answered three questions, and that is enough,'
Said his father; 'don't give yourself airs!
Do you think I can listen all day to such stuff?
Be off, or I'll kick you downstairs.'

LEWIS CARROLL, 'Father William'

8. There is beauty in the bellow of the blast,
   There is grandeur in the growling of the gale,
         There is eloquent out-pouring
         When the lion is a-roaring,
   And the tiger is a-lashing of his tail!
         Yes, I like to see a tiger
         From the Congo or the Niger,
   And especially when lashing of his tail!

   Volcanoes have a splendour that is grim,
   And earthquakes only terrify the dolts,
         But to him who's scientific
         There's nothing that's terrific
   In the falling of a flight of thunderbolts!
         Yes, in spite of all my meekness,
         If I have a little weakness,
   It's a passion for a flight of thunderbolts.

W. S. GILBERT, from The Mikado

9. Sea Shell, Sea Shell,
      Sing me a song, O please!
   A song of ships, and sailormen
      And parrots, and tropical trees.

   Of Islands lost in the Spanish Main
      Which no man ever may find again,
   Of fishes and corals under the waves,
      And sea horses stabled in great green caves,
   Sea Shell, Sea Shell,
   Sing of the things you know so well.

AMY LOWELL, 'Sea Shell'

10. Oh, but he was a tight-fisted hand at the grindstone,
Scrooge! A squeezing, wrenching, grasping, scraping, clutching,
covetous old sinner! Hard and sharp as flint, from whom no steel
had ever struck out generous fire; secret and self contained and
solitary as an oyster. The cold within him froze his old features,

nipped his pointed nose, shrivelled his cheek, stiffened his gait, made his eyes red, his thin lips blue; and spoke out shrewdly in his grating voice.

CHARLES DICKENS, A Christmas Carol

11. If I were not a little mad and generally silly,
    I should give you my advice upon the subject, willy, nilly;
    I should show you in a moment how to grapple with the question,
    And you'd really be astonished at the force of my suggestion,
    On the subject I shall write you a most valuable letter,
    Full of suggestions when I feel a little better,
    But at present I'm afraid I am as mad as any hatter,
    So I'll keep 'em to myself, for my opinion doesn't matter!

W. S. GILBERT, from Ruddigore

12. Roll back the tide of eighteen hundred years. At the foot of the vine-clad Vesuvius stands a royal city. The stately Roman walks its lordly streets, or banquets in the palaces of its splendors. The bustle of busied thousands is there; you may hear it along the thronged quay; it rises from the amphitheatre and the forum. It is the home of luxury, of gaiety, and of joy. It is a careless, a dreaming, a devoted city. Lo! there is blackness in the horizon, and the earthquake is rioting in the bowels of the mountains! Hark! a roar! a crash! and the very foundations of the eternal hills are belched forth in a sea of fire! Woe for that fated city! The torrent comes surging like the mad ocean! It boils above wall and tower, palace and fountain—and Pompeii is a city of tombs!

ANONYMOUS, Pompeii

13. Oh, when I am safe in my sylvan home,
    I tread on the pride of Greece and Rome;
    And when I am stretched beneath the pines,
    Where the evening star so holy shines,
    I laugh at the lore and the pride of man,
    At the sophist schools and the learned clan;
    For what are they all, in their high conceit,
    When man in the bush with God may meet?

R. W. EMERSON, 'Good-bye'

Appendix A

SINCE voice and speech, from an acoustical point of view, are nothing more than a complex of sound waves, theoretically at least it should be possible to describe and explain all of the characteristics and qualities of vocal communication in terms of what is known of the nature and behavior of sound. Within limits it is possible, and profitable, to do this. Certainly a basic knowledge of sound will enable one to understand more clearly just how tone is produced in the larynx, how it is modulated into speech sounds through the operation of resonance and articulation, and how the expressive characteristics of the voice resulting from variations in pitch, time, loudness, and quality are derived.

SOUND AS A PHYSICAL AND A PSYCHOLOGICAL PHENOMENON

There are two traditional points of view from which sound can be defined and described—the psychological and the physical. These points of view are clearly illustrated in the well-known dilemma of the meteorite falling and exploding in the middle of a desert with no living creature within hundreds of miles. The problem is: Does the explosion make any sound? From the psychological point of view, it makes no sound, since there is no one there to hear it. To the psychologist sound is merely the brain's interpretation of certain sensations received through the mechanism of the ear; sound is what we hear. To the physicist, however, sound consists solely of waves, or more properly, periods of rarefaction

419

and condensation in some elastic medium—in the case of the exploding meteorite, air. Sound can also travel through many other substances, such as water, wood, metal, and the tissues and bones of the body. In comparison with the rate of travel of light rays and radio waves, sound travels slowly, its velocity in air being a little less than 1100 feet per second.

While the psychological point of view is probably more important than the physical in enabling one to understand why and how certain interpretations become attached to vocal symbols, still it is necessary to consider the physical aspects of sound also, since it is those aspects which in the final analysis determine what we hear. Therefore, if we are to understand voice and speech as such, we must understand sound.

SOURCES AND NATURE OF SOUND

Sound originates as the result of activity of some vibrating agent. This vibrating body may take a vast number of forms —a bar, as in the xylophone; a string, as in the violin or piano; a reed, as in the clarinet; a tightly stretched membrane, as in the drum; a rod, as in the tuning fork; or merely blades or sheets of air itself, as in the flute and piccolo. These objects are all set into vibration by being bowed, plucked, struck, or in some other way having force applied to them.

The nature of their vibration may be explained very simply as a periodic swing, or back and forth motion, very much as in the case of the pendulum, except, of course, much more rapid. This rapid swing operates to set up disturbances in the surrounding medium, in most instances air, which disturbances are transmitted from one particle to the next, as force applied to one end of a line of billiard balls is transmitted from one ball to the other until the last one is reached, without any of the balls having materially changed its position. In the case of sound these successive waves of force strike the drum membrane of the ear, causing it to vibrate back and forth, and it is these pulsations, conveyed first to the inner ear and thence to the brain, which we interpret as sound.

It should be noted that in this process the air itself does not travel to convey the sound, but rather the particles of air vibrate back and forth, their movement being transmitted in this way to surrounding particles, which operate in a similar fashion to 'carry' the sound waves or, more properly, sound pulsations. A familiar analogy can be found in the waves set up on the quiet surface of a pool of water when a stone is dropped into it. Here the waves travel in concentric circles out from the source of their origin conveying a portion of the force released by the impact of the stone on the water. The important point illustrated by this example is that the water itself does not travel from the stone to the shore. The wave literally passes through the water. So it is with sound in air.

Tone as Opposed to Noise. The terms *tone* and *noise* are psychological concepts employed to describe the effect, largely one of pleasantness or unpleasantness, which different types of sounds produce upon us. But, in common with other psychological interpretations of sound, they have their basis in more or less definite physical characteristics. The chief distinction between tone and noise, so far as sound itself is concerned, is based upon the regularity, or periodicity, of the sound waves. The more regular and predictable the form which the sound wave pattern takes, the more the sound becomes what we identify as tone. The more irregular and haphazard the pattern, the more the sound approaches what we call noise. Tones can also be recognized as having a clearly defined pitch, but noises are sounds to which no definite pitch can be assigned.

The analogy of the pool of water may again be employed. If only one stone is quietly dropped into a still pool, the resulting waves will be regular and of a definitely set form.

Or if a second stone is dropped a moment after the first one and in the same spot, the wave form, while now becoming more complex, will still have a definite order and periodicity. If, however, a handful of pebbles are thrown into the pool, or a number of stones are cast indiscriminately here

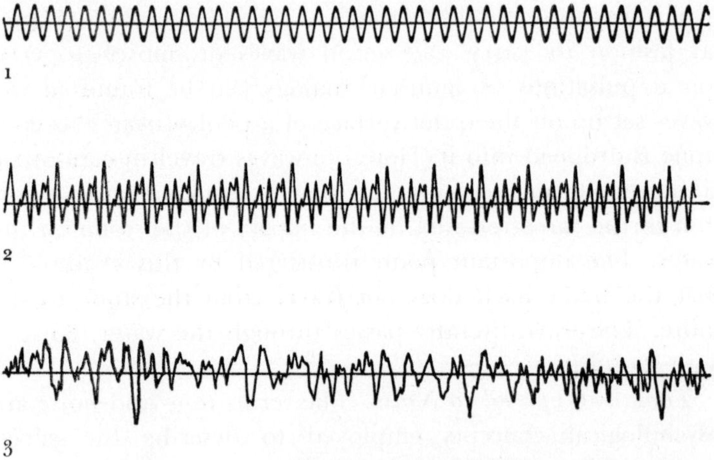

1

2

3

(Courtesy of the Bell Telephone Laboratories and D. Van Nostrand Company, Inc.)

FIG. 19. Oscillograms illustrating a typical wave form of: (1) A pure tone of 500 cycles; (2) The vowel [a], as in *father*, intoned at 183 cycles; (3) Street noise.

and there over the surface, the resulting waves will form a jumbled and irregular pattern. The first of these conditions represents tone, the second noise.

The feature of periodicity, or regularity of pattern, is shown in Figure 19, which illustrates a simple tone as produced by a tuning fork, a complex tone such as the human voice or a musical instrument produces, and a jumbled, patternless wave form characteristic of noise. It should be pointed out in passing that simple, or pure, tones such as those made by the tuning fork are seldom found outside the laboratory; virtually all of the sounds we hear every day represent some degree of complexity, and many of them would have to be classified as noises.

One should note, however, that there is no sharp line of demarcation between tone and noise, considered either psychologically or from a physical point of view. With respect to the individual's own judgment and preference, much depends upon his social inheritance and training. Many of the sound combinations which to the Oriental, for example, constitute enjoyable music strike harshly upon the Western ear as unpleasant noise. Our distinction, therefore, between what we identify as tone and as noise is within limits largely a matter of taste—what we are used to and what we expect to hear. Likewise the physical distinction between the two is a relative one; there are degrees of regularity and irregularity of pattern. Furthermore, a tone that has basically a regular wave pattern may have noise elements mixed with it in the form of sporadic and unrhythmical vibrations.

Speech sounds embody the use of both noise and tone. Vowel sounds, such as the [ɑ] of *father* and [o] in *coat,* for example, when properly sounded, are relatively pure tone. Certain voiced consonants, on the other hand, such as [z] and [g] (gun), have a basic element of tone with a component of noise superimposed upon it, while the voiceless consonants, of which [s] and [k] are examples, are largely noise. Such noises, of course, are a regularly accepted part of the speech process, and a necessary part, since clearly formed consonants account for intelligibility. If the noise elements become too prominent, however, unpleasantness results as in the case of a hissing [s] or a noisily exploded [t] or [k].

It may be noted in passing that in the production of speech sounds, tones normally originate in the larynx, while noises result from the various adjustments made by the articulatory mechanism—tongue, teeth, lips, and other agents. Of course, when proper conditions for good tone production in the larynx are lacking, unpleasant noise elements may also be added directly to the vocal tone at its source in the form of breathiness, hoarseness, or harshness.

THE BASIC FACTORS OF SOUND

Physicists are in general agreement that there are four basic factors or characteristics of sound with respect to which it may be studied and described. If speech and voice are nothing more than patterns of sound, then these same four factors must of necessity underlie any analysis or study of the voice. These characteristics have been designated as *time, pitch, loudness* or *intensity,** and *quality* or *timbre,* as it is sometimes called. Let us inquire into the physical nature of these basic factors and examine their relationship and significance to voice production and voice training. How these four characteristics should be managed for enhancing the communicative ability of the voice forms the principal discussion of Chapter V.

Time. The factor of time, which refers simply to the duration of the sound, when applied to speech is concerned with the duration of vowel tones and with the length of the pauses between words and phrases. These two elements lie at the basis of tempo in speech and to a certain extent of rhythm also. An increase in the factor of time means a slower tempo, more tone and hence better carrying power in the voice, and usually clearer, more careful articulation.

Speaking voices generally would be improved if more time were given to the vowel tones. Too often undue emphasis is placed upon the articulation of consonants when as a matter of fact it is the vowels that should be formed and molded more carefully. In the first place, as was stated in a previous paragraph, an increase in the proportionate emphasis placed upon consonants means an increase in the noise elements in

---

* While the terms *intensity* and *loudness* are not synonymous, the interests of simplicity and clearness will be better served if no delimiting definitions are attempted and if the term *loudness* alone is used to denote this particular characteristic of sound.

speech—the hisses, explosions, and friction noises which make up our consonant sounds. An increase in vowel tone, on the other hand, means an increase in the sonorous, musical, pleasing elements of speech. As a demonstration of this point, contrast the effect produced by such sentences as *Peter Piper picked a peck of pickled peppers* and *Sister Susie seemed to suspect that something was missing* with such sentences as *We are all well* or *Over the rolling waters go.* In the first examples we have a preponderance of voiceless consonants and short vowels while in the second voiced continuants and longer vowel tones predominate. While for the sake of clearness of speech, consonants should by no means be slighted, the basic quality of the voice can be improved only by giving attention, and time, to the vowels.

Pitch. Pitch is the psychological interpretation of the frequency or rapidity of a vibration.* An object vibrating rapidly has a high frequency, which is heard as a high pitch; one vibrating more slowly has a low frequency, which is heard as a low pitch. Remove the cover of a piano and study the action of the various strings, or experiment with a guitar. The strings producing the lowest tones vibrate so slowly that the movement of the string can be seen, while the strings giving forth the very high tones vibrate so rapidly that no movement is observable.

Most objects that vibrate do so with a characteristic frequency determined by their structure. Clock pendulums vary in the rapidity of their swing, the short ones having a more rapid swing, or vibration, than the longer ones. Large bells produce a lower pitch than smaller ones, and a tightly stretched string will vibrate more rapidly than a looser one. This pitch, in each case, is known as the natural frequency of the object.

What determines the frequency of a vibrating body and

* Each complete vibration is referred to as a 'cycle,' and the frequency, or pitch, of a sound is commonly expressed in cycles per second.

hence the pitch which will result from its movement? Three factors are responsible: (1) the length, (2) the weight or mass per unit of length, and (3) the tension. Pitch varies directly with tension, but inversely with length and weight. That is to say, pitch rises as tension rises, but falls as length or weight is increased. In most musical instruments all three of these factors are independently controlled, and when one is varied, the other two remain constant. The pitch-changing mechanism of the voice, however, is far more complex than that of any musical instrument, since a change in any one of these factors is accompanied by a change in the other two, necessitating a readjustment of the entire mechanism. This complexity of adjustment explains why it is very difficult, if not impossible, for even a trained singer to maintain an exact pitch for any appreciable length of time. Although the ear may not be able to detect it, the tone will waver slightly above and below the pitch the singer is attempting to hold. In speech, and singing too, the picture is also greatly complicated by the relationship between pitch and breath pressure, explained in more detail in Chapter III.

Range. Range is a musical term defined as the interval between two tones, one higher than the other. Very often in the common use of the term, however, these defining limits of range are thought of as being the extreme limits as well. Considered in this sense, the range of the piano, for example, would be the interval expressed in octaves between its lowest and highest tones, or notes. The untrained singing voice will have a range of two octaves or less, while the trained singer may exceed these limits by as much as an octave or more in some cases.

The total range of the vocal mechanism, meaning the fundamental tone, including the voices of both men and women, extends almost four octaves from a low bass tone of 70 or 80 cycles per second in the male voice to upwards of 1024 in the female voice. However, the range of the entire speech mechanism is considerably greater than that, extending from the low tone of the male voice mentioned above to the high frequency hiss of the consonant [s] produced by the articulatory mechanism. This sound, which is quite independent of voice as such, has frequencies in it running to 6000 or 8000 cycles per second. Yet this extreme range of voice and speech is still well within the range of human hearing, which extends from approximately 20 cycles per second to 20,000. It may be noted in passing, however, that the frequencies involved in voice and speech lie within that portion of the auditory range where hearing is keenest. Below and above the speech range auditory acuity falls off rather markedly; especially is hearing likely to be deficient at the higher pitch levels. The high frequency sounds, therefore, especially the voiceless consonants, are usually the first to be lost or the most likely to be defective in the speech of an individual whose hearing is at all seriously impaired, in accordance with the well-established principle that the ability to produce a given speech sound, under ordinary conditions, is contingent upon the individual's ability to hear it.

Loudness. Loudness is the product of the amplitude or extent of vibration when the factor of pitch is held constant. And amplitude is dependent largely on the resiliency of the vibrating body and on the strength of the activating force which sets it in motion. Thus, if a piano string is struck very lightly, a relatively weak tone is produced, but if the string is struck a vigorous blow, the amplitude or width of swing is increased to the point where the vibrations of the string can be plainly seen and a much louder tone is the result. However, if the activating energy is not renewed, the vibrations gradually subside with a consequent decrease in loudness, just as a swing finally comes to rest when children 'let the cat die.' Loudness is also closely related to the distance which the sound waves are required to travel, being greater at points near the source of the sound than it is at points more removed.

In the voice loudness is the product of three conditions: (1) the pressure exerted upon the outgoing breath, which determines the amplitude or swing of the vocal folds; (2) the efficiency with which the folds vibrate, for obviously any condition which interferes with their action or allows unvocalized breath to escape between them will operate to decrease loudness; and (3) the degree of reinforcement supplied to the tone by the resonance chambers. The first of these three factors is discussed in the chapter on breathing, the second is dealt with in the chapter on phonation, and the third is treated in the chapter on resonance.

Just as speech sounds vary in pitch, so do they differ even to a greater extent in intensity, or phonetic power, the strongest sound in English speech, the vowel [ɔ], as in *awe*, having an intensity value 680 times greater than the weakest sound, the voiceless consonant [θ], as in *thin*.* As would be expected, the vowels are much stronger than the consonants, the more open vowels such as [ɔ], [ɑ], and [æ] (cash), having the greatest phonetic power of all speech sounds. Among the weakest consonants are [θ], [f], and [p]. These facts lend weight to the argument that greater attention given to the vowels increases the power and carrying ability of the voice. They also explain why such consonants as [f], [t], [d], and [k] are often lost in speech unless one articulates them very carefully.

Quality. Besides differing in time, loudness, and pitch, sounds are also distinguishable on the basis of a fourth factor, quality. It is quality that enables one to identify a trombone, a clarinet, or a violin when all three are playing the same note, with equal loudness, and for the same duration of time. It is likewise quality that enables us to distinguish the voice

* Fletcher, Harvey, *Speech and Hearing in Communication*, p. 86, D. Van Nostrand Company, New York, 1953.

of Jim from the voice of Fred, even though both may speak with similar pitch and inflectional patterns.

While pitch results from the frequency of vibration, and loudness is the product of the amplitude of vibration, quality is related to the complexity of vibration. It owes its existence to the fact that most objects which are capable of producing sound through vibration do not vibrate in a simple back and forth or up and down motion as a pendulum swings, but rather they vibrate in small sections or segments, each segment contributing its own peculiar frequency, or pitch, to the sound complex as a whole. These segmental vibrations are known as partials or overtones.

This phenomenon is best explained if a vibrating string is used for illustration. When a taut string is struck or plucked, it vibrates not only as a whole but also in segments, each segment constituting an equal division of the complete string, a half, a third, a fourth, a fifth, and so on. The frequency of the string vibrating as a whole, which we identify as the 'pitch' of the string, is called the fundamental. This fundamental frequency, as we learned in a previous paragraph, is determined by the length, weight, and tension of the string. A further application of this principle to the frequencies of the segmental vibrations, or overtones, reveals that since weight and tension remain constant while length is broken up into common fractions of the original length, the frequency or pitch of each segment will be an exact multiple of the frequency of the fundamental. That is, the various overtones will have frequencies two, three, four, five, and so on, times the fundamental. When this simple relationship prevails, as it does in the case of the string, the overtones are also known as harmonics.

From a physical point of view quality can be defined as resulting from (1) the number and (2) relative intensities of the overtones, and (3) their relationship in pitch to the fundamental; and it is the variations in one or all of these factors that account for differences in quality among various tones. Bear in mind that all of these vibrations, the fundamental and the numerous overtones (some musical instruments may have as many as twenty or more), are not heard as separate frequencies, but rather as one integrated tone-complex which we recognize as quality. Elimination or amplification of certain of the overtones will result in a noticeable change in the quality of the resulting tone. Certain musical instruments have fewer overtones than others; in some the fundamental and lower overtones are strongest, while in others the fundamental may be comparatively weak but the higher overtones will be more prominent. All will differ markedly in quality.

Virtually all of the sounds we hear from day to day are complex ones, differing in quality as well as in the other characteristics. Only with certain types of electrical apparatus or with well-constructed tuning forks is it possible to produce a simple, or pure, tone consisting solely of a fundamental. This explains why all tuning forks always sound alike, so far as the quality of tone is concerned. Moreover, when all of the overtones have been eliminated from the tone-complex produced by an instrument such as a piano, violin, or horn by being passed through a specially constructed electrical transmission system, these instruments are indistinguishable. The resulting tone in each case is that of a tuning fork; they have lost their characteristic quality.

No musical instrument can equal the voice in the possibilities for variation in the quality of tone which it produces. Such variability makes possible the expressiveness of the voice in mirroring not only attitudes, thoughts, and feelings of the speaker, but fundamental personality and character traits as well. Moreover, as explained elsewhere, even the different vowel sounds are merely variations in the quality of the laryngeal tone.

RESONANCE

While the total number of overtones present in a complex tone and their relationship in pitch to the fundamental are determined largely by the essential structure of the vibrating agent, the relative *intensities* of the various overtones can be materially altered through the operation of resonance. And what is resonance? This interesting and very important phenomenon of sound cannot be explained easily in simple terms. However, perhaps the nature and function of resonance can be understood more clearly if some of its characteristics, or manifestations, are explained briefly.

Forced Vibration. Forced vibrations result when a vibrating body is placed in direct contact with another object and the second object is forced to vibrate with the same frequency as the first. For example, a vibrating tuning fork merely held in the hand can be heard only if it is within a few inches of the ear. But when the shank of the fork is placed upon a table top and pressed against it, the tone can be heard throughout a large room. The explanation is not difficult to understand. The tone produced by the tuning fork alone results from vibrations of two small prongs of metal which cause relatively weak sound waves. However, when the fork is held against the table top, the vibrations are transmitted directly to the table top which acts as a sounding board, causing the whole surface to pulsate and give off much stronger sound waves.

Note that it is unnecessary for the two objects to respond naturally to the same frequency; through actual contact the second object, the sounding board, is forced to vibrate 'in tune' with the first, the actuator. One further point should be understood—the sounding board does not increase the total energy output of the vibrating body; it merely permits the energy to be used up faster. For example, the tuning fork, when struck, will vibrate for a longer time when held in the hand, but will sound louder for a shorter time when pressed against the table top.

This sounding-board form of vibration is found in many types of musical instruments of which the piano is a good example. As a matter of fact, it plays a prominent part in virtually all of the stringed instruments, the vibrations of the strings being conveyed directly through the bridge to the vibrant body of the instrument itself.

There is little doubt that this sounding-board effect is also operative in voice production, though there is considerable question with respect to its actual influence on the final tone. For example, the vibrations which can easily be felt in the chest when a low tone is sung are in all probability the result of forced vibrations conveyed directly from the larynx to the ribs and the sternum through the tissues of the neck and the bones of the spinal column. A sensitive stethoscope will pick up similar vibrations from many other points on the surface of the body, particularly from bones protruding near the surface, not only in the region of the chest, but at the points of the shoulders, around the neck, and all over the surface of the head. It is possible that a considerable portion of the entire body operates in some fashion as a sounding board for the voice-producing mechanism, and appreciable amplification of tone may result therefrom.

Resonance Vibrations. Resonance vibrations can easily be demonstrated by sitting at the piano, depressing the 'loud' pedal so that the strings are left free to vibrate, and singing various tones up and down the scale. Within a very short time a pitch will be found that will set up an easily audible vibration in one of the strings of the piano. What has happened? In your singing you have chanced to strike a pitch that corresponded to that of one of the strings, and the alternating periods of condensation and rarefaction of the air, which constitute the sound wave, exerted sufficient force to set the string into vibration.

Observe that in order for resonance vibrations, sometimes referred to as sympathetic vibrations, to function, the two vibrating mediums must be in tune; that is, the natural frequency of the two vibrating bodies must be similar. Moreover, the second object, the one that vibrates 'sympathetically,' must have sufficient resiliency to permit an easy and ready response even to a very weak stimulus. It is doubtful whether we have sympathetic vibration, in the form just described, operative in the voice. It is true that the term is found in discussions of voice production, but its meaning has not always been carefully delimited, and as a result the term has at times been used to describe conditions which were in reality examples of forced vibration.

Resonance in Partially Enclosed Cavities. While the form of resonance which can be designated as cavity resonance is in reality merely another manifestation of sympathetic vibration, possibly the use and function of resonance in the human voice can be explained more clearly if a slight distinction is made between them. Cavity resonance is the form usually referred to when the unrestricted term *resonance* is used in connection with the voice.

As an example, let us take a tuning fork representing for convenience middle C, which has a pitch, or frequency, of 256 cycles per second, and experiment with a collection of jars and bottles of varying shapes and sizes. If our collection is sufficiently extensive, undoubtedly we shall find at least one that will greatly amplify the tone when the vibrating fork is held over the opening. When we blow across the mouth of this bottle, we discover that the sound it makes— its natural frequency—has the same pitch as the tuning fork.

Now let us proceed in a slightly different way. This time we take a large jar with a relatively small opening, and as we hold the vibrating fork over the opening we pour water slowly into the vessel. Eventually as we thus change the capacity of the cavity and hence the volume of the air contained in it, we shall find a size that corresponds to the pitch of the fork and a reinforcement of the tone will again result. If a fork of 512 vibrations is used, considerably more water must be poured into the jar to reduce further the size of the resonance cavity. Thus, the smaller cavity resonates the higher pitch. This principle is well illustrated in the musical instrument that best exemplifies this form of resonance, the marimba. The resonators for the low tones are long tubes; those for the high notes are small and short.

The chief point to be noted in this connection is that cavity resonators are tuned resonators. That is, they will respond to only one frequency with maximum efficiency and to a relatively narrow band of frequencies with diminishing efficiency as the pitch of the vibrator departs more and more from the natural pitch, or frequency, of the resonator. This natural pitch is determined mainly by two factors that are of primary interest to students of voice: (1) the volume of the cavity, and (2) the size of the opening. As we have already seen, the larger the cavity the lower the pitch to which it will respond, but the larger the opening the higher the pitch which it will resonate. That is, a low tone requires as a resonator a large cavity with a small opening, a high tone a small cavity with a large opening. This principle explains why a certain tongue and lip position must be assumed for the production of each of the several vowel sounds. This fact, together with the necessity for careful 'tuning' of all of the adjustable resonators of the voice, is of supreme importance in voice training and is dealt with in considerably more detail in several chapters of this book, particularly in Chapter IV.

The Relation of Resonance to Quality. One should not make the mistake of confusing resonance and quality and thinking of the two as being synonymous. While resonance may be considered quantitatively, quality should not be thought of from this point of view. One voice does not have more quality than another, but rather a different quality.

Similarly the concept of resonance is often confused; a voice having a disagreeable quality or lacking in general effectiveness is not necessarily lacking in resonance—it may have too much of the wrong kind. Mere resonance alone does not make a superior voice.

In other words, since the principal resonators of the voice are tuned resonators, they function selectively to amplify only those frequencies to which they are tuned. And thus by changing the shape, size, and relationship of the various cavities of the resonance mechanism, the proper overtones in the vocal tone can be amplified to produce the desired quality. Therefore, while some weak voices may actually need more resonance, those in which there is a noticeable defect of quality need instead the proper kind of resonance. Finally, then, resonance can be said to function selectively to determine quality and to modify it. Aside from the actual initiation of the tone itself, the development and management of proper resonance is the most important single aspect of the entire process of voice production, and plays an important role in the formation of speech sounds, especially the vowels.

Appendix B

THE most convenient tests for the measurement of sensory abilities related to speech are the Seashore tests of musical ability, called specifically 'Measures of Musical Talent.' These tests, which include measurements of pitch, time, rhythm, timbre, tonal memory, and loudness, are available on long-playing phonograph records from The Psychological Corporation, 304 East Forty-fifth Street, New York 17, New York. Norms and directions for administering and scoring the tests accompany the records.

The sensory ability most directly related to speech skills is probably pitch discrimination, the capacity to recognize differences in pitch between tones. With respect to this ability, the average person is able to detect a difference of four c.p.s. or approximately 1/100th of an octave between two tones at 435 c.p.s. Occasionally an individual is discovered, however, who finds it impossible to recognize pitch differences of as much as twenty or more c.p.s. between two tones at this same pitch level. Such a person approaches the condition known as tone deafness.

While there is no close relationship between pitch discrimination and voice production generally, such wide variations from the normal as this are often reflected in an unusual monotony of voice. According to some authorities, a causal relationship between pitch discrimination, or the lack of it, and absence of adequate variety in the voice may be suspected when the limit of the person's discrimination is

9 c.p.s. or more. This would place the individual's score at about the 25th percentile on the Seashore pitch test. 'In the absence of all other causes tending toward monotony of voice, a tone-deafness with a limit of 15 c.p.s. or more may be regarded positively as the cause.' * This would place the score around the 10th percentile or below on the Seashore test.

However, as was explained in Chapter V, lack of sensitivity to pitch differences is only one of several possible factors which may operate to cause monotony of speech. Nevertheless in cases of pronounced monotony it is one of the factors that should be investigated.

* West, Robert, Ansberry, Merle, and Carr, Anna, *The Rehabilitation of Speech,* p. 220, Harper and Brothers, New York, 3rd ed., 1957.

Bibliography

Akin, Johnnye, *And So We Speak,* Prentice-Hall, Englewood Cliffs, N. J., 1958.

Barbara, Dominik, *Your Speech Reveals Your Personality,* Charles C Thomas, Springfield, Ill., 1958.

Barnes, Grace, *General American Speech Sounds,* D. C. Heath, Boston, 1946.

Bender, James F., *How To Talk Well,* McGraw-Hill Book Company, New York, 1949.

Brigance, W. N., and Henderson, F., *A Drill Manual for Improving Speech,* J. B. Lippincott, New York, rev. ed., 1955.

Brodnitz, Friedrich S., *Keep Your Voice Healthy,* Harper and Brothers, New York, 1953.

Bronstein, Arthur J., *The Pronunciation of American English,* Appleton-Century-Crofts, New York, 1960.

Cartier, Francis A., *The Phonetic Alphabet,* Wm. C. Brown Company, Dubuque, Iowa, 1954.

Curry, Robert, *The Mechanism of the Human Voice,* Longmans, Green, New York, 1940.

Desfosses, Beatrice, *Your Voice and Your Speech,* Cattell and Company, New York, 1946.

Eisenson, Jon, *The Improvement of Voice and Diction,* The Macmillan Company, New York, 1958.

Fairbanks, Grant, *Voice and Articulation Drillbook,* Harper and Brothers, New York, rev. ed., 1960.

Field-Hyde, F. C., *The Art and Science of Voice Training,* Oxford University Press, London, 1950.

Fields, Victor A., and Bender, James F., *Voice and Diction,* The Macmillan Company, New York, 1949.

Froeschels, Emil, *Twentieth Century Speech and Voice Correction,* Philosophical Library, New York, 1948.

Greene, Margaret, *The Voice and Its Disorders,* The Macmillan Company, New York, 1957.

Hahn, Elise, *et al.*, *Basic Voice Training for Speech*, McGraw-Hill Book Company, New York, rev. ed., 1957.

Heltman, Harry J., *Trippingly on the Tongue*, Row, Peterson and Company, Evanston, Ill., 1955.

Kaplan, Harold M., *Anatomy and Physiology of Speech*, McGraw-Hill Book Company, New York, 1960.

Karr, Harrison M., *Developing Your Speaking Voice*, Harper and Brothers, New York, 1953.

Kenyon, John, *American Pronunciation*, George Wahr, Publisher, Ann Arbor, Mich., 1951.

Kenyon, John S., and Knott, Thomas A., *A Pronouncing Dictionary of American English*, G. and C. Merriam Company, Springfield, Mass., 1944.

Lawson, Franklin D., *The Human Voice*, Harper and Brothers, New York, 1944.

Levy, Louis, Mammen, Edward W., and Sonkin, Robert, *Voice and Speech Handbook*, Prentice-Hall, New York, 1955.

Manser, Ruth B., *Speech Correction on the Contract Plan*, Prentice-Hall, New York, 3rd ed., 1951.

Manser, Ruth B., and Finlan, Leonard, *The Speaking Voice*, Longmans, Green, New York, 1950.

Morgan, Lucia C., *Voice and Diction Drillbook for Students in Speech*, Wm. C. Brown Company, Dubuque, Iowa, 1951.

Moses, Paul J., *The Voice of Neurosis*, Grune and Stratton, New York, 1954.

Mulgrave, Dorothy, *Speech*, Barnes and Noble, New York, 1954.

Needleman, Morriss H., *A Manual of Pronunciation*, Barnes and Noble, New York, 1949.

Negus, V. E., *The Comparative Anatomy and Physiology of the Larynx*, Grune and Stratton, New York, 1949.

Pear, T. H., *Personality, Appearance and Speech*, George Allen and Unwin, London, 1957.

Stanley, Douglas, *Your Voice*, Pitman Publishing Corp., New York, 1945.

Thomas, C. K., *An Introduction to the Phonetics of American English*, Ronald Press, New York, rev. ed., 1958.

Thomas, Charles K., *Handbook of Speech Improvement*, Ronald Press, New York, 1956.

Van Dusen, C. Raymond, *Training the Voice for Speech*, McGraw-Hill Book Company, New York, 1953.

Van Riper, Charles, and Irwin, John V., *Voice and Articulation*, Prentice-Hall, Englewood Cliffs, N. J., 1958.

Van Riper, Charles, and Smith, Dorothy E., *An Introduction to General American Phonetics*, Harper and Brothers, New York, 1954.

Wise, Claude M., *Applied Phonetics*, Prentice-Hall, Englewood Cliffs, N. J., 1957.

Wise, Claude M., and Morgan, Lucia, *A Progressive Phonetic Workbook for Students in Speech*, Wm. C. Brown Company, Dubuque, Iowa, 1948.

Index of Topics

Abdominal muscles, 31
Accent, 395
Adenoids, 22, 122
Adolescence, change of voice in, 81-3
Affricates, 280-82
Alphabet, phonetic, 241-4
Ansberry, Merle, cited, 437
Articulation, 125, 126, 245ff.
  developing clearness of, 245-8
  of difficult sound combinations, 404-6
  dynamic nature of, 126, 246, 406-8
  exercises for, 251-5
  faults of, 125, 248-51, 395-9, 409-11
  organs of, 246, 336
  tests of, 17, 18
  and unstressing, 398, 399
Arytenoid cartilages, 59
Aspirate quality, see Breathiness
Aspiration of consonants, 70, 95, 271
Assimilation, 276, 406-11
  breathiness, 45, 69; exercises for, 94-6
  nasality, 116, 344, 349; exercises for, 136-40
  and speech standards, 409-11; exercises for, 413
Attitudes, harmful to voice, 6, 175-7, 208, 214, 220, 222
  revealed through voice, 157, 167, 168
Autonomic nervous system, 212, 216

Back vowels, 124, 338
Breath, pressure and pitch, 65-7
  wastage, 42-5
Breathiness, 42, 68-72
  exercises for overcoming, 42ff., 93ff.

Breathing, biological functions of, 21, 22, 32-5
  with the diaphragm, 35-7
  economy of breath, 44, 45; exercises for, 46ff.
  effect of emotion on, 33, 213
  exercises for control of, 39ff.
  exhalation, 30-32, 34; exercises for control of, 41ff.
  flexibility of breath control, 36, 48, 49ff.
  inhalation, 27-30
  mechanics of, 29-32
  muscles of, 27, 28
  proper habits of, 35-9
  role of, in voice training, 37-9
  for speech, 34-9, 48, 49, 76
  supporting the tone, 32, 53, 54
Bronchi, 22

Carr, Anna, cited, 437
Carrying power, 144ff.
Carry-over, exercises for pitch, 107-10
  exercises for general expressiveness, 202-5
  exercises for general voice, 111
Cartilages of larynx, 58-60
Cavity resonance, 433
Change of pitch, 161-3
Change of voice, 81
Chest, 24ff.
  resonance in, 112-14
Consonants, classified, 268-70
  defined, 260-62
  discussed in detail, 271ff.
  [p] and [b], 271; exercises for, 272-4
  [t] and [d], 274-6; exercises for, 276-8
  [k] and [g], 278; exercises for, 279

443

Index of Selections and Authors

451